Shopping Center Management

Editorial Consultants
Harold J. Carlson, CPM®
Robert D. Oliver, CPM®
John W. Phelps, CPM®

Joseph T. Lannon
Publishing and Curriculum Development Manager

Caroline Scoulas
Senior Editor

Shopping Center Management

Alan A. Alexander, CPM®
Richard F. Muhlebach, CPM®

Institute of Real Estate Management
of the **NATIONAL ASSOCIATION OF REALTORS®**
430 NORTH MICHIGAN AVENUE • CHICAGO, ILLINOIS 60611

This publication is designed to provide accurate and authoritative information in regard to the subject matter covered. Forms or other documents included in this book are intended as samples only. Because of changing and varying state and local laws, competent professional advice should be sought prior to the use of any document, form, exhibit, or the like.

This publication is sold with the understanding that the publisher is not engaged in rendering legal, accounting, or any other service. If legal advice or other expert assistance is required, the services of a competent professional should be sought.

The opinions expressed in this book are those of the authors, Alan A. Alexander, CPM®, and Richard F. Muhlebach, CPM®, and do not necessarily reflect the policies and positions of the Institute of Real Estate Management.

Library of Congress Cataloging-in-Publication Data

Alexander, Alan A.
    Shopping center management / Alan A. Alexander, Richard F.
Muhlebach.
      p. cm.
    Includes index.
    ISBN 0-944298-68-0 (hard cover)
    1. Shopping centers--Management.   I. Muhlebach, Richard F., 1943-
    II. Title.
HF5430.A45 1992   91–40796
658.8'7--dc20   CIP

Printed in the United States of America

1 2 3 4 5 6 7 8 9 10 Printing / Year 01 00 99 98 97 96 95 94 93 92

To my loving wife, Jeanne, who is
always there when I need her.
                                    A.A.A.

To my wife, Maria, who in the early
years of our marriage shared the life
of a mall manager. To my children,
Kathy and Eric, who grew up
at their father's mall.
                                    R.F.M.

Preface

Shopping Center Management was written to provide the reader with a hands-on practical approach to managing, marketing, and leasing shopping centers and retail properties. The principles found in this book apply to shopping centers of all sizes—from small strips to specialty centers to enclosed super regional malls. This book is intended to be a resource for shopping center managers, marketing directors, leasing agents, asset managers, developers, and property owners.

Chapter 1 reviews the origin of the shopping center, its evolution, and recent changes in the industry and discusses the necessary components for making such operations successful. Chapter 2 reviews the processes of developing and rehabilitating shopping centers, and chapter 3 discusses development of a successful retail component in nonretail properties—e.g., an office building and a mixed-use development (MXD). It considers the pitfalls of retail tenancies in other types of properties along with what particularly makes them successful.

Chapter 4 addresses development of a management plan for a shopping center; chapter 5 covers the management responsibilities of the shopping center manager, and chapter 6 discusses daily operations. Tenant relations and tenant retention are two critical areas of responsibility for property managers in the 1990s, and chapter 7 provides helpful suggestions for developing and implementing a tenant relations program.

Nearly one-third of the text is devoted to the importance of developing a comprehensive marketing and leasing program. Chapter 8 discusses tenant mix and its importance to the success of every shopping center. Chapter 9 describes step-by-step the marketing and leasing of shopping centers and retail space. Chapter 10 describes the lease document and explains the financial and operational implications of specific provisions in a shopping center lease.

One of the components of a successful shopping center of any size is an effective marketing, advertising, and promotions program. Chapter 11 outlines different approaches to marketing and promoting a shopping center to the consuming public.

Administration, record keeping, and budgeting are fundamental responsibilities of a property manager, and these aspects of shopping center management are covered in chapter 12.

In addition, the multiple appendixes provide adjunct information relevant to several issues in shopping center management. First there is a discussion of retailing principles that will help the property manager qualify prospects and work with established tenants in a shopping center to foster their success. There is also a comprehensive discussion of insurance as a form of risk management and its application to the shopping center and retail tenants. In addition, there is a series of maintenance forms (inspections and janitorial specifications) and example bylaws for a merchants' association. The last appendix is a list of publications and organizations that are resources on shopping center management.

Acknowledgments

We would like to acknowledge Chuck Orton of MacDonald Miller in Seattle and Sue Matthews of the Roofing Industry Education Institute in Englewood, Colorado, for the forms they provided. Jack Smith of American Building Maintenance in Seattle provided information on security guards, and Jim Hebert of Hebert Research, Inc., in Bellevue, Washington, supplied market survey information.

We appreciate Bob Bearson's insights into the retail skills appropriate for property managers. As a consultant, he provides specialized training on retailing (ABM—Advisors to Business Management in Long Beach, California).

We also appreciate the advice and expertise of our fellow shopping center managers who served as editorial consultants: Harold J. Carlson, CPM®, of Harold J. Carlson Associates, Inc., Rosemont, Illinois; Robert D. Oliver, CPM®, of JMB Properties Company, Boston, Massachusetts; and John W. Phelps, CPM®, Fullerton, California.

Thanks to Karin Grice who assisted in preparing the initial drafts, and our utmost appreciation to Caroline Scoulas, IREM's senior staff editor, for editing our manuscript.

The Urban Land Institute and the International Council of Shopping Centers provided valuable studies, reports, and publications that we found useful. *Dollars & Cents of Shopping Centers* (from ULI) is the industry standard for percentage rates, tenants' sales per square foot, and a wealth of other valuable information (examples are included in this book with their permission). We encourage the reader to become familiar with both ULI and ICSC.

We would especially like to recognize the Institute of Real Estate Management for our twenty-plus years' relationship and for the valuable education we received toward our CPM® designations and from IREM conferences and meetings.

Alan A. Alexander, CPM®
Richard F. Muhlebach, CPM®

About the Authors

Alan A. Alexander, CPM®, CSM, CRE, is Senior Vice President of Woodmont Managements, Incorporated, in Belmont, California, specializing in the management, leasing, and consulting for shopping centers. He has provided problem-solving consultation on properties throughout the United States.

Previously, he was President of Alexander Consultants of San Bruno, California, specializing in managing and consulting for income-producing properties. Mr. Alexander is a former Senior Vice President of Fox and Carskadon Management Corporation with responsibility for a portfolio of properties in four Western states that had values in excess of $300 million. As Director of Leasing for Fox and Carskadon Financial, he was responsible for leasing all shopping centers owned by the company throughout the United States.

Mr. Alexander is on the National Faculty of the Institute of Real Estate Management and is a past President of that organization's San Francisco Bay Area Chapter. He is a frequent speaker at International Council of Shopping Centers programs, including Idea Exchanges, the Annual Convention, Management and Maintenance Institutes, and the University of Shopping Centers. He has been the moderator and speaker for more than 200 seminars on the developing, managing, and leasing of shopping centers and small office buildings for the Northwest Center for Professional Education.

Mr. Alexander is coauthor of *Managing and Leasing Commercial Properties* and *Managing and Leasing Commercial Properties: Forms and Procedures,* both published by John Wiley & Sons, Inc., in New York. He has written numerous articles on commercial leasing and management published in the *Journal of Property Management (JPM)* as well as articles on other real estate subjects published in *Journal of Real Estate Development, Real Estate Business,* and elsewhere. He was inducted into the IREM "Academy of Authors" in 1984.

In addition to the CPM® designation from IREM, Mr. Alexander holds the CRE designation (Counselor of Real Estate) from the American Society of Real Estate Counselors (ASREC) and the CSM award (Certified Shopping Center Manager) given by the International Council of Shopping Centers.

Richard F. Muhlebach, CPM®, CSM, CRE, RPA, is President of TRF Management Corporation in Bellevue, Washington. He is also Director of Leasing for TRF Pacific, a developer of shopping centers, malls, and office buildings on the West Coast and in Alaska. TRF Management Corporation is responsible for the management and leasing of approximately five million square feet of shopping center, office building, and industrial park space in the Northwest and Alaska.

Mr. Muhlebach has 20 years' experience managing, leasing, developing, and rehabilitating commercial buildings. Previously he served as vice president for Tishman West Management Corporation and was the general manager of The City—a two-million-square-foot mixed-use development in Orange County, California—and was responsible for converting The City shopping center (a distressed open regional center) into a successful enclosed mall. He also supervised the management of several high-rise office buildings in Los Angeles.

Previously, Mr. Muhlebach served as Vice President and Director of Property Management of the Lusk Company—a major residential and commercial developer in Irvine, California. He has managed and leased neighborhood shopping centers to multilevel regional malls, low- to high-rise office buildings, medical buildings, industrial parks, commercial and residential condominiums, and major residential developments. He has managed properties from San Diego to Fairbanks and in locales ranging from rural communities such as Eagle River, Alaska, to major metropolitan areas such as Los Angeles.

In 1985, Mr. Muhlebach received the "CERTIFIED PROPERTY MANAGER® of the Year" award from the Western Washington Chapter of the Institute of Real Estate Management, and he received the same award in 1979 from the Orange County Chapter. He has served as a Regional Vice President of IREM and is that organization's Senior Vice President of Education for 1992.

Mr. Muhlebach is a senior instructor for the Institute of Real Estate Management and an instructor for the International Council of Shopping Centers and the Institute of International Research, and he has taught real estate management and leasing at the college level for five years. He is a frequent lecturer in Singapore.

He is coauthor of *Managing and Leasing Commercial Properties* and *Managing and Leasing Commercial Properties: Forms and Procedures,* both published by John Wiley & Sons, Inc., in New York. As author of more than 30 articles on real estate subjects, he has been published in the *Journal of Property Management (JPM), Shopping Center World, National Mall Monitor, Journal of Real Estate Development, Real Estate Finance, Real Estate Today,* and *Buildings* magazine as well as journals published in Asia. He received the *JPM* "Article of the Year" award in 1983 and 1984, and Honorable Mentions in 1986 and 1987. He is a member of the IREM "Academy of Authors." Mr. Muhlebach has also served on the editorial review boards for three IREM publications—*Leasing Retail Space, Principles of Real Estate Management (Thirteenth Edition),* and *Before Disaster Strikes: Developing an Emergency Procedures Manual.*

In addition to the CPM® designation from IREM, Mr. Muhlebach holds the CRE designation (Counselor of Real Estate) from the American Society of Real Estate Counselors (ASREC), the CSM award (Certified Shopping Center Manager) given by the International Council of Shopping Centers, and the RPA designation (Real Property Administrator) from the Building Owners and Managers Association (BOMA).

About the Institute
of Real Estate
Management

The Institute of Real Estate Management (IREM) was founded in 1933 with the goals of establishing a Code of Ethics and standards of practice in real estate management as well as fostering knowledge, integrity, and efficiency among its practitioners. The Institute confers the CERTIFIED PROPERTY MANAGER® (CPM®) designation on individuals who meet specified criteria of education and experience in real estate management and subscribe to an established Code of Ethics. Similar criteria have been established for real estate management firms that are awarded the ACCREDITED MANAGEMENT ORGANIZA-TION® (AMO®) designation.

In 1990, the Institute's membership included nearly 9,000 individuals as CPM® members and nearly 550 AMO® firms. Among U.S. commercial properties alone, CPM® members managed nearly 30 percent of the shopping centers and 25 percent of the office buildings under professional management. The Institute of Real Estate Management publishes books on real estate-related subjects, primarily related to property management, and offers numerous educational courses and seminars for career training in professional real estate management. This publication is part of the Institute's continuing efforts to provide quality education in the professional management of income-producing properties.

Contents

Shopping Centers in Perspective

The future promises to be very challenging for those involved in shopping center management. The shopping center industry has experienced unprecedented growth over the past 40 years, and that growth is likely to continue—but with many changes in the size, amenities, and tenant mix of individual shopping centers. Over the years, the shopping center industry has had to overcome recessions, overbuilding, and major shifts in anchor tenants' economic situations and space requirements as well as changes in the characteristics of shoppers. In spite of all these challenges, the industry has grown and prospered, as can be seen from a review of how shopping centers evolved to their current position of prominence.

EVOLUTION OF THE CONCEPT

The concept of the shopping center dates back to the beginnings of the historical era. In Europe and elsewhere, the center of town was used as a marketplace where one farmer might exchange vegetables for another farmer's grain, and townspeople could barter their "wares" (e.g., pottery) for agricultural products. The market became not only a place to buy and sell goods but also a social occasion. Permanent shops were established around the town square to take advantage of the farm traffic and to offer goods and services not provided by the farmers. Eventually, the town square or main street became the central business district of a bustling city.

The same pattern evolved in the United States, and there was little reason to change that pattern until the invention of the automobile and the beginning of Americans' love affair with it. The automobile made it possible to live outside the central city and still work and socialize there. Individuals could travel where they wanted, when they wanted—provided there were roads to their destinations. The migration out of the city and the rise of the suburbs provided a unique opportunity for developers to create a revolutionary retail experience—the "shopping center."

The first shopping center in the United States was Country Club Plaza, built outside of Kansas City, Kansas, in 1922. Having foreseen the coming success of the automobile, J. C. Nichols (the developer of Country Club Plaza) located his center south of town, and he included all of the elements considered necessary for a shopping center today—free paved parking, broad tenant mix, central management, controlled architecture, and pleasant landscaping.

Several factors converged after World War II and set the stage for the rapid growth of the shopping center industry. Government-backed home loan programs—especially FHA (Federal Housing Administration) and VA (Veterans Administration) loans—made home ownership much more easily attainable. This fostered homebuilding in suburban areas outside large cities. The development of an interstate highway system made it easier to get from one place to another and, more importantly, made it possible to live in the suburbs and work in the city. With the population moving to the suburbs, astute merchants soon realized that they could move their businesses to the suburbs as well.

Grocery chains were the first to open stores in the suburbs. Having stores located close to the customer base made grocery shopping more convenient. Sears, Roebuck, & Company was one of the first department stores to open branches in the suburbs. The stores were freestanding buildings, but they soon became focal points for development as independent merchants opened smaller stores adjacent to Sears. These other retailers had quickly realized the value of being located near a department store like Sears, and that realization gave rise to the distinction of having "anchor" tenants in a "shopping center."

From the 1950s into the 1970s, malls were the most obvious form of new shopping center construction, with a decided trend toward "enclosure." An enclosed mall provides a pleasant atmosphere in which to shop no matter what the weather is like outside. It can be 102 degrees in the shade or there can be two feet of snow on the ground, but the climate *inside* the mall will be just right.

However, beginning in the late 1970s and into and through the 1980s, this trend changed, and new development was dominated by smaller, "neighborhood" centers. Although development of large regional and super regional malls continued during this time, fewer sites were available for such large projects. In addition, construction materials were more costly, and financing became more difficult to obtain. At the same time, development of new residential tracts had slowed, limiting population growth in some areas and therefore precluding adequate numbers of consumers to support additional large centers. Also during this same period, more and more women who would otherwise have been full-time homemakers chose to work outside the home. These career women had less and less time for shopping and the regional center shopping experience; they sought shopping convenience compatible with their dual responsibilities—holding down a job *and* running a household.

Added to this was the Tax Reform Act of 1986, which had a tremendous impact on the shopping center industry. With one stroke of the pen, the economics of all income-producing properties were changed drastically. The sudden change was devastating, particularly to syndicators, but there were many in the industry who thought the changes were good for the long term. On the positive side, the Tax Reform Act of 1986 requires future projects to be based on sound economics—not just a tax write-off. In the early 1980s, in particular, many shopping centers and other income-producing properties were built solely because of the tax advantages they provided for investors, with little regard for their long-term viability. The hope was that a project would survive for a number of years on the tax advantages, by which time inflation (which had been in double digits) and a stronger market would bring the economics into line. Unfortunately, a recession and a drop in the inflation rate prevented this from happening, and numerous shopping centers failed. This rather gloomy economic picture continued into the early 1990s.

Components of Shopping Center Success

Of the various income-producing properties, shopping centers are generally considered the most complex to operate. In order for a shopping center to be successful, it must have the right location, easy access, high visibility, good management and marketing, and the right tenant mix for the demographic profile of the population it serves.

Location, Access, and Visibility. The best *location* for a particular shopping center depends on the type of center being built. Typically, a regional or super regional shopping center will be located in a densely populated area near an expressway exit or along a major arterial street. A neighborhood center must have an adequate population of shoppers and a location at the intersection of two well-traveled streets or, at the very least, facing a well-traveled street. A strip center should be located close to its customer base, preferably on a street with heavy traffic, and designed for easy access and convenient parking. Discount, off-price, and outlet centers are typically located beyond the outskirts of cities, usually at an expressway exit or near a tourist area. Specialty or so-called "theme" centers are generally located in the midst of a tourist area where there are other attractions as well.

Access is critical for all types of shopping centers. Modern shoppers value convenience, and they will not spend an extra twenty minutes in their cars waiting to get into a shopping center—they will shop somewhere else. Good access will include convenient, defined left-turn lanes; safe "stacking" lanes, if needed (for deceleration of inbound and acceleration of outbound vehicles); well-timed signals; wide driveways that are well-marked; good internal circulation in the parking lot; and well-designed, appropriately angled parking stalls.

If there were only one shopping center in a town, it could be located almost anywhere and people would find it readily enough; they would have no other convenient choice. However, most shopping centers have competition, and that is where *visibility* becomes essential. Visibility is what reminds customers that the center is there, even when they have no immediate need to shop. From the street, it should be easy to see how attractive the center is and how easily it can be accessed. In some cases—notably strip centers—customers must be able to see what shops are located in the center.

Management and Marketing.   The tremendous success of shopping centers over the years can be attributed, in part, to their *management*. The management of a center provides specific direction to all of its parts. It keeps the merchants focused on the trade area so their merchandise and pricing remain a good "fit" with the customer base. It fosters good business practices, encourages advertising, and provides a clean attractive environment for shoppers.

Marketing is increasingly important in the shopping center industry. Management and marketing personnel at regional and super regional centers have long understood the value of marketing, and they typically budget large amounts to pay for aggressive advertising and promotional campaigns throughout the year. Smaller centers have not followed that lead, for a variety of reasons. According to The Urban Land Institute, 76 percent of super regional centers now have either a merchants' association or a marketing fund; 59 percent of regional centers have one or the other, or both; and 51 percent of community centers have some form of marketing effort. Only 35 percent of neighborhood centers participate in centerwide promotional efforts, but that percentage is higher than had been reported previously. The most likely reason for this new-found interest in marketing is competition. If there are four neighborhood centers at an intersection, and they are all about the same in terms of tenant types, convenience, accessibility, etc., the one with the best marketing program is most likely to have the largest volume of sales and the easiest time leasing vacant spaces.

Tenant Mix and the Demographic Profile.   *Tenant mix* is critical to a shopping center, much more so than in an office building or an apartment complex. This is because retail tenants require customer traffic to generate the sales that are the measure of their success. To be successful, a shopping center must have complementary store types that will maximize the attraction to its prospective customers. The "right" tenant mix for a particular center will depend on a number of factors, among them the type of center being built, availability of specific tenant types in the area, economic and other factors related to the leasing terms, etc. The selection of store types is based on the characteristics of the marketplace.

To create a proper tenant mix for a shopping center, one must study the population of prospective customers to determine what they are likely to buy. Data on population size, age, and family or household composition; levels of education, income, and homeownership (versus renting); and ethnic considerations are available to the shopping center industry from numerous governmental agencies and private commercial sources. These data comprise the *demographic profile* of a shopping center's *trade area.*

The U.S. Department of Labor, Bureau of the Census, and industry sources such as *Sales and Marketing Management* magazine (August and October issues), can provide information about what consumers buy and how much they spend on different types of merchandise. The International Council of Shopping Centers (ICSC) is another source for marketplace information. Statistics on income reflect the potential buying power of the consumers in a given marketplace, and sales levels of established merchants can be estimated fairly accurately. From such data, it is possible to determine the *sales potential* or market share available for businesses at a proposed shopping center. These statistics should be studied carefully *before* specific retailers are approached to become tenants. Once tenants are in place, their sales and merchandise must be monitored to assure that the shopping center remains "right" for the customers in the trade area.

A demographic profile can yield many different scenarios. There may not be a large enough population to support a particular type of shopping center at the time it is planned. If the area population is expected to grow substantially over the next few years, it may be appropriate to develop a new center in phases, matching it to the growth of the population and its buying power. On the other hand, sales in the area may be quite strong, but an oversupply of space may mean too many merchants are competing for too few dollars in that location. The marketplace may be changing, and that may be for the better—or for the worse.

An understanding of the ongoing changes in the demographic profile of the trade area will help the manager make the best decisions to keep the shopping center competitive and extend its useful life. The manager's objective is to create a tenant mix that will best provide the goods and services required by a particular population. In a shopping center located in an affluent community, the shops are more likely to be upscale, with particular emphasis on personal services and an aesthetically appealing ambience. On the other hand, in a shopping center serving a lower-income area where shoppers are generally more price-conscious, the tenants are more likely to be offering value-oriented merchandise in a self-service environment. Ambience as such may be somewhat less a concern, but it should still be a clean, pleasant place to shop.

In general, it is not advisable to include both upscale merchandise and bargain-basement goods in one center. A shopping center is rather like a very large department store, with each "department" operated independently. If there is a store like Kmart on one end and one like Nieman-Marcus on the other, shoppers will become confused and may not complete their shopping at that location. The manager should always strive to provide a tenant mix that offers the broadest range of goods and services consistent with the demographic profile of the area. There is no one "right" tenant mix for a type of center; rather, the tenant mix at a given center must be tailored to the needs of the customers it will serve. For example, a center located in a retirement community is not likely to include the kinds of shops that appeal primarily to young people (e.g., jeans shops). A value-priced cafeteria may be more appropriate for that type of location than an expensive sitdown restaurant. A used book store and a drug store are other likely prospective tenants.

Types of Shopping Centers

Shopping centers are classified primarily by their size, tenant mix, and anchor tenants. There are eight basic types of shopping centers: convenience, neighborhood, community, regional, super regional, outlet or off-price, power, and specialty. In each type of center, the anchor tenant is the main traffic draw. The tenants in the smaller shops may be local, regional, or national retailers. Depending on the type of center, some stores may be leased to service companies, businesses, or medical, dental, or legal professionals as office space. Pads or outlots (freestanding buildings) are typically leased to regional or national fast food operations or locally owned restaurants, or to branch banks (often for drive-up services), although there are numerous other tenants for those types of spaces—e.g., drive-up drop-off photo services, video rental stores, automotive service stations (with or without gasoline), and florists.

Convenience (Strip) Shopping Centers.   This type of shopping center usually has between 5,000 and 50,000 square feet of *gross leasable area (GLA)* and is designed as one continuous row of shops—thus the term "strip" center. Though the ideal location is on a corner, a convenience shopping center can be located anywhere along the street. Most of the tenants are service or food operations. If there is an anchor tenant, it is usually a convenience grocery store such as 7-Eleven. This type of shopping center may well be developed throughout multiple business districts in a large city and can be successful with a small population base (1,000–2,500).

Neighborhood Shopping Centers.   The typical neighborhood shopping center ranges in size from 50,000 to 150,000 square feet of GLA. They usually include at least one anchor tenant but may have two or more. A supermarket is the most common anchor; alternatives are drug or home improvement stores. The small shop spaces are occupied by a mix of services, specialty food stores, and business or professional (medical, dental, legal) offices. Beginning in the 1980s, retailers selling soft goods have been occupying less space in neighborhood shopping centers than they did in the 1960s and 1970s. Pads or outlots may be leased to fast food or full-service restaurants, banks, etc. This type of center can do well with a trade area population of 5,000–40,000.

Community Shopping Centers.   These shopping centers typically range in size from 150,000 to 400,000 square feet of GLA. They usually have three or more anchors from among the following: junior department store, discount department store, supermarket, super drug store, variety store, home improvement center. The small shops are predominantly occupied by retail, service, and specialty food tenants. Most community shopping centers are large open-air strips, although some are developed as enclosed malls, and they need a population base of 100,000–150,000.

Regional Shopping Centers.   These centers typically range in size from 400,000 to 1,000,000 square feet of GLA and are anchored by two or three major retailers, at least one of which is a full-line department store. Other anchors may include specialty, junior, and discount department stores. The tenant mix for the small shop spaces is developed around the quality and price of merchandise sold by the anchor tenants. If the anchor tenants are high-end department stores, the other tenants should offer medium- to high-end merchandise. Fashion, gift, jewelry, and food service retailers occupy most of the shop space. Regional shopping centers are usually developed as enclosed malls, and they require a minimum population of 150,000–300,000.

Super Regional Shopping Centers.   A super regional shopping center is just a larger version of a regional shopping center. It encompasses more than 1,000,000 square feet of GLA, has more than 100 shop tenants, and is anchored by at least four full-line department stores. A population in excess of 300,000 is required to support it.

Specialty Shopping Centers.   These centers are also known as theme or festival shopping centers, and they usually range in size from 50,000 to 300,000 square feet of GLA. Often they are created by conversion of an existing old building to a new use (adaptive use) although some are new structures. Many perpetuate an architectural theme suggested by the original use of the building or the location. Specialty centers require a minimum population of 150,000 to survive, and they are often located in tourist-oriented areas that already have good traffic (most of them do not have traditional anchor tenants). Often their main attraction is food services and entertainment establishments, and smaller shops are usually one-of-a-kind boutique and specialty stores. Seldom do national or regional retailers locate in a specialty shopping center unless they are food operators. Faneuil Hall Marketplace in Boston and Ghirardelli Square in San Francisco are classic examples of such specialty centers. Faneuil Hall was originally a row of three industrial and public market buildings near the waterfront; Ghirardelli Square had been a chocolate factory.

Outlet or Off-Price Shopping Centers.   *Factory outlet stores* sell manufacturers' surplus merchandise, which may be seconds, irregulars, or overruns. *Off-price retailers* sell first-quality brand name merchandise at low prices. (They make special bulk purchases and pass the savings on to the customer.) Off-price and outlet stores are frequently found in the same shopping center, which can be an open-air strip or an enclosed mall. These centers are located away from traditional retailers; usually they are in smaller communities, adjacent to a major freeway, and one or two hours' drive from a major metropolitan area. A population of 150,000-plus is generally required for their survival.

Power Centers.   First developed in 1984, these shopping centers were originally known as promotional centers. They are large strip centers anchored by several large promotional, warehouse, or specialty stores that dominate their merchandising category. A prime example is Toys R Us. Promotional retailers are *destination* stores—customers tend to visit the shopping center to shop at that one store. As a result, power centers have only a small percentage of their GLA devoted to small shops. Generally, 75–80 percent of the power center's GLA is occupied by anchor tenants. Successful power centers have the draw of a regional mall from a minimum population of 150,000.

THE IMPORTANCE OF SHOPPING CENTERS

Shopping centers are a very important part of our economy. The different sizes and arrangements of shopping centers are all planned with two purposes in mind—to provide an optimum retailing environment for the tenants and to meet the shopping needs of consumers. Organized centers for shopping are a twentieth century phenomenon. As this century draws to a close, shopping centers are becoming increasingly important for the services they provide to individual consumers and the many ways in which they benefit the communities in which they are located. No other property type has the impact on a community that a shopping center does. In particular, it provides substantial revenue, a variety of employment opportunities, the convenience of one-stop shopping, and a testing ground for new businesses.

Many communities encourage development of shopping centers, especially the large regional and super regional shopping centers, because they are major sources of revenue for local and regional (municipal) governments. The two primary types of revenue they yield are sales tax and property tax. Almost all states and municipalities assess a sales tax, but they may exempt some items—commonly foods and restaurant purchases.

The fiscal impact of a shopping center on a particular community can easily be calculated. Take the example of a 135,000-square-foot neighborhood shopping center anchored by a 40,000-square-foot supermarket, a 30,000-square-foot super drug store, and a 35,000-square-foot home improvement center, with the remaining 30,000 square feet divided into several small shops. Assuming annual sales for the shopping center are $24,250,000 and the supermarket's share of those sales is $10 million or $250 per square foot per year, the remaining space yields $14,250,000 in sales or $150 per square foot per year. If the sales tax is 6 percent, and supermarket sales are totally exempt from sales tax, the shopping center would generate $855,000 in sales taxes on the total taxable sales of $14,250,000. If *only* food sales are exempted for the supermarket, the sales tax amount would be substantially larger.

A regional or super regional shopping center will generate significantly greater sales and tax revenues than a neighborhood shopping center. An example is a super regional mall with 1,250,000 square feet of GLA that is anchored by four department stores. If sales are $300 per square foot per year, and none of the sales are exempt from sales tax, the center would generate annual sales of $375,000,000. Using the same 6 percent tax rate as in the preceding example, this super regional mall would yield $22,500,000 in sales taxes. Nationwide in 1990, according to ICSC, shopping centers generated more than $28.5 billion in sales taxes on $723.3 billion dollars in retail sales. That represented well over half of all nonautomotive retail sales across the United States.

Shopping centers are also taxed as real estate. Most municipalities assess property taxes by first determining a property's value and then multiplying that value by the property tax rate. If a community values shopping centers at $100 per square foot, the assessed valuation of the example 135,000-square-foot neighborhood shopping center would be $13,500,000. At a property tax rate of .015—1.5 percent of the property's assessed valuation—the real estate taxes on the shopping center would be $202,500. If the example 1,250,000-square-foot super regional mall is similarly valued at $100 per square foot, its assessed valuation would be $125,000,000. At the same 1.5 percent rate, real estate taxes on the mall would be $1,875,000.

Another major benefit shopping centers provide for the community is jobs. A shopping center offers substantial employment opportunities at several levels, and people are attracted to retailing because it is exciting and fun. Businesses in a shopping center offer numerous entry-level positions that are filled by teenagers, senior citizens, and people entering the work force for the first time. Most shopping centers employ people both full time and part time. Retailing also offers seasonal positions, primarily during the Christmas selling season that traditionally starts the Friday after Thanksgiving and extends to the end of the year. Nationwide, shopping centers employ more than 10 million people directly. That represents some 9 percent of the total non-agricultural employment in the United States. In addition, development of new centers creates thousands of jobs in the construction trades—roughly one full-time construction job for every 1,000 square feet of GLA built.

Shopping centers are a convenience for consumers. Neighborhood and community shopping centers with the right tenant mix—e.g., a supermarket, a drug store, and service tenants—allow consumers to do most, if not all, of their routine shopping in one place. A regional or super regional mall usually has several stores of one type all under one roof and therefore provides opportunities for customers to comparison shop for fashions, gifts, and other items. The primary alternative to shopping at a shopping center is visiting a number of retailers scattered over a wide area. This usually requires more time to visit all the stores and may actually result in less actual shopping being done. By comparison, the shopping center provides one-stop shopping, and the enclosed mall provides one-stop shopping in an attractive, climate-controlled environment.

Because part of the American dream is to own a business, a retailer just starting a business in a shopping center can benefit from both the synergy of the tenant mix and the traffic generated by anchor tenants. If the shopping center has a merchants' association or marketing fund, the new business will have opportunities for joint advertising with its neighbor merchants. Promotional activities and coordinated sales and merchandising events will bring additional traffic to the shopping center. None of these benefits exists for a business that is located in a freestanding building or on the ground floor of an office or residential building. The majority of opportunities for new retail businesses are found in strip centers and smaller enclosed malls; most regional and super regional enclosed malls accept only national and regional retail chains and local merchants with a proven track record.

A shopping center is a self-contained operation that provides most of its own services. Because the shopping center is private property, the property manager will contract for all maintenance—including parking lot sweeping, snow removal, and sidewalk cleaning—whereas in a downtown area, the municipality contracts and pays for street and sidewalk maintenance. Regional and super regional shopping centers—and many large specialty shopping centers—provide their own security services; local police seldom handle incidents on these properties.

Shopping centers, in particular regional and super regional shopping centers, have become focal points of the communities they serve. Girl Scout troops, Little League teams, and similar local groups may be allowed to use shopping center facilities for membership drives, project displays, and fundraisers. Many enclosed malls provide a community booth where people may distribute information on local activities and issues. Space to hold meetings may be made available to nonprofit organizations free of charge. All of these types of "community services" attract people to a shopping center.

Regional and super regional shopping centers, along with smaller enclosed malls, provide entertainment activities for the community. Most regional malls have annual marketing budgets exceeding $150,000, while those of super regional malls often exceed $250,000. A part of these funds is used for promotional activities such as auto, bridal, and arts and crafts shows and photos with Santa Claus. Another part is used to promote and coordinate merchandising events such as fashion shows, sidewalk and moonlight sales, back-to-school sales, and year-end sales. Often the center provides specific entertainment or contests in conjunction with these events.

In some communities, the impact a shopping center has on traffic can be controversial. Some people say that a shopping center creates additional traffic, and this is true in the immediate area of the shopping center. However, analyses of shopping center traffic patterns have revealed that many shopping centers actually reduce the amount of traffic throughout the community at large. If a neighborhood shopping center or regional mall did not exist, people would drive farther and be on the road longer to travel to the nearest shopping center. Because shopping centers provide one-stop shopping, they reduce the amount of travel time, the number of stops, and the number of shopping trips consumers must make to complete their shopping. One can argue, in general, that a shopping center reduces traffic community-wide, thus helping to eliminate or minimize traffic congestion and reduce gasoline consumption.

CHANGES IN THE SHOPPING CENTER INDUSTRY

The shopping center industry has gone through many changes in recent years. In the last decade, value-oriented centers were being built all across the United States. They were, and in most cases still are, quite successful. These centers were developed in three distinct types—manufacturers' outlets, discount centers, and off-price centers—though many are combinations of all three. More recently, the industry has seen the rise of the so-called power center, very large stores called superstores, specialty use centers where all the merchants are focused on a particular market niche (e.g., automotive services), and centers with no anchor at all.

A *manufacturer's outlet* is a store operated by the manufacturer of a type of merchandise. Liz Claiborne, Van Heusen, and Corning Ware are examples. These manufacturers wholesale their merchandise to department stores and other retail outlets and also sell direct to the consumer—often at lower-than-

retail prices—in their own outlet stores. Though originally intended as outlets for manufacturing "seconds" (slightly flawed) and overruns, manufacturers' outlets were so successful in many cases that they began to carry a full
line of merchandise all year round.

Off-price stores feature brand-name merchandise at bargain prices. Examples are Loehmann's and Marshalls. Initially, shoppers at these stores had a
limited selection, and not all items were available at any one time. However,
this concept, too, was so successful that the selection was improved, and these
stores are kept stocked all year round.

Discount stores have been around for a long time, but in the last decade,
discount merchandising really expanded and became a major force in retailing. Some of what they sell may be brand-name merchandise, and some may
be "private label" merchandise manufactured for the discounter; all of it is
sold at lower prices. Kmart and Wal-Mart are two discounters that have had a
tremendous impact on retailing in recent years.

The typical "bargain" center is built in a strip, although some are designed as enclosed malls or configured as "villages" of shops. In recent years,
several traditional shopping centers and even older well-located buildings
were converted to bargain-type shopping centers. Such *adaptive use* of warehouses, post offices, and other structures that no longer serve their original
purposes has become an economical means of bringing retailing back into
urban business centers. Interestingly enough, the first centers of this type
were very spartan in nature; the thought was that people looking for low
prices were not interested in ambience. Over the years, however, public demand has led to improved aesthetics. Instead of piling merchandise on tables
or stacking open shipping crates, these centers now offer an attractive shopping environment with merchandise displayed as nicely as it might be in a
typical department store.

Discount merchandising has become a growth business in the United
States—from a few dozen "outlet" centers in the late 1970s to some 275 such
centers with sales of $6.5 billion in 1990. New ones are being built in popula-
tion centers (rather than outlying areas), and some rival large-scale retail centers in size and amenities. The 2.2 million-square-foot Gurnee Mills north of
Chicago will have 200 stores when it is finished along with two food courts
and parking for 10,400 cars.

Power centers were another innovation. They differ from the traditional
shopping center because they are dominated by destination-type tenants with
very large stores. These "category killers" are heavily advertised, high-
volume/low-markup operations. Their success depends on moving large
amounts of merchandise. A power center with 250,000 square feet of GLA
may comprise only eight or ten stores, with most—or all—of them being so-
called category killers. Most power centers have between 250,000 and
350,000 square feet of GLA, but there is one with 1.2 million square feet—
Scottsdale Pavillion.

Power centers need a very large population base from which to draw customers, so they are generally located in or near major metropolitan areas and close to an expressway exit or on a major arterial street. Because of the large volumes of business they generate, traffic in power centers is much heavier than that in traditional shopping centers. For this reason, they tend to have higher *parking indexes*—six spaces per 1,000 square feet of GLA rather than the traditional four to five spaces per 1,000 square feet of GLA recommended by the Urban Land Institute. Typical tenants include Home Depot, Circuit City, Pier One Imports, Nordstrom's Rack, and Toys R Us.

Another newcomer is the *superstore* or *hypermarket*. Generally these are supermarkets that have been expanded to 100,000 square feet of GLA so they can carry many lines beyond the traditional supermarket merchandise mix, often at discount prices. These stores are trying to fill two needs, enhancing their profitability by selling items that have a higher markup percentage and increasing their appeal to shoppers by offering a broader selection of merchandise. While many of the first such stores were quite successful, there is a cloud looming on the horizon. These large stores are often considered difficult to shop and that causes customer frustration. Because they are also vying for the same consumer dollars, some supermarkets are downsizing their stores to make shopping easier and increase merchandise turnover, therefore enhancing their profitability. Only time will tell which approach is "best," and very likely both will continue to have a niche in the marketplace.

Another type of center that has come into its own is the *specialty use center*. Usually located in large cities, these shopping centers are merchandised to a very narrow segment of the marketplace. An example is an automobile care and maintenance center whose tenants specialize in seat covers, tune-ups, mufflers, tires, paint jobs, major repairs, air conditioners, car phones, etc. Another center may feature goods and services related to the home (furniture, paint, draperies, floor coverings, lamps, upholstering, interior decorating, cabinetry). Specialty use centers vary widely. There is one very large center in Colorado that is strictly new car dealers. One might think car dealers are too competitive to be together in one location, but they actually like it. The proximity allows customers to shop and compare—and come to a decision quickly. The dealers believe they each get their share of the market in this setting. At the other end of the spectrum is a small shopping center in Phoenix, Arizona, that is devoted entirely to weddings. In one stop, the bride and groom can order invitations, rent a tuxedo, buy a bridal gown and bridesmaid's dresses, order the flowers, arrange for catering and photography, register silver and crystal patterns for gifts, make travel arrangements for their honeymoon, and drop off their dry-cleaning after the ceremony.

Along these same lines, there are shopping centers whose tenants are all restaurants. Some are all "fast food" operations; others have all sit-down restaurants with different ethnic approaches (e.g., Italian, Mexican, Continental, Chinese, etc.). As this book was being written, a new concept was being introduced—the all-entertainment center. This type of center is expected to include restaurants plus a variety of specific entertainments (e.g., billiard parlor, video game center, etc.). All of these concepts aim to make it easy and convenient for the customer.

The *anchorless strip center* has made a strong showing, but many in the industry are skeptical about its potential to be successful into the future. Economically, this type of center benefits the developer because all the spaces are smaller and they typically command higher rents. However, what makes anchor tenants desirable is their customer draw. Unless the public is attracted strongly enough to the center itself, the chances of its long-term survival are not good.

Overall, the last decade has been good for the industry. There were 36,650 shopping centers of all types in the United States at the end of 1990, with GLA in excess of 4.5 *billion* square feet. Some 15,000 new shopping centers had been built during the previous decade—an unprecedented period of growth—but new construction starts each year and the total GLA built each year have been declining significantly in recent years.

Throughout its history, the shopping center industry has worked diligently to know and understand consumers' needs and desires and to fulfill them. The results of a consumer poll commissioned by ICSC indicate that the industry is doing an excellent job in that regard. Consumers were asked to rate shopping centers in comparison to seven other common institutions, and shopping centers were ranked third overall—just slightly below hospitals and churches. Respondents also believed that shopping centers contribute substantially to the local economy and considered them to be major employers. Some 80 percent responded that there were *not* too many shopping centers and, rather surprisingly, more than 50 percent favored local authorities granting zoning and tax considerations to encourage development of more shopping centers. In fact, 77 percent preferred to shop at shopping centers (rather than downtown), and their opinions were very favorable with regard to such issues as access, parking, variety of stores, customer services, and safety and security. Respondents also expressed interest in and satisfaction with specific amenities at shopping centers (e.g., seating areas, directories, public restrooms and telephones, and entertainment or special events).

Statistical data from ICSC tend to reaffirm the poll's results. In a typical month, 174.4 million adults (94 percent of the population over age 18) shop at shopping centers. Some 70 percent of adults shop at regional malls—on average, nearly four times in a month; and 89 percent of adults shop at smaller (neighborhood and community) centers an average of seven times a month. Shopping centers, in all their forms, have become an accepted—indeed, desirable—part of the American landscape, and they should continue to grow and prosper. To assure that growth and prosperity, developers and managers must continually seek to understand the needs and desires of shoppers and make their shopping centers responsive to the demands of a changing consumer marketplace.

The next decade will see continued changes in the demographic profile as an aging baby boom population becomes more affluent and is interested in quality rather than quantity. The American family is expected to have both husband and wife working outside the home and a growing need for convenience. This segment of the population prefers to shop close to home, eats out more than previous generations did, and has the money to spend on what it wants.

Developers and managers of shopping centers in the future will be increasingly involved with the public and public institutions. No longer is it the exclusive purview of the developer to decide how the shopping center will be built, what amenities it will provide, or how it will be operated. Local planning agencies and interested public-spirited citizens will have a strong say in many aspects of shopping center development. While this may make the development process somewhat cumbersome and remove some of the entrepreneur's prerogatives, it should also improve a shopping center's acceptance by the community and the likelihood of its financial success. The coming years will see many changes and offer many challenges to the shopping center manager—changes and challenges that provide opportunities to succeed.

Development and Rehabilitation

Development of income-producing real estate is a speculative business. The developer builds space for lease based on an understanding of the demand for the type of property. A development that has been built as budgeted, leased at the rates anticipated, and opened on time is usually enormously successful. If the project's cost is significantly over budget, or if the rental rates or lease-up time do not meet the leasing projections, the development will not be profitable for the developer. Developing real estate is a high-risk business, but developers are willing to take the risks inherent in building a shopping center because the potential financial rewards are tremendous.

DEVELOPMENT OBJECTIVES

Opportunities exist for developing new shopping centers, expanding existing shopping centers, and rehabilitating older ones. Developers can be merchant builders, or they can build for their own account—i.e., to retain ownership and benefit from ongoing rental income. The merchant builder's intent is either to presell the project or to sell it immediately after completion. The primary objective of development is to generate a substantial profit. "Profits" for the shopping center developer derive from several sources. In addition to the development fee, there can be leasing commissions, management fees, operating income (cash flow), and revenue from the sale of the property.

The shopping center *pro forma,* which projects the costs of development and the return on the investment, includes a development fee. The fee typically ranges from 3 to 7 percent of the actual construction costs and is included as a construction expense. This fee is an important source of income for a development company because it covers the development company's overhead. If several shopping centers are being developed concurrently, development fees can easily exceed the developer's annual overhead.

Another potential source of income for a developer is leasing commissions. A developer has three approaches to leasing a shopping center, and the approach used determines the commission income earned. First, an in-house leasing team can be created to lease all the space in new projects. They would have exclusive authorization to lease, and cooperation with other brokers would be limited or nonexistent. In that case, the development company would earn all the leasing commissions projected in the pro forma, and these can be substantial. For example, the leasing commissions for a 120,000-square-foot strip center anchored by a supermarket and a super drug store can range from $250,000 to $350,000. The second approach is for the developer to negotiate the leases with anchor tenants and hire a leasing company to market and lease the small shop spaces. This approach is used when the developer has a rapport with anchor retailers and is in a better position than anyone else to negotiate their specific leases. In this situation, the developer would earn only the commissions for the anchor leases. The final approach is to hire a leasing firm to negotiate all the leases, in which case, the developer would not earn any commission income.

A third source of income is management fees. If the developer's business includes a management department or management company, a fee can be earned for managing the property for the development company or for the purchaser of the property. If the developer retains ownership of the property, cash flow is a fourth source of income.

When a development achieves its goal and is built and leased per the original pro forma, substantial value is created in the property. This value can be realized by either selling or refinancing the property. If the shopping center is a joint venture with another company or with other individuals, the developer may act as the broker when the shopping center is sold and earn a commission on the sale—in addition to an ownership share of the proceeds.

In addition to the financial considerations, there are numerous intangibles such as pride of ownership and the developer's sense of accomplishment. Many developers take great pride in the projects they create. They want the shopping center's design and layout to be compatible with the community's objectives and the property to become an asset to the community. Lenders and prospective anchor tenants evaluate developers based on their prior shopping center projects. When the developer has a successful track record, lenders and prospective anchor tenants are more inclined to become involved with the project.

The developer of a shopping center risks losing considerable money. The risks may not always be obvious, but they can be substantial. Perhaps the most important ones to note here are those risks that relate directly to the shopping center as a form of investment property. *Functional risk* is related to the shopping center's location, design, size, etc., and its utility for retail enterprise. *Interest-rate risk* arises because changes in value are often attributable to variations in interest rates and availability of financing. *Inflation/ deflation risk* is a measure of the effects of changes in purchasing power on the value of the shopping center. Successful retention of quality tenants at acceptable rent levels is *marketability risk*. Real estate occasionally loses value and, because real property is almost always developed (at least in part) with borrowed money, the value need not drop to zero for the owner's entire equity in such an investment to be lost. Risk accompanies most investments, and shopping center developers and their financial advisors are expected to make intelligent estimates of the risks inherent in such projects.

The opportunities for generating tremendous profits and creating great value in a property are the driving forces behind development. Being entrepreneurs, developers may view risk differently than others do, or they may permit the anticipated profits to obscure the potential risks. The overbuilding of commercial properties in the last decade—including and especially shopping centers—is an example. In the typical real estate investment, risk is equated with chance of loss. The degree of risk depends on the difference between expected and actual outcomes. If the expected outcome is guaranteed, the risk is negligible; if there is great uncertainty about the outcome, the risk is high. In order to succeed, the development must be based on all the criteria for a successful shopping center.

THE DEVELOPMENT TEAM

Developing a shopping center is a very complex process that requires the knowledge and experience of many individuals, each with a separate expertise. Each member of the development team brings specific expertise to the project with one objective in mind—to develop a successful shopping center. The central or focal point of the development team is the *developer* who will typically assign a *project manager* to orchestrate the team's efforts and take the project from concept through lease-up to opening. A *construction manager* supports the project manager's efforts. The project manager will select the other members of the team, which comprise an architect, a general contractor, a leasing agent, a property manager, and various consultants. In some projects, the lender is also a member of the team. The project manager must allow the other team members to express their points of view. In the early stages, differences of opinion should be encouraged in order to obtain a complete analysis of all sides of each issue and aspect of the development process.

The *architect* creates a layout and design for the proposed shopping center based on the vision of the developer. From such information as the proposed anchor tenants, a suggested number of pads or outlots, and a range of sizes for the other shop spaces, the architect proposes an arrangement of store spaces. The well-developed creative skills of a knowledgeable and experienced shopping center architect will augment the developer's vision. The architect should also be able to provide a rough estimate of the costs of constructing the proposed shopping center as designed.

The project manager and the construction manager will interview and select a *general contractor.* Traditionally, the general contractor's main function has been to construct the project according to the plans and specifications previously prepared by the architect and approved by the developer. While this remains the principal role of the contractor, many developers make greater use of the contractor's construction expertise. During the design stage, developers often ask the general contractor for opinions about other aspects of the property's construction. In an economy where rising construction costs are the norm, the general contractor's knowledge of how to keep costs down without sacrificing quality can benefit the developer. To guarantee that the project is economically feasible, the developer should arrange a series of meetings between the architect and the general contractor during the initial design and drafting stages.

It is often necessary to hire additional experts as *consultants* to the development team. An appraiser may conduct a market study to verify for the lender and the developer that there is a demand for the retail space and that the projected rental rates are achievable. The expertise of civil and mechanical engineers, landscape architects, and environmental and wetlands consultants may be needed as well.

Land, construction, and financing costs can be estimated with a fairly high degree of accuracy. The one outcome of the development process that cannot be predetermined, unless a project is fully preleased, is the leasing. This makes the *leasing agent* a critical member of the development team. Projected lease-up time and rental rates are estimates based on the best information available to the developer. If space in the shopping center is leased at rental rates significantly lower than those projected, or if the lease-up period extends far beyond the time projected, the development is a candidate for failure regardless of whether the other components of the pro forma are on budget. The project manager must select the leasing agent who is most qualified to market and lease the shopping center. The person (or persons) selected may be an in-house leasing agent, an agent from a brokerage firm, or the property manager.

The *property manager* should be included during the design stage to contribute a management perspective on the development process. The layout of the shopping center should be reviewed to detect any spaces that may be difficult to lease. The manager should examine the layout of the shopping center and evaluate the proposed building materials from maintenance and operations perspectives (e.g., care, repair, safety, security, etc.). Also at this stage, the property manager should review the projected rental rates and lease-up schedule and either verify them or offer another perspective on the market.

One of the results of the savings and loan crisis was a tightening of lending practices, and many lenders now require the developer to obtain approval for over-budget and nonbudgeted pro forma items. They often retain the right to approve each proposed lease, too. In essence, these controls include the *lender* as a member of the development team.

SITE SELECTION AND ACQUISITION

Both selection and acquisition of the site depend on careful analysis. In the development process, the developer evaluates demographic information to determine whether the site is viable for a shopping center. If development is feasible from this market standpoint, the developer will take an option on the site or enter into a sales contract contingent on certain requirements being met—e.g., a commitment from one or more anchor tenants, appropriate rezoning, availability of financing, etc.

Most developers will not acquire title to a property until they have a commitment from one or more anchor tenants. If no major retailers are interested in the site, the shopping center will normally not be developed—most shopping centers are anchor dependent.

The development process continues during the option period as the developer's architect draws a preliminary site plan of the center that shows the locations of anchor tenants, shops, and pads or outlots. The site and building plans must be submitted to the municipal building department for approval and permits. The first approval is for *zoning.* Zoning ordinances are the means by which a municipality exercises control over land use. If the site is not zoned for shopping center use, the developer may apply for a variance, and the option to purchase the site will be contingent on appropriate rezoning.

Environmental issues are also considered in the analysis of the site. An environmental audit is conducted to determine if any hazardous substances are present. Development of wetlands requires a specific permit. Development of a shopping center can be affected by environmental laws issued by state and local governing bodies in addition to the federal regulations enforced by the U.S. Environmental Protection Agency (EPA). Requirements for such things as testing, monitoring, approvals, and construction and operating permits add to development costs, and some outcomes of environmental analyses may preclude development of a selected site.

Based on the preliminary site plan, the developer can prepare a pro forma financial analysis that lists the costs of developing the site and projections of income, expenses, and cash flow. The developer negotiates a loan to finance the project based on the cost to develop the shopping center, the amount of equity the lender will require, and the property's *net operating income (NOI)*.

When it is a certainty that the anchor tenants have committed, all governmental requirements for approval have been met, and financing has been obtained, the developer can exercise the option to purchase the property and proceed with development.

Importance of Anchor Tenants

Anchor tenants are crucial to shopping center development. The size and positioning of anchor space affects the design and placement of all the other tenant spaces in the center. The type and caliber of the anchor's merchandise affects both the mix of tenants and their placement in the center. The financial arrangements with the anchor tenant will affect development costs, and they may affect the leases for the other tenants and the financial arrangements with them. For these reasons, negotiation of anchor leases usually takes place very early in the development process. The developer must be assured of the anchor tenants' commitment to the project well in advance, both to attract other tenants to the center and to secure construction and other financing. Lenders often require lease commitments as a condition for shopping center development loans. (Negotiation of anchor leases is discussed in chapter 9.)

Anchor Store Location.   Retailers use several criteria when evaluating and selecting a site for a store. The old saying that the three most important things in real estate are "location, location, and location" definitely applies to shopping centers. Major retailers that occupy anchor spaces and many national and regional retailers that lease shop spaces will thoroughly analyze a site using criteria they have developed to measure their stores' success. Location means more than just the actual site and is evaluated in several ways. When retailers or shopping center developers say "location," they also mean the demographic profile of the area and competition in relation to the site as well as site accessibility and any impediments to development.

A retailer normally evaluates an area to determine its sales potential. An analysis of demographic data for the area will allow the retailer to profile its "typical customer" and project sales volume figures. The demographic profile of a trade area includes the size of the population and its dominant age ranges, household and family sizes, income levels, types of employment, and levels of education. Using such information, a discount retailer will most likely look for family income levels that are low to medium, while a fine jeweler will seek income levels that are medium-high to high. An auto supply store that depends on blue-collar workers and a strong teen and young adult population for its success would not be located in an area populated primarily by senior citizens. A specialty book store requires a well-educated population. Toy stores and children's wear retailers need a large population of families with young children if they are to thrive.

A major retailer's selection of the site is one validation that a shopping center could succeed there. The developer must be cautious, however. Just because a major retailer has selected a site is no guarantee that other retailers will be successful at that location. An anchor tenant draws customers from a larger trade area than is available to the tenants in the smaller shops. If the demographic profile in the immediate area is inadequate or inappropriate to their customer profile, shop tenants may fail. Anchor tenants are able to draw their customers from an area beyond the immediate vicinity of the site because of their size, their array of merchandise, and their ability to promote themselves more widely.

Another criterion that is examined today is the psychographic "profile" of the trade area. This analysis goes beyond numbers and dollars to examine values, attitudes, and similar phenomena. These characteristics of a population are more likely to be manifested in lifestyle choices—i.e., the differences between two music lovers, the rock-and-roll concert fan versus the opera-goer. Such distinctions do affect how and when people spend their money.

Retailers are also concerned with location in relation to competition and the number of competitors in the area. Another consideration is the location of a site in relation to their other stores. All of these factors will affect tenants' sales volumes. The final consideration is the impact of future developments in the area on a retailer's success at this site. New competition moving into the general area has the potential to reduce an established retailer's market share.

Customer Draw.   An anchor tenant usually occupies a large proportion of the available GLA and is the tenant that will draw the majority of the customers to the shopping center. The type of retailer that serves as the anchor tenant varies with the type of shopping center. Department stores (Sears, Nordstrom, Dayton-Hudson, etc.) are anchor tenants for regional and super regional malls. Discount stores (e.g., Kmart, Wal-Mart) more frequently anchor community shopping centers but may be found in regional and even some neighborhood centers. Junior department stores such as Mervyn's anchor community or regional shopping centers. Supermarkets, super drug stores, and home improvement centers serve as anchor tenants for neighborhood and community centers. Restaurants are often anchor tenants for specialty or theme centers. A small strip center may be anchored by a convenience store such as 7-Eleven or Circle K.

Neighborhood, community, and regional shopping centers must have one or more anchor tenants to be successful. Shopping center owners have found that the traffic draw of the anchor tenant or tenants is essential to the success of the entire shopping center. The tenants in the smaller shop spaces collectively do not have the drawing power to attract sufficient traffic for each tenant to be successful. Many small shop tenants, especially independent retailers and service businesses, need the continual exposure that results from the significant amount of traffic generated by the anchor tenant. A large center developed without an anchor tenant is referred to as "anchorless"; many such centers have either failed or met with only marginal success.

Specialty or theme shopping centers are an exception to the rule that most shopping centers need anchor tenants. Many such centers are the result of adaptive use of "landmark" structures, and the location and unique features of the design of the building or its historical nature is the traffic draw. For instance, Ghirardelli Square, located at the end of a cable car line and near the waterfront in San Francisco, is an old chocolate factory converted to a specialty shopping center. Trolley Square in Salt Lake City has combined the uniqueness of an old trolley barn with entertainment facilities and boutiques. Most major U.S. cities have some such development.

A few major regional or super regional mall developers are experimenting with including a large amusement park within the enclosed mall as a major draw. Amusement areas in malls are being developed because malls have long been among the entertainment centers of the community. Such areas provide an additional reason for a family to shop at the mall. The West Edmonton Mall in Alberta, Canada, has 5.2 million square feet of GLA and includes such entertainment features as an indoor amusement park, ice palace, sea life cavern, submarine ride, miniature golf, dolphin lagoon, water park, and nineteen theaters. It is too early in the development of malls with amusement parks to know whether they will be successful over the long run.

Tenant Mix. Anchor tenants often establish the price range of the merchandise sold by the other tenants. A mall anchored by Neiman-Marcus, Sak's Fifth Avenue, and Nordstrom would have shops offering merchandise that is generally higher in price. Shopping centers anchored by discounters (e.g., Kmart) and "popular price" stores (e.g., Mervyn's) will have other tenants whose merchandise is priced similarly—i.e., a particular discounter may sell low-priced *or* high-priced items; the common bond is the discount pricing.

The anchor tenants also set the tone for the tenant mix of the shopping center. When a shopping center is anchored by a supermarket or a super drug store, or both, the majority of the smaller shop spaces will be leased to services such as dry cleaning, shoe repair, and insurance agents, and to food vendors such as restaurants, delis, and bakeries. These are called destination tenants. Supermarket and super drug store customers know what they want, and they shop for predetermined items at the centers anchored by these stores. They are not looking for a leisurely shopping experience, and they are not likely to shop impulsively.

Regional and super regional shopping centers are tenanted by fashion, gift, jewelry, and food retailers. These specialty tenants complement the merchandise offered by department stores. The department store will draw the majority of the traffic to the shopping center and, by placing department stores at opposite ends of the mall, the shop tenants benefit from the cross traffic between or among the shopping center's department store anchor tenants. (Tenant mix is discussed in detail in chapter 8 and elsewhere in this book.)

Lender Considerations.   Lenders for shopping centers recognize the importance of the anchor tenant to the success of the shopping center. Developers usually cannot obtain a loan commitment until one or more anchor tenants acceptable to the lender have committed to the project. With some anchor tenants having financial problems due to leveraged buyouts in the mid- and late 1980s, lenders now carefully evaluate the financial status of the anchor tenant.

Lenders generally require a certain percentage of the shopping center's income to be from creditworthy tenants in general. There is no industrywide ratio for the percentage of the shopping center's income, the number of tenants, or the amount of GLA to be attributable to creditworthy tenants. However, shopping center investors prefer that anchor tenants *not* occupy too large a percentage of the shopping center's GLA. For instance, an investment group may set a criterion that not more than 65 percent of the GLA is to be occupied by anchor tenants. Because anchor tenants negotiate lease terms favorable to themselves that include long-term leases and limited rent increases, many investors believe that a shopping center with an extraordinarily high percentage of GLA occupied by anchor tenants will have limited upside income potential. A good balance between anchor tenants and shop tenants is a key factor in a shopping center's success.

Prospective Anchor Tenants.   When a developer is proposing a neighborhood or community shopping center, there may be only one or two supermarkets as potential anchor tenants. This occurs when some of the supermarkets are already represented in the immediate area and many of the other supermarkets are concentrating their expansions elsewhere. For instance, in many areas of the country, there may be only two dominant supermarkets, such as Safeway and Albertson's in the Northwest, and several small supermarket chains that are associated with one or two cooperative purchasing organizations.

On the other hand, a regional or super regional shopping center usually will have two to five anchor tenants. In the Seattle area in the early 1990s, for instance, there were only five full-line department stores, two junior department stores, and four large discount operators. If a developer wants a super regional mall in the Seattle area to be anchored by four full-line department stores, there are only five potential candidates. Among these five candidates, some may already have stores that serve part or all of the trade area of the proposed super regional shopping center; others may not be expanding their operations (increasing the number of stores), while still others may have expansion plans that are limited to other areas of the country.

Major retailers know their importance to the shopping center as anchor tenants. They also know there are a limited number of anchor-type tenants available for each proposed shopping center. Seldom are there *more* potential anchor tenants available than the shopping center can accommodate, and rarely do these retailers bid against one another for a site in a particular shopping center.

Preparation of the Development Pro Forma

A developer will prepare and revise the pro forma for a proposed shopping center several times. The entire development team contributes to the evolving pro forma. The developer will contact major retailers and negotiate the terms of their anchor leases. The leasing agent will provide income projections from rents for the shop spaces, pads, and outlots. The construction manager will obtain firm bids from several general contractors. While the construction costs are being acquired, the developer will negotiate with a lender for a loan commitment. The property manager will verify the income projections and prepare estimates of grand opening event costs and operating expenses. The initial pro forma will be based on the estimation of projected income and construction costs. If it appears from the rough numbers that the proposed shopping center is economically viable, the developer will pursue the project.

The example pro forma in exhibit 2.1 permits analysis of the cost to develop the shopping center, projections of income and the landlord's nonreimbursable operating expenses, and calculation of NOI and return on investment. The costs of developing the shopping center include land acquisition, design and consultation fees, construction costs, and the cost of financing these activities. Also to be considered are off-site infrastructure costs, impact fees, construction and operating permits, etc., which can add substantially to development costs.

Projected rental income from the property is based on the GLAs of anchor tenant spaces, small shop spaces, and pads or outlots. However, developers and lenders are primarily interested in the revenue the center is likely to produce on an annual basis over time rather than what it could produce if it were always 100-percent occupied and all rents were paid in full. It is prudent to anticipate some loss of income due to tenants vacating and rents being received late or not at all. Lost income from vacancies has usually been projected as 5 percent of the small shop space, with no vacancy factor applied to anchor spaces (anchor leases have long terms, and these tenants are usually verified to be creditworthy). However, this varies in practice. *Vacancy loss* may be estimated based on a time period, say three months, at the market

E X H I B I T   2.1

Draft Pro Forma

Date: _____   Project: _____

[*Company Name*]

Areas

Total Site   _____ Sq Ft   (_____ Acres)
Less Nonusable   _____ Sq Ft
Net Site   _____ Sq Ft
Building Area   _____ Sq Ft
Common Area   _____ Sq Ft

Costs

A. Land _____ Sq Ft @ $_____/Sq Ft $_____

B. On Site _____ Sq Ft @ $_____/Sq Ft $_____
   Off Site _____ Sq Ft @ $_____/Sq Ft $_____
   Total for Site Work (B) $_____

C. Buildings
   1. _____ _____ Sq Ft @ $_____/Sq Ft = $_____
   2. _____ _____ Sq Ft @ $_____/Sq Ft = $_____
   3. _____ _____ Sq Ft @ $_____/Sq Ft = $_____
   4. _____ _____ Sq Ft @ $_____/Sq Ft = $_____
   5. _____ _____ Sq Ft @ $_____/Sq Ft = $_____
   6. _____ _____ Sq Ft @ $_____/Sq Ft = $_____
   7. _____ _____ Sq Ft @ $_____/Sq Ft = $_____
   8. _____ _____ Sq Ft @ $_____/Sq Ft = $_____
   9. Tenant Allowances _____ $_____
      Total Buildings (C) $_____
      Total Buildings *plus* Site Work (B + C) $_____

D. Architecture and Engineering _____ % of (B + C) $_____
E. Annexation and City Liaison $_____
F. Sales Tax _____ % of (B + C) $_____

G. Lease Commissions
   1. Anchor _____ Sq Ft @ $_____/Sq Ft
   2. Shops _____ Sq Ft @ $_____/Sq Ft
   3. Pads   _____ Sq Ft @ $_____/Sq Ft
   4. _____ Sq Ft @ $_____/Sq Ft
   5. _____ Sq Ft @ $_____/Sq Ft
      Total Lease Commissions (G) $_____

H. Fees and Permits $_____
I. Survey, Soils, Texts, and Inspections $_____
J. Legal, Environmental, Appraisal, and Market Study $_____
K. Real Estate Taxes $_____
L. Assessments $_____
M. Bond/Insurance _____ % of (B + C) $_____
N. Escrow $_____
O. Clean-Up—Punch List $_____
P. Grand Opening and Promotion $_____

E X H I B I T   2.1 (*continued*)

Q. Miscellaneous Costs $_____
R. Development Fee _____ % of (B + C) $_____
S. Contingency $_____
T. Financing $_____
        _____ Points $_____
     Interim _____ % _____ Months _____ % $_____
            Total Financing (T)
                                                                                        $_____

U. Land Carry
                                                                                        $_____

Income Statement

A. Rental Income
     1. Anchor _____ Sq Ft @ $_____/Sq Ft $_____
     2. _____ Sq Ft @ $_____/Sq Ft $_____
     3. _____ Sq Ft @ $_____/Sq Ft $_____
     4. Shops _____ Sq Ft @ $_____/Sq Ft $_____
     5. _____ Sq Ft @ $_____/Sq Ft $_____
     6. _____ Sq Ft @ $_____/Sq Ft $_____
     7. Pads _____ Sq Ft @ $_____/Sq Ft $_____
     8. _____ Sq Ft @ $_____/Sq Ft $_____
     9. _____ Sq Ft @ $_____/Sq Ft $_____
            Total Rental Income (A) $_____

B. Expenses
     1. _____ % Vacancy $_____
     2. Management Fee _____ % $_____
     3. Nonreimbursable Maintenance $_____
     4. Vacancy CAM/Tax/Insurance @ $_____/Sq Ft $_____
     5. Merchants' Assn/Market'g Fund @ $_____/Sq Ft $_____
     6. Other Expenses $_____
            Total Expenses (B) $_____

C. Net Operating Income (NOI) [A − B] $_____

Cash—Loan—Equity Analysis

Economic Value—Cap Rate _____ % of NOI $_____
Loan _____ % of Value—Coverage _____ $_____
Debt Service _____ %—_____ Year = $_____ K $_____
Cash Flow $_____

Total Cost $_____
− Loan Amount $_____
Equity Requirement $_____

$_____ ÷ $_____ = _____ %
  (Cash Flow)   (Equity Required)   (Rate of Return on Investment)

Common area usually includes space allotted for parking. *Off-site costs* may include infrastructure items. *Equity requirement* would include any downpayment (amounts paid upfront by the developer and/or ownership partners) and may reflect the developer's investment of time and expertise (part or all of the "development fee") and prior investment in the land.

Pro forma compilation and calculations are intended to project a reasonably accurate estimate of construction costs, and operating income and expenses. Other items may be incorporated as appropriate.

rate prevailing at the time of lease expiration, and *collection loss* may be calculated as a percentage of the gross receipts (e.g., 2 percent of the anticipated gross rental income from all tenants except the anchors). Subtraction of vacancy and collection losses from gross rental income yields a projection of *effective gross income* or the actual receipts likely to be collected for the shopping center.

Next, the nonreimbursable *operating expenses* are estimated. These include the pass-through charges—e.g., common area maintenance (CAM), taxes, and insurance—that are attributable to the vacant spaces and which the landlord therefore pays, as well as other nonreimbursable expenses which cannot be collected from or passed through to other tenants, such as merchants' association or marketing fund dues, utility costs for vacant spaces, legal fees, and possibly the management fee. Note that if anchor tenants' leases exclude them from paying some CAM expenses and the other tenants' leases prorate CAM expenses in relation to the entire GLA of the center (including the GLA of the anchor spaces), the anchors' shares of the CAM expenses become nonreimbursable operating expenses of the landlord and should be included in the development pro forma estimates to assure their accuracy.

Subtracting the operating expenses from the effective gross income yields the property's *net operating income (NOI)*. Finally, the annual debt service on the loan (payments of principal and interest) is subtracted from the NOI to determine the *cash flow*. This cash flow figure is used to project the developer's *return on investment (ROI)* as part of the development pro forma.

Importance of Financing

A critical element in the development process is financing. Without an outside source of funds—either a lender or a joint-venture partner—a shopping center will not be developed. A project is usually developed with two loans. The first is a *construction loan,* which is a short-term loan that covers the cost to develop the project and is usually funded by one or more commercial banks. The primary lender negotiates with and provides the loan to the developer. Often the primary lender will share the risk in making the loan by having other lenders participate in it. Such participating lenders then provide the funds for a portion of the construction loan. A construction loan is usually a *recourse loan,* meaning the borrower is required to guarantee the repayment of the loan (the lender can claim other assets of the borrower in addition to the collateral if the loan is defaulted).

Subsequently, a *permanent loan* is taken out to replace and pay off the construction loan. In the past, a permanent loan was typically a long-term loan for a period of 20–30 years. Today, however, such loans are as likely to have a term of five, seven, or ten years, with their amortization (installment payments) comparable to those for a 25- or 30-year loan and a final balloon payment to pay off the outstanding principal. Long-term loans typically were *nonrecourse loans* (the borrower who defaulted had no personal liability for the loan beyond the property pledged as collateral), but this is not always the case today.

In the early 1990s, lenders required a percentage of a commercial project to be preleased either before construction or before the permanent lender would provide the loan for the development. For shopping centers, lenders will require a lease commitment from one or more anchor tenants before they will make a loan commitment.

Sources for Financing.   The developer's goal is to obtain 100-percent financing. In such a situation, the developer would have no cash invested in the project; he or she would receive a substantial development fee and still own the project. Prior to the early 1980s, this goal was achievable. If a developer could demonstrate that the value of a shopping center was 133 percent of the cost to develop it, and the lender was willing to provide a loan at 75 percent of value, the loan would be for 100 percent of the development cost (133 percent x 75 percent = 100 percent). Once operational, the center's NOI was usually sufficient to service the debt on the loan because interest rates were traditionally below 10 percent.

In the early 1980s, however, interest rates reached the highest levels in the history of the United States, soaring into double digits and exceeding 20 percent in some areas. Understandably, few proposed developments would generate sufficient NOI to service a loan at such a high interest rate. As a consequence, developers sought alternatives to traditional financing. Two sources of such funding were common during the high-interest-rate years of the early 1980s, and both reduced the developer's *equity* (outright ownership) in the project.

Many institutions, especially insurance companies, stepped in to provide the funds for development of commercial projects. For providing all of the development funds, the institution would receive a 50-percent share of the equity—there would be no loan or loan payment as such. Often the institution would receive either a guaranteed or a preferential return on the investment. A *guaranteed return* would provide the institution with an agreed-upon rate of return on the funds it contributed. The guarantee would be for either a limited period (e.g., two or five years) or the entire term of the joint ownership of the property. If the cash flow from the property was not sufficient to provide the guaranteed return, the developer would have to make up the difference from personal funds. A *preferential return* would provide the institution with the first distribution from the cash flow of the property until it received a prescribed percentage return on the amount contributed (e.g., 12 percent). The developer would then receive the next distribution from the cash flow, which would be equal to the amount paid to the institution. Any additional cash flow would be divided equally between the institution and the developer for distribution. A distinct advantage to this arrangement is that when all the funds necessary to develop the project are contributed, there is no debt service—in essence, the NOI of the property is its cash flow.

The second source was lender-participation loans. The lender would provide a loan at an interest rate below the market rate and receive either (1) an equity position in the property or (2) a percentage of either the cash flow from the property or its appreciation upon sale.

During the early 1990s, developers were confronted with another type of financing crisis. The savings and loan industry tightened its lending practices, and lenders required developers to put cash into their projects. The typical loan was for 70–80 percent of the project cost, and developers were required to make up the difference between the project cost and the loan amount, from either their own funds or those of an *equity partner* who would receive a substantial percentage of ownership in the project.

SHOPPING CENTER DESIGN

Shopping centers are commonly designed either as a single row of stores facing a parking lot (a strip center) or as a double row of stores facing each other and separated by a walkway called a mall. Most open shopping centers are strip centers, while most regional and super regional shopping centers are enclosed malls. Many specialty centers also are enclosed because they are developed in old buildings. Examples of these are Jackson's Brewery in New Orleans and The Pavilion in the Old Post Office in Washington, D.C.

Strip shopping centers may be configured in several different ways. Typically they are either aligned in a straight strip or L-shaped; occasionally they are U-shaped. The size and shape of the parcel of land will determine the configuration of a strip center. Exhibit 2.2 shows a plan for a typical straight strip with a single anchor *(top)* and with three anchors and a few shops along one side *(bottom)*. Exhibit 2.3 shows an L-shaped center with several anchors clustered on one leg of the L *(top)* and the more typical arrangement with an anchor tenant on each end of the L *(bottom)*. Exhibit 2.4 shows a U-shaped center with anchors in the middle and near each end. (See pages 32–35.)

Malls are often developed with department store anchors positioned at either end to generate traffic between them, as in the dumbbell-shaped design shown in exhibit 2.5. Malls anchored by three department stores are usually T-shaped (exhibit 2.6, *top*). When there is a fourth anchor, the mall is usually cross-shaped (exhibit 2.6, *bottom*).

Malls can be built either all on one level (horizontal) or on several levels (vertical). When a mall has two or more levels, the anchor tenants should have entrances on each level to equalize traffic flow. If the multilevel mall has garage parking, each level of the mall should be accessible from the garage.

Such an arrangement is usually not possible in downtown multilevel malls. There, parking may be on building levels other than those of the mall or in a separate building.

The layouts shown in the following exhibits are representative but not universal. Obviously, the configuration of a particular shopping center will depend on the size, shape, elevation, and other physical features of the parcel of land where the center is built as well as limitations imposed by local zoning ordinances.

Planning and Design

When planning and designing a shopping center, the development team must satisfy two customer bases. The first customer base is the tenant or space user; the second is the consumer—the shopper. In the early years of shopping center development, tenants were almost exclusively retail or service uses. More recently, though, the primary tenant base of retail and service uses has been expanded to include offices, medical professionals, and governmental agencies. The consumer base has also changed over time. People who shop at convenience centers are looking for a quick trip. They know what they want to buy, and they want to be in and out of the shopping center and the store or stores as quickly as possible. When the same people shop at an enclosed fashion mall, they have different expectations—usually they want to comparison shop in a more leisurely atmosphere. No matter how beautifully designed, how well-built, or how well-maintained it is, a shopping center will not succeed unless the people in the community accept and support it by shopping there.

Changing Tenant Requirements.   The requirements of shopping center tenants vary with the type of center. For instance, most tenants in a strip shopping center are concerned with their visibility from the parking lot or the street. They are also concerned that customers will be able to walk directly from their cars into the stores. A convenience grocery store such as 7-Eleven, a dry cleaner, or a video rental store needs parking close to its storefront. Such tenants will locate in strip centers ranging in size from small (10,000 square feet) to large (e.g., open-air community centers in excess of 200,000 square feet). On the other hand, a fashion store in an enclosed mall is concerned with (1) the relationship between its location and the locations of the other stores (both anchor tenants and small shops) and (2) the amount of foot traffic passing by its store. A *center court* location in an enclosed mall— midway between two department store anchors—will usually have the greatest amount of foot traffic, while an unanchored wing will usually have the least. The design of each type of shopping center must be planned to meet the needs of each type of tenant that will locate in that center.

The changing needs of retailers can be traced over the past two decades.

E X H I B I T   2.2

Representative Straight Strip Shopping Centers

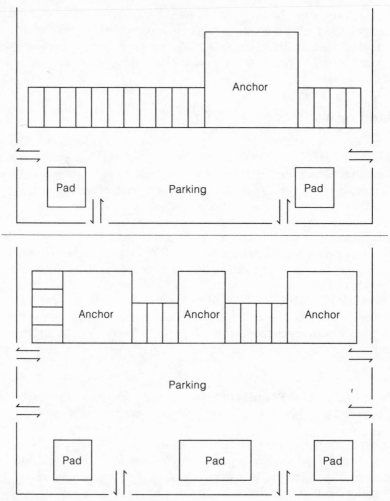

Top, single-anchor strip. A straight strip design, typical of a neighborhood or community shopping center, commonly includes one anchor store (e.g., a supermarket) and may have one or more pad spaces leased to a fast food restaurant or a bank. *Bottom,* three-anchor strip. This example includes three anchor stores plus small shops and pad spaces. The combination of anchors might be a supermarket, a drug store, and a home improvement center; the pads might be leased to restaurants and a bank.

E X H I B I T   2.3

L-Shaped Shopping Center Designs

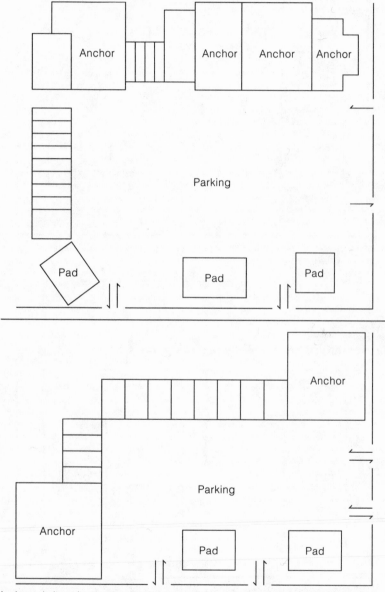

An L-shaped shopping center may have several anchors clustered along one leg of the L *(top)*; this example includes several pad spaces as well. However, an L-shaped design typically places an anchor at the ends of both legs of the L, with small shops aligned between them *(bottom)*; there are also pad spaces in this example.

Representative U-Shaped Shopping Center Design

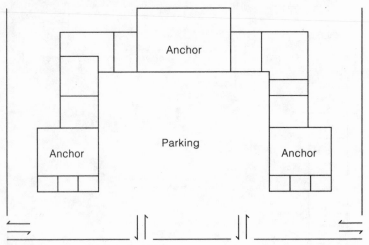

In a U-shaped center, anchors typically occupy spaces in the center of the U and at the ends of the two arms.

Representative Dumbbell-Shaped Shopping Center

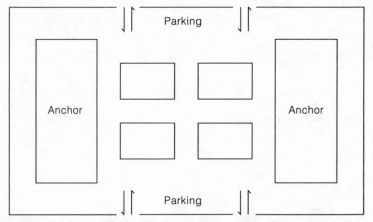

The dumbbell shape is typical of a mall with anchors at either end and small shop spaces between them. Today, malls are commonly enclosed, but some older existing centers have clusters of small shops along an open walkway or mall between anchors.

E X H I B I T   2.6

Representative Mall Configurations

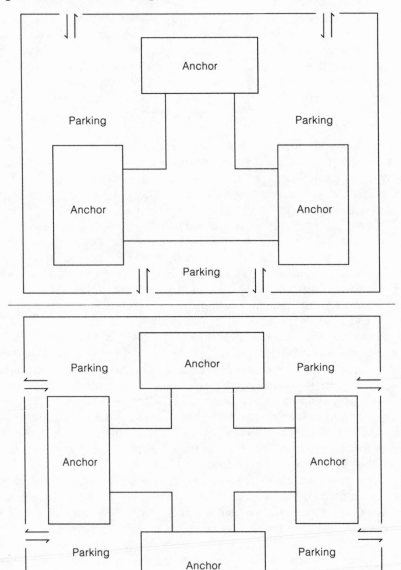

When a mall has three department store anchors, they are usually arranged in a T shape *(top)*. Shopping centers with four anchors are usually arranged in a cross shape with the anchors positioned at the extreme ends *(bottom)*.

The most obvious changes have been the increasing store size of the super-market, which is the primary anchor tenant for neighborhood and commu-nity shopping centers. Supermarkets have been expanded from 25,000-square-foot stores in the 1960s to 40,000-square-foot or larger stores in the 1990s. Today, a neighborhood shopping center developed on 10 acres with a supermarket anchor would devote more of its GLA to the supermarket and less to the small shop spaces than one developed in the 1960s, the 1970s, or the early 1980s. Because the tenants in the small shop spaces pay more rent per square foot than a supermarket does, the income would be lower from a center with proportionately less GLA devoted to small shops than to anchor space.

The larger supermarkets have also changed the tenant mix of the shop-ping centers they anchor. A 50,000-square-foot supermarket carries a wider array of merchandise than a 30,000-square-foot grocery store. Such large su-permarkets often include a fresh fish market, a deli, prepared food for carry-outs, a cafeteria, and an extensive selection of wines and liquors. Some even include a camera department in addition to selling film and film processing. All of these "departments" used to be potential uses for the small shop spaces. Often when the anchor tenant expands its line of merchandise, it pre-cludes some other tenants from leasing smaller spaces in the shopping cen-ter. An independent fish market or deli may not want to compete—indeed, may not be able to compete—with a supermarket that has greater buying power and an extensive advertising program.

Another specific change in retailing in the late 1980s was the advent of the "category killers." These stores are larger than the typical stores in their categories, and they carry the full breadth and depth of their merchandise lines. Their selection of merchandise is so complete and their pricing so com-petitive that they often discourage competition in the immediate area. Ex-amples are Blockbuster Video—whose stores are four to five times the size of the typical (1,500 square foot) video rental store—and the 25,000–40,000-square-foot linen stores that overwhelm the typical (1,750 square foot) bath shop. Toys R Us is another example.

While these expansions are widespread, they are not necessarily univer-sal. In fact, the majority of retailers have decreased their store sizes. In the 1970s, a women's shoe store usually had more than 2,000 square feet of GLA; in the early 1990s, the typical women's shoe store had approximately 1,450 square feet of GLA. Many of the apparel stores that formerly had more than 5,000 square feet of GLA now have 2,000–3,500 square feet of GLA. Such stores were downsized initially to reduce occupancy costs. After downsizing, retailers found that by merchandising their entire store area—the floor, the walls, and even the ceilings—they generated greater sales than they did in larger stores. Downsizing also meant they either eliminated or reduced the size of their stock rooms and managers' offices. Developers must respond to the downsizing of these nonanchor tenants by building stores that are smaller.

However, retailers still want the same amount of frontage for visibility, so the stores have to have less depth.

The increasing size of supermarkets combined with the downsizing of most of the tenants for shop spaces has changed the design of the shopping center over the years. In the 1960s, a neighborhood shopping center was designed with a 25,000-square-foot grocery store and smaller shop spaces that were 100 feet deep. In the 1970s, the same type of center was designed with a 35,000-square-foot supermarket and shop spaces with depths of 70–85 feet. In the early 1990s, however, neighborhood shopping centers are being designed with a 45,000-square-foot or larger supermarket and shop spaces with depths of 50–60 feet.

The constant changing of tenants' space needs and the advent of the category killers have had their impact on the tenant mix of existing and proposed shopping centers. The shop spaces in some older centers are too large for many current shop tenants while their anchor spaces are too small to accommodate a state-of-the-art supermarket. Centers with shop spaces that are too large will have leasing problems. There are few potential tenants for shop spaces in neighborhood and community shopping centers where the spaces are larger than 2,500 square feet, especially where store depths are 80–100 feet. Consequently, these spaces rent for less per square foot than the spaces that are in high demand. Monitoring the trends in retailing enables a developer to plan and design a shopping center that will meet the space needs of its tenants and have a high probability of success.

Changing Shopper Needs.   Just as the requirements of shopping center tenants have changed over the years, so have the needs of shoppers changed, and the shopping center must meet those changed needs, too. An example of one such adaptation is the changes in the hours that malls and anchor tenants in strip centers are open. With a larger percentage of women in the work force, retailers have had to change their hours. Most enclosed malls are open longer, including evenings and weekends. Twenty years ago enclosed malls closed at 5:00 p.m. on Saturdays and Sundays. Today most malls stay open until 6:00 p.m. on both days, some till as late as 9:00 p.m. on Saturdays. During the Christmas holidays, many malls stay open until midnight on Fridays and Saturdays between Thanksgiving and Christmas Eve. Supermarkets may be open 24 hours a day to meet the needs of their customers who can thus shop at any time of the day or night.

The needs of the shoppers also vary with the type of shopping center. A shopper expects a neighborhood or community strip center to have easy vehicular ingress and egress, convenient parking, a well-lighted parking lot, and stores that are visible and accessible from the parking lot. The strip center, whether small or large, must be designed to meet these demands. When shoppers are looking for convenience, they seek out a shopping center with the right mix of stores that is easy and convenient to reach, well-maintained and well-lighted, and a place where they can feel secure. When shoppers are looking for a shopping experience, they will shop a regional or super regional shopping center. Here they want a tenant mix that provides comparison shopping for apparel, shoes, accessories, gifts, jewelry, and specialty items. Shoppers usually prefer the climate-controlled environment of an enclosed mall. They are looking for comfort and convenience—mall seating, clean restrooms, telephones, a place to have a snack or a meal. Convenient parking and a safe environment are also important. Some malls offer valet parking either all year round or during the Christmas season.

When the customers' needs are not met and alternative shopping is available, they will shop elsewhere. When a shopping center loses its customer base of shoppers, it will ultimately lose its customer base of tenants. Since the retailer is the shopping center's customer, and the shopper is the retailer's customer, the interaction of the two can greatly affect the entire shopping center.

Owners of existing shopping centers and developers of new ones must monitor the changing needs of both retailers and shoppers. When the needs of either of these shopping center customers changes, the shopping center must be adjusted to remain competitive. Developers must be aware of the changing needs of their prospective customer bases, and the design of a new shopping center must incorporate adaptations to these changes. The planning and design stages of development of a proposed shopping center are the times when changes can be incorporated most cost effectively. Remodeling or rehabilitation of an existing center often is essential to maintain its competitive position in the market. When the developer or property owner ignores or is unaware of the changing needs of the retailer, the shopping center will have a built-in leasing problem. When the needs of shoppers are not met, the shopping center will have built-in obsolescence that may or may not be curable.

Site Planning

An early concern of the developer is how the maximum gross leasable area (GLA) can be designed into the shopping center, and this effort can lead to a critical design error. When the primary design criterion is to maximize GLA, the result is often a shopping center with built-in leasing problems—space is designed that is difficult to lease. Spaces may be too deep or odd-shaped. They may have little frontage and wide rear areas, or they may have poor visibility to shoppers. They may be isolated from the primary traffic flow of the shopping center or tucked away in a corner. The developer attempts to maximize the amount of GLA on the site because the larger the GLA, the higher the income projection. However, this is a fallacy—the amount of GLA should be based on the demand for space. If the demand for space is less than the total amount of GLA that the site can accommodate, it is usually prudent to develop the shopping center in two or more phases. The cost to carry the undeveloped portion of the shopping center is considerably less than the cost to carry vacant space.

Specific Design Challenges.   Though the site plan is the creation of the developer's architect, the anchor tenants will have considerable input into the final layout of a shopping center. An anchor tenant will want to be certain that its store is positioned in the shopping center to meet its needs and the needs of its customers. Among the specific concerns of all shopping center tenants are visibility of their stores, accessibility of the center, parking, and customer amenities.

Visibility is critical for most tenants in a strip center. Tenants in small centers (5,000–30,000 square feet of GLA) must be visible from the street. Because these centers have no strong anchor tenants, their tenants' success is partially dependent on people seeing them on a repeat basis as they drive by and eventually becoming regular customers. Store spaces in larger strips— neighborhood and community shopping centers—should have good visibility from the street and the parking lot. An important component of the concept of visibility is signage. The shopping center sign criteria should allow each tenant to have a sign that is sufficiently large and properly placed so that it can be seen easily. Enclosed mall tenants have no visibility from the street; they are concerned with visibility to the mall traffic.

In evaluating whether or not to locate in a particular shopping center, a major concern of all prospective tenants is *accessibility*. Most shopping centers are located on a corner so that there is access from two streets. Strip shopping centers must be located on streets with substantial volumes of traffic, and convenience shopping centers must be convenient for the shopper— they must have good ingress and egress flow patterns.

Shopping centers should be accessible to traffic flowing in both directions. If there are no left turn lanes into a shopping center, many shoppers will drive by it enroute to the next shopping center. The entrances to and exits from the shopping center should provide a clear view. A driver's view on entering or exiting a shopping center should not be blocked by landscaping or a large identification sign for the center. The ideal location for a regional or super regional shopping center is adjacent to a freeway exit ramp or at the intersection of two freeways. When this is not possible, location on a major thoroughfare and within a short distance from a freeway is a minimum requirement. The heavy volume of automobile traffic to a regional shopping center makes location near a freeway imperative.

After accessibility, the next concern is *parking* lot layout and traffic flow. The parking lot or parking garage should provide pedestrian walkways. *Lighting* is a critical element in a shopper's decision to visit a shopping center at night, and all areas of the shopping center must have adequate lighting. The *landscaping* plan, including selection and placement of plants, should be evaluated from perspectives of aesthetics, safety, and maintenance. *Customer amenities*—seating areas, public telephones, and bike racks for all shopping centers, along with restrooms, children's areas, and community and information booths for enclosed malls—must also be planned.

Service facilities are important for tenants' operations. Placement and accessibility of loading areas are important to store efficiency. Loading areas for strip shopping centers are located behind the stores. These areas must be accessible by large trucks. All of the stores in an enclosed mall may have direct access to the parking lot for loading, but this is not always possible. Usually only some of the stores, primarily the anchors, have such direct access, and the loading areas for the remainder are behind the stores in corridors that lead to a service exit to the parking lot.

Management and maintenance requirements must also be considered. Storage rooms, access to the roof, locations of utility meters and shutoff valves, hose bibbs, and a management office must be included in the site plan and design for enclosed regional and larger shopping malls.

Specific Design Problems.   The design of each space will determine its marketability. The anchor tenant will provide the design and layout for its premises, and its architect will work with the shopping center architect to coordinate the placement of the anchor tenant's premises in the shopping center. The remaining store and shop spaces must have good visibility, and they must be placed where they can benefit from the traffic generated by the anchor tenant or tenants. The following are some typical shopping center design problems.

- *Spaces too deep.* Because most retailers have downsized, they seek spaces with shallower depths. Centers with store depths greater than 75 feet find fewer and fewer potential tenants.
- *Spaces too large.* In neighborhood shopping centers, spaces that are larger than 1,800 square feet have fewer potential uses, and spaces larger than 3,000 square feet have limited uses.
- *Spaces too narrow.* Tenants want as much frontage and as little depth as possible. Spaces with more than 1,000 square feet of GLA and widths less than 15 feet are difficult to lease.
- *L- and T-shaped spaces.* Space that is L- or T-shaped, with the wider portion in the rear, will have limited appeal.
- *Pie-shaped spaces.* Spaces in the middle of an L-shaped strip of shops are sometimes triangular or pie-shaped. These large spaces have little frontage and a wide rear area, which is not a desirable configuration.
- *Spaces with poor visibility.* Most small shop tenants need good visibility. Too many buildings on pads or outlots in front of a neighborhood shopping center can block the visibility of small, in-line shops. A shop-

ping center may front on a major street and also have shops on the side of the center facing a poorly traveled street (see configuration in exhibit 2.2).

- *Malls too wide.* The mall area between stores should range from 30 to 40 feet wide. When the width exceeds 40 feet, the customer does not see the stores on both sides of the mall as easily.
- *Side hallways in a mall.* Many malls have secondary exits to the parking lot, usually from hallways that are tenanted by small shops. Because these areas receive little traffic, many retailers find them undesirable.
- *Unanchored malls.* Small shops in an enclosed mall that has no anchor tenant have neither a major draw nor visibility. The small shops collectively are not strong enough to draw shoppers into the mall. Enclosure of the mall eliminates storefront visibility from the street.
- *Unanchored wings of a mall.* Expanding a mall by developing a wing of small shops without an anchor tenant can be deadly. Without a major draw, this area of the mall will have little traffic, poor sales, high tenant turnover, and large numbers of vacancies.
- *Mall with no anchor on second level.* Two-level malls with an anchor tenant such as a junior department store or a major discounter on the first level, but no anchor tenant on the second level, will have a great disparity in traffic between the first and second levels. The second level will be slow to lease and have a high turnover of tenants.
- *U-shaped centers.* In U-shaped neighborhood and community shopping centers where the anchor tenants are on the ends of the U, there is little traffic drawn to the small shops in the area of the U between the anchors.
- *Anchor tenants grouped together.* A shopping center design that groups the anchor tenants together instead of locating them at opposite ends of the center clusters the smaller shops away from the anchors, in areas where they will receive little traffic.
- *Minimalls.* Division of large vacant spaces into multiple small shops to create an enclosed "minimall" is rarely successful in the long term. When W. T. Grant, a national variety store, closed all of its 50,000-square-foot stores in the early 1970s, some owners converted these stores to minimalls. They created an aisle (mall) down the middle of the space and developed small shops on both sides of it. The owners were able to increase the rent on the space from the $2–$3 per square foot that W. T. Grant usually paid for the entire store to $8–$15 per square foot for the small shops. However, most of these minimalls failed because the small shops could not attract sufficient traffic to generate adequate sales.
- *Second-level office space.* Shopping centers with second level office space often have incompatible uses. The office space usually becomes

less-desirable, Class B space. The office employees who park all day may occupy valuable customer parking. Quite often the office space suffers from a high turnover of tenants and a high vacancy rate.

Errors in planning and design are either impossible to correct or costly, if correctable, and they lower both the income and the value of the shopping center. In evaluating such "errors," it is important to distinguish between *economic obsolescence* resulting from changes in the marketplace or the impact of governmental regulations and *functional obsolesence* because the design or components are out of date. The loss of value due to functional obsolescence may be curable, but the desirability of a cure depends on the cost of replacement being equal to or less than the expected increase in value.

Parking Requirements

Americans depend heavily on the automobile for transportation, a dependence that is greater in suburban areas—where most shopping centers are located—than in urban areas. Because the American consumer travels by automobile to shop, parking areas must meet the shopper's needs. Parking is one criterion a shopper considers in deciding where to shop.

The following criteria are used to evaluate the convenience of parking in a shopping center.

- Convenience of access to and exit from the parking area
- Adequacy of the number of parking stalls
- Ease of parking
- Level and quality of maintenance of the parking area
- Level and quality of lighting of the parking area
- Security of the parking environment
- Safety and ease of access to the shopping area from vehicles

A shopper will be discouraged from patronizing a shopping center if any one of these criteria is not met. If several of the criteria are not met, the shopper will patronize the center only out of necessity.

One of the objectives in developing a shopping center is to maximize the amount of GLA at the proposed site. The main design criterion that will affect the amount of GLA a site can accommodate is how much of the site is dedicated to parking. The shopping center architect will usually design a shopping center to have the maximum amount of GLA and the minimum amount of parking allowed. To determine the allocation for parking, municipal parking requirements will have to be reviewed.

The size of a parking area is determined from the number of parking stalls required by the municipality or demanded by the anchor tenants and the amount of space the municipality requires to be devoted to landscaping.

The specific requirements will be expressed in either a parking area ratio or a parking index. A *parking area ratio* expresses the relationship between the square footage of the parking area and the square footage of the building. If the municipality requirement is three square feet of parking area to one square foot of building area, the parking area ratio is three to one (3:1).

A more accurate assessment of shopping center parking needs is to establish a relationship between the number of parking stalls and the amount of GLA. A *parking index* expresses the number of parking stalls provided for every 1,000 square feet of GLA. An index of 5.0 means there are five parking stalls for every 1,000 square feet of GLA. The parking index is used most frequently to express the parking needs or requirements of a shopping center— or a particular tenant. An anchor tenant may negotiate parking requirements to be stated in the lease. For example, the lease for a supermarket may include a provision whereby the landlord is required to maintain a parking index of no less than 4.5 parking stalls for every 1,000 square feet of GLA.

Alternatively, parking requirements may be expressed as the number of stalls in the entire shopping center or within a defined portion of the shopping center. The supermarket lease in the previous example might state a requirement for a minimum of 450 parking stalls in the shopping center and a minimum of 250 parking stalls in a specific area in front of its premises.

The Urban Land Institute (ULI), in cooperation with the International Council of Shopping Centers (ICSC), conducted two studies on the number of parking stalls needed for different-sized shopping centers. The first study, *Parking Requirements for Shopping Centers,* was published in 1965. It found that 5.5 parking stalls per 1,000 square feet of GLA would be more than adequate to meet the parking needs of a shopping center for all but the 10 hours of greatest parking demand during the year.

The second parking study (published in 1982) found that considerably less parking was needed in all types of shopping centers and that parking demands differ based on the size of the shopping center. The study indicated that fewer parking stalls were needed in neighborhood and community shopping centers than in a regional or super regional shopping center. This difference can be explained by how long a customer's car is parked while shopping for convenience goods and services as compared to shopping for fashion and gift items.

A major consideration in calculating the number of stalls that can be designed in an area is whether stalls for compact cars are included in the parking layout. "When more than one out of three vehicles parked at a center are compacts, it is appropriate to consider special accommodation of these vehicles." The greater the percentage of the parking area allocated for compact cars, the greater the number of parking stalls. By increasing the number of stalls—by including parking for compact cars—the parking capacity can be increased. This may forestall the need for additional parking area or permit conversion of part of the parking lot to expand the GLA at the site.

Another consideration in determining the minimum adequate number of parking stalls is the amount of GLA that will be occupied by food services. The study found that additional parking stalls were needed when the shopping center had food service tenants. The recommended parking ratio increases as the size of the shopping center is increased.

The study also analyzed the impact a cinema has on the parking demands of a shopping center. The study concluded that peak parking demands at a cinema did not coincide with the peak parking demands of the retailers. Consequently, dual use of the shopping center parking area was possible. This dual use of parking results in a slight increase in the parking index for a shopping center with a cinema.

The following is excerpted from *Parking Requirements for Shopping Centers: Summary Recommendations and Research Study Report* published by the Urban Land Institute in 1982 (see also exhibit 2.7, page 46).

Recommended Parking Indices. The following values were developed through analysis of design hour parking demands at over 135 centers and are adequate to serve the needs of all patrons, visitors, and employees during the 20th busiest hour of the year except where modifications are required for offices, cinemas, and food services which need special consideration.

- Design hour parking demands at smaller centers with GLA between 25,000 and 400,000 square feet, which exhibit less peaking during the Thanksgiving and pre-Christmas shopping seasons and where parking durations are shorter, require 4.0 spaces per 1,000 square feet of GLA.
- At centers with 400,000 to 600,000 square feet of GLA, the parking demand index increases from 4.0 to 5.0 spaces in a linear progression as size increases, with an average index of 4.5 spaces per 1,000 square feet of GLA.
- Centers larger than 600,000 square feet require 5.0 spaces per 1,000 square feet of GLA. At centers having over 1.2 million square feet of GLA, the number of required spaces declines from 5.0 spaces per 1,000 square feet of GLA. The number of centers with over 1.2 million square feet of GLA participating in the study was insufficient to quantify this reduction in demand; thus, it is suggested that the demand for these centers be addressed on a case by case basis.

Adjustments for Food Service Tenants. For food services occupying up to 10 percent of the total GLA at centers with 100,000 square feet or less, or up to 5 percent of the total GLA of centers larger than 100,000 square feet, the differential parking demand is the following:

- A center with more than 25,000 and less than 100,000 square feet of total GLA requires an additional 10 spaces per 1,000 square feet of food service tenant area.

- A center having 100,000 but less than 200,000 square feet of total GLA requires an additional 6.0 spaces per 1,000 square feet of food service tenant area.
- A center having 200,000 but less than 600,000 square feet of total GLA requires no additional spaces for food services.
- A center with 600,000 square feet or more of GLA can reduce the required parking (as calculated by using the recommended index of 5.0 spaces per 1,000 square feet of GLA) by 4.0 spaces per 1,000 square feet of GLA devoted to food services.

Adjustments for Cinemas. Because one vehicle may serve 3.0 to 4.0 cinema patrons while, typically, the same vehicle would only serve 1.5 to 2.5 shoppers, the parking demand associated with movie trips is reduced proportionately:

- A center with less than 100,000 square feet of GLA requires a nominal three additional parking spaces for every 100 cinema seats for cinemas occupying up to 10 percent of the total center GLA.
- Centers having 100,000 to 200,000 square feet of GLA can accommodate up to 450 cinema seats without providing additional parking. For every 100 seats above the initial 450 seats, a nominal 3.0 additional spaces per 100 seats are required.
- A shopping center with over 200,000 square feet of GLA can accommodate up to 750 seats without providing additional parking spaces. For every 100 seats above the initial 750 seats, a nominal three additional spaces are required.

The second criterion used in determining the size of a parking area is the amount of landscaped area required by the municipality. Municipal authorities recognize that a sea of asphalt is unsightly, and they attempt to beautify or soften a parking area by requiring that a minimum percentage of the area be landscaped. Sometimes the types and sizes of plants that must be included in the landscaped areas are also specified.

The final parking area design must take into consideration all of the preceding concerns and also provide parking for employees and handicapped shoppers.

Sometimes the use of the parking area can be maximized through dual use. Dual use is a sharing of the same or a portion of the same parking area by different property uses. A cinema in or adjacent to a shopping center has already been mentioned; another example is parking shared between an office building and a shopping center. Parking is needed for an office building primarily Monday through Friday from 8:00 A.M. to 5:00 P.M. The parking lot for an office building is almost totally empty during peak shopping times—evening hours Monday through Friday and late mornings and afternoons on weekends.

Municipal regulations may allow for an office building and a shopping center to plan for 85-percent dual use of parking, in which each property may

EXHIBIT   2.7

Parking Requirements

Center Size	Parking Index	Additional Parking Spaces over Index	
sq ft of GLA	Spaces/1,000 sq ft of GLA	per 1,000 sq ft of Food Service GLA	per 100 Cinema Seats
25,000–100,000		10	3
100,000–200,000	4.0	6	0 up to 450 3/100 over 450
200,000–400,000		none	
400,000–600,000	4.0–5.0 (Av. 4.5)		0 up to 750 3/100 over 750
>600,000	5.0	**reduce** number by 4.0 spaces	

Compiled from *Parking Requirements for Shopping Centers: Summary Recommendations* (Washington, D.C.: The Urban Land Institute, 1981). Reproduced with permission.

share 85 percent of its required parking stalls with the other property. However, caution must be exercised when considering the ratio of dual use parking. If the parking requirements of one property should increase, the amount of parking available for the other property will be reduced.

REHABILITATING SHOPPING CENTERS

As conditions favorable to new developments decline in the 1990s, developers and property owners are exploring opportunities to rehabilitate existing shopping centers. Since most shopping centers were developed after 1970, rehabilitation is not being done because of deterioration of their physical plants. Rather, shopping centers are being rehabilitated for two other reasons—either to enhance the value of the property or to maintain its existing value (or halt its decline).

Many shopping centers are excellent candidates for rehabilitation for several reasons.

- An existing shopping center has an established trade area. New shopping centers are often developed on the fringe of growth, and it may take several years before the trade area is developed.

- An existing shopping center has a group of tenants who are successful and whose businesses are well established.
- The center's physical plant is intact; usually it needs only minor modification.
- Most importantly, the shopping center that is a candidate for rehabilitation has an existing income stream.

The first step in determining whether or not to rehabilitate a shopping center is to develop a pro forma. One important component of the pro forma is a projection of net operating income (NOI) that takes into account the changes resulting from rehabilitation.

The first component of the NOI formula is income, and evaluation of the rehabilitation of a shopping center starts with an existing income stream. The income from the existing GLA is projected based on three factors: (1) rental and other income from existing tenants through the remainder of their lease terms; (2) anticipated rental increases when existing leases expire; and (3) projected income from existing vacancies. A fourth possibility is additional income if the shopping center is expanded.

First to be considered is the income from existing tenants. Their rents are usually low compared to the rental rates that will be expected from tenants after the rehabilitation is completed. Many of the present tenants will not be able to generate the sales necessary to support a substantial rent increase. They may be only marginally successful paying low rent and may not have the merchandising ability to produce significantly higher sales regardless of any changes to the shopping center. The developer must anticipate that these marginal tenants will not renew their leases. Other tenants will welcome improvements to the shopping center and be able to afford the rent increases.

Another step in the income projection is to estimate how long existing vacancies—and the vacancies created when existing tenants do not renew—will endure. A market survey must be conducted to accurately project the property's rental rates after the rehabilitation. If tenants lease and occupy space prior to the rehabilitation, they may have a two-tiered rental rate; their leases will show an initial rental rate that reflects the value of space in the shopping center prior to the rehabilitation and include an automatic rental increase that commences on the date the rehabilitation is completed.

Next, income is projected for additional GLA. This could be rent and other income from new pad or outlot space or from space in new buildings. It may be possible to expand the GLA of the site without adding land or a parking garage. If the shopping center originally had a parking index of 5.5 or 6.0 parking stalls per 1,000 square feet of GLA, additional GLA may be added to the site if the parking index can be lowered to 5.0 or 4.5 parking stalls per 1,000 square feet of GLA. The developer should check with the municipality to see if the parking index has been changed since the shopping center was developed. If the parking index has not been changed, the developer may petition for a variance or suggest to the city's building department that it consider changing the municipal parking index. Information from the Urban Land Institute report, *Parking Requirements for Shopping Centers,* may be provided to the building department or city council as supporting documentation. Another consideration is existing leases for both anchor and shop tenants which may include provisions that restrict the number of parking stalls. The leases and the shopping center operating agreement must be reviewed to determine the existence and extent of any restrictions that limit changes to the parking area or rehabilitation or expansion of the center.

Another source of income to be evaluated is reimbursement of operating expenses that are passed through to tenants, such as common area maintenance, taxes, and insurance. If the shopping center will have a higher occupancy after rehabilitation, additional income from pass-through charges can be projected.

After the income from all sources has been projected, a realistic vacancy factor should be projected and income adjusted accordingly. A vacancy factor is seldom applied to the anchor spaces because of the length of their lease terms. For the small shop space, however, the industry uses a rule-of-thumb vacancy rate of 5 percent.

The second component of NOI is operating expenses. The operating expenses for a shopping center will be budgeted in either two or three separate groupings. The first is the landlord's nonreimbursable expenses, which include the landlord's contribution to the merchants' association or marketing fund dues, the cost to maintain the vacant spaces, partnership audits, legal expenses, utilities in vacant spaces, and the management fee if it is not included in the CAM expenses. The second is for maintenance of the parking lot and exterior common areas. The budget for an enclosed mall will have a third group of expenses for maintenance of the mall common areas. Each of these groups of expenses will undoubtedly increase after the rehabilitation.

One outcome of rehabilitation of a shopping center is an upgrade in the appearance of the common areas and the buildings. The improvements that will be most noticeable are those made to the landscaping and parking lot and any added lighting. In addition to an increase in expenses for these items, the overall maintenance cost for the shopping center will increase. The additional value created in the shopping center will also result in increased taxes and insurance costs. Most of these expenses are passed through to the tenants, and that will increase their occupancy costs.

Subtracting the operating expenses from the income projection will provide the property's projected NOI.

Another component in the pro forma for rehabilitating a shopping center is an estimate of the construction cost. Structural and mechanical surveys should be done to determine the integrity of the physical plant. The extent of needed repairs and the costs to make them should be estimated. Areas that should be considered for upgrading include the roof, parking lot, landscaping, lighting, and signage. If the shopping center is an enclosed mall, additional areas to consider for upgrading are mall flooring, restrooms, directories, and seating areas. A review of the local building code should reveal any specific upgrades that are necessary to meet code requirements. For example, installation of sprinklers and fire walls and provision of parking and access for the handicapped (added ramps, special doors) may have to be done if these were not part of the original construction. An environmental impact report (EIR) may be required by the local municipality. Certainly it is prudent to conduct an environmental audit, which may include a soil survey, to determine if any hazardous substances are present. Potential hazards in a shopping center include wastes classified as toxic substances (e.g., spent dry cleaning fluid), PCBs from transformer leakage, and asbestos used as a construction material. The costs of the surveys and of any changes necessitated for full compliance should be included in the construction cost estimate.

Another item in the pro forma is the cost to market and lease the new space and to re-lease existing space when tenants vacate. The amount of this expense can be projected accurately; however, the timing of the payment of commissions will be only an estimate because it is based on when space is leased.

The next expense to evaluate is promotions and advertising. The landlord, through the merchants' association or marketing fund, will provide additional funds to promote and advertise the shopping center both during the period of construction and for a grand reopening. The extra advertising and promotion are to let the community know that the shopping center is open during construction and to promote the shopping center's new image. The amount needed for advertising and promotion of a neighborhood shopping center will range from a few thousand dollars to $25,000, while this expense for a regional shopping center will likely exceed $100,000.

The cost of the rehabilitation may be funded from the property's cash flow, an equity infusion, financing, or any combination of these sources. The development pro forma, the NOI when the property is stabilized, and the stabilized cash flow will be used to determine whether or not to proceed with the rehabilitation. Once the decision is made to go ahead, the developer must determine the extent of the work to be done.

The rehabilitation may be only cosmetic improvements such as painting the building, minor upgrading of the landscaping, and parking lot repair and restriping. Alternatively, the work may include extensive redesign of the building (e.g., changing the facade, roof line, and exterior material) in addition to major changes to the parking lot, landscaping, and exterior lighting. Rehabilitation may include altering the tenant mix to revitalize the merchandise and services offered to meet the needs of the changing demographic profile of the shopping center's trade area.

A successful marketing and leasing plan will validate the decision to rehabilitate the shopping center. This program starts with the rental or market survey. Once the market rental rates are established for the shopping center, each existing space and all new spaces must be priced on the basis of their value to a retailer or service tenant. Next, a survey is conducted to determine which tenant uses are over- and under-represented in the shopping center's trade area. The existing tenant mix is analyzed to determine the shopping center's strengths and weaknesses. Introduction of new anchor tenants may call for a different tenant mix. The marketing and leasing program should be targeted to specific tenant uses. Prior to or during the construction phase is an excellent time to extend some tenants' leases. All tenants should be encouraged to remodel their stores to present a fresh, new image when the shopping center has its grand reopening.

Tenants will be concerned that the construction phase will have a negative impact on their sales. Surprisingly, many tenants' sales increase during the construction period. The additional advertising and promotion, new tenants moving in, and shoppers' curiosity often result in increased traffic at the shopping center and, thus, in higher sales. If a tenant's loss of sales is expected to be severe, it may be appropriate to convert the tenant's lease for the duration of the construction phase to require payment of percentage rent only—i.e., a percentage of the retailer's sales in lieu of the minimum or base rent required under the lease. For tenants located in an area that will be demolished, buy out of their leases or temporary (or permanent) relocation within the center may be explored.

Several operating issues must be addressed prior to and during the construction phase. Seldom are shopping centers totally vacant during the construction. A plan must be developed to keep the tenants open for business during construction. The plan should incorporate a concern for the safety of shoppers and employees. Safety issues may be addressed by barricading construction staging areas, building protective walkways, and fencing off construction activities. Keeping the parking lot and sidewalk clear of all construction debris is mandatory. It may be necessary to assign security personnel to keep people out of construction areas and provide a liaison with construction workers.

It is important for the property manager to communicate with the tenants before and during the rehabilitation. A general meeting of all the merchants should be called to announce the rehabilitation. This meeting should include a presentation by the architect. The architect or general contractor should explain the construction sequencing and how each tenant will be affected during the construction phase. The property manager or the marketing director should present the advertising and promotion plans for the construction period and beyond.

Following the general meeting, the property manager should meet regularly with each merchant to explain the progress of the rehabilitation, what will happen next, and what effect this will have on the tenant. Memos on advertising and promotions, new tenant leases, and construction progress should be sent out regularly to all the tenants.

It is important to avoid doing construction during the Christmas holiday period. Ideally, construction should be started as early in the year as weather permits and completed prior to Thanksgiving.

Rehabilitating a shopping center presents opportunities to enhance the value of the property. For every opportunity to succeed, however, there is a corresponding opportunity to fail. A thorough analysis of the proposed rehabilitation is necessary to assure that it will be a success.

Retail in Other Property Types

In addition to discrete shopping "centers," substantial retail space is often incorporated into office buildings, either during initial development or as part of a revitalization of an established property. This has been especially true in downtown areas. In addition, complex multiple-use properties that include retail space have been developed. Often the scale of the retail component approaches that of a freestanding shopping center.

Such mixed use of a site is not a totally new idea. The Agora in ancient Greece, the medieval market square, and European residential-commercial blocks also had multiple uses. What is new is the intentional development of an entity with a singular identity that includes several different types of specific uses on a very large scale.

The manager responsible for operating the retail components in office buildings and mixed-use properties must understand how they are similar to and different from true shopping centers.

RETAIL AREAS IN AN OFFICE BUILDING

Frequently, high-rise office building developments will include a retail component. Certainly retail and service businesses can expand the base of potential users for office space. They also add amenities to the building which make it more marketable to office tenants, and they generate additional income for the building owners. If specific areas in the building are more valuable to a retail or service tenant, the base rent charged for these areas can be increased above the rate an office user would pay. In addition, the leases for retail tenants and for many service tenants can include a percentage rent clause such that if their sales exceed a predetermined volume, they will pay percentage or overage rent in addition to their base or minimum rent. (Percentage rent, commonly required under shopping center leases, is discussed in later chapters.)

Location of the Retail Space

Spaces for retail and service tenants are usually located on the ground floor of the building, although a restaurant or business club may occupy the top floor. Sometimes less-desirable space in the building can be leased to health clubs or daycare facilities. Some major office building developments include multiple floors for retail and service tenants, starting at the ground floor.

Ground-Floor Retail Space   A ground-floor location provides maximum visibility to and access by potential customers walking past the building. Placement of ground-floor retail and service space may be planned in four different ways, and any one or all four methods may be used for a particular building. The first method is to have all of the ground-floor retail and service space in the front of the building, with direct access to the street. Street access often has more value to a retail or service tenant than to the typical office user because these tenants usually prefer a prominent and easily accessible location. The value of this space to a retailer or service tenant depends primarily on the sales volume the tenant can expect to achieve. The anticipated sales volume is directly related to the size and demographic profiles of two discrete populations—the people who work and live in the immediate area and the people who walk by the office building every day. (Suburban locations usually do not have sufficient numbers of either group to support ground-floor retail or service operations.)

The second method of designing space for retail or service tenants in an office building is to provide significant space in less-desirable locations at a lower rental rate than the rest of the building. For example, basement areas may be leased to large destination uses such as a health club or a printer.

The third method is to develop one or two small shops in the lobby area, usually near the building entrance or next to the elevators. Once called "smoke shops," these spaces are suitable for merchants whose merchandise is mostly "convenience" items and whose sales are totally dependent on the captive population of building employees and visitors. These shops are usually open early in the morning before the office tenants open for business, and they may close in the afternoon or shortly after the office tenants close. They are not open on weekends.

The fourth method is to design a *concourse* area, which can be likened to a small enclosed mall with no anchor tenant. A concourse area is usually located on the ground floor, but occasionally it may be one level below or above the ground floor. A concourse consists of several retail or service tenants located along a single corridor. It can be single-loaded (tenants on one side only) or double-loaded (tenants on both sides). Because most, if not all, of the spaces in the concourse area have no direct access to the street, these tenants' sales are dependent on people who work in and visit the building. Concourse tenants are usually *destination uses*—e.g., a travel agent, an office supply store, a florist, or a coin shop. A variation of the concourse shopping area may be developed if several office buildings are joined together by an underground passage. This provides an opportunity to merchandise the sides of the passageway.

Top-Floor Retail Space.   A retail or service business may occupy the top floor or penthouse in an office building. Usually this is a quality full-service restaurant with a cocktail lounge or a private business club for executives. Some developers will lease top-floor or penthouse space at a rate below that which an office user would pay because these types of tenants add prestige and identity to the building. In addition, the restaurant or private club may provide unique amenities, which can be a plus in the building's marketing and leasing program.

Multilevel Retail Space.   Another approach to developing an office building project is to create multiple levels for the retail and service component. The dedicated area usually comprises the first two to four levels of the building, and its development is similar to that of a multiple-level enclosed mall. However, most of these areas are developed without an anchor tenant.

Tenant Mix and Customer Base

The proposed *tenant mix* for a multilevel retail component of an office building must be carefully analyzed. In the absence of a retail anchor tenant such as a department store, it is doubtful whether fashion retailers can be successful in such a project. (Most fashion retailers need the synergism created by other fashion stores and the traffic draw of one or more department stores to be successful.) Without fashion stores, the project will have service, food, and nonfashion retailers as tenants. This might include a bookstore or a card and gift store.

The first considerations are, "Who will be the customers, and where will they come from?" Without a fashion element, the *customer base* for the project will be drawn largely from two sources—the employees of the office tenants in the building and people who work in adjacent buildings. The fact that the primary customers will be employees in the building raises two concerns: First, the building must be of sufficient size to have tenants with enough employees to support the retail component of the building. Second, the office component of the building may lease up slowly, in which case, the sales of the service, food, and retail tenants will be significantly affected. Often the retail component will not be successful until the office space is almost fully occupied.

The secondary customers for the retail and service tenants—people working in adjacent and nearby buildings—are most likely to shop the retail areas of the building during their lunch breaks. A large proportion will be women who are working downtown in increasing numbers. The boundaries of the trade area—the buildings from which people will come to shop this project—can be determined fairly easily. Most of these shoppers will be within a short, easy-to-walk distance of the building, probably no more than 10–15 minutes away. Their time to shop will be limited, and most of their purchases will be preplanned (e.g., lunch, a greeting card, a book, etc.). A suburbanite working in a downtown office building has a completely different buying orientation than other shoppers. The normal percentage distribution of sales or merchandise categories becomes heavily skewed toward consumables and services, with emphasis on specialty foods, although cosmetics, hair styling, shoe repairs, banking, and travel agencies are also popular. The opportunities for gift and jewelry merchants improve as the number of people working in the area increases.

A third potential customer base is people who are visiting the city—tourists, convention delegates, and business travellers.

A retail component adds to the amenities and identity of an office building and broadens the market from which prospective tenants can be sought. However, caution must be exercised when adding this component to an office building. The process of selecting retailers and service businesses to be tenants in an office building is no different than the one used to select tenants for a shopping center. In other words, consideration should be given to the trade area, the demographic profile of the customer base, the volume of traffic that passes the building, compatibility of the retail uses with the existing tenants and the building's location, and the physical needs of the tenant. Part of the analysis of the design phase of an office building should include consideration of space for retail and service tenants.

THE RETAIL COMPONENT IN A
MIXED-USE DEVELOPMENT

A *mixed-use development (MXD)* has been defined by the Urban Land Institute as a large-scale real estate project having three principal characteristics. The first is incorporation of three or more *significant* revenue-producing uses (e.g., retail, office, residential, hotel, recreation). In well-planned projects, the uses are all mutually supporting. Most include substantial areas devoted to parking, and in urban MXDs in particular, parking can be an additional source of revenue. The second characteristic is a significant physical and functional integration of project components and, thus, an intensive use of land. Although this integration can take many physical forms, its main objective— interconnection of the uses—is often achieved via uninterrupted pedestrian walkways. Integration can be achieved by:,

- Vertical mixing of project components into a single tower occupying only one city block.
- Careful positioning of key project components around centrally located focal points—arrangement of retailers in a shopping gallery; a hotel containing a larger central court; a central open-air plaza; a park or water feature within the MXD.
- Interconnection of project components through an elaborate pedestrian circulation network such as subterranean concourses, walkways and plazas at grade level, or aerial bridges between buildings.
- Extensive use of escalators, elevators, moving sidewalks, and other mechanical means of facilitating horizontal and vertical movement of pedestrians.

The third characteristic is conformance of the development to a coherent plan. Minimally, this plan will set forth the type and scale of uses, permitted densities, and related items.

The most frequently found use in an MXD is offices. However, retail uses can be a significant component in mixed-use developments or provide ancillary services to the other uses. Office buildings serve their own tenants and visitors, hotels are used primarily by out-of-town guests, and apartments and condominiums are oriented toward their residents. In contrast, retail and entertainment uses open the MXD to the general public. An Urban Land Institute survey found that 98 percent of MXDs include retail uses. The average size of the retail space is slightly less than 200,000 square feet, and 21 percent of the MXDs that include retailing have at least one department store. Though merchants can derive many benefits from locating in an MXD, if the primary customer base is not the people who live and work in the MXD, the retail component must draw customers from the general public to be successful.

Retail businesses add life and vitality to a mixed-use development. Managing, leasing, and marketing of the retail component are complex, and the individual who assumes these responsibilities must have specialized knowledge and experience. The manager's expertise is the key to maximizing the benefits to retailers of locating in an MXD. Being present in a mixed-use development will not, by itself, make the retail component successful. The location of the MXD and the design and integration of the retail component into it, coupled with the right tenants for the trade area, are the essential criteria for a successful retail component in an MXD.

Evolution of the Mixed-Use Development

The first "mixed-use" developments were large, almost monolithic office towers that included some retailing on the lower floors. A good example is Rockefeller Center, a New York landmark since the 1930s, which is dominated by office buildings and includes a multitude of "uses" but does not have three or more major revenue-producing uses. (In particular, there is no residential component.) In the 1960s, the typical MXD was gigantic, averaging 2.2 million square feet in size. As the number of MXDs grew, however, the structures were made smaller. By the end of the 1980s, MXDs averaged only 1.1 million square feet in size, and the retail, hotel, and entertainment components were expanded at the expense of office space.

Mixed-use developments are found in both urban and suburban locations. Downtown areas have always been the center of commerce; until the development of regional malls, downtown was the retail center of the community. In any size community but mostly in large cities, downtowns have always served as the primary locations for the finest hotels, live-performance theaters and entertainment, and the community's night life. Thus it is not surprising that the first MXDs were developed in downtown areas.

Urban MXDs consist of one or more vertical structures developed on a relatively small parcel of land. Many urban MXDs are dominated by one use while others have a relatively equal distribution of space among uses. One of the first urban MXDs, Penn Center in Philadelphia, has three uses—offices, retail space, and a hotel. Chicago has several MXDs in its extended downtown area, each of which originally created a separate identity that emphasized its different uses.

- *Marina City,* a 1.6 million-square-foot MXD situated along the Chicago River, is dominated by two circular 65-story residential towers, with adjacent structures enclosing 16 floors of office space (180,000 square feet) and three movie theaters, all rising above two levels of retail and service shops. As built, the project included a marina, a health club, a bowling alley, and a skating rink, plus parking for 900 automobiles. The residential use is dominant—originally rental apartments, the twin towers were converted to condominium apartments. Entertainment uses are no longer prominent, and retailing is not a major component.
- *John Hancock Center,* on North Michigan Avenue, is a 100-story, 2.8 million-square-foot office and residential project, with more than 800,000 square feet of office space and 705 condominiums—plus parking for 650 automobiles. The retail component on one level below grade comprises mostly small shops and services. (Bonwit Teller origi-

nally occupied space on the first five floors.) There is an enclosed observation deck and restaurant on one of the upper floors.

* *Water Tower Place,* across the street from the John Hancock Center, is internationally known for its vertical regional mall. The eight-level, 613,700-square-foot retail component is anchored by two high-end department stores—Marshall Field's and Lord & Taylor. This MXD includes a 450-room Ritz Carlton Hotel on 20 floors, approximately 200,000 square feet of office space, and 260 luxury condominiums along with parking for more than 650 automobiles and entertainment functions. Its dominant feature is the grand atrium leading to the vertical mall.

In each of these three urban MXDs, retailing plays a significant, but distinctly different, role. Marina City is known primarily as a residential project, the John Hancock Center as an office building, and Water Tower Place as a shopping center. Each, however, has other uses that are a significant part of the success of these projects.

Suburban MXDs are large-scale projects covering many acres and located away from the downtown area. Often they are developed on a tract of land in excess of 100 acres. There are usually several buildings ranging from small low-rise office or retail buildings to large high-rise office or residential towers. Each use may occupy its own building or buildings connected to the other buildings in the MXD by pedestrian walkways. The Houston Galleria is one of the earliest suburban MXDs. Developed in stages beginning in 1967, it has a fairly equal distribution of office, retail, and hotel space. While this MXD is best identified by its 1.6 million-square-foot super regional mall, it also includes one million square feet of space in high-rise office buildings and a 22-story, 405-room luxury hotel (800,000 square feet).

Two other suburban master-planned developments that broke ground on the first phases of their developments in the late 1960s are The City and Newport Center, both in Orange County, California. The City occupies 175 acres at the junction of three freeways in the center of Orange County. The heart of this MXD is a 700,000-square-foot regional mall that was originally developed as an open-air center but was converted to an enclosed mall in 1978. Adjacent to the mall are a low-rise office building and a high-rise office tower. A four-lane ring road encircles these interior buildings. Outside the ring is surface parking. Additional office buildings, a large garden apartment complex, and a high-rise hotel are located on the perimeter of the project. There are entertainment facilities, two multiscreen theaters, a health club, and several restaurants in freestanding buildings located throughout the development.

In contrast to the mixed-use development is the *multi-use development.* Newport Center, a 622-acre development in the affluent coastal community of Newport Beach, is an example. In the center of this development is Fashion

Island, a super regional mall containing primarily high-end department and specialty stores. A six-lane ring road encircles the mall and its self-contained surface parking. Office and medical buildings, freestanding restaurants, two multiscreen theaters, and residential complexes are located outside the ring road. Though this project has multiple uses, it lacks physical integration because it is spread over such a large area. Therefore, it does not conform to the definition of an MXD.

Multi-use developments encompass three broad categories: (1) densely configured developments that achieve physical and functional integration but include only two uses; (2) mixed-use developments as described earlier; and (3) developments with two or more uses that lack physical and functional integration, usually because of their large scale, low density, or lack of a coherent plan.

Advantages and Challenges of the Mixed-Use Development

The MXD presents unique management, marketing, and leasing advantages. Along with these advantages are the challenges related to its mixture of uses. Because retail businesses create a focal point in the community, provide services to adjacent businesses, often pay higher rents than other uses, and are successful in a variety of locations, they are an important component in the success of many MXDs. The concept that "the whole is greater than the sum of its parts" aptly describes an MXD and the benefits to retailers of locating there. The MXD offers unique advantages that cannot be found in a strip shopping center or an enclosed mall. Each separate use has a built-in customer base so each component benefits the others and, in particular, all the other components benefit the retailers. Office, hotel, and entertainment uses draw people to the MXD from beyond the retailers' primary and secondary trade areas. Hotels attract out-of-town customers—tourists, conventioneers, and business travelers. Office buildings provide a base of professional and white-collar workers who will patronize retailers during two periods when store sales are normally slow—lunchtime and immediately after work—and few of these workers will live nearby. A residential component (condominium or rental apartments) usually houses people in the middle- to upper-income brackets who will patronize the retailers.

If the development is a landmark in the community and has an atmosphere of prestige and success, a retailer's image and identity will benefit from its being located in the MXD. Retailers must remember, however, that locating in an MXD does not guarantee success. The criteria retailers use to analyze a shopping center location must be applied similarly to a location in an MXD.

For its part, the retail component adds vitality to an MXD and extends its active life into the evenings and weekends. Without the retail and entertainment components, the MXD would be primarily an office park appealing only to a small segment of the population. Retailers broaden its appeal to the entire community.

Specific Advantages.   A well-conceived mixed-use development offers many advantages over a single-use development.

- Each use provides an amenity to the other uses.
- Large size will make it a landmark.
- A luxury hotel will add to its prestige.
- Retail, restaurant, and entertainment uses create community awareness and add an array of services.
- High-end specialty department stores add a mystique to the development.
- Moderate-price merchants provide convenient shopping for office workers and residents.
- Office workers and condominium or apartment residents provide a stable customer base for the other uses.
- Mixed uses provide for higher density.
- Multiple uses are an added benefit in marketing and leasing each individual use.
- Management operations can be more cost-effective.
- Shared use of parking reduces the area devoted to parking and allows more area for buildings.
- Large suburban sites can be developed more rapidly as MXDs—because each building in the MXD shares the infrastructure of the project, multiple uses can be developed simultaneously.

Specific Challenges.   Each component in the MXD—office, retail, residential, hotel, entertainment—must be able to succeed on its own without the benefit of the other uses. A use that by itself would be a failure will not thrive in an MXD even if other uses in the project are successful. If a site is not a good location for an office building, creating an MXD with a major office building as a component use will not make the office building successful. Similarly, a poor retail site cannot be made successful as a shopping center by massing office buildings around it.

People who work in an office building will shop primarily for convenience items and food during their lunch breaks, and they seldom make major retail purchases. If the shopping center must rely on office workers for its primary customers, it will fail. While office workers, hotel visitors, and residents in an MXD are a captive market for retailers and restaurants, they will only improve an already successful business. Few, if any, retailers can survive on a customer base limited to these groups.

The massiveness of the MXD can be a drawback for shoppers. While the retail component in a downtown vertical MXD may be located on the lower floors with easy access from the street, the retail component in a suburban MXD may be in the middle of a sprawling complex or even hidden behind rows of office buildings. Entrances to the retail component, whether by pedestrian or vehicular traffic, must be prominently identified by signage and easily accessed.

Prospecting for Retail Tenants. If the MXD has a substantial amount of retail GLA, this area should be leased by a retail leasing specialist or a retail leasing team. If a team is used to recruit retail and service tenants, the areas of responsibility can be divided by merchandise categories to maximize each team member's efforts and avoid contacting the same prospects. For example, one member may be assigned to clothing and shoes, while another is assigned to accessories, gifts, and jewelry, and a third to food services and miscellaneous merchandise. The retail leasing team must coordinate its efforts with those who are leasing the other property uses.

In addition to the leasing strategies commonly used for shopping centers, the MXD offers the leasing agent additional selling points and opportunities. Some prospective tenants may find it difficult to grasp the concept of an MXD. The flow of traffic within the MXD, how each component is related to the others, and the demographic profiles of the people living and working at the MXD all require explanation. Office employees and residents represent captive customers, so demographic studies of these groups should be conducted. A well-structured study will reveal the size of each group and their distribution by age and gender—and, possibly, income level. Information can be gathered in several ways. Questionnaires can be distributed to every resident and office worker. A resident profile can be determined from a summary of applications for rental apartments. The number of visitors can be estimated by counting the people who enter the office building between the hours when most of the people employed there arrive for work and go home (excluding lunch hours). When members of the leasing team approach prospective tenants, they should be able to characterize the unique aspects of the MXD and the specific benefits of locating there.

The leasing and marketing staff must use special leasing tools in working with prospective retail tenants. While a model of the project as a whole can be used to highlight the location and features of the retail section, a video or slide presentation may be necessary to explain the magnitude of the MXD. Photographs (including aerial photos of the surrounding area), a rendering, and descriptions of the adjacent buildings and the general area are essential components of the leasing package, along with a demographic profile of the trade area that includes the people who live and work in the MXD.

Internal Promotion of the Retail Component. The MXD itself provides a unique opportunity for marketing and promotion. Typically, the thousands of people who work and live in the nonretail segment of the MXD and the hundreds of people who visit it daily are a captive customer base for the retail and service tenants. Following are several inexpensive ways to reach that captive customer base.

- *Newsletters* can be sent to every resident and office worker each month. Upcoming promotions, new merchants, and stores that are adding new merchandise can be featured, along with profiles of established merchants and general information on the management and operations of the mall and the MXD.
- *Promotional flyers* can be placed in a brochure rack, distributed to tenants, or posted on bulletin boards in the recreation rooms of residential buildings or in lunchrooms or mailrooms in office buildings. Merchants should be encouraged to provide the property manager with flyers promoting their sales or new merchandise.
- *Elevator signs* can be used to promote a different tenant or category of merchandise each week. Merchandising and promotional events can also be announced in this manner. A glass-enclosed frame can be mounted inside each elevator to hold professionally designed, 8-inch by 11-inch signs. If several elevators serve each floor, each elevator can carry a different sign. This will increase the promotional impact because workers will use different elevators during the week.
- *Posters* promoting upcoming events can be displayed throughout the MXD.
- *Mall brochures* can be placed in the lobby of every building. These should be pocket-sized, list every merchant, and include a layout of the mall.

Promotional literature can also be placed in conference rooms, lunchrooms, and mailrooms in the office buildings and in the recreation room in apartment buildings. Many shopping centers provide a community room for use by nonprofit groups and organizations, and an MXD can do the same. Flyers, brochures, and signs—even photos of past promotions—can be displayed in the community room.

Special Programs. Entertainment and educational programs for people who live and work in the MXD can be coordinated by the marketing director of the retail center. Fashion shows, merchandise displays, and lectures—even seminars on financial planning—can be presented in the evenings in the recreation room of a residential building or in the community room of the MXD. Programs for people working in the office buildings can be presented at lunchtime. A tenant's conference room, the conference room of the building, or a vacant office may be the right size. Another possible site is a theater in the complex.

Special Promotions. Sidewalk sales, arts and crafts shows, and entertainments that normally occur on the weekends can be started on Thursday or Friday morning. This will permit workers in the office buildings to participate in such events. Special noontime events can also be aimed at office workers (e.g., special fashion shows on business clothing and accessories). Frequent shopper discounts can be granted to residents and office workers in the MXD by issuing special identification cards that will be honored by the retail and service tenants.

The number and type of activities to promote the retail component to the other buildings in the MXD is limited only by the imaginations of the property manager and the marketing director of the mall.

A final point about marketing the MXD. Promotional activities for one use can also benefit the other uses—e.g., a merchandising event on the mall will increase the traffic to the MXD, and the other restaurants and entertainment facilities can capitalize on this increased traffic. The entire spectrum of marketing activities outlined here can be utilized throughout the MXD. Joint coordination of the marketing of each property type using a unified logo and theme will establish the identity of the project as a whole and promote the relationship of the component uses to each other.

Management

Mixed-use developments typically are large projects exceeding one million square feet of GLA. The synergism created by the multiple uses is nurtured by cooperative management and marketing of each property type. One challenge to coordinating the management and marketing is the possibility that individual buildings or portions of buildings may be under different ownership. In a large suburban MXD, the regional mall may have been built by one developer, the office buildings by a second developer, and the residential component by a third. A convention center or other public facility in an MXD may be owned by the city or one of its agencies. The size and scope of MXDs reduces the likelihood of single ownership generally. A development company may sell some or all of its buildings to one or more investment groups.

In such multiple ownership situations, the individual owners are likely to be responsible for managing their own buildings, or they may contract separately for property management services. However, the owners usually will agree on central management of the common areas, especially if some facilities (e.g., mechanical and HVAC equipment) are shared, as is often the case if the entire MXD is located in one or two high-rise buildings. To accomplish this, the owners may enter into a formal management and maintenance agreement among themselves. Management of the common areas and facilities may be assigned to one party and include responsibility for security, maintenance, design approval, HVAC and utilities services, and financial accounting. The agreement among the owners of the MXD should address several issues in particular as noted below. (Note that the management agreement between ownership and a property manager or a property management firm is a separate document, as described in chapter 5.)

- Effective management of common areas and internal boundaries between two uses
- Uniform standards for maintenance, operations, and use—regardless of ownership
- Mutual protection for all owners against deterioration and adverse use of surrounding property
- Promotional mechanisms and responsibilities, with fair representation of diverse interests
- Equitable sharing of financing by the project's beneficiaries
- Continuity in public participation, where appropriate, despite policy or organizational changes in the public agency's participants
- Mechanisms for change and flexibility, as appropriate, to deal with unforeseeable circumstances and events

From a property management perspective, the ideal arrangement is to have the entire MXD under one management. An exception to this would be the management of a hotel, which is likely to be autonomous in its operating hours, parking requirements, and provision of security. The success of most major hotels depends on the national reservation network of a hotel chain. In addition, hotel management is a specialized field of property management and is often contracted to a major hotel chain operator.

The reality is that each property type in an MXD is usually managed independently. Each use requires specific knowledge and skills, and few property managers have extensive experience and expertise in the management, marketing, and leasing of multiple property uses. An exception may be made if one property use is comparatively small—i.e., if the retail component consists of only 100,000 square feet of GLA, the property manager of the office building is likely to also be responsible for the retail sector.

Operations

Operating differences can have an adverse effect on the management of each property type as well as the entire MXD. The property manager for each component of the MXD must recognize and appreciate the varying needs of the other property types. Each component should have a coordinated management plan that will maximize the benefits of being a part of an MXD and resolve any conflicts that occur. Effective property managers understand that in terms of overall operation, the good of the entire MXD must take precedence over that of any one component.

Hours of operation is a good example of the differences in operational requirements. An office building is operated primarily between 8:00 A.M. and 6:00 P.M. on weekdays. Shopping centers and their retail tenants are typically open from 10:00 A.M. to 9:00 P.M. on weekdays and noon to 6:00 P.M. on weekends, with extended hours before the holidays. Entertainment facilities operate from 11:00 A.M. or noon to midnight seven days a week, although some cinemas have only evening screenings except on weekends. The residential component, whatever its nature (e.g., rental apartments, condominium, or hotel) is a round-the-clock operation.

The differing hours of operation vary the demands for maintenance and security. Maintenance of residential projects is generally performed during business hours on weekdays. In office buildings, maintenance and repairs may be done during the day, but janitorial work is done in the evening and early morning hours. Most maintenance in a shopping center is done on weekdays—general cleaning and policing of the grounds seven days a week during shopping hours; heavy janitorial work after the shopping center is closed. The parking lot is swept in the early morning hours, while litter is picked up throughout the day.

The parking demands of each commercial use parallel the hours the tenants are open for business. Office building tenants require long-term parking on weekdays, while retail customer parking is needed through the evening hours on weekdays and in the afternoon on weekends. Special selling hours may extend those times periodically. The parking required for customers of entertainment facilities may extend past midnight.

Availability of ample and convenient parking for their customers is a major concern of retail tenants. In a suburban MXD with acres of surface parking for the entire complex, employees of the office tenants may park in the prime areas for retail customer parking. To reduce this problem, property managers must designate customer parking, notify the office building workers where *not* to park, and possibly use chains to close off some of the retail parking areas until 9:30 or 9:45 A.M. During the lunch break, these areas may have to be patrolled to discourage office workers from parking there. The entrances and exits of the different parking areas must be clearly delineated and have good directional signage. In general, the directional signs in an MXD must be easy to read and provide clear directions on how to move about the project and how to locate tenants.

Emergency procedures must be coordinated among all the buildings in the MXD. All security and maintenance personnel should be able to communicate with one another to warn of potential problems and to request assistance in emergencies.

The complex nature of the MXD makes it essential to account for operating expenses accurately and to bill each building and its tenants correctly. As is usual in commercial properties, most or all of the operating expenses are passed through to the commercial tenants by the landlord. However, in an MXD, there may be some expenses that are charged to each building separately, while other expenses must be allocated among all of the buildings. Common area expenses, taxes, and insurance premiums are among the most difficult to allocate fairly. Utilities can be separately metered to each building and submetered to each tenant. Allocation of operating expenses should be based on a master plan that utilizes a single formula to prorate each building's share. The basis may be the leasable area of the building, proportionate use of the service, or the comparative value of one building in relation to the values of the other buildings. Whatever the basis for the master formula, allocation of common area and joint expenses must be fair and defensible. Once a formula is developed, it should not be changed unless the size of the MXD changes or a substantial formula error is discovered. Accurate accounting of operating expenses and proper allocation of the cost to each building or use is in everyone's best interests.

Planning for Management

It is almost impossible to do an effective job of managing a shopping center without a *management plan*. Unless the manager and the property owners have goals for both the short and long term, many of their decisions could be counterproductive to achieving the highest and best use of the property. The success of a shopping center depends on a thorough management plan that states the objectives and financial terms of the investment and provides short- and long-range recommendations for achieving them. An effective management plan is the result of gathering all the pertinent information, analyzing it, presenting the results of the analysis in a usable format, and making specific recommendations that will guide the operation of the property.

The management plan is an organized pool of information about the property that should guide the decisions that must be made about its day-to-day operation and prepare the property manager to meet the challenges posed by a changing business environment (e.g., market conditions, legal guidelines, financing alternatives, interest rates, etc.). Managers often learn of better ways to maintain the property, or they may become aware of specific trends in the area—more families with small children moving in or increasing commercialization, or consumers' buying power dwindling because the area is suffering from a depressed economy—and they must be able to take advantage of their new knowledge. In short, flexibility is imperative because the property itself and the environment in which it must exist are changing constantly. To prepare the manager to do what is most important—i.e., being able to operate a property in a changing economic climate—this chapter will focus on the management plan as a meaningful decision-making tool for the owner of a shopping center and the property manager who runs it.

The management plan must be as accurate as possible if it is to provide effective guidelines. Otherwise, decisions based on the plan are likely to have negative outcomes—e.g., reduced income, adverse effects on the tenant mix, and an inability to realize the property's full value.

The recommendations contained in the management plan will address such considerations as rental rates that tenants should pay, lease terms, a maintenance schedule, staffing requirements, alternative programs for improvements, and the financing needed to achieve them. To assure its flexibility as a decision-making tool, the management plan should be updated as necessary to reflect changes in the local market (trade area) and in the local (community) and national economies.

COMPONENTS OF A
MANAGEMENT PLAN

A management plan begins with a full *market survey* that notes all of the factors that affect the shopping center. This market survey includes studies of the region (e.g., Pacific Northwest), the community (town or neighborhood where the center is located), and the trade area. A major component of these analyses is a demographic profile of the population that includes trends and changes in its size and characteristics. A psychographic profile of local lifestyles is also helpful.

Included in the plan is a comprehensive analysis of the shopping center itself. This *property analysis* should begin with a thorough physical inspection (type of construction, age, general condition of the physical plant) and include an evaluation of the common areas (including entrances and exits), a review of the tenant mix, and an assessment of current vacancies. The same types of information are compiled for all centers in the trade area that compete with or have an effect on the subject property. The objective is to determine how the subject property compares to its competition.

The comparison data should also include rental rates. This information will be used in the third component of the management plan—a *rent analysis*. In order to set optimal rents, the manager must know what rents are charged at other shopping centers and how rates at the subject center compare to those of its competitors.

The fourth component of a management plan is an *analysis of alternatives*. This is a study of the property to determine its highest and best use. Few properties would not benefit from having a great deal of money spent on them, but the objective of the manager's analysis is to determine the optimum investment by comparing expected benefits to likely costs. Such an analysis should include the economic feasibility of leaving the property as is and compare that with the benefits of investing in modernization, rehabilitation, or a change of use.

Finally, if the management plan recommends changes to the property, it should also include a recommendation for *financing* the changes. It is not unusual for a remodeling program to look good on paper but not make sense financially. The financing market is extremely complex, and the manager should be able to provide valid reasons for selecting one form of financing over another, taking into account the financial structure of the shopping center and the likely alternatives. To be able to make such recommendations, the manager must understand available financing and apply the form of financing that best suits the investment. However, financing is such a complex and important matter, it is also recommended that the investor obtain the advice of a mortgage banker.

Although the management plan is an analysis of the property, its recommendations must also reflect consideration of the financial capability of the owners, their reasons for owning the property, and their long-term objectives for it. Equipped with the management plan and a thorough understanding of the owners' investment needs, the manager is in a position to recommend the best course of action for the property. The property owners should receive a complete copy of the management plan, including a list of the steps the management team must take to achieve the owners' stated goals for the property.

Market Analysis

A unique aspect of investment in a shopping center is the interest in the market that is shared by both the owner and the tenants. In this type of real estate investment, more so than any other, the owners' income is directly related to the tenants' economic success, and the market—the consuming public—ultimately determines whether the tenants and the shopping center will prosper. Therefore it is essential that the management plan include a thorough analysis of the market. For an existing shopping center, this will define current conditions. The market may have changed substantially over the period since the center opened, especially if it is more than ten years old. Changes in the market may suggest or necessitate changes in the center's tenant mix or its operations or both to make it profitable now. Analysis of the market is also critical to the decision to build in the first place. (See chapter 2, Development and Rehabilitation.)

Regional and Community Analyses.   The manager is interested in learning the vital statistics of the region, and this usually begins with an analysis of the population—the number of people and their distribution by age and income as well as any past and projected trends (the demographic profile). Other considerations include family and household composition, income level, and buying habits. Ethnic composition may also be important.

These data can be obtained from census reports, although the property manager should be aware that demographic data can change quickly. Information from the decennial census is updated annually, and more current figures may be found in the *Statistical Abstract of the United States*. The *Census of Retail Trade* and the *American Housing Survey* are conducted on five-year and three-year cycles, respectively. The use of computers has facilitated comparative analysis of demographic data, and numerous commercial sources are also available (see appendix E, References and Resources).

Many other aspects of the region can affect planning for a shopping center. Climate, available natural resources, local industries, recreational facilities, schools, and competing businesses in the area will all affect the investment, and the manager should analyze each of these factors on an ongoing basis. Information on types and levels of employment is also particularly useful. Evaluation of the dominant industry should provide an indication of the region's stability.

A geographic obstruction such as a major lake, a river, or a mountain range will probably affect the region and the property. Any such natural barrier should be mentioned in the management plan along with an expert's opinion of just what it means to the area and the property.

Manmade conditions must be analyzed as well. If the shopping center is located in a major tourist area or if the location is dominated by office buildings, this should be noted in the management plan and its likely impact on the investment projected. Local ordinances and regulations (e.g., zoning) should also be evaluated and noted in the management plan because they can affect both current and future operations as well as any alterations to the property.

Because the future of the property as an investment is the ultimate concern, the property manager must understand the current economic picture to be able to project the economic prospects for the region. Various federal agencies can provide data on economic trends in a region. The municipal or county government and their planning departments, trade associations, real estate brokers, appraisers, local chambers of commerce, utility companies and financial institutions, and the local library are all possible sources for economic information on the regional and local scenes.

Trade Area Analysis.   The management plan for a shopping center should contain an analysis of the trade area. This represents the shopping center's drawing power. The trade area from which customers come to a shopping center can be divided into primary, secondary, and tertiary trade areas, often also called "zones" to distinguish the parts from the whole. The *primary zone* is the area from which most of the center's customers come (70–75 percent of sales). Its size will vary from center to center and depends on such things as center size, anchor stores, dominance in the marketplace, and the extent and effectiveness of the competition. The *secondary zone* is the source of customers who will shop at the center less frequently (some 20–25 percent of sales). It extends some distance from the property and is shaped by many of the same center-specific factors mentioned above. The *tertiary zone* is the source of occasional or one-time customers (perhaps 5 percent of sales) and may extend many miles beyond the center. This small percentage of sales also represents people who may travel a considerable distance to take advantage of a special sale or visitors to the area who may shop on their way to or from somewhere else. In analyzing the trade area, the manager should focus on the primary zone. However, the demands of and limitations on shoppers from the other two zones should also be taken into account.

Although it is important to identify and analyze all the trade area zones for every type of shopping center, careful evaluation of the primary zone is critical to the success of neighborhood centers because they attract customers from an extremely small geographic area. For any type of center, the population of the primary zone must be sufficient in both numbers and buying power. It is usually impossible to attract enough customers from the secondary and tertiary zones to support a shopping center of any size. The exception to this is the specialty center developed intentionally as a focus for tourists— Faneuil Hall Marketplace in Boston is an example. The descriptions of the various types of shopping centers presented elsewhere in this book (see chapter 1) indicate the consumer population they require for survival. Except for those living in isolated rural areas, most people will usually travel only a short distance (1½ miles) to purchase groceries and convenience items, while they will travel much farther (8–10 miles) to comparison shop for a major appliance. These travel distances are another consideration in determining the boundaries of the trade area zones for each type of center.

The market analysis should also include the results of a physical inspection of the area. Valuable insights may be gained from observing the general appearance of homes as well as noting the average prices at which they are selling, the numbers of factories, businesses, and schools in the area, and the overall condition of highways and expressways. Attitudes at the local government level should also be investigated. A "no-growth" sentiment may be evident from zoning ordinances restricting commercial development; zoning codes can impose strict limitations on changes to an existing shopping center or prohibit development of a new one. (Market analysis is also important to leasing; see chapter 9.)

Property Analysis

For a management plan, the property analysis should include both physical and fiscal considerations. Nearly all investors work with limited funds, and the property manager must recognize what the demands of the property will mean in financial terms. That the property is clean and smooth-functioning will remain ongoing concerns (see chapter 6, Operations). A well-maintained property will help foster good management-tenant relations, and it serves as one of the best promotions for attracting a continual flow of shoppers.

The key to analysis of the property is a thorough *physical inspection* and an evaluation of what is observed. The property analysis is the basis for comparison of the shopping center with its competition. It also provides a basis for development of an *operations manual* which will facilitate day-to-day and long-term management of the property. Because the primary source of income for the property is rents, an important element to be included is a *rent analysis.* Comparison with rental rates at competing properties will indicate the center's position in the marketplace as well as establish a basis for setting new rates at the property.

Inspection. A physical inspection of the property is always necessary. Ideally it will be conducted before the survey of the competition because it will give the manager an idea of minimum standards for the comparison. However, these standards are not essential to the property analysis, and the manager may want to set specific goals for the property. A record of the inspection is usually compiled on a specific form (see examples in appendix C, Maintenance Forms). The level of detail may vary, but the objective is to establish the current condition and note any specific repairs that must be made to restore the physical plant to optimal operating condition. Obvious deferred maintenance should be recorded in this initial inspection as well as any other information that can be used to plan and schedule routine maintenance and repairs.

The manager should conduct the physical inspection in a manner that will maximize familiarity with the property. Carrying a camera and taking pictures will provide a record not only of conditions but also of location and orientation of various elements of the property. Of particular concern are those aspects and features of the property that may be important considerations for insurance coverages. Items to be located and photographed should include center signage and directories, lamphoods, bicycle racks, benches and other seating areas, trash receptacles (baskets or containers, bins or dumpsters), roof access ladders and roof equipment, fire safety equipment (extinguishers, sprinkler heads, controls), timers and switches, directional arrows in parking areas, and locations of utility meters. Because photographs also serve as reminders, the manager should also take pictures of items that need to be repaired.

A thorough physical inspection may take several days, but it will be well worth the manager's time. Through such an inspection, the manager obtains a broad view of the property and becomes familiar with the location of specific items. Ultimately, the information gathered during this initial inspection will be used to prepare budgets, predict future capital expenditures, allocate funds for maintenance and personnel, determine the need for maintenance and other service contracts, respond to tenants' complaints, and react promptly to emergencies.

Operations Manual.   The operations manual is a separate item from the management plan, but because it serves many of the same purposes as parts of the plan, it is appropriate to develop it concurrently. The operations manual should contain information about the center for situations that demand quick decisions. It should include the following items.

- A site plan showing locations and names of all tenants
- Plot plans that indicate locations of essential features, fixtures, and controls
- A list of key personnel to contact for each tenant (store owner, store manager) with store phone numbers plus their home addresses and emergency phone numbers
- A lease summary sheet for each tenant
- Lists of exclusives granted by the landlord (owner) and restrictions that are imposed on tenants—either by other tenants (usually the anchors) or to comply with legal requirements (e.g., zoning)
- A listing of property files and their contents
- A list of employees who comprise the management staff, including their positions and their home addresses and phone numbers
- A list of maintenance and service contractors, including company and individual names, addresses, and business and emergency phone numbers

The operations manual should be a ready reference that will answer most of the operating and management questions that will arise on a daily basis. Use of a looseleaf binder will facilitate both organization of the contents and addition of new information. When the manager is out of the office or away from the property, the operations manual serves to guide the other staff members in maintaining the status quo.

Plot plans are scale drawings of the site that indicate locations of such key elements as parking lot light controls; roof access points and ladders; incoming water lines and distribution piping, as well as effluent piping and storm and sanitary sewer lines; fire sprinkler valves, extinguishers, and alarms; electrical wiring patterns and master controls; and various utility meters, including a complete list of what they serve at the center. These make it easy to pinpoint problems and facilitate access to control systems to shut off utilities during repairs.

A *lease summary form* is a record of the tenancy and the leased space that includes such information as the store area, rental rates (base rate, rent escalations, percentage rate), pro rata bases for pass-through charges, utilities, merchants' association or marketing fund contributions, insurance re-quirements, and specific lease terms (including options, if any, and lease re-strictions). The information on this form provides ready answers to questions about specific tenants and specific leases. (An example form is included in chapter 12, Administration, and its use is discussed there in greater detail.)

An *exclusive use* clause reserves to the tenant the right to conduct a cer-tain business exclusively in the shopping center during the term of the lease. A list of these special provisions prevents errors when new leases are being negotiated. There should also be a complete list of *restrictions* that apply to the shopping center. These may include local zoning ordinances as well as separate agreements negotiated with anchor tenants. The latter may refer to such things as easements granted or parking rights or limitations. (Restric-tions are addressed in more detail in chapter 9, Leasing.)

The manager is responsible for maintaining the property files and records even though they belong to the property owner. Preparation of a list for the operations manual is one way to ascertain the completeness of the property files. The property manager must be certain that the files contain at least the following:

- Deeds of trust and mortgage papers for the property
- Restrictive agreements that apply to the center (e.g., easements, etc., negotiated with anchor tenants)
- Current zoning laws that apply to the property
- Records of property taxes
- Insurance policies and premiums
- Tenants' leases and records
- Covenants, conditions, and restrictions in the leases
- Rent increases
- Sales records (bases for percentage rents)
- Common area maintenance expenses and prorations
- Property tax allocations to tenants
- Tenant correspondence and payment records
- Correspondence from public officials
- Contracts
- Employee and payroll records

Rent Analysis.   Establishing rental rates that are fair for all parties involved is critical for assuring the profitability of the shopping center as an invest-ment. A lower-than-market rent may attract tenants to the center, but even-tually it will have a negative impact on the property's value. If an owner de-cides to lease a 1,000-square-foot store for ten cents per foot per month less than the market would actually allow, the rent loss will amount to $100 per month or $1,200 per year. At a conservative capitalization rate of 10 percent, the value of the center will have been reduced by $12,000. While ten cents per square foot per month may seem insignificant, it obviously is not. Any amount of reduced rent is likely to cut deeply into the investor's profits. If rents are too high, it may be extremely difficult to lease space in the center. Spaces that are vacant for long periods—or even multiple short-term vacancies—can give the shopping center a troubled look and compound other problems on the property. Vacancies also reduce income.

On the other hand, setting rents at the proper level can be a frustrating exercise, but there is a systematic approach that managers can take to set optimal rental rates. First, they should check rental rates at competing centers—by requesting information about rental rates when "For Lease" signs are seen in retail spaces, reading classified ads in newspapers, contacting local appraisers, and directly approaching retailers in the trade area. Information from these sources should provide an idea of the "going rate" in the trade area. After these figures have been obtained, more objective comparisons must be made. The manager should evaluate the competing centers, scrutinizing their geographic locations and the populations they serve as well as the availability of public transportation. *Vacancy rates* at competing centers—the ratio of vacant space to total leasable areas—should also be determined. All of these factors relate to rental rates.

The manager should then analyze specific aspects of the subject shopping center. Prospective tenants will want to know particulars about the retailing mix (types of tenants and merchandise) and the anchor tenants, the aesthetics of the interior of the center and maintenance of the property as a whole, and the convenience of the location. All of these factors affect their willingness to lease space at a specific rental rate.

After all this information has been compiled, the manager should prepare a grid that lists both positive and negative aspects of the subject and the competing properties. (A useful form for this purpose is the Shopping Center Survey shown in chapter 9.) Many decisions about rental rates will depend on this final comparison. Typically, new centers can command a higher rental rate than older centers. If small-sized shop spaces rent for $14.00 per square foot at competing sites and the subject center is new, the new space probably can command $14.50 or $15.00 per square foot. Other factors will have to be considered, however. Space built out for a tenant, rather than leased as a shell, will command a higher rent. The type of lease is also especially important. A *net lease* will yield a lower base rent than will a *gross lease* because it requires the tenant to pay both rent and a proportionate share of some or all of the costs of operating the center, usually including common area maintenance, repairs, insurance, and taxes. Under a gross lease, on the other hand, the landlord pays these operating expenses, and the tenant pays only the "base" rent.

Ultimately, the rental rate is a subjective decision, but it should be based on objective market conditions. The shopping center will suffer if rents are either too high or too low. The manager must understand how optimal rents will increase the income and therefore the value of the property. For a variety of reasons, the owner of a shopping center may decide against charging the highest rents possible, but the manager should know what the rents could be.

Once a fair market rent has been set, the base rate will actually apply to only some of the spaces in the shopping center. Different types of retail businesses will command different rental rates based primarily on their size. For example, most supermarkets operate on a high volume of sales with a low markup. They occupy large store spaces and pay low base rates and low percentage rates (often only 1 percent). Jewelry stores, on the other hand, operate on a low volume of sales and a high markup; they occupy small store spaces and pay substantial base and percentage rental rates (usual range is 5–10 percent). A supermarket occupying more than 25,000 square feet of GLA may have sales approaching $300 per square foot and pay total rent amounting to only 1 percent of gross sales including percentage or overage rent, while a jewelry store may occupy only 1,500 square feet of GLA and have sales of $200 per square foot but pay a total rent approaching 10 percent of gross sales when percentage or overage rent is included.

Generally, smaller spaces rent for higher rates per square foot than do larger spaces. Although there are fewer potential tenants for very large spaces, the laws of supply and demand are only a partial explanation for the rate variations. Smaller spaces actually cost more per square foot to build than do larger spaces—a restroom, a doorway, etc., cost the same regardless of the size of the store. The rent a particular tenant will pay depends on several factors.

- *Size and location* of the leased space in the shopping center—small spaces with good visibility in areas of heavy pedestrian traffic (e.g., kiosks in mall corridors, corner locations, spaces close to anchors) command higher rental rates than odd-shaped spaces and those on side corridors away from the anchors. Also, the more mall frontage a space has, the higher the rent.
- *Type of business,* which determines potential for percentage rent—supermarkets have large volume sales at a low markup and usually pay a very low base rent and a low-rate percentage rent (this can be very profitable for the shopping center owner because a 1-percent rate will yield $1,000 of percentage rent for each $100,000 of sales over the amount of the base rent); a jeweler or furrier usually pays a high base rent and a substantial percentage rate because these types of businesses have few sales at high unit prices and a substantial markup.
- *Desirability* of a particular tenancy—if having a branch of the premier local store in the area will add to the center's attraction, image, sales, or all three, negotiation of a lease may require a compromise or concession that provides for a reduction in the rent (although a reduction in base rent may be compensated by percentage rent).

If all spaces were leased at the same rental rate, prospective tenants would seek out only the best locations, and the owner would be left with vacancies in the less-desirable spaces. Usually, however, it is only when one or two spaces remain to be leased that rent reductions as such will be discussed.

Tenant Mix.   The management plan should contain an analysis of each tenant. Because sales volume is the true measure of retailing success, a review of past sales records is a good starting point for evaluating individual tenants. Each tenant's performance should then be compared to the performance of similar merchants in the trade area.

It is at this point that all of the analyses of the market and the property should come together. The property analysis should have indicated whether the property can or does satisfy the needs of the current tenants and whether the tenants are, in fact, suitable for the center. The market analysis should have indicated what types of tenants are most likely to succeed at the center given the economic conditions and demands in the trade area. The tenant analysis should have revealed any disparities between probability and actuality of success, and these should be evaluated further. A specific tenant may no longer be suitable for the mix of the center based on the current demographic profile for the trade area and the existing competition. In particular, fads in merchandise are usually short lived. The center may need one or more new tenants to create a new image or so that it can more effectively compete with other shopping centers in the market. The manager may find, to the contrary, that the center is actually outperforming the competition. Whatever the situation, without this thorough analysis, the manager and the owner may not know which tenants are best for the trade area and the shopping center, and they could enter into leases that are actually harmful to the future of the property.

A final, critical component of the analysis of the property is an evaluation of its financial status. A straightforward calculation of cash flow will indicate whether the property is being operated profitably at its current level and serve as a benchmark for comparing income and expense projections for other sections of the management plan, especially in the analysis of alternatives. Cash flow is calculated as follows:

	Gross Possible Rental Income
minus	Vacancy and Collection Loss
plus	Miscellaneous Income
equals	Effective Gross Income
minus	Operating Expenses
equals	Net Operating Income (NOI)
minus	Debt Service (Principal and Interest)
equals	Cash Flow

When percentage rent is to be included in the calculation, it should be a separate line item added to the income.

Analysis of Alternatives

In analyzing the alternatives for an established shopping center, the property manager searches for what is called the *highest and best use* of the property. At best, this is a subjective determination. *Highest use* refers to financial returns, suggesting that the success of an investment depends purely on economic factors; however, each developer's expectation of the return on an investment will be different. *Best use* refers to that which makes one use more appropriate than another—i.e., if a shopping center rather than condominium apartments would be more beneficial for the area. If the shopping center is also likely to prosper, the developer has chosen the highest *and* the best use. If an existing property is doing well financially, and it fits into the growth patterns of the area, then it is probably at its highest and best use—in which case, the appropriate "alternative" would be to maintain status quo.

Assume, however, that the shopping center is operating at less than its highest and best use. The owner in this situation faces a major decision about the shopping center, and the choice is whether to continue trying to optimize profits in the context of its limitations or to change it. Basically, there are five options that can be considered: (1) do nothing, (2) modernize, (3) rehabilitate, (4) enclose, or (5) convert. Each alternative will have a different cost, so it is understandable why investors analyze them all very carefully. Note that while the choice to do nothing has no upfront costs, financial projections for long-term operation without change should be made as a basis for comparison. This may, indeed, be the preferred option. The other four alternatives require investment upfront.

The evaluation of alternatives should include a *cost-benefit analysis* that projects the impact of the particular change on operating income (NOI) and cash flow and compares that impact to the cost of making the change. The costs to be considered should include any financing and the time required for the change to pay for itself. If a change is to be economically feasible, the projected increase in income (and related increase in property value) must clearly outweigh the costs involved.

Modernization.   With the exception of doing nothing, this is generally the least costly option. *Modernization* refers to the removal or upgrading of original or existing features primarily to reflect technological improvements (e.g., installation of energy-saving light fixtures in the parking lot). The purpose of a modernization program is to replace outdated equipment that is adding significantly to the cost of operating the property. Modernization should reduce financial losses due to changing modes of operation, a process referred to as *functional obsolescence*.

Sometimes modernization is more important for a center's image. Many shopping centers built during the 1950s and 1960s were well-planned and are still architecturally sound. They are in good locations, but their exteriors date them. A modernization program can benefit these centers greatly. Older shopping centers are recognizable from the steel columns along their walkways and the corrugated iron overhead. While quite functional, these items are not aesthetically pleasing, and they appear quite dated compared to more recently designed shopping centers. Often for a reasonable cost and with minimal disruption of operations, the property owner can remove and replace such elements that age a center.

Signage, in particular, becomes outdated. In the past, shopping center owners generally imposed few limitations on signage. Each tenant tried to surpass the others in the size, brightness, or attractiveness of their signs. That has changed, however, and most centers now have guidelines that all tenants must follow. The idea that the center is a unit, and that tenants must plan all their promotional efforts in relation to the whole, is the basic purpose for such coordination. The same philosophy holds true for all design elements at the center, from paint colors to sidewalks and lighting. The design must be coordinated or the shopping center will look chaotic. A modernization program related to signage can be very inexpensive. In fact, it can cost the landlord virtually nothing. New signs can be leased with little capital outlay, and this will improve the appearance of the center. A request that merchants remove paper advertising signs from their windows costs nothing, and yet this simple act may greatly improve appearances.

Other cosmetic changes that can be made at relatively small cost are installation of new benches and trash receptacles, sealing and striping the parking lot, and replacing the lens covers on canopy lights. Also, items that are no longer useful can be removed. Unsightly or incorrect signs, old flag poles, broken roof drains, and abandoned pipes fall into this category.

Many early shopping centers had very little landscaping, but those built more recently have extensive lawns and shrubbery. It is not unusual for a new center to have 15–20 percent of the site landscaped to comply with local governmental requirements. Although existing landscaping may be "modernized," extensive changes exceed the objectives of a modernization program.

Modernization alone can accomplish much for little cost, but it will correct only minor, mostly cosmetic, problems. It cannot change a poor layout of buildings, nor will it solve such problems as poor access or poor visibility. The management plan, if properly done, will distinguish between those problems that can be corrected by simple modernization and those that require major renovations.

Rehabilitation. The second alternative relates to major structural changes on the property. *Rehabilitation* may involve complete removal of a building or addition of a new one. It can entail complete relandscaping or total remodeling of tenant spaces. Sometimes it is possible or desirable to create additional leasable space by altering (reducing) the common area. Whatever the changes, rehabilitation is intended to restore a property to its original condition, without changing its basic use.

Rehabilitation is generally done in an operating shopping center, which creates the added concern that the construction workers may disturb customers and tenants (see also the discussion of rehabilitation in chapter 2). How much rehabilitation is necessary will be determined largely from evaluation of the competition in the area. Because a compromise on the improvements could eventually preclude the best merchants from leasing space at the center or mean that rents will be below the market rate, the analysis of alternatives should indicate the proper level of improvements to the shopping center to make it competitive once more.

Generally, rehabilitation becomes necessary either because of neglect of the property or because of major changes in the trade area. If the underlying problem is a complex socioeconomic condition within the trade area population, no single project—no matter how extensive—is likely to change that situation. It is more likely, however, that changes in the shopping center and retailing industries will make a particular center obsolete.

Economics are always a consideration. The solution to the problem may be quite clear, but the owner may not have the resources to see it through. The manager must determine what the actual problems are and, using the resources available, work toward the best solution within the limitations that exist. Without sufficient money, however, even a well-prepared property manager will face great obstacles in trying to turn a decaying property into a prosperous one.

In planning a rehabilitation program, the manager should consider every aspect of the shopping center and assure that each part of the program conforms to the owner's objectives. With regard to the property as a whole, the basic layout may be a detriment or there may be improvements that will reduce insurance costs. Each retail space should be evaluated for deficiencies as well. The owner may decide to improve the interiors of the stores, for which the tenants in those spaces should pay a higher rent. If clauses in their leases prevent such rent increases, it may be possible to negotiate a higher rent in exchange for rehabilitation of the exteriors of the tenants' stores as well.

If the improvements appear to be economically sound and the necessary financing has been secured, the owner would be well advised to proceed with the rehabilitation program as soon as possible despite any limitations related to leases. In an inflationary economy, the cost of construction will only escalate in the future. While phased construction—completing small discrete projects and rehabilitating the property gradually over a longer period—is an alternative to be considered, it can affect the earning power of the investment as well as reduce the impact of having an "all new" shopping center to promote to the public. The cost-benefit analysis of doing improvements over an extended period must also examine the attendant disruption of tenants' business and loss of rents, and all of these considerations must be weighed against the specific costs and benefits of completing the work quickly and efficiently.

Enclosure. Because the consuming public has grown accustomed to shopping indoors, there is always the possibility that the absence of an enclosed mall may be harming the investment in an open center. *Enclosure* is the conversion of part of the common area of an open shopping center to a "mall" that is fully enclosed by a roof and walls. This can be erection of a simple canopy or a complex, million-dollar project (most enclosures are also heated and air conditioned). It should be pointed out, however, that enclosure in and of itself does not create a mall; the enclosed space must be designed appropriately for it to function as a true mall.

Many factors must be considered in the decision to enclose a center. While economic issues are paramount, they are not the only considerations. The owner will certainly want to know if enclosure will yield additional income and whether that will justify the cost. While enclosure can be a rationale for raising rents, other considerations will also be important to the decision. If the competition is enclosed and the subject center is not, the open center is more likely to lose customer support and tenants are more likely to move out when their leases expire. In such circumstances, enclosure is preferable even if there are no immediate economic benefits. Here the intent would be to preserve the asset rather than to achieve immediate financial gain.

Climate is also a factor. In areas with severe winters, enclosure will probably improve business at the center. The same is true in areas with very hot summers. In these instances, enclosure is likely to produce greater traffic and thus increase tenants' sales volumes.

Change of Use. As trade areas change and the shopping center industry evolves, there are many opportunities for shopping center development that did not exist when some of the first centers were built as early as the 1930s. *Change of use* is becoming more common as a development alternative. Examples are the specialty centers developed in strong markets through *adaptive use* of old nonretail buildings, many of which were once landmarks (e.g., train stations, post offices, warehouses). Even conversion of existing shopping centers provides developers with many possibilities. To a large extent, the market survey will determine how the property should be altered. If the owner is considering changing a convenience center into a discount center, the demographic profile of the trade area will indicate whether the latter would be more profitable. The location and success of other discount operations in the area—the competition—should also be evaluated because the market may already be saturated.

For any contemplated change of use, the data for the area must indicate a real need for the proposed shopping center. Otherwise, the project will be a mistake. The demographic profile must be appropriate for the types of stores that will be at the center, and tenants must be found whose merchandise fits the proposed product array. In some parts of the United States, anchor tenants for new sites are plentiful but tenants for small shop spaces are not. In other areas, the reverse is true. There must be a market (tenants) for all the space that will be created, and tenant mix must be given special consideration.

Financing

Many excellent real estate projects have not been developed because the would-be investor could not obtain proper financing. When this happens, it can be a statement about the project or about the marketplace. In some instances, the high cost of funds may render a project unfeasible. Financing is therefore an important consideration in the analysis of alternatives.

Several lenders should be approached with a brief explanation of the project and a description of its current financing to find out if they are active in the market. This type of loan shopping should yield an acceptable form of financing that is suited to the project. Assuming there is more than one choice, the financing package that best meets the owner's goals for the investment should be selected. It should be pointed out, however, that financing is a very specialized subject, especially in relation to a shopping center. More suitable financing may be obtained by a professional mortgage banker or a loan broker who is familiar with the various lenders and the types of projects they prefer to finance.

The terms of any loan should be considered carefully along with the fees that must be paid. *Points* paid for loans are upfront percentage fees that are intended to increase the yield to the lender—one point equals one percent of the face value of the loan. Points play a big part in the financing of shopping centers. Because such loans frequently are for millions of dollars, points will be measured in tens of thousands of dollars. On a long-term loan, the points will not have much impact, but on a short-term loan (3–5 years), the points can make a substantial difference in the yield to the lender. On a construction loan with a term of 24 months, the points are a critical consideration. It is also not uncommon for an investor to pay additional points upfront in exchange for a lower interest rate (and, as a consequence, lower debt service payments), thereby making the loan possible.

Refinancing.   Sometimes evaluation of the financial condition of a shopping center provides specific insights. It may be appropriate to refinance the investment as a means to lower periodic debt service payments or just to make more money available for improvements. The decision to refinance an existing shopping center is one that should not be taken lightly. It is especially important to determine how the owner's short- and long-term goals for the property will be affected by refinancing before a decision is made. Because points have to be paid on a new loan, refinancing may not be worthwhile if the property will be sold in a year. On the other hand, refinancing with a loan that is assumable may make the property more attractive and therefore easier to sell. The terms of the existing debt should be scrutinized as well. If the owner has a first loan with a very low interest rate, it may be more advantageous to seek secondary financing for the short term and retain the original loan for the long term.

Before proceeding with plans for an alternative, the manager and the owner must review the profitability of the property in its present state and anticipate the effects of each proposed change. Both income and expenses must be scrutinized. A modernization program that permits more efficient operation of the shopping center may effectively lower operating expenses (e.g., for heating, air conditioning, lighting). A rehabilitation program that includes work on the individual store spaces may lower expenses because of greater efficiency of operation and generate additional income because the store spaces can command higher rents. Enclosure to create a mall will increase operating costs, especially if new common area is created. However, enclosure should also make it possible to raise rents. Another consideration is that common area maintenance expenses are among those most commonly passed through to tenants, so much of the increase in operating cost resulting from enclosure will be borne by the tenants. (Whether and how much expense can be passed through will depend on the language of existing leases, which should be reviewed by legal counsel. It may be necessary to renegotiate the leases to include an appropriate pass-through provision.) A comparison of current income and expenses to projected income and expenses will indicate how the net operating income and, ultimately, the cash flow of the shopping center will be affected by the change.

Wraparound Financing. Wraparound (or wrap) loans have a very specific application and are generally used when current interest rates are significantly higher than the rate on the existing first mortgage. With a wraparound loan, the first loan remains in place. However, the terms and amount of the first loan are combined with (wrapped around) the terms and amount of the additional funding needed. The combined debt is the basis for a new loan at an interest rate somewhere between that on the existing loan and the current market rate. The borrower receives the difference between the face amount of the wrap loan and the amount of existing debt, and the wrap lender assumes responsibility for payment of the debt service on the prior loan. The borrower then makes payments only to the wrap lender. This is how a wrap loan works: Assume that a property owner has a current loan balance of $350,000 and needs $200,000 to make improvements to the property. Instead of creating a second mortgage, the lender writes a loan for $550,000 with a single periodic payment due from the borrower, and the wrap lender assumes responsibility for the $350,000 loan.

Recasting an Existing Loan.   For many shopping center investments, a logical means of obtaining additional funds is to recast an existing loan. The lender merely puts up the additional funds and renegotiates the interest rate. Because the lender is already familiar with the property, its owner, and the existing financial arrangements, the recast loan closes faster. Not only is this an efficient way for the owner to obtain the needed funds, it also generally reduces the loan fees and penalties.

Once the owner and the manager have considered the alternatives for financing the shopping center, they must remember that the financing plan they discuss with a lender today may not be available for very long. It is not unusual for a lender's commitment for specific terms to be viable only for a very short time. If the financing market moves upward, the lender will not want to make a loan that is no longer attractive. While a lender may agree to commit to a project, the borrower must realize that market conditions will dictate the final terms of a specific loan. All of these considerations must be part of the management plan because they are central to the success of the shopping center investment. Not all property managers are involved in the financing of the shopping centers they manage, however. The amount of responsibility granted to the property manager will vary depending on the owner.

THE OWNER'S OBJECTIVES

Thus far this chapter has focused on the shopping center itself. However, it is also necessary to understand the owner's objectives for the property. In choosing among alternatives for operating or changing the shopping center, analysis of each possibility must include consideration of the owner's goals and objectives. Investors own income-producing properties for many reasons, and their ownership objectives will have a bearing on which alternative will be chosen for a specific property.

Extreme examples will make the point. Suppose the owner is a single, elderly woman who expects the investment's cash flow to provide her with income during her retirement years. This owner will probably reject a plan to use the entire cash flow to modernize the center because that would eliminate her income. In addition, because her need is immediate, she will probably have little interest in any long-range plan to improve the center's profitability, especially if achieving that objective will conflict with her immediate need for cash flow. On the other hand, suppose the owner is a professional investor on a small scale who is seeking short-range tax benefits and long-range capital appreciation. For this type of owner, cash flow is generally secondary, and appearance of the property and long-term appreciation will be primary concerns. For this owner, the manager should investigate alternatives whose long-term possibilities will maximize the property's value.

Valuation

The principal goal of most investors who buy shopping centers is long-term appreciation of the property's value. What they expect will increase is its market value, but it is not that simple. First the property manager must understand the two types of value that apply to investment real estate. *Market value* is the price at which a seller would willingly sell the property and a buyer would willingly buy it if neither were acting under unusual pressure. Market value is based on the implication that both buyer and seller are acting as "typical" participants in the transaction. On the other hand, *investment value* is the price that an investor bound by special circumstances and restraints will agree to pay. Investment value relates to equity ownership and may be more useful in decisions regarding refinancing or sale of a property already owned. The return on the investment, income taxes, and alternative investment opportunities also affect investment value. Investment value and market value will be equal only when the investor's requirements are typical of willing buyers and sellers in the prevailing market situation.

There are three approaches to determining property value based, respectively, on (1) replacement cost, (2) comparable sales in the market, and (3) the income the property generates. Each of these approaches has some inherent problems. Ideally, all three methods will be used, and each method will serve as a cross-check on the others. Ultimately, however, only a willing buyer and a willing seller will decide the real (market) value of a property. (A professional appraiser should be consulted to obtain an accurate estimate of property value.)

Cost Approach.   This method determines the value of a property based on the cost to replace the improvements on it. That cost will depend on whether the intent is to reproduce the improvements using the same materials or to replace them using modern materials and techniques. While the cost approach may be used as a cross-check on the other approaches, in reality, replacement cost has little bearing on the value of a property—a single-use concrete building may cost a lot to replace but have little actual value in the marketplace. Used along with the other approaches to valuation, however, and assuming that the property itself is useful, the cost approach may reinforce a decision about the property.

Underlying the theory of replacement is the theory of substitution. This theory implies that a buyer will not knowingly pay more for a property than it would cost to build a new, identical property. If this were true, however, why would developers ever build shopping centers in the first place? They simply would not. The reason new shopping centers are built is because the property is worth much more than the sum of its replacement parts. Tenants lease space in the center, and their rents provide the income of the property—income that increases as rents are raised and as the tenants prosper and pay larger amounts of percentage rent.

In computing value on the basis of replacement cost, the property manager takes into account each element in the building and prices each component part in the current market. The manager may also confer with architects, engineers, cost estimators, and developers to determine how much it would cost at current prices to replace the improvements on the property. The calculation must include the value of the land (estimated as vacant), development costs (including the developer's overhead and profit), and an allowance for depreciation (loss of value). When all of these factors are taken into account, the value determined for the property using the cost approach should be close to the values obtained using the other approaches.

Market Approach.   This method determines the value of a property by comparing it to similar properties that have been sold recently. The main advantage of this approach is that it directly reflects the market. However, no two properties—in particular, no two shopping centers—are exactly alike, and this is the basic problem with comparable sales analysis as a basis for value. If the manager does use this approach, special care must be used in selecting "comparable" properties. Factors such as age, location, condition, layout, tenant mix, financing, surrounding area, and possibly even a personal problem of the seller may all affect the final sale price in a transaction. In some cases, the seller may offer favorable financing terms in exchange for a higher price, or a higher interest rate may be paid for financing in exchange for a lower selling price. It is therefore imperative for the manager to learn as much as possible about each sale before accepting it as a basis for comparison.

Income Approach.   In this method, value is determined on the basis of the property's ability to generate income. Although the method is not perfect, it is considered the most accurate way to determine the market value of income-producing property. Most sophisticated investors use the income approach to value.

Because the ability to generate income will be dependent on the property remaining in good condition, all long-term improvements to it (e.g., roof replacement) must be taken into account, even if the property has only recently been built. Managers will often prepare an income statement without accounting for vacancies or possible emergency maintenance. The developer or former owner may agree to manage the property for an extremely low fee, which will lower expenses for the new owner, but only for a short time. An appraiser will adjust for such variations to develop a "stabilized" NOI for use in estimating value. Regardless of the specifics, the more accurate the estimation of stabilized net operating income (NOI), the more accurate the estimation of value. Value is estimated by dividing NOI by a capitalization rate—the formula being

$$V = \frac{I}{R}$$

The *cap rate* is a rate of return used to estimate value based on the net operating income. Capitalization is therefore the process of translating a property's estimated income stream into an estimate of value. The cap rate is the percentage rate of return (yield) on the investment (purchase price) that the investor expects to obtain from the property. Ultimately, the market cap rate reflects the "typical" buyer's evaluation of risk. The higher the cap rate, the greater the risk—assuming that the real estate market sets prices efficiently—but the higher the return from the investment. Because the cap rate is divided into NOI to estimate market value, a high cap rate yields a lower value for the property and a low cap rate yields a higher value for the property using the same NOI.

In the real estate market, the cap rate for a particular property can change for many reasons. The condition of the property, the safety of the investment and, above all, market conditions—the rental levels of the property compared to others in the market and competing non-real estate investment opportunities—may change for the better or the worse, and these factors are all reflected in the cap rate. Ultimately, the market determines the prevailing cap rate. If many investors in the area are willing to buy property at a 7-percent cap rate, the investor who is only willing to buy at a 9-percent cap rate is unlikely to find many properties of similar perceived risk available for purchase. The rate difference does not make either investor right or wrong but, in this case, the other market participants have bid the cap rate—i.e., the rate of return—to a lower level than the investor is willing to accept.

Income Capitalization.   As has already been noted, the income approach is the most accurate of the three methods of determining property value, yet it too has inherent problems. The main problem is finding an accurate cap rate. Through the years, practitioners have used many different methods to obtain cap rates. Some of the more common methods are described in the following paragraphs.

In the early years of real estate investment, managers often calculated a cap rate using *comparable sales* in the market—the net income of the property at the time of the sale divided by the purchase price produces a percentage (yield) rate for each transaction. Unfortunately, there are many problems inherent in this method, including the difficulty in finding comparable properties. Also, the buyer's net income figure may be higher than the seller's, or vice versa, and the method ignores the cost of improvements. Furthermore, financing arrangements (terms), which do affect the value of the investment, will change from one transaction to the next. Rarely are two real estate transactions alike in all respects.

Another method divides the sales prices of comparable properties by their effective gross incomes to arrive at a *gross rent multiplier (GRM)* for the specific investments. Multiplying the income of a property by a GRM gives an estimated sale price or market value. Expressed as a percentage, the GRM is similar to a cap rate. Although this method is straightforward, it implies that expenses will be the same among properties in the sample and that is seldom true. In actuality, a GRM is rarely used for commercial properties. There are too few truly comparable shopping centers to permit the development of a statistically accurate model. However, the method does reflect the market, and from that standpoint it can be a useful check on other methods.

The *band-of-investment method* paved a new road for investment real estate. It was the first method to use elements of first and second loans and equity in establishing the cap rate. However, this method relies completely on the current availability and terms of financing and does not take into account individual buyers' behavior. A refinement of the band-of-investment considered more accurate by practitioners today is the *debt-equity band-of-investment method.* This combines two critical elements of investment real estate, namely debt constant and equity dividend. The method recognizes the principle that the market depends on financing, and that interest rates often change over time and from one property to the next. It also recognizes that investors want to measure their equity cash flow. The debt-equity band-of-investment method takes into account both debt and equity components and assumes that the investment can and will be financed or refinanced at conventional rates with conventional terms.

Many factors in the present U.S. economic picture frustrate attempts to arrive at an acceptable market cap rate. The cap rate reflects the relative risk of an investment. Under normal economic conditions, a new property with no deferred maintenance would be expected to have a lower cap rate and, therefore, a higher price than an older, neglected property, and the buyer of the new property could expect a higher rate of return. In recent years, however, cap rates have been lower than interest rates, making most large loans imprudent. Cap rates may range from 7 to 9 percent, while interest rates may be as high as 10 or 11 percent. Unless the property is purchased with cash or the downpayment is extremely large, the cost of borrowing money is so high that the property will operate with a negative cash flow (loss). This means that more money is going into the property than is coming out of it. As a result, the buyer of a clean, new property can no longer assume that the investment will yield a return with less risk.

More recently, another factor has entered the picture. The number of foreign investors is growing for a variety of reasons. Real estate prices in the

United States are low compared to those in their own countries, and some see the United States as the most stable real estate market in the world. Others fear nationalization of their assets in their own countries. Foreign ownership of U.S. real estate is also increasing because some of those investors accept terms that American investors will not. If a foreign investor will buy property at a lower cap rate, it brings down the cap rate for domestic investors as well. Analysis of a property may indicate that 9 percent is a prudent rate, but if a foreign investor has a lower cost of financing and, thus, is willing to buy at 7 percent, domestic investors will be outbid. To remain in the market, real estate investors have been forced to bid on a competitive basis regardless of what their own analyses indicate.

The cap rate can change dramatically if the investor obtains a large loan on attractive terms. The better the financing package, the more affordable the investment. For instance, the seller may be willing to offer a 7-percent loan for a specific period of time in exchange for a higher selling price. All else being equal, the price paid may indeed be higher.

The Manager's Role

Regardless of the owner's specific objectives, the manager should always prepare a thorough management plan. Development of a management plan is an integral part of the property manager's job regardless of whether information in the plan is used. What is important is that the manager present a comprehensive plan for the property, complete with a program for its current operation and recommendations for its future. The property manager is a *professional*—an expert who should understand all aspects of the property—and a well-prepared management plan is evidence of the manager's professional expertise.

The manager's responsibilities for the management, maintenance, and remodeling of a shopping center remain constant, regardless of the owner's objectives. If appropriate action is not taken to maintain or improve the present position of a shopping center in the marketplace, it is likely to decline economically as an investment. Ultimately, if the present owner is unwilling to invest the necessary money, the manager may want to recommend selling the shopping center to someone who is willing to invest in the necessary improvements. Once a shopping center has reached the latter stages of deterioration, it is very difficult and extremely expensive to turn it back into a positive investment. Not every investor is prepared to undertake major remodeling and upgrading of a poorly producing property.

Management Responsibilities

The type of ownership and the investment goals the owners have for a particular property determine how the property will be operated day to day and over the long term. All property owners expect to profit from their investment, and the best way to do that is to hire professional management.

While shopping centers may be owned by individual investors, sole proprietors are more likely to be outright owners of smaller, less-complex properties (e.g., a two- or three-story building that contains one or more street-level store spaces below apartments or offices, a strip center developed on the corner of a city block, etc.). Large-scale developments such as regional and super regional shopping malls that require investment of millions of dollars are more often owned by development companies, investment partnerships, or other institutions that have access to large amounts of capital. In the United States, institutional ownership of shopping centers—by insurance companies, pension funds, real estate trusts, etc.—grew throughout the 1980s and into the 1990s because these entities had become primary sources of financing for such developments.

KEY MANAGEMENT PERSONNEL

The success of any shopping center depends on two critical factors—(1) the relationship between the landlord and the tenants and (2) the acceptance of the shopping center by the community. To achieve good results in both of these areas requires effective management of the shopping center by certain key personnel—the asset manager, the property manager, and the marketing and promotions director.

The Asset Manager

When institutions own shopping centers, the management of the investment is usually more complex. They commonly appoint an asset manager to oversee the management and operation of the center from a financial standpoint. The asset manager acts as an agent of the institutional owner and, in fact, may be responsible for several shopping center holdings.

Professionals within the real estate industry will sometimes use the terms "asset management" and "property management" interchangeably. The differences between them can be drawn more clearly by describing them within a hierarchy of management. The Real Estate Research Corporation, a national real estate advisory and appraisal firm, distinguishes among three different levels of involvement. *Portfolio management* is the allocation of investor equity among various types of assets (e.g., stocks, bonds, venture capital, cash), including real estate. *Asset management* focuses on one type of asset (e.g., real estate) and the addition of value to it. *Property management* is involved with the day-to-day operation and maintenance of specific buildings or land. In the context of shopping center management, the asset manager assumes the role of the landlord, authorizing the expenditure of funds. The property manager implements the plans of the asset manager-landlord and works directly with the tenants to create the property income.

There are eight key functions of asset management. These represent ways in which the value of a property is increased during the period of ownership.

1. *Acquisition* includes review of candidate properties (particularly their operating expenses and revenue potential), review of performance projections, and assessment of future opportunities for re-tenanting and rehabilitation.
2. *Property management* includes the selection and supervision of on-site managers and property management companies, authorization of operating expenditures, review and approval of leases, and monitoring conditions in the local market.
3. *Performance monitoring and control* involves generation of management information at regular intervals (monthly, quarterly, annual), periodic visits to the site, strategic review of the property's potential, preparation of long-term capital budgets, and analysis (and sometimes appeal) of property tax assessments.
4. *Re-tenanting and rehabilitation* encompass design and execution of planned programs.

5. *Peripheral development* includes review of assets for existing expansion opportunities, preparation of development plans and carrying out the necessary additional construction, or selling or leasing part of a property to generate cash.
6. *Refinancing* involves monitoring of the national financial market and current techniques for restructuring of debt, renewing mortgages at more attractive terms, and designing new financing as a means to reduce equity or fund improvements.
7. *Restructuring of ownership* may consider transfer of partial ownership via sale or lease of a portion of a property or evaluate buy-out options in a joint venture.
8. *Disposition* involves monitoring the life-cycle position of a property to identify an optimum time for sale, consideration of a sale if the local market position is threatened, and evaluation of all unsolicited offers to buy.

The asset manager selects and hires the property management firm and works directly with the property manager. Because asset managers' schedules usually do not allow them to visit an individual property very frequently, day-to-day management, operations, and leasing responsibilities are assigned to the property manager. However, some of the duties and responsibilities of the asset manager and the property manager overlap as they work together to enhance the value of the property.

The Shopping Center Manager

The shopping center manager is considered to have six areas of responsibility—administrative, fiscal, operations, tenant relations, leasing, and marketing and promotions—many of the specific duties of management will be delegated to administrative or operations personnel.

Administrative
- Collect rent
- Obtain and review tenants' sales reports
- Administer risk management (e.g., insurance policies)
- Hire, train, supervise, and terminate management staff
- Evaluate tax assessments
- Assist with litigation
- Administer leases

Fiscal
- Develop NOI projections, operating and capital budgets (annually)
- Prepare operating statements (monthly)

- Authorize expenditures
- Monitor financial activities (budget versus actual)

Operations

- Develop management plan
- Prepare management reports (monthly)
- Develop and implement emergency procedures
- Develop and implement programs for maintenance management
- Evaluate and establish a program for security of the property
- Coordinate or supervise tenant improvements
- Coordinate remodeling and rehabilitation

Tenant relations

- Develop a program to retain tenants
- Establish lines of communication with tenants
- Be responsive to tenants' needs

Leasing

- Determine market rental rates and concessions
- Develop and implement a program to identify, contact, and follow up with prospective tenants
- Negotiate leases
- Coordinate leasing activities

Marketing and promotions

- Supervise marketing and promotions director
- Develop community relations program
- Represent property owner in the merchants' association or marketing fund

The manager works closely with the marketing director to develop and administer specific programs directed to the community at large (discussed later in this chapter). The following chapters address the property manager's role in shopping center operations, tenant relations, and leasing activities, respectively, and discuss the contents of the lease document. The roles of the property manager and the marketing director in promoting the shopping center to the consuming public are the subject of chapter 11, and the manager's fiscal responsibilities and reporting requirements are detailed in chapter 12.

The Marketing and Promotions Director

One of the key personnel on the management staff of a large shopping center is the marketing and promotions director. First of all, this individual must have the creative skills and ability to develop and implement programs to promote the shopping center to consumers. In addition, he or she must have

strong observational and analytical skills because the marketing director will
be called on to help evaluate the competition and promote the shopping center to prospective tenants. This person works closely with the shopping
center manager and with the tenants in the operation of the center's merchants' association or marketing fund.

The responsibilities of the marketing and promotions director include:

- Conduct periodic market research
- Prepare annual advertising, marketing, and promotions calendar
- Develop a public relations program
- Implement advertising, marketing, public relations, and promotions
  program
- Maintain rapport with the media
- Develop annual marketing and promotions budget
- Review and approve invoices for marketing expenses
- Develop and operate the accounting system for the marketing program
- Visit periodically with merchants
- Maintain close working relationships with managers of major stores
- Participate in merchants' association or marketing fund meetings
- Adhere to the bylaws or rules and regulations of the merchants' asso-
  ciation or marketing fund
- Hire, train, and supervise marketing and promotions staff

MANAGEMENT AGREEMENT

The property manager's responsibilities for management of a specific shopping center are spelled out in a management agreement. If the property manager is employed by a management firm, the agreement will be between the
management firm and the shopping center owner.

A management agreement is a legal contract between ownership and
management that establishes the manager's duties, authority, and compensation and states the owner's obligations to insure the shopping center, provide
sufficient funds for its operation, and assure its compliance with building and
construction codes and environmental regulations. In general, the operating
expenses of the property, the wages of personnel employed to maintain the
property, and the taxes, insurance premiums, and other costs of the property
are the responsibility of ownership. However, it is the manager who is responsible to collect the rental income from the tenants and to pay the bills for
the expenses.

For the management services provided, the manager is compensated
with a fee that is usually defined in the agreement as a percentage of the gross
rental income of the property. A minimum monthly amount should also be

stated to assure compensation for management regardless of the level of rental income. Calculation of this *management fee* should take into account the full range of duties and activities to be undertaken by the manager or the management firm and, if not otherwise specifically provided, the wages and benefits paid to employees who work as management staff. It may also be appropriate to provide for additional specific fees to compensate the manager for such costs as payroll and common area maintenance administration.

Because the leases for shopping center store space are usually for terms longer than one year and negotiation of the specifics related to them—rents, renewals, prorated operating expenses, tenant improvements, etc.—is complex, the shopping center manager usually receives additional compensation for leasing. A specific *commission schedule* and the leasing parameters acceptable to ownership may be appended to the management agreement and incorporated in it by reference.

The management agreement should state the types and frequencies of reports to ownership and the timing and issuance of the budget for the following year. It should designate responsibility for compliance with employment laws and filing of reports on employment taxes withheld from wages. The manager may seek indemnification from certain liabilities, as may ownership, and the indemnifications they agree to should be stated. Because federal, state, and local laws determine liability under and compliance with environmental and other specific regulations, legal advice should be sought regarding what may apply in a particular situation.

The management agreement may cover other particulars related to the legal arrangements for management of a shopping center. The specific property to be managed and the names of the parties to the agreement (ownership and management) should be stated along with the authority of the parties to enter into the arrangement. These agreements usually cover a specified period and are subject to renewal by mutual agreement. Beginning and ending dates of the term and conditions of renewal should be specified. It is also appropriate to include provisions for termination of the agreement other than at the expiration of the term and for compensation to the parties if such termination occurs. Provision for notification of the parties and a statement of the relationship between ownership and management are other important inclusions. The manager is authorized to act as the owner's agent and, as such, is *not* an employee of the owner. Also to be included are statements regarding ownership of records related to the management of the property and provisions for the transfer of records from ownership to the manager at takeover of the property and their return to ownership at termination.

The specific provisions of a particular management agreement should reflect the responsibilities assumed by the manager to achieve the owner's objectives for the investment in the property. The complexity of the document will vary with the size and complexity of the property and the array of duties assumed by the manager. Both parties to the agreement should consult their

respective legal advisors to assure that their interests are properly represented and protected by the provisions of the management agreement.

MANAGEMENT DUTIES AND RESPONSIBILITIES

Included among the property manager's specific duties is responsibility for
administering the property's risk management program. This includes maintaining records of insurance coverages and ensuring on-time payment of the
premiums. The property manager also administers the details of individual
leases. In working directly with individual tenants to assure compliance with
lease requirements, the manager has frequent opportunities to observe their
business operations and identify potential problems. Sometimes the manager
can help solve those problems.

Insurance

The property manager usually administers the insurance program for the
shopping center. However, the manager usually does *not* determine the types
and amounts of insurance coverages. This is because few managers have specific expertise in insurance and, in case of a loss, they could be held liable for
inadequate coverage. The owner should determine the insurance requirements in consultation with a qualified insurance agent. A shopping center
should be insured against losses resulting from physical damage to the structure (due to fire, natural disasters, etc.) and, because shopping centers are
open to the public, against liability for injury to persons or damage to others'
personal property. The types of risks involved and the range of coverages that
can apply to shopping centers are described in more detail in appendix B,
Insurance and Risk Management. (Note that specific types and values or limits
of coverage may be set by state laws; an insurance agent who writes commercial policies can advise on local and state requirements.)

A property management firm usually employs individuals who perform a
variety of specific functions, ranging from administrative activities performed
in an office (accounting, record keeping) to maintenance of equipment at a
managed site. Often the firm's personnel handle clients' funds (rent collections, bank deposits, etc.). Insurance for a management firm includes fidelity
and other surety bonds, coverage for damage to or loss of office equipment
and personal property, automobile liability for company cars, and workers'
compensation. The firm may also offer insurance as an employee benefit—
most commonly including life, health (hospitalization, major medical, dental), and disability coverages. The property management company is subject

to liability as the owner's agent, and for this reason it is advisable for the firm to carry errors and omissions insurance (professional liability coverage).

Lease Administration

The relationship between the property manager and the tenant begins with a review of the operations of the shopping center. It is the property manager's responsibility to assure that the tenants abide by the center's rules that regulate store hours (opening and closing times), employee parking, and use of the common areas. Because each of these issues affects the tenant mix and the shopping center's image in the community, they should be addressed specifically in the leases the tenants sign. (Lease clauses are discussed in chapter 10.) In particular, the property manager must work to prevent problems that can be caused by a tenant's manner of doing business.

A tenant moving into a shopping center is prepared to operate a business but may be unaware of how to do this within the shopping center milieu. The property manager should meet with the tenant just before or after the lease is executed and discuss the shopping center's rules and regulations. The newcomer should be provided with a *tenant kit* that contains pertinent information regarding shopping center operations (exhibit 5.1). The kit should also include suggestions for how to handle different emergencies such as fires, accidents, bomb threats, arson, and power outages and good housekeeping practices to prevent fires and accidents. Depending on the geographic location of the shopping center, specific natural disasters (earthquakes, floods, tornados) should also be mentioned. The tenant kit should have sufficient extra capacity that correspondence from the property manager and the marketing director can be kept at the back of it. It should be accompanied by a letter welcoming the tenant and explaining the contents of the kit. The letter should also request the following items from the tenant.

- Certificate of insurance
- Certificate of occupancy
- Construction drawings
- Signage drawings
- Estoppel certificate
- Tenant emergency information (home phone numbers of store manager and assistant manager) and the home office (headquarters) phone number.

Compliance with the financial requirements of the lease also has to be monitored. On-time receipt of rents, operating expenses, common area charges, and other payments from the tenants is imperative because these

EXHIBIT   5.1

Contents of a "Tenant Kit"

- **Estoppel certificate**—what it is and why the landlord needs it.
- **Grand opening**—a summary of plans for the grand opening of a new shopping center or the re-opening of one that is being rehabilitated.
- **Hours**—when the shopping center is open on weekdays, weekends, and holidays as well as the days the shopping center is closed. In a strip center, tenants usually set their own hours.
- **HVAC**—the name and phone number of the company to call for service and how the tenant will be billed (if the landlord is responsible for the maintenance) or a request for a copy of the tenant's service contract (if the tenant is responsible). Instructions for setting the thermostat are included.
- **Insurance**—the names of the property owner and the property management firm to be included on the tenant's insurance policy as additional named insured parties (referring the tenant to the insurance provision of the lease).
- **Keys**—how to obtain the keys to the store (with a suggestion that the tenant immediately rekey the premises and a notice that the landlord does not keep a key to any leased spaces).
- **Mail**—how to initiate service and where mail is delivered.
- **Maintenance**—which areas within the premises are the tenant's responsibility.
- **Merchants' association or marketing fund**—the name and phone number of the marketing director (or ad agency), dates and places of scheduled meetings, the names of the officers, and a copy of the calendar of events.
- **Parking**—a copy of the shopping center plot plan with employee parking areas highlighted and a reminder of the fine for violating the employee parking regulations.
- **Sales reports**—when sales reports are due, to whom they are sent, and how to calculate percentage rent owed.
- **Security**—the guard's hours (with a note that they are subject to change) and instructions on how to contact a guard (provided the shopping center has such personnel).
- **Signage**—a copy of the centerwide sign criteria, along with the procedures for the landlord's review of a tenant's proposed sign.
- **Tenant construction**—procedures for having plans approved by the landlord and how to contact the local building department.
- **Utilities**—the names and phone numbers of the utility companies that serve the area.
- **Waste management**—the schedule for trash pickup and any special instructions regarding an in-place recycling program.

---

funds are critical to the shopping center's net operating income and cash flow. (Collections and other economic factors of lease administration are discussed in chapter 12.)

Shopping Center and Store Hours.   One of the critical components of a successful retailing community is uniform store hours. The consumer will want to know that most (if not all) of the stores will be open during specific periods each day. Because most consumers have limited time periods during the day when they can shop, they will shop preferentially at those centers where they can do as much as possible of their shopping at one time.

Uniform store hours are also important to the tenants. The primary bene-fit for a tenant to locate in a shopping center is the synergism created by the variety of retailers and service tenants. Each tenant plays an important role in creating that synergism because each merchant's customer traffic benefits the other merchants. In the same manner, every vacant space and every merchant that is closed while the other stores are open weakens the synergism and less-ens the traffic draw.

Uniform store hours are extremely important to both the shopping cen-ter's tenant mix and its leasing program. When retailers are open longer hours, they have higher levels of sales. Extended hours and the increased sales that result enable a tenant to be more successful and increase the possi-bility (and probability) that the tenant will pay percentage rent.

The hours that stores are open have changed over the past 30 years as a result of retailers responding to changing consumer lifestyles. When consum-ers' preferences, tastes, and lifestyles change, shopping centers must also change in order to maintain their competitiveness. In the late 1960s, ICSC conducted a survey of evening openings and sales volume. The survey, pub-lished in 1969, found that 62 percent of the 570 shopping centers that re-sponded were open at least five nights a week. This represented 73 percent of the enclosed malls, 51 percent of the open malls, and 68 percent of the strip centers that reported. Today, being open five nights a week is standard in malls and in most strip shopping centers.

Only 12 percent of the shopping centers reported that center manage-ment established store hours; the other shopping centers reported that either the major tenants established the shopping center's hours or the individual stores established their own hours. It is interesting to note that almost 65 per-cent of the shopping centers surveyed in the late 1960s reported that they did not have a coordinated marketing effort (e.g., merchants' association or mar-keting fund). Yet in the early 1970s, it was the merchants' association that de-termined the store hours or had an important influence in establishing the centerwide hours.

In 1971, ICSC published the study, "Sunday Opening in Shopping Cen-ters." Of 49 chain stores surveyed, 75 percent reported that they were open on Sundays. Stores do business for fewer hours on Sunday—opening at ei-ther 11:00 A.M. or noon and closing at 5:00 or 6:00 P.M.—but Sundays gener-ate the highest sales per hour of any day of the week. Saturdays produce the highest sales for any full day of the week. On weekdays, evening sales exceed daytime sales.

The reasons for having evening and Sunday openings, as reported in the 1969 and 1971 ICSC studies, indicate how retailers and shopping centers ad-justed to changing lifestyles. Aside from the strong competition from discount centers, which initiated Sunday openings, three trends apparently affected the change in shopping center operating practices.

1. The shift to living in the suburbs and the greater dependence on the automobile for commuting often tied up a family car so that the only time available for shopping was in the evenings or on Saturday and Sunday.
2. The more affluent economy of the period (beginning in the late 1960s) greatly increased the demand for discretionary purchases which involved family group decision-making.
3. The strict religious dominance over Sunday activity waned, and a more permissive society became tolerant of activities that were once prohibited.

It is interesting to see just how much shopping habits in the United States have changed since the late 1960s. Families now often have more than one automobile; so-called "blue laws" that once prohibited Sunday openings in many communities and states have been rescinded in most locales; teenagers have become a major purchasing segment of our population; and the primary shopper, the woman, must balance homemaking with a career. The additional family automobiles provide greater mobility and allow people to shop wherever they please. Today's working parents have limited time to shop compared with their parents' generation, and fewer shopping trips are a social outing with the family or friends.

In the 1990s, store hours are being established by the shopping center management, and evenings and Sundays are recognized as the busiest times during the week. Because property owners and property managers know that the issue of store hours is too important to the success of the shopping center to let merchants determine their own hours, the lease includes provisions that establish the tenant's store hours and give the landlord the right to change them. Large shopping centers and malls are typically open Monday through Friday from 10:00 A.M. to 9:00 P.M.; Saturdays from 10:00 A.M. to 6:00 P.M., and in some malls, to 9:00 P.M.; and Sundays from 11:00 A.M. or noon until 5:00 or 6:00 P.M. During the Christmas season, many malls extend their hours until 10:00 P.M. weeknights and stay open until midnight on the two Fridays and Saturdays before Christmas Day.

A shopping center lease requires tenants to maintain specific store hours. In an enclosed mall, tenants that do not have a customer entrance from the parking lot generally will not be allowed to remain open when the mall is closed. Anchor tenants, as well as some restaurants in malls, have both mall and parking lot entrances. Tenants that have such outside entrances may open earlier and close later than the mall itself does. When the mall includes a movie theater, the entrances near the theater are kept open until 30–60 minutes after the last movie is over. In a strip center, however, tenants may maintain extended hours regardless.

It is important that all tenants maintain the hours specified in their leases. When tenants do not maintain their required store hours, the tenant mix, the shopping center's reputation, tenant morale, and the potential for percentage rent are all affected. Some leases provide for a penalty if the tenant opens late or closes early. The penalty for repeated violations can range from a monetary fine to lease termination. Closing for an entire day is a violation of the continuous operation clause, and some shopping center leases give the landlord the right to cancel the tenant's lease if a store is closed for a day or longer.

A program should be developed to monitor tenant compliance with shopping center hours. If the shopping center has management, maintenance, or security personnel on site, one of them can be assigned to walk past all the stores each morning and evening and record whether they were open or closed and whether that fact agreed with their posted store hours—which should be in compliance with the lease. In the absence of on-site personnel, it is not likely that store hours will be monitored on a daily basis. In that case, the property manager should visit the shopping center periodically at the times when the stores should open or close and note their posted (and actual) opening and closing times. Frequent visits and discussions with the merchants may also disclose violations of the store hours clause. (An example form for monitoring store hours as a report from security to the property manager is shown in exhibit 5.2.)

Employee Parking. Occupancy of a prime parking stall can turn over eight to ten times in a day at a mall and even more frequently at a convenience center. This turnover refers to the numbers of *shoppers* who park in the stall each day. One of the criteria for a successful shopping center is convenience. When prime parking stalls are taken by tenants' employees, the shopping center becomes less convenient for shoppers. To avert this problem, employee parking rules and regulations should be established and enforced.

An important early step in an effective program for enforcement of employee parking is to explain to the store operators (owners, managers) the importance of providing convenient parking for shoppers. Another key step is designating a specific area for employee parking. This may be an area in the parking lot that is some distance from the shop buildings or behind them. A map of the parking lot with the employee parking area highlighted should be provided to each tenant. (For purposes of security, the parking lot itself should *not* be marked.) Regular monitoring is required to assure that tenants' employees are parking in the designated area—the level of occupancy of the assigned area will indicate the level of compliance. However, a more effective method is for the center management to require the tenants to supply the license number for each employee's vehicle or to issue a numbered sticker and require that each employee place it in the window of his or her vehicle.

Some regional malls rent nearby parking areas or garages during the Christmas season and require employees to park in these areas during peak

E X H I B I T   5.2

Example Form for Monitoring Store Hours

To: Property Manager
From: Security

Shopping Center: _____
Date: _____

STORES	OPENED	CLOSED	STORES	OPENED	CLOSED

Reproduced with permission from Alexander, Alan A., and Muhlebach, Richard F.: *Managing and Leasing Commercial Properties: Forms and Procedures* (New York: John Wiley & Sons, Inc. 1991).

traffic periods—evenings and weekends. Free shuttle service between the off-site parking areas and the mall may also be provided. Off-site parking possibilities include the parking lots of adjacent office buildings and schools, both of which are usually empty in the evenings and on weekends. In locations where safety is questionable, it may be necessary or appropriate to provide security guards in off-site parking areas. Use of a buddy system in which employees walk together to their vehicles should also be encouraged.

Tenants' leases should include a provision that allows the landlord to fine the tenant for each of its employees who violates the parking rules. The fine should be assessed against the tenant because the landlord's relationship is with the tenant and not the employee. (A sample employee parking lease provision is shown in exhibit 5.3.)

E X H I B I T   5.3

Example Lease Clause—Tenant and Tenant's Employees Parking

Tenant and Tenant's agents and employees shall park only in those areas designated by Landlord or Landlord's agents. Tenant shall pay a fine to Landlord of $20.00 per violation for each parking violation of Tenant, Tenant's employees, or Tenant's agents or licensees.

NOTE: This is the first of many example lease clauses provided in this book. The reader is advised to seek appropriate professional guidance before using this or any other such example.

Merchandising Beyond the Lease Line.   The lease line is the divider between the tenant's premises and the common area. Except for centerwide "sidewalk sales" and similar promotional events, shopping center reciprocal easement agreements (REAs) and common area agreements usually prohibit tenants from using the common area for selling. Nevertheless, tenants frequently place merchandise in front of their premises. It is not uncommon for a mall tenant to position a "Sale" sign in a holder two or three feet into the mall corridor. Some will move a table with sale merchandise on it outside of their lease line. In a strip center, tenants may stack merchandise in front of their stores.

The property manager is responsible for enforcing the reciprocal easement or common area agreement and the lease. Before discussing possible lease-line violations with a tenant, these documents should be reviewed. If any of them prohibit lease-line violations, the property manager should visit either the store owner or the store manager and explain the rule and its purpose. Because many store managers never see the lease itself, they may be unaware that they are violating a lease provision or ignorant of the limitations established through an REA or a common area agreement. If lease-line violations are permitted, the shopping center will develop an unsightly appearance. Eventually more tenants will move merchandise beyond their lease lines—most of it "sale" merchandise—and the shopping center will soon look like a flea market.

Avoiding Tenant Problems

Shopping centers have more tenant problems than any other type of commercial property. Apart from business failures, a particular tenant's use may create a problem. Use and disposal of hazardous substances, offensive odors, rowdy clientele, and long-term parking (usually by tenants' employees) are a few of the problems associated with specific uses. The best way to handle tenant problems is to anticipate their potential and address them in the lease. Tenants, leasing agents, and property managers may all bemoan the length of a shopping center lease, but this complex document has evolved out of necessity. Almost every provision in a lease addresses a problem experienced by a landlord at one time or another. While the lease is intended primarily to protect the landlord's investment, it frequently is not appreciated or fully understood until the property manager has to resolve a tenant problem.

Most retail tenants do not cause problems. However, some categories of businesses have greater potential to create disturbances and problems than others do, and the property manager must be aware of these types of tenants and address the potential problems they can cause both in the lease document and in the shopping center's operational procedures. The ultimate solution to such problems—if they cannot be controlled or eliminated by any other means—is the landlord's exercise of the right to terminate the lease. Provision of this right should be included in the lease document regardless of the potential for specific problems.

Hazardous Wastes.   The use and disposal of hazardous substances is a major concern of landlords and property owners. Illegal use and disposal is a particular problem. The cost to remove hazardous waste and clean up a site usually starts in the tens of thousands of dollars and can easily exceed $100,000. For example, when a landscaped area behind the shop building at a center managed by one of the authors was discovered to be contaminated with cleaning fluid, the cost to clean the site was more than $50,000. (In this case, it was thought that one of the tenants had disposed the material—without the property manager's knowledge.)

Businesses that handle or use hazardous materials in their operations include service stations, automotive service centers, dry cleaners, and photo-processing plants. Doctors and dentists are generators of uniquely hazardous wastes because medical wastes can create problems related to the public health. Tenants' leases should prohibit illegal use of hazardous materials and require appropriate safeguards when such materials are used legally. Hazardous wastes also require special labeling and transport for disposal. The landlord or the landlord's representative (i.e., the property manager) must be allowed to inspect the premises periodically, and the tenant should be required to pay all fines and clean-up costs associated with the use or disposal of hazardous substances (both legal and illegal). The property manager should inspect the premises personally or contract this type of inspection with a consultant. In the latter situation, tenant payment of the cost of the inspection should have been included in the lease. If the tenant violates the hazardous waste provision of the lease, the landlord should have the right to terminate the tenant's lease, to charge the tenant for the cleanup, or both.

Offensive Odors.   Adjacent tenants and their businesses can be affected adversely by repulsive odors that penetrate their premises from hair salons, nail sculpture studios, or other such businesses. A possible solution is to build the demising walls of such tenants' spaces all the way to the roof. These types of operations may require additional ventilation as well. Their leases should state that the cost to eliminate the transfer of odors to adjacent stores is a tenant expense.

Rowdy Behavior.   When a tenant's clientele become rowdy or vandalize the shopping center, not only the landlord but also the other tenants and their customers are affected. Taverns, billiards establishments, and video arcades are among those categories of businesses that can engender rowdyness among their clients and create high levels of noise in general. Some landlords will not lease to these businesses either because they do not fit the tenant mix or because their potential problems outweigh the benefits of their presence. If it is believed that the clientele of a particular business may cause problems, that business should not be considered a prospective tenant. When a lease is offered to such a business, it should include provisions to minimize or eliminate potential problems. One solution is for the lease to require the tenant to have a uniformed security guard on the premises. Also, the landlord should have the right to charge the tenant for security personnel in the parking lot if problems arise there.

There is less likelihood of problems with video arcades in enclosed malls than in strip centers. Enclosed malls usually have security; they are not open late in the evening, and there are more shoppers in the immediate area. When a video arcade is in a strip center, however, the parking lot in front of the arcade may become a place where young people congregate and "hang out." The lease for a video arcade should require the operator to have an adult attendant on site while the arcade is open. The provision that will eliminate the problem is the landlord's right to cancel the lease.

Long-Term Parking.   Office tenants in a shopping center may cause parking problems because they are likely to have more employees than a retailer leasing the same amount of space. It is important that office employees park in the designated employee parking area. For example, a real estate office may have more than twenty salespeople attending weekly meetings. The office manager of the real estate firm must tell these employees where they are required to park. The tenant's lease should include a fine for employee parking violations, and if a tenant has the potential to become a major violator of this lease provision, the monetary penalty should escalate with each violation.

Business Failures.   Occasionally when a local (mom and pop) business in a shopping center fails, the operator may blame the landlord. The tenant may try to get the landlord to cancel the lease with no penalty or threaten to sue the landlord for an alleged breach of promise. The promise may have been an inferred "guarantee" from the landlord or the leasing agent that a

EXHIBIT   5.4

Example Lease Clause—Entire Agreement

This lease contains the entire agreement of the parties hereto and any and all oral and writ-ten agreements, understandings, representations, warranties, promises and statements of the parties hereto and their respective officers, directors, partners, agents and brokers with respect to the subject matter of this lease and any matter covered or mentioned in this lease shall be merged in this lease and no such prior oral or written agreement, understanding, representation, warranty, promise or statement shall be effective or binding for any reason or purpose unless specifically set forth in this lease. No provision of this lease may be amended or added to except by an agreement in writing signed by the parties hereto or their respective successors in interest. This lease shall not be effective or binding on any party until fully executed by both parties hereto.

---

particular retailer would lease space in the center or that the center would have a certain percentage of its spaces occupied by a particular date. This is a difficult situation to avoid. However, as with other types of problems, a well-crafted lease provision that addresses this issue specifically may avert it. (An example of an "entire agreement" clause is shown in exhibit 5.4.) As addi-tional protection against alleged breach of a promise to lease only to retailers, the leasing brochure should not state "retail space for lease," but rather "re-tail, service, and office space for lease."

Helping Tenants Succeed

Shopping center managers generally have more interaction with their tenants than do managers of office buildings or industrial properties. This occurs be-cause the tenant's business is affected by the operation of the shopping cen-ter, and the success of the shopping center is determined by how well the tenant conducts its business. Sometimes when a tenant is having difficulties, the manager may be able to help turn the situation around. In order to do this effectively, however, the manager must understand how retailers operate their businesses (see appendix A, Retailing Basics).

Seminars for Merchants.   The rent a retailer can afford to pay is directly related to its sales volume. Parent corporations of national shop tenants and franchisees commonly provide them with ongoing education and training. However, local merchants have limited opportunities and little time to pur-sue education. As a consequence, they generally do not have the expertise and sophistication of the national retailers. Local merchants also represent the majority of so-called problem tenancies—rent collection difficulties, re-luctance to advertise and participate in promotions—and have the highest percentage of business failures.

The property manager can help these merchants succeed by providing the education and training they need. One approach is to develop a series of seminars for presentation once a month at night or in the morning. Retailing consultants can be brought in to discuss markdown timing, window displays, merchandise presentation, in-store promotions, and other merchandising issues. If selling skills need polishing, motivational sales training can be included. A banker can discuss financing to purchase inventory and the availability of and requirements for loans from the SBA (U.S. Small Business Administration). A police representative can discuss shoplifting and credit card fraud. Another approach is to have retail consultants present a series of three or four mini-seminars during the course of a week followed up with one-on-one meetings with the merchants to discuss their store operations.

Such seminars can be invaluable to the local merchants, but they will have to be encouraged to attend. The tenants should be involved in the selection of topics and speakers from the beginning. After the program is developed, the property manager should meet with each of the merchants and personally encourage them to attend and bring along as many of their staff as possible. To further promote the program, the merchants should be sent a bulletin one month before the start of the program, followed by a reminder notice a week before the program and a telephone call the day before.

Landlord sponsorship of these seminars is appropriate because investment in the tenants' merchandising abilities is an investment in the shopping center. Regardless of whether seminars are feasible, the landlord may want to consider purchasing copies of *The Retail Challenge* (the ICSC newsletter for retailers) for distribution to the merchants.

Working with Financially Troubled Tenants.   Throughout the life of a shopping center, there will be the occasional merchant who experiences financial problems. These problems may be the result of an economic downturn or a consequence of the shopping center losing its competitive edge. The merchant may not be particularly adept at retailing or the problems may be totally unrelated to his or her store operation.

One of the first signs that a merchant is having financial problems is slow payment of rent. This problem must be dealt with immediately. Otherwise, before long—within only a month—the tenant will be two months behind in paying rent. Other indications of a tenant wrestling with financial difficulties are a shortening of store hours (closing earlier), reduction of inventory, lessening of advertising, and layoffs of personnel. The property manager must decide whether to evict the delinquent tenant or work with the tenant to turn the situation around. In making this decision, several factors must be considered.

First and foremost is the impact on the shopping center of the tenant's failure and another vacancy. If there are already several vacancies, one more will weaken the tenant mix further, lower the morale of the other tenants, and add to the difficulty of leasing space in the center.

The condition of the leasing market—how soon the space can be re-leased and how much it will cost to replace the tenant—is another important factor to be considered. The turnover cost will include loss of income in the forms of rent and tenant charges for an unknown period; added to this are payment of a leasing commission and, possibly, the cost of new tenant im-provements. However, if the shopping center has a high occupancy, or the leasing market is strong, or both, the best course may be to replace the tenant.

Also to be considered is the value the tenant has contributed to the shop-ping center. The tenant may have been successful for many years but is now experiencing personal problems or being affected by a downturn in the economy. In such a case, it may be desirable to work with the tenant to over-come this short-term problem. The prospect of a successful turnaround—and its costs—must be weighed against the likelihood of the tenant be-coming so far behind in paying rent that recovery is impossible. Careful evaluation beforehand and continuous monitoring throughout the period of recovery are required.

In choosing to work with the merchant, the landlord may offer monetary or nonmonetary assistance. Monetary assistance usually is some form of rent relief, either a deferral or a waiver of lease requirements. When rent is de-ferred, payment of present and future rent is delayed until another time. For example, a tenant's monthly rent of $2,000 may be temporarily lowered to $1,000 (e.g., for the next 12 months), with the tenant being required to pay back the deferred amount during another specific period (perhaps the last 12 months of the lease). A requirement to pay percentage rent only is a waiver of the minimum rent for a specific period, with the tenant having to pay only a percentage of its sales. When rent is waived, part or all of past or (and) future rent is forgiven. Waiver of a portion of the future rent may require the tenant to spend part of the waived amount on additional advertising. Alternatively, the tenant's security deposit may be applied to past due or future rent. The program for a particular tenant should be tailored to that tenant's needs, and ways to address the problem over the longer term should be explored.

Nonmonetary assistance also may take different forms—e.g., reduction of the size of a tenant's premises or relocation to a space where the rent is lower. However, a tenant's particular problems may require a different ap-proach altogether, in which case, the landlord may choose to hire a retailing consultant to evaluate the tenant's operations and recommend ways to im-prove them.

When monetary or nonmonetary assistance is offered, the tenant's lease must be amended appropriately. The lease should be reviewed, and provi-sions that are onerous (from the landlord's perspective) should be renegoti-ated. While it may be most desirable to eliminate an exclusive or an option previously granted to the tenant, other provisions should be scrutinized as well—specifically the use, assignment, merchants' association or marketing fund, signage, store hours, and advertising clauses.

Although monetary or nonmonetary assistance is not advocated (or appropriate) for every merchant having financial problems, it can offer a temporary solution to a center's immediate problem—in some shopping centers, it may be the only solution. Partial rent and a merchant in operation may be better than no rent and another vacancy.

Other Tenant Programs

In large shopping centers and malls, it is often possible to develop supplementary programs that benefit both the tenants and the center. Major retailers commonly discount merchandise sold to their own employees. A centerwide discount program can be an employee benefit for everyone working at the center. While department stores and other major retailers usually have ample space in which to promote their merchandise, smaller merchants—especially those whose stores are in less-frequented areas of a mall—may welcome additional, low-cost display opportunities. Strategically placed display cases are one such opportunity. Similar use of vacant storefronts is a productive alternative to boarding them up.

Employee Discounts.   Many shopping centers develop an employee discount program to encourage shopping centerwide, create loyalty to the center, and provide a benefit for working at one of the stores. To make such a program work, tenants' employees should be issued a special identification card and given a list of the stores that offer the discount. Each merchant should be encouraged to participate; however, there may be a few who cannot. While for some businesses nonparticipation may be related to a corporate policy, others may not participate because their merchandise and pricing policies preclude such discounting.

When there is an employee discount program, the mall management and operations staff should be included as participants. However, if there is no such program, the property manager should never ask for a discount or seek any special favor from a tenant. Such requests only lead to problems. If a property manager accepts a special favor or a discount not offered to all employees of the shopping center, he or she will be indebted to the merchant and may develop a reputation for being "on the take" or using the management position to take advantage of tenants. In addition, such indebtedness may render the property manager unable to deal objectively with the tenant on other issues—i.e., lease violations.

Mall Display Cases.   These are four-sided, freestanding rectangular units, four or five feet high. Their top halves are glass enclosed and include shelves for displaying merchandise. Mall display cases are used to generate additional income, focus attention on a particular area of the mall, and allow merchants the opportunity to promote their stores in other areas of the mall. When display cases are planned, they should be designed to match the architecture of the mall and constructed from quality materials.

Merchants may be allowed to use the display cases on a rotating basis, and a fee may be charged for their use. If they are intended to attract attention to an area of the mall with poor traffic or where tenants have poor sales, the fee may be waived. Regardless of how or why they are used, overuse of display cases reduces their impact. Also, too many display cases give the mall a cluttered appearance and may detract from nearby merchants' stores.

Merchandising Vacant Space.   Whether true or not, vacancies send two messages: (1) that some businesses at the center failed and (2) that the shopping center is having leasing problems. To overcome these negative impressions, vacant spaces can be "merchandised" albeit on a temporary basis. This can benefit the community as well as the center's merchants and eliminate the unsightly appearance of an obvious vacancy.

Retailers in the shopping center can be offered free use of the display windows or areas in vacant spaces and allowed to decorate them with merchandise and signs indicating their store locations. Possible users include card shops, book stores, and hobby and craft stores as well as clothing, accessories, and record stores and service tenants. Merchants should be discouraged from displaying expensive items, however.

Alternatively, community groups can be allowed to place displays in the windows of vacant stores. The YMCA, scout troops, Little League, school classes, and senior citizens groups are just a few organizations that may welcome such an opportunity. Vacant space may be donated to charitable organizations for short-term use for fundraising and other activities they sponsor (e.g., collecting toys for needy children at Christmas, a haunted house at Halloween). Use of vacant space as a community room is discussed later in this chapter.

CUSTOMER SERVICES AND COMMUNITY RELATIONS

Major malls often become the shopping areas of the nearby communities, replacing the older downtown or uptown retailing districts. The areas immediately surrounding the malls may be developed into support retail areas, while the older downtown may be transformed from the prominant retail district to primarily an office and service area. When the mall gains such prominence, there is an opportunity to provide valuable services to the community—once the purview of businesses in the downtown area—and further enhance the mall's focal position through interaction with community groups and development of community loyalty to the mall.

A wide array of services and activities which can be sponsored by or offered at the mall are valuable to the community either directly or indirectly. Examples include specific shopper services, individual activities, and holiday entertainments, as well as meeting rooms for community organizations and possible use of the center as a public forum. The size of the shopping center or mall will often determine the extent of the specific programs.

Customer Services

Shopping center services and programs that benefit individuals generate goodwill in the community at large. Senior citizens and teenagers are two groups that patronize malls frequently and deserve special attention. Because consumers generally patronize shopping centers that offer more conveniences, attention to shopper services is important, too.

Information Booth.   Most regional and super regional malls include an information booth in or near center court. During the hours the mall is open, staff in these booths answer shoppers' questions, provide assistance in finding lost children, and help people with car problems. The information booth may also be the answering service for the mall. Individuals staffing the booth should be trained to handle varying situations—from lost children to irate customers to bomb threats.

Services commonly offered at such booths include rentals of strollers and wheelchairs and sales of shopping bags (imprinted with the center's logo) and gift certificates that can be used at any store in the center (usually in $10 or $20 increments). Wheelchairs or strollers may also be provided at no charge. Regardless of the arrangements, identification should be required before a wheelchair or stroller is released to a customer. The person in charge of the booth may also be responsible for cleaning the item when it is returned.

Senior Citizens Programs.   The number of senior citizens in American society is increasing steadily, and usually they have substantial amounts of disposable income. Property managers should encourage senior citizens to patronize the shopping center by providing services directed to them. Some shopping centers develop specific discount programs and provide participants with special identification cards. Others sponsor a free or reduced-fare shuttle or bus service between local senior housing facilities or recreation centers and the shopping center.

One popular program is the mall walkers, which may be coordinated with a local hospital or community agency. The mall doors are opened early in the morning for senior citizens and other members of the community to exercise by walking in the mall. Registered participants receive a mall walkers' pin; their distances are recorded, and they are given a certificate when they reach specific milestones.

Teens on the Mall.   The mall has become a favorite place for teenagers to hang out. Regardless of the weather or the time of year, there is always something to do at the mall. Fashion fads, restaurants, music stores, video games, in-mall theaters, and promotions all attract teens. They seem to consider the mall a place where they can meet their friends and be seen. Parents often encourage teens to "hang out" at the mall because it is one of the safest places in the community. The wise property manager will welcome teens for several reasons. They have much more disposable income than their parents did when they were teenagers, and in a few years, they will represent a major segment of the mall's customer base.

The teen years are a period of growth and high energy levels, and sometimes teenagers become unruly. This type of behavior can be frightening to others in the mall, especially elderly shoppers. Some malls have been taken over by teens during certain times of the day or night. The property manager may want to welcome teens, but it is also important to maintain an orderly and safe shopping environment for all mall customers. Any program developed to encourage all the consumers in the community—including teenagers—to shop at the mall must include means of preventing groups of teens from creating problems for other shoppers.

Gangs, Graffiti, and Other Problems.   Graffiti may be the first indicator of potential gang problems. Gangs mark their turf with messages and symbols, and the police can often identify which gang is active in the area by the types of graffiti. (Removal of graffiti is discussed in chapter 6.) If teen behavior or gang activity becomes a problem, the police should be asked to participate in the development and implementation of a solution to it. Teens are more likely to congregate in or near the food court, center court, video game rooms, record shops, and areas near in-mall theaters. Security staff should be alert, and teens who become unruly should be informed that they are welcome at the mall only as long as they do not disturb others. Preventing large crowds from gathering in one place and discouraging teens from loitering in one area (e.g., the food court) will go a long way to avert problems.

Some malls have taken a "get tough" policy. They ban teens from the mall on Friday and Saturday evenings if they are not accompanied by an adult and bar unruly teens from returning to the mall for a period of time. Teens are handed pocket-sized cards listing the mall's rules and regulations, and parents are called when the teenager's behavior is unacceptable. There is a difference of opinion among mall managers as to whether such a policy is effective or only serves to aggravate the situation.

Mall security staff will have to be trained to deal with teenagers. A bully approach does not work and may aggravate a sensitive situation. Some malls have a customer representative whose responsibility includes working with teens and handling teen problems. Good lighting in the parking lot and other areas of the shopping center is a particular deterrent to rowdy behavior. Music has been found to affect behavior, and restaurants have changed the music they play specifically to discourage a rowdy clientele.

A Positive Approach.   There are any number of approaches to dealing with teenagers in the mall, including having the police become advisors to the mall management. One approach that can be very effective is to develop and implement a specific program to cultivate a relationship with the youth of the community. This can be done by creating an advisory board at each high school in the mall's primary trade area and a teen board at the mall. A representative from each school's advisory board is appointed to the teen board at the mall. The advisory board may be invited to suggest promotions for the mall, assist in presenting fashion shows, and coordinate school-related activities at the mall. In conjunction with merchants in the mall—through either the merchants' association or the marketing fund—it may be possible to develop a work-study program with the local high schools. The school's advisory board would then serve as the job-placement liaison with the mall management and the stores. Specific promotional events can be developed in honor of the schools and the students. If there are only one or two high schools in the area, the mall may become a sponsor or supporter of an athletic team or another student activity or organization.

Christmas Community Programs.   Holidays bring out people's charitable instincts, and community programs can be initiated that will benefit those in need, generate goodwill in the community, and promote the shopping center. One popular program is an angel tree—a Christmas tree decorated with paper angels, each bearing the name and age of a needy child. Shoppers can select an angel, purchase a gift, attach the angel to the gift, and place it under the tree. The program is coordinated with a local social service agency (e.g., the Salvation Army) that provides the names and ages of the children, and the gifts are distributed just before Christmas. It may be appropriate to stipulate that gifts should not be wrapped. Otherwise, wrapped gifts may have to be unwrapped (to assure that the gift is appropriate) and rewrapped. An angel tree program may also include the names of needy adults.

Another popular offering is a gift wrapping service provided by a community group. Space in the mall may be donated to a local charitable organization to set up a gift wrapping booth. No rent or fee is charged for the space, and the organization is expected to provide the gift wrapping materials (paper, bows, etc.). The fees charged for the gift wrapping earn a "profit" that will fund other activities of the organization. In addition to providing a source of funds for a worthy cause, the gift wrapping booth provides an added service for shoppers.

One of the oldest community service activities is the selling of live Christmas trees. Most typically, a strip center will allocate a corner of its parking lot for Christmas tree sales, usually to benefit a community service or charitable organization. Regional malls are less likely to participate in this activity because their entire parking lots are needed for parking during the holiday season.

Other Christmas-related items such as wreaths and handmade seasonal decorations may also be sold by charitable groups. However, specific offerings must be scrutinized beforehand. Items sold to benefit charities should not compete directly with tenants' merchandise. It must be remembered that holiday sales represent a major portion of most retailers' annual sales, and a successful holiday season is the measure of their business year.

Valet Parking.   During the Christmas season, some malls provide valet parking as a convenience to shoppers loaded with purchases who have a long walk to their cars. It also relieves the concern some shoppers may have about safety late in the evening. If shoppers feel more comfortable and secure, they are more likely to patronize the shopping center. Valet parking may be provided at no charge or for a standardized fee.

Specific Community Services

Programs addressed to the community at large will strengthen the shopping center's position in the community as well as provide valuable services to those who live and work there.

Community Room.   A community room in a shopping center provides a place for organizations to meet. Many developers will design a permanent community room for a mall, usually in an area that would be difficult to lease to retailers. However, provision of a community room may have to be on a temporary basis. If a strip center or enclosed mall has several vacancies, one of those spaces may be converted to a community room. If there is a great demand for use of the community room and other vacancies are not expected to be leased for a while, additional community rooms may be created. Because community rooms can be easily reconverted to leased space, reservations for their use should not be accepted more than two months in advance. This will facilitate future leasing.

To allow as many groups as possible to use the community room, and to minimize problems that can arise from such use, a set of policies and guidelines should be developed. Such policies may establish conditions for use, set priorities for accepting reservations, and prohibit specific activities. Following are some examples of issues to be addressed in policies.

- Reservations should be made no less than two weeks and no more than two months before the intended use.
- No group should be permitted to use the room more than twice in one month.
- Use of the room may be limited to nonprofit organizations only, or nonprofit groups may be given priority.
- A fee may be charged for use of the room (nonprofit groups may be allowed to use the room at no charge).
- A security deposit may be required.
- Certain activities may be prohibited—sales of services or merchandise, distribution of handbills outside the room, loudspeakers, loud music.
- The user should be required to clean the room and return the tables and chairs to their original positions.
- Hours for the use of the room should be established.
- Organizations should be required to sign a hold-harmless agreement that indemnifies the center and its management against liability arising out of the organization's activities on the property and includes rules and regulations for the use of the community room.

There may be other conditions or limitations required for a community room in a specific shopping center. The program and policies governing its use should be thought through carefully before the first use of the community room, and the landlord's (owner's) potential for liability should be investigated. Insurance coverages may preclude some kinds of activities, and state and local laws may proscribe others. Advice of legal council should be sought before proceeding.

Establishment of a community room offers a unique opportunity to market the shopping center to a captive audience. The walls can be used to display a list of the merchants, a separate list of the restaurants, and a calendar of upcoming promotional events as well as posters promoting past events and photos of them. The community room itself should be promoted. It offers an opportunity for publicity and community goodwill. A description of the community room and an invitation to use it can be sent to local nonprofit organizations, and announcements (press releases) can be sent to all the media. Basic equipment for a community room consists of folding tables (at least two, usually eight feet long) and a number of folding or stacking chairs (usually at least 20–30).

Community Booth. While it may be desirable to permit individuals or groups to promote their activities within the community, such permission may also require provision of time and space for promotion of controversial issues and organizations. There have been varying and conflicting rulings by the U.S. and state Supreme Courts regarding the right to use the shopping center as a public forum. Both state and federal laws may have to be researched in addition to local ordinances to understand the situation fully. Allowing use of the common areas for dissemination of information may be required under the law. Because this can be a sensitive area, legal advice should be sought regarding public rights and the owner's (landlord's) obligations to allow individuals or groups to disseminate information at the shopping center. It may be appropriate to develop a specific policy regarding use of the shopping center as a public forum.

If the shopping center owner chooses or is required to permit such a use of the common areas, reasonable and nondiscriminatory rules regarding such use must be established. Specific rules may (1) require advance reservations and payment of a reasonable and refundable deposit, (2) set limitations on the duration of use, location, and signage, and (3) prohibit use of a public address system and interference with the tenants. To accommodate such public use, a booth may be set up in a mall in an area that is visible and accessible by shoppers. In a strip center a discrete area may be designated in lieu of a booth. Individuals should be required to remain in the booth or designated area, and they should be prohibited from distributing handbills outside of their area.

Other Use of the Shopping Center.   Many shopping centers donate space or charge nominal rent for city and county agencies to use space in the mall. Space leased to the U.S. Postal Service for a post office, a postal substation, or an express mail drop box provides a customer convenience and is therefore a useful amenity.

Space that is difficult to lease or less desirable from a retailing standpoint may be donated for local use as a branch public library, a police substation, a youth community room, or an art museum. Police and fire departments and area hospitals may be provided space to conduct training sessions—e.g., cardiopulmonary resuscitation (CPR). Space may be set aside in the parking lot for recycling bins.

Legal responsibilities and liabilities should be explored and understood before any specific arrangements are made.

Customer Surveys

Keeping up with population changes, evolving tastes, and new competition requires frequent monitoring of the needs and preferences of the consumer. The shopping center is designed, leased, marketed, promoted, and managed to meet the needs of the community. An effective means to discover what the residents in the area want is to ask them. Surveys may be conducted prior to development of a new center or when a property owner is planning to rehabilitate an established center to find out which categories of tenants and which specific merchants should be in the center—i.e., what the shoppers want.

Regular customer surveys provide valuable information for evaluating and assisting the leasing, marketing, and operations of a shopping center. A customer survey can be conducted to determine the demographic profile of a trade area or to characterize a center's regular shoppers and determine their preferences. Surveys are used to determine the most effective media for the center's advertising, and shoppers' preferences for radio stations and newspapers are also commonly sought. Shoppers may be asked which promotions they attended and what other types of promotions they would like presented, as well as their opinions of the security, maintenance, and convenience (or inconvenience) of the shopping center.

A customer survey may include questions regarding advertising and promotions, leasing and tenant mix, management and operations, frequency of shopping, and the competition, as well as specific demographic information. (A questionnaire used by one of the authors is shown in exhibit 5.5.) The customer survey is intended to evaluate many aspects of the shopping center and to compare the shopping center to its competition. Once a survey is completed, the results are tabulated and evaluated and shared with the tenants, if appropriate. Customer surveys can be invaluable for maintaining the shopping center's competitiveness.

There are several methods for conducting customer surveys. Different methods are used to obtain different types of information, and the cost of each method will vary. Five methods are described below.

1. *Intercept.* This type of survey is conducted *at* the shopping center. The shopper is "intercepted" and asked questions regarding the leasing, marketing, and operations of the center. Interviews take between 7 and 12 minutes, and 300–500 interviews are required for the results to be valid. It must be remembered that such an intercept surveys only consumers who shop at the mall; it does not obtain the opinions of consumers who do not shop the mall.

2. *Bag stuffer questionnaires.* A simple questionnaire may be placed in the bag along with the purchased item. A mall-wide survey might ask questions about where the purchase was made (store name), what was purchased and the price paid, when the purchase was made (time of day, day of the week), whether it was an intentional (destination) or unintentional (impulse) purchase, how often the mall is shopped, and some very basic demographic data (e.g., shopper's age, distance traveled).

   The shopper who returns the questionnaire may be given a token gift, or the survey may be included in a drawing for a larger item (a major prize), in which case a name and address would be required. The response rate for this type of survey is low, and the validity of the results is questionable. However, it is a very inexpensive method and may produce good public relations.

E X H I B I T   5.5

Example Customer Survey Questionnaire

Advertising and Promotions

1. To help us in the proper placement of our advertising, please indicate which newspaper(s) you regularly read.

   _____ Seattle Times   _____ Kirkland Tribune
   _____ Seattle Post Intelligencer   _____ Highlander
   _____ Eastside Journal American   _____ Other _____
   _____ Redmond News   _____ None. Do not regularly read a newspaper.

2. Which radio station(s) do you listen to regularly?

   _____ KING-AM   _____ KTIP-FM
   _____ KOMO-AM   _____ KUOW-FM
   _____ KIXI-AM   _____ KROX-FM
   _____ KPIX-AM   _____ KOLD-FM
   _____ KROO-AM   _____ KREX-FM
   _____ KIRO-AM   _____ KING-FM
   _____ Other AM _____   _____ Other FM _____

3. What do you think is the best medium for advertising Northway Mall?

   _____ Newspaper ads   _____ Mailers
   _____ TV   _____ Ads in weekly shopping news
   _____ Radio   _____ None of the above
   _____ Other _____

4. Which newspaper is delivered to your home?
   _____   _____ None

5. Do you subscribe to cable TV?   _____ Yes   _____ No

6. Did you or anyone in your household attend the following events at Northway Mall?

   _____ January sidewalk sale   _____ Boat show
   _____ February Valentine's promotion   _____ Bridal show
   _____ Easter show   _____ Summer fashion show

Leasing and Tenant Mix

1. At which store(s) did you shop during the past week?
   _____

2. Which store(s) did you visit today?
   _____

3. In which store(s) did you make a purchase?
   _____

4. Are there any additional stores you would like to see at Northway Mall?
   _____

5. Which stores do you shop that are not located at Northway Mall?
   _____

E X H I B I T   5.5 (*continued*)

Management and Operations

1. Please rate all of the following aspects of Northway Mall.

	Excellent	Good	Fair	Poor	No Opinion
Selection of stores	_____	_____	_____	_____	_____
Selection of merchandise	_____	_____	_____	_____	_____
Quality of service	_____	_____	_____	_____	_____
Parking facilities	_____	_____	_____	_____	_____
Access to the center	_____	_____	_____	_____	_____
Mall cleanliness	_____	_____	_____	_____	_____
Decor/attractiveness	_____	_____	_____	_____	_____
Mall amenities/facilities	_____	_____	_____	_____	_____
Eating facilities	_____	_____	_____	_____	_____

2. If you are dissatisfied in any way with Northway Mall, please tell us about it. (Please be as specific as possible.) _____
_____

Frequency of Shopping and the Competition

1. How often do you shop at Northway Mall?

   _____ Twice a week or more   _____ Once a month
   _____ Once a week   _____ Less than once a month
   _____ Twice a month   _____ This is my first visit

2. Which of the following describes the length of your typical shopping visit?

   _____ Less than one hour   _____ Two to three hours
   _____ One to two hours   _____ Three hours or more

3. How did you arrive at the shopping center?

   _____ Car   _____ Walk
   _____ Bus   _____ Bicycle
   _____ Other _____

4. Please tell us which shopping center you shop regularly.

   _____ Southcenter   _____ Bellevue Square
   _____ Northgate Mall   _____ Alderwood Mall

5. At which shopping center do you shop most frequently?
   _____

6. What do you like best about that shopping center?
   _____

7. Why don't you visit Northway Mall more often?
   _____

E X H I B I T   5.5 (*concluded*)

Demographic Information

1. The shopper is _____ Male; _____ Female

2. Home zip code _____

3. Occupation _____

4. Your age
   _____ Under 18   _____ 18 to 24   _____ 25 to 34   _____ 35 to 44
   _____ 45 to 54   _____ 55 to 64   _____ 65 & over

5. Are you married?   _____ Yes; _____ No

6. Total family income
   _____ Under $20,000   _____ $20,000 to $40,000   _____ $40,000 to $60,000
   _____ $60,000 to $100,000   _____ Over $100,000

7. Number of children under age 18 living in your household _____

8. Number of adults living in your household _____

9. Which of the following categories best describes the number of years of education you have completed?

   _____ Up to 11 years   _____ 4-year college graduate
   _____ High school graduate   _____ Graduate school
   _____ 1–3 years of college   _____ No response

---

3. *License plate survey.* Copying license plate numbers and asking the state department of motor vehicles to identify the town and street address where the owner of the vehicle lives was popular for many years. Today, however, many states will not give out this information. So, a license plate survey can only be useful in determining what percentage of shoppers are from another state. Shopping centers located in states that border on Canada may use this method to determine the number of Canadian shoppers. A more appropriate methodology is to track vehicle stickers. Most municipalities tax vehicle owners, and the windshield stickers (decals) they issue feature the town's name prominently.

4. *Focus groups.* These consist of six to eight randomly selected individuals who are recruited by telephone to meet in the office of the research company. Usually they are compensated for their time with cash or merchandise. The results are subjective rather than objective and not statistically significant, but the forum-like environment fosters conversation and can provide interesting information and opinions.

5. *Direct observation.* This has become a popular survey technique. It involves primarily counting exercises, from which patterns of shopper

behavior in a particular center can be determined. Specific observations include

—people leaving the shopping center with bags,

—traffic counts, and

—when people shop at the mall (time of day).

Direct observation will yield some interesting specifics and answer questions of who, when, and how many. Estimated percentages of shoppers leaving with bags indicate customers (buyers) as compared to shoppers (lookers). Traffic counts taken in different areas of the shopping center, at different times of the day (including and especially evenings), and on different days of the week (especially Sundays) indicate peak shopping times and areas. Observation of specific groups at specific times pinpoints customer habits. Senior citizens may shop late mornings and early afternoons, homemakers during the afternoon, teens in the late afternoon, and working people in the early evening. This information can be used to help plan specific events.

Prospective tenants may conduct their own observation surveys to determine which areas of the shopping center have the highest traffic or where particular groups of shoppers spend more of their time. Observation techniques are relatively inexpensive compared to other forms of surveys.

Operating the Physical Plant

The responsibilities of the property manager have evolved from simply responding to problems to include the establishment and implementation of programs that will enhance the value of the property, fulfill the landlord's lease obligations, and respond to community needs and environmental mandates. An effective maintenance management program assures a high-quality shopping environment while preserving and upgrading the condition of the property and enhancing its value. Energy conservation and recycling programs are not only sound economic measures, but also socially responsible actions. Appropriate security and an emergency procedures plan will address shoppers'—and tenants'—concerns about safety. While improvements to their leased spaces are typically the tenants' responsibilities, the landlord must establish the guidelines for such construction to assure that the integrity of the building is maintained. Each of these programs will have a different impact on the tenant, the community, and the value of the shopping center.

MAINTENANCE

There are several reasons to have an effective maintenance program. The economic life of a building is a consequence of its physical condition. Value diminishes when a property is neglected and maintenance is deferred. Good maintenance will extend a building's physical life. The landlord has a responsibility to the tenants and the community to provide a well-maintained facility.

Pride of ownership is another reason to have a maintenance management program, but the most important reason is to assure the safety of both shoppers and tenants.

General Maintenance Management

A maintenance management program will include custodial, corrective, and preventive maintenance. *Custodial maintenance* is the ongoing cleaning and upkeep of a property that includes janitorial activities as well as mowing the lawn and sweeping the parking lot. *Corrective maintenance* is the ordinary repairs that must be made to a building and its equipment on an ongoing basis. *Preventive maintenance* is a program of regular inspection and care that prevents potential problems or at least detects them early and permits their being solved before major repairs are required. It includes routine servicing of major equipment (e.g., HVAC) to assure its smooth, continued operation and control the cost and frequency of repairs.

Inspections.   The first step in implementing a maintenance management program is an inspection of the shopping center. This initial inspection is necessary to determine what types of maintenance tasks have to be performed on the property, how frequently each task should be performed, and whether the work should be done by the center's maintenance personnel or contracted to professionals. The roof, landscaping, parking lot, and vacant spaces should be inspected thoroughly, not only to assess the need for specific maintenance, but also to identify requirements for capital improvements. Inspection is vital to the development of both operating and capital budgets.

The property manager is responsible for conducting all inspections. Periodic inspections enable the property manager to be totally familiar with the general physical state of the shopping center. However, it is advantageous for other management and maintenance personnel to inspect the property periodically because each person will see the shopping center differently. The maintenance schedule may require the property manager to conduct every other inspection and assign the in-between inspections to various maintenance, management, and administrative personnel.

How often a property is inspected depends on its age and condition. An older property or one that is in disrepair will have to be inspected more frequently than one in good condition. The volume of customer traffic is another consideration. Heavier traffic will necessitate more frequent inspection. Other variables include the relative locations of the property and the property manager's office and the time the manager has available to conduct such inspections.

As a rule, a shopping center—including the parking lot—should be thoroughly inspected at least once a month. High-traffic areas in a mall and areas where trash receptacles are located should be inspected more frequently. Daily or even hourly inspections of restrooms, center court amenities, and food courts may be necessary, especially during busy periods (e.g., the holidays), and these inspections may be conducted by janitorial employees. On the other hand, leased spaces are seldom inspected. They are the responsibility of the tenants—i.e., the store owners or managers. However, unoccupied store spaces should be inspected each time a property inspection is conducted. Roofs should be inspected no less than twice a year. (Roof and parking lot maintenance are discussed later in this chapter.)

To assure a thorough inspection, an appropriate form should be used. Usually there are separate forms for the interior and exterior common areas of a shopping center. (Examples are included in appendix C, Maintenance Forms.) Use of the same form each time a property is inspected provides a historical record of maintenance and repairs. That record can become important documentation if someone is injured on the property—i.e., in a slip-and-fall suit, inspection forms may provide the evidence that the shopping center is well-maintained.

The person conducting the inspection should be required to note the status of each item listed on the form. This will assure that every item is properly inspected. Inspection forms completed by administrative and maintenance personnel should be given to the property manager who will review them, take necessary and appropriate actions, and file them as a record. Copies may be provided to the property owner in the monthly management report.

Maintenance Personnel. In developing a maintenance management program, one of the property manager's earliest decisions is whether to contract for maintenance services or establish an in-house maintenance staff. Neither approach is particularly better than the other, so the advantages and disadvantages of each should be weighed to determine the most efficient and cost-effective approach for a particular shopping center.

Two variables that will affect the decision are the size of the shopping center and its location. A strip center with less than 300,000 square feet of GLA usually cannot support a full-time maintenance person. Because the tenants are responsible for maintaining their premises, the maintenance person would only be responsible for the common areas—in this case, primarily the parking area—and the roofs. Unless the center has unusual maintenance or security requirements, there would not be enough work to occupy someone on the site full time. Policing the grounds, minor repairs, and landscape maintenance for neighborhood and community strip centers often can be done by one person working part time. A community center with an enclosed mall may need one or more people working full time to maintain the mall and the parking lot. As an alternative, a management firm responsible for numerous properties may employ one maintenance person or a maintenance crew to travel between and maintain several shopping centers. If the distance between the centers is too great, however, the maintenance personnel may spend more time traveling between locations than performing maintenance.

Contract Labor. The advantages of contract maintenance are many. First, the price is known and agreed on before the work commences; the fee for a particular job is the same regardless of how long it takes. Often a contractor's technical knowledge exceeds that of any in-house person. Contractor's usually have the ability to meet short-term needs for specialized labor. Supervision of the contractor's maintenance staff is provided by the contractor, and the property manager communicates primarily with that supervisor. The property manager is relieved of responsibility for interviewing, hiring, training, and—when necessary—terminating maintenance personnel as well as employee administration and replacement of workers when they are ill or on vacation. The shopping center does not have the expense of purchasing and maintaining equipment, and the contractor's insurance will cover damage caused by its personnel.

In-House Staff. There are also advantages to having an in-house maintenance staff, the first of which is direct control over scheduling and quality of the work. The cost to perform the task may be less because the contractor's profit is saved, but there may be concern as to how long the job will take. Employees are more loyal to their direct employer—in this case, the shopping center. Additional personnel are available to handle emergencies, and their schedules can be adjusted to respond to maintenance problems more quickly. However, specific skills may have to be contracted anyway because it is not practical for a shopping center to have an in-house staff with expertise in every area of maintenance.

Using Both Contract and In-House Personnel. The property manager's analysis of the maintenance needs of the shopping center will determine in large measure whether in-house staff or contract maintenance is the most effective way to maintain a particular center. For large shopping centers, a hybrid approach is frequently taken, with technical maintenance contracted and in-house personnel handling minor repairs and maintenance tasks that require general labor. Smaller shopping centers typically contract all maintenance or contract the technical maintenance and hire a part-time employee to police the grounds. Enclosed malls generally have the most complex systems and equipment to be maintained. For these properties, maintenance and repairs that require specific expertise are contracted (e.g., HVAC, elevators, escalators), while tasks that can be performed by unskilled labor are assigned to in-house staff.

Janitorial Specifications.   No commercial income property type has as much daily traffic as a shopping mall. Malls are open to the public between 70 and 75 hours a week; during the Christmas season, they may be open 80 or more hours a week. A mall must be kept clean regardless of the amount of traffic or the weather. In addition to cleanup, rain poses a hazard because it makes the floors slippery. In winter, long periods of accumulated snowfall mean that melted snow, sand, and salt will be tracked in and deposited on the mall flooring. Ongoing cleanup is necessary, not only for its own sake, but also to minimize the potential hazard of a slippery floor surface and prevent possible damage to the flooring material.

Shopping centers are unique in that they are cleaned while they are in use. The number of janitorial or housekeeping personnel needed for a particular center will vary with the selling season and the volume of promotional activity. To facilitate housekeeping, the design of the mall should include janitorial closets and storage areas located strategically throughout the building. Hot and cold running water and drains are required for scrubbing machines, so storage areas should include appropriate plumbing.

Janitorial work is scheduled in two phases—general cleaning and policing the grounds while the mall is open and heavy cleaning and floor care when the mall is closed. There are three approaches to handling janitorial tasks.

1. Contract all such work
2. Establish an in-house program
3. Contract the after-hours heavy cleaning only and have an in-house crew with direct control over the cleaning while the mall is open.

The combination approach precludes the purchase of heavy equipment and supervision of late night work crews. Daytime janitors at a mall are assigned duties that include dusting prominent surfaces, polishing the floor, cleaning the restrooms, keeping the glass in directories and doors clean, and policing the mall and the parking lot—including the landscaped areas.

However janitorial service is provided, the key components to an effective program are (1) supervision and (2) comprehensive janitorial specifications. (Specifications for the after-hours cleaning of an open or enclosed mall are included in appendix C, Maintenance Forms.) Strip shopping centers do not have the amenities, restrooms, and common areas found in enclosed malls, and their requirements for janitorial work per se may be limited to policing the parking lot and washing the outsides of windows. However, tenants may contract with an independent window-washing service, especially if they want their windows cleaned on a specific schedule.

The property manager must communicate regularly with and supervise the janitorial foreman, who must then closely supervise the janitorial staff—each of whom must have a job description listing all of their duties. The janitorial specifications are provided to the supervisor of the in-house janitorial staff or attached to the janitorial contract as an addendum.

Food Court Operations.   Food courts are popular components of malls, often becoming major gathering places. The typical food court has 9–12 small food vendors and common seating for approximately 400 people— roughly 35–40 seats per vendor. (Food courts and their tenants are also discussed in chapter 2, Development and Rehabilitation, and chapter 9, Leasing.) Ideally, restrooms and a janitorial closet with hot and cold running water and floor drains will be adjacent to it. A sufficient number of trash receptacles is essential. Natural lighting, interior landscaping, and attractive signage create a special ambience.

The combination of food service with high traffic requires special attention from the property manager. No other area of a mall will have such fluctuations in traffic volume during the day. There is generally a primary traffic peak at noon, and a second peak period for the evening meal. The number of janitorial staff working in the food court will change throughout the day; some individuals will be reassigned to other areas of the mall during slow traffic periods. Although the concept of a food court is one of self-service, and customers are expected to dispose of their food and paper waste in the receptacles provided, substantial policing of the area is still required. The main janitorial responsibilities are wiping tables and chairs, cleaning (possibly mopping) the floor, emptying trash receptacles, and keeping the adjacent restrooms clean. If the food court area is not cleaned properly, grease deposits will accumulate on surfaces. Together with a dirty floor, they make an eating area uninviting. Care should be exercised in selecting the cleaning agents; they must be authorized for use around food. Cleaning is especially important because food wastes are breeding grounds for insects.

Waste disposal is another potential problem. Receptacles for wet trash (including food waste) should be stored in close proximity to the food court. If the trays used in the food court have to be cleaned for reuse, facilities and equipment to wash the trays must also be close to the food court. The alternative is vendor-provided, disposable trays, which are expensive and will add to the volume of waste being disposed.

Often a separate budget is established for maintenance of the food court, and food court CAM costs are passed through to the vendors. Some malls also have a separate marketing fund to promote the food court and its tenants. Because a food court is an amenity and a traffic draw, and has the potential to generate high revenue, it should be managed with attention and care—as though it were a fine restaurant.

Graffiti.   A common problem that demands immediate attention is the presence of graffiti. Although graffiti may be the result of enthusiasm for a local event (a winning team, a graduating class), they are often intentional acts of vandalism and may signal the presence of gang activity. Gangs commonly identify their territories with particular symbols and words, and police can usually identify which gang is active in an area from the graffiti. Buildings covered with graffiti messages are not inviting places to visit. Shopping centers, with their large numbers of daily visitors and long and massive walls, are prime targets for graffiti "artists." Any such markings must be removed as soon after their discovery as possible. If not removed, they may inspire additional graffiti. Also, when graffiti are not removed, the public may rightly assume that the property owner does not care about the exterior of the building and that the interior is equally uninviting.

Shopping center personnel should be on the lookout for graffiti every time the property is inspected. Even if graffiti are not present, it is a good idea to develop an action plan to combat this potential problem. The first phase is preventive action which may include applying an anti-graffiti coating to surfaces that are easy targets. Beware, however, that the coating material can penetrate the surface of the wall and may darken it, an effect that may be undesirable aesthetically.

Other preventive approaches may be more desirable. Good lighting may be all that is necessary to discourage random acts of vandalism, including the application of graffiti. Adjusting the schedules of maintenance and security personnel to place them in specific areas at particular times of the day may also serve as a deterrent. A major preventive, of course, is denying the "artist" a showcase by removing or painting over graffiti as soon as they are found. That is the second phase of the action plan.

Graffiti "artists" use a wide array of media that include spray paint, felt tip markers, lipstick, nail polish, and shoe polish, none of which are water soluble. The appropriateness of a particular removal procedure is dependent on the finished surface of the building—i.e., whether it is porous or nonporous, rough or smooth, layered or nonlayered. The type of surface will also determine the materials that can be used to remove the graffiti. In deciding how to proceed, it is best to choose the safest, most gentle process that will yield the best results.

There are two basic approaches—use of *chemicals* such as acids and alkalis (both water-based) or solvents (oil-based, organic) and *mechanical treatments* such as water blasting, sandblasting, and steam. Because each of these methods can damage a building, an experienced chemical or equipment contractor or supplier should be consulted before any attempt is made to remove graffiti.

Tenants' and Landlord's Separate Responsibilities. The maintenance responsibilities of the landlord and the tenant are spelled out in the lease. Typically, the tenant is responsible for maintaining the area inside the demised premises, the storefront (including the windows), and the entrance and rear doors. The landlord is responsible for maintenance of the common areas, the roof, and the HVAC unit. Roof maintenance is typically a CAM charge, and maintenance of the HVAC unit is billed directly to the tenant. Some managers and assistant managers of retail operations may not have seen the leases for their stores and therefore will not know all of the tenants' responsibilities. On-site maintenance personnel for the shopping center should be instructed *not* to perform maintenance in the tenants' premises except in an emergency or special situation. Because store personnel may not know whom to call for specific maintenance work, the property manager should provide each merchant with a list of acceptable maintenance contractors and vendors. Usually this is included in the tenant kit (see chapter 5).

Access to Occupied Spaces. Once a store space is occupied, responsibility for everything inside the store is transferred to the tenant. Unlike the arrangements in office buildings, *the property manager should not keep keys to occupied store spaces.* When a space is leased, all the keys should be turned over to the tenant; the lock should be taken off the master key, and the tenant should be encouraged to re-key the doors. When keys are retained by management, there is greater liability. If a tenant's store is broken into and merchandise is stolen, the property manager and shopping center staff could become suspects. If an after-hours emergency requires entering a tenant's locked space, the door can be forced open, or if necessary, the glass in the door can be broken to provide immediate access. This particular situation will likely occur only once or twice in a property manager's career.

Maintaining Vacant Spaces. Vacant spaces must be ready to show at all times. This means electrical power (for lighting) must be continued at the landlord's expense and the spaces must be inspected and cleaned periodically.

The inspection form should include a section to record inspections of vacancies (see example in appendix C, Maintenance Forms). These areas are easily forgotten otherwise. It is most embarrassing and frustrating for a property manager or a leasing agent to take a prospective tenant to a vacant space and find that it is dirty or being used as a storage area. A showing should not have to begin with an apology for the condition of the space that is being offered.

Vacancies should be inspected no less often than once a month, and maintenance personnel should be reminded about the need to have vacancies ready to show at all times. A vacancy may be used as a lunch area and trash left scattered on the floor. Workers may not have removed all the debris after maintenance has been performed in a vacant space. When a store is vacated, the prior tenant's fixtures should be removed and the space returned to broom-clean condition. The windows should be washed on the inside at least once every six months and on the outside every two to three months. Two areas in vacancies are frequently overlooked—restrooms must be cleaned, and water-stained or missing ceiling tiles must be replaced. Anything stored in a vacant space should be stacked neatly in the rear. Windows should not be covered with paper unless something inside the premises should not be in public view. If the vacancy does not have a storefront, a plywood wall can be built to keep people out and eliminate the unsightly appearance. The plywood can be painted or covered with wallpaper-like material showing graphic designs or the name of the shopping center.

Specific Maintenance Requirements

Although a shopping center is a large and complex property, there are usually only three major items that themselves require regular, detailed inspections and ongoing preventive maintenance—the heating, ventilating, and air-conditioning (HVAC) system, the roof of the building, and the parking lot.

The HVAC System.   Customers will spend little time shopping in a store or mall that is too hot or too cold. The HVAC system is intended to provide a comfortable environment in which to shop. The adequacy of heat and air conditioning will depend on the type and size of the HVAC system. In particular, the system should be appropriate to the climate of the region and the size of the property. Correct equipment, a good preventive maintenance program, and proper use of the system components and controls will assure year-round comfort for all.

Strip Center HVAC.   The HVAC systems for strip shopping centers almost always consist of rooftop package air conditioners with heat pumps. A package unit for a typical shopping center space may use either electricity or natural gas to provide heat, and it will have a cooling capacity of 2–5 tons. Tenants whose cooling loads are significantly larger than normal often have supplementary air-conditioning units. Restaurants, in particular, will require additional air-conditioning equipment, and they almost always have specialized exhaust hoods and recirculating fans in the kitchens.

Enclosed Mall HVAC.   There are two basic approaches to meeting the HVAC needs of an enclosed mall—multiple rooftop package units or a large-capacity central system.

When multiple package units are used in multilevel enclosed malls, the units that serve the tenants on the top floor are the same type as those used in strip centers. Split-system air conditioners consisting of ceiling-mounted air-handling units connected by refrigeration piping to roof-mounted, air-cooled condensers are used to serve the tenants on the lower levels, and the common areas are air conditioned using larger capacity rooftop package units (typically 20–50 tons).

A central system for an enclosed mall may utilize cooled air or chilled water as the air-conditioning source. *Cooled-air systems* consist of medium-capacity (60–100 tons) variable-air-volume (VAV) air-conditioning units capable of cooling 24,000–40,000 square feet of tenant space. Each zone is supplied by a VAV distributor controlled by a thermostat, and each tenant's space will most likely comprise two or more zones for heating and air conditioning. These systems use an electric heater and a fan mounted on the VAV boxes to heat the exterior zones.

Chilled-water systems have traditionally been supplied by large-capacity centrifugal compressors that vary in size (capacity) from 300 tons to more than 1,000 tons. Usually there are two or three such chillers to assure partial cooling in case one unit fails. Chilled-water installations also require circulating pumps and a cooling tower to dissipate the heat removed from the water. Each zone is then cooled via an air-handling unit (blower) coupled with a chilled-water coil. Electricity is used to provide heat in the exterior zones.

Another system commonly used in enclosed malls is a hybrid of these two (chilled water and cooled air). A central cooling tower is used to eject the heat generated in all the tenants' spaces. The tower is connected to individual tenant spaces via a cooling-water condenser loop. Water-cooled air conditioners are installed in each tenant space, and electricity is used to supply heat to the exterior zones. The common areas, on the other hand, are cooled by constant-volume rooftop package air-conditioning units with capacities in the 20–50-ton range.

HVAC Maintenance.   The maintenance of the HVAC equipment at strip centers has evolved from one where the tenant bore both responsibility and cost to one in which the landlord retains the responsibility but the tenant pays the cost. Maintenance of the central heating and air-conditioning systems in enclosed malls is the responsibility of the landlord, with the cost prorated and billed to the tenants as a CAM expense.

Through the 1950s, 1960s, and 1970s, the landlord's requirement that tenants in strip centers maintain their own HVAC units resulted in different levels of maintenance. The units broke down more frequently and were more costly to repair because of the lack of proper maintenance. In the late 1970s and early 1980s, landlords modified the lease provision covering HVAC maintenance so that the tenant remained responsible for the cost to service and repair the HVAC unit but the landlord assumed responsibility for having the work done. This allowed the landlord complete control over the standard of preventive maintenance for shop tenants' HVAC equipment. Regardless of the arrangements for the shop tenants, major tenants are typically responsible for maintaining all the HVAC equipment in their stores.

Contracts for HVAC Maintenance.   The volume of service required at one site should enable the property manager to negotiate a very competitive service contract. When only one service contractor is used, traffic on the roof is reduced and so is the potential for damage to it. More importantly, when a tenant vacates, the landlord knows that the HVAC unit has been properly maintained and is in good working condition.

When the property manager is seeking bids on HVAC service and repairs, each contractor should be required to bid on the same specifications. The type and number of filter changes and the number of times the units are serviced should be standardized. The specifications should be developed from the manufacturers' recommendations for the specific equipment. (If copies of service manuals are not in the property files, the manager should obtain them.) The type and frequency of service will vary with the type of equipment and the geographic area. If each contractor provides a bid based on its own specifications, the maintenance tasks to be performed under the service contract will not be comparable. (Exhibit 6.1 shows both sides of a two-page preventive maintenance work order form for a package HVAC unit.) When bidding HVAC service contracts, the following points should also be considered.

- The contractor's experience with the type of equipment
- Contractor training of service personnel on an ongoing basis
- The contractor's availability and charges for after-hours service
- Any limitations on the amount of time to be spent servicing each unit
- What parts are routinely carried in service trucks
- Extra charges for filters
- The types of insurance coverage carried by the contractor

A good preventive maintenance program will extend the life of the HVAC equipment, reduce the frequency and cost of repairs, and provide a comfortable, climate-controlled environment for both shoppers and tenants.

The Roof.   The roof of a neighborhood shopping center may cover a total area of 2–4 acres; that on a super regional mall may extend over 15–25 acres of both tenant space and common areas. A roof that is not well-maintained will eventually become deteriorated and damage the building, resulting in extensive, costly repairs and premature failure of the roofing system.

The basic components of a roofing system are a roof deck, a vapor-retarding barrier, insulation, and a surface membrane. The majority of commercial (low-slope) roof systems have built-up roofing (BUR) membranes—two or more alternate plies of saturated or coated felts or similar materials layered in place and cemented together with asphalt or pitch to make the system waterproof. A typical BUR membrane comprises between three and five felt plies, with three plies generally considered minimum for a BUR membrane (finished thickness less than one-half inch). The felts reinforce the roofing system, protect the bitumen from water degradation, and add fire-retardant properties to the membrane. Single-ply roofing (SPR) systems that consist of only one layer of a water-tight, weatherable membrane are also used. However, this type of roofing is more vulnerable to piercing than are BUR membrane systems.

EXHIBIT 6.1

Example Work Order Form

PREVENTIVE MAINTENANCE	WORK ORDER	NO:		OUT
ADDRESS:				
CITY:	STATE:		ZIP:	
AUTHORIZED PERSONNEL:				
SERVICEMAN #1:		#2:		
CONSTRUCTION JOB NO:		SALESMAN:		
START UP DATE:		WARRANTY DATE:		
SPECIAL INSTRUCTIONS:				

1. ANNUAL
2. SEMI-ANNUAL
4. QUARTERLY
6. SEMI-MONTHLY
12. MONTHLY
26. BI-WEEKLY
52. WEEKLY
F. FILTERS

NOTE: DO ENCIRCLED OPERATION NUMBERS ONLY:

S – SCHEDULED FREQ.   ✔ – WORK COMPLETED-OK   X – WORK COMPLETED-SEE NOTES

#	S	SCHED. "A" REFRIG. & COOLING SYSTEMS ✔/X	#	S	SCHED. "C" COOLING TOWERS & CONDENSER ✔/X
1		Check drive and belts & adjust	1		Lubricate bearings
2		Check head and suction pressures	2		Check drive and belts & adjust
3		Check oil levels and pressures	3		Check spray nozzles and clean
4		Add oil if required	4		Clean basin and sump
5		Check compressor controls & adjust	5		Add chemicals & check auto feed
6		Tighten head bolts	6		Check float control and adjust
7		Check rotation	7		Clean line strainers
8		Check water valve and adjust	8		Set constant bleed
9		Check unloader operation	9		Check oil in gear box
10		Check sight glass	10		Check coils for scale
11		Check refrigerant controls & adjust	11		Clean air intake screen
12		Lubricant bearings	12		Check water meter
13		Check for refrigerant leaks	13		Check operational cycle
14		Check operational cycle	14		Check fan for alignment & operation
15		Clean drip pan and drain	15		Check sump heater operation
16		Clean chilled water strainers	16		Check electrical connections
17		Check for vibration and noise	17		
18		Check filter-dryer	18		
19		Check txv's superheate & adjust	19		
20		Check amperage draw	20		
21		Check electrical connections	21		
22			22		
23			23		
24			24		

#	S	SCHED. "B" PUMPS ✔/X	#	S	SCHED. "D" FILTERS ✔/X
1		Lubricate bearings	1		Change disposable filters
2		Clean line strainers	2		Clean washable filters
3		Check pressure gauges	3		Check electronic air cleaners
4		Inspect packing glands	4		Check air filtration efficiency
5		Check mechanical seal	5		Check manometer operation
6		Check amperage draw	6		
7		Check electrical connections	7		
8			8		
9			9		

FILTERS REQUIRED

QTY	SIZE	TYPE	LOCATION/UNIT	QTY	SIZE

	F	52	26	12	6	4	2	1	WEEK G	WEEK B
									1	27
									2	28
									3	29
									4	30
									5	31
									6	32
									7	33
									8	34
									9	35
									10	36
									11	37
									12	38
									13	39
									14	40
									15	41
									16	42
									17	43
									18	44
									19	45
									20	46
									21	47
									22	48
									23	49
									24	50
									25	51
									26	52

TYPE   LOCATION/UNIT

This form covers scheduled maintenance of HVAC equipment and accessories. Each client receives a master form on which the vendor has indicated the scheduled frequency of particular maintenance items (see frequency list at top right; e.g., 12 in the S column means do monthly; an asterisk with a number denotes "or as needed"). The form is copied and specific items are circled each time work is to be done.

Reprinted with permission from MacDonald-Miller Company, Seattle, Washington.

E X H I B I T　6.1 (*continued*)

SCHED. "E" — HEAT PUMPS

#	S	Item	✓/x
1		Check defrost control & cycle	
2		Check & lube condenser fan motors	
3		Check refrigerant charge	
4		Check operational cycle	
5		Check electrical connections	
6		Check 4-way valve operation	
7		Check resistance heating coils	
8			
9			
10			
11			
12			

SCHED. "F" — A.H.U. & EXH. UNITS

#	S	Item	✓/x
1		Lubricate bearings	
2		Check drive belts & adjust	
3		Clean air intake screens	
4		Check air volume	
5		Check air temperature	
6			
7			
8			
9			
10			
11			
12			

SCHED. "G" — ELECTRICAL

#	S	Item	✓/x
1		Check electrical connections	
2		Check voltage and amperage draw	
3		Check fuses, change as necessary	
4		Check starters, breakers and resets	
5		Spot test switches and receptacles	
6			
7			
8			
9			
10			
11			
12			
13			
14			
15			

SCHED. "H" — BOILERS

#	S	Item	✓/x
1		Clean traps, strainers & valves	
2		Check boiler controls & water level	
3		Check electrical connections	
4		Check boiler water level	
5		Clean and inspect burner	
6		Lubricate bearings	
7		Check operational cycle	
8		Check drive and belts & adjust	
9		Adjust electrodes	
10		Clean & lube comb. air fan	
11		Check heat exchanger	
12		Check flue pipes	
13		Change oil filter	
14		Check oil pump pressures	
15		Check for oil leaks	
16		Add chemicals as required	
17		Check for fire hazards	
18			

SCHED. "I" — FURNACES

#	S	Item	✓/x
1		Lubricate bearings	
2		Check for gas or oil leaks	
3		Check electric coils	
4		Check pilot and burner operation	
5		Check safety shut-off controls	
6		Check drive and belts & adjust	
7		Check operational cycle	
8		Check heat exchanger	
9		Check flue pipes	
10		Check operation of Thermocouple	
11		Check for fire hazards	
12		Check electrical connections	
13			
14			
15			
16			
17			
18			

SCHED. "J" — CONTROLS

#	S	Item	✓/x
1		Check air comp., drain moisture & change oil	
2		Check damper motors, & adjust	
3		Check thermostats, clean and calibrate	
4		Check minimum O. A. damper settings	
5		Inspect relays	
6		Check voltages @full load	
7		Check electrical connections	
8		Check all safety controls	
9		Inspect contactor points	
10		Check lock-out controls	
11		Check, capacitors	
12		Check economizer controls	
13		Check operation of time clocks	
14			
15			
16			
17			

SCHED. "K" — PLUMBING

#	S	Item	✓/x
1		Check valves and faucets	
2		Check for leaks	
3		Check flush tanks	
4		Check flushometer	
5		Clean traps and drains	
6		Clean roof drain strainers	
7		Check traps and pipes for freezing	
8		Check safety devices	
9		Check sump pumps	
10		Check sewage disposal pumps	
11		Check sprinkler control system	
12		Check hot water system	
13			
14			
15			
16			
17			
18			

SCHED. "L" — PERIODIC MAINT.

#	S	Item	✓/x
1		Clean condenser tubes	
2		Drain chiller	
3		Drain, clean tower & condenser	
4		Clean chiller tubes	
5		Clean heating and cooling coils	
6		Pump down refrigerant system	
7		Clean boiler, drain, flush & refill	
8		Clean heat exchangers	
9		Change oil and oil filters	
10		Change refrigerant driers	
11		Test oil sample	
12		Test water sample	
13		Inspect & service purge unit	
14		Check bearing wear	
15		Check all electric motors	
16		Clean and paint equipment	
17		Clean & paint mech. rooms	
18			

SCHED. "M" — MISC.

#	S	Item	✓/x
1			
2			
3			
4			
5			
6			
7			
8			
9			
10			
11			
12			
13			
14			
15			
16			
17			

A roof is a major investment for a property owner. The most important reason for regular roof maintenance is to protect that investment. A good maintenance program will not only add years to the life of the roof, but also detect minor problems before damage is widespread and avoid interruption of internal operations of the building. To facilitate development and execution of a roof maintenance program, the property manager should have as-built drawings of the roof deck, flashings, and roof system, plus a roof plan showing construction details (all vents and rooftop installations, updated to show new additions). A history of the roof should be kept on file, including its age, the dates and descriptions of any resurfacing, and copies of inspection reports. (A representative historical record is provided in exhibit 6.2.)

An effective roof maintenance program will consist of inspections and corrective action (removal of debris, minor repairs, consultation with a roofing contractor as appropriate). Inspections should be conducted no less than twice a year—preferably in the late spring or early autumn—and after any severe weather (e.g., torrential rains, high winds) or other natural occurrences (e.g., earth tremors). The inspection and maintenance schedule for the roof should incorporate other related elements as well. Skylights require frequent inspection and maintenance, and drains and gutters require regular cleaning.

Items to inspect include the parapet walls, counter flashing, metal work, coping, roof penetrations, equipment supports, curbs, drains, gutters, and downspouts. During the inspection, the roof material should be observed for the following conditions: water ponding, bubbles and blisters, splits, dry felts, wrinkles, exposed laps and fish mouths, oxidation, and alligatoring. Each of these defects requires immediate action. (A semiannual roof maintenance inspection checklist is shown in exhibit 6.3.)

There are four possible courses of action when a roof requires repairs.

1. *Patching* with material that is compatible with the existing roof materials.
2. *Recoating* of the roof surface when the felts are in good condition.
3. *Recovering* by applying another roof system over the existing one.
4. *Replacement* of the old roof system with a completely new one.

In general, traffic on the roof should be kept to a minimum, and a professional roofing contractor should be consulted when there are major problems. Because every penetration threatens the integrity of the roof membrane, it may be desirable or necessary to install a special walkway. This is particularly true for SPR membrane roofs. If a tenant wants to install equipment on the roof, permission to do so should require the work to be performed to strict specifications, and the property manager or assigned maintenance personnel should be present during the installation. The installation should be inspected as soon after completion as possible.

E X H I B I T   6.2

Example Historical Record Form

Historical Record

1. Building & Location

	Firm	Contact	Telephone
Architect			
General Contractor			
Roofing Contractor			
Roof Consultant			
Test Laboratory			
Roofing Mat'ls. Manufacturer			
Deck Contractor			
Decking Mat'ls. Manufacturer			
Others			

2. Materials and Specifications (As-Built)

Roof Deck (Type, thickness or gauge, coating or treatments, method of attachment, side lap fastening, lap requirements, span, etc.)

Roof Drainage (Designed slope, slope of valleys, use of crickets, scuppers, drains set in sumps, etc.)

Vapor Retarders (When used, identify trade names, mil thickness, how sealed at ends and side laps, penetrations, describe quantity of adhesive and method of application. Describe edge seals if used.)

Thermal Insulation (List all trade names, thickness and type of each layer, define published 'R' values, method of attachment to substrate and layer to layer. Identify code numbers, U.L. or F. M. labels, method of breaking joints, etc.)

Roof Membrane (List all trade names, retain samples 8½ × 11 of each type sheet material. If Bituminous, list all bitumens used by ASTM designation and quantities specified for interply and surfacing. If elastoplastic, describe all adhesives or solvents used, method of attachment i.e. loose-laid, partial, etc. Describe lapping, exposure, other details of importance.)

Roof Surfacing — List materials (i.e. ⅜" Dia Gravel in 60 lb. flood coat nominal 400 lbs/100 ft² of Type I asphalt; 1½" Dia Rounded Gravel at 1200 lbs/100 ft²). Note walkway materials, if any and method of attachment.

Flashings (Describe base flashing materials such as cant strips, types of films or felts used, priming of walls, trade names and description or thickness, specified fasteners and frequency, surfacing, list flashing spec numbers and manufacturer's details.)

Sheet Metal (Describe types used, detail no.'s, fascia details, lapping, stripping, securement, etc. as applicable.)

3. Date of Completion of Initial Roof Application _____ _____

Roof Guarantees by _____ Expiration Date _____

4. Building Usage (include interior temperature, relative humidity, chemical processing, vibration, etc.)

5. Previous Maintenance, Surfacing or Repairs (Briefly summarize and attach previous reports.)

This form is used to record information about roof installation and care.

Reproduced with permission from *Roof Maintenance* (Englewood, Colo.: The Roofing Industry Educational Institute, 1988).

E X H I B I T   6.3

Example Semiannual Maintenance Inspection Checklist

Building _____   Date _____   Date of previous inspection _____

Location _____   Inspected by: _____

I. Supporting Structure	OK	Problem Minor	Major	Observation	Date of Repair
Exterior and Interior Walls					
Expansion/Contraction					
Settlement Cracks					
Deterioration/Spalling					
Moisture Stains/Efflorescence					
Physical Damage					
Other					
Exterior and Interior Roof Deck					
Securement to Supports					
Expansion/Contraction					
Structural Deterioration					
Water Stains/Rusting					
Physical Damage					
Attachment of Felts/Insulation					
New Equipment/Alterations					
Other					
II. Roof Condition					
A. General Appearance					
Debris					
Drainage					
Physical Damage					
General Condition					
New Equipment/Alterations					
Other					
B. Surface Condition					
Bare Spots in Gravel/Ballast Displaced					
Alligatoring/Cracking					
Slippage					
Other					
C. Membrane Condition					
Blistering					
Splitting					
Ridging/Wrinkling					
Fishmouthing					
Loose Felt Laps/Seams					
Punctures, Fastener Backout					
Securement to Substrate					
Membrane Shrinkage					
Membrane Slippage					
Other					
III. Flashing Condition					
A. Roof Perimeter Base Flashing					
Punctures or Tears					
Deterioration					
Blistering					
Open Laps					
Attachment					
Ridging or Wrinkling					
Other					

Reproduced with permission from *Roof Maintenance* (Englewood, Colo.: The Roofing Industry Educational Institute, 1988).

The Parking Lot.   At a small strip center, the parking area may be only a quarter of an acre, but the parking lot at a super regional mall can cover more than 50 acres. Regardless of the size of the center, the parking lot typically covers the largest area of the property.

Most shoppers' first contact with a shopping center occurs when they get

E X H I B I T　6.3 (*continued*)

III. Flashing Condition (cont'd.)	OK	Problem Minor	Problem Major	Observation	Date of Repair
B. Counter Flashing/Termination Bars					
Open Laps					
Punctures					
Attachment					
Rusting					
Fasteners					
Caulking					
Other					
C. Coping					
Open Fractures					
Punctures					
Attachment					
Rusting					
Drainage					
Fasteners					
Caulking					
Other					
D. Perimeter Walls					
Mortar Joints					
Spalling					
Movement Cracks					
Other					
IV. Roof Perimeter Edging/Fascia					
Splitting					
Securement					
Rusting					
Felt Deterioration					
Fasteners					
Punctures					
Other					
V. Roof Penetrations					
A. Equipment Base Flashing-Curbs					
Open Laps					
Punctures					
Attachment					
Other					
B. Equipment Housing					
Counter Flashing					
Open Seams					
Physical Damage					
Caulking					
Drainage					
Other					
C. Equipment Operation					
Discharge of Contaminants					
Excessive Traffic Wear					
Other					
D. Roof Jacks/Vents/Drains					
Attachment					
Physical Damage					
Vents Operable/Screens Cleaned					
Other					
VI. Expansion Joint Covers					
Open Joints					
Punctures/Splits					
·Securement					
Rusting					
Fasteners					
Other					
VII. Pitch Pockets					
Fill Material Shrinkage					
Attachment					
Other					

Reproduced with permission from *Roof Maintenance* (Englewood, Colo.: The Roofing Industry Educational Institute, 1988).

out of their cars in the parking lot. They are not likely to notice that it is well-maintained. However, when it has potholes, cracks, and chunks of broken asphalt, shoppers get a negative impression of the shopping center before they reach the stores. Shoppers will avoid such a poorly maintained parking lot and the center will lose customers.

When a shopping center first opens, the parking lot is attractive and safe, but its condition deteriorates over time as it is damaged by both weather and use. An appropriate maintenance program will extend the useful life of the parking lot and minimize the need for repairs.

General Maintenance. At the very least, a parking lot should be swept regularly, especially when landscaping debris (fallen leaves, seed pods, etc.) makes it look unkempt. Because it is the shopper's first impression of the shopping center, the maintenance schedule should include daily policing and removal of wastepaper and other litter from the parking lot.

The parking lot should be inspected regularly by simply walking the area from side to side and from one end to the other. Large parking lots can be divided into sections and each section inspected on a different day. A well-maintained parking lot will improve the aesthetics and safety of the shopping center and reduce maintenance and repair expenses.

Snow Removal. The best retail selling period during the year is the Christmas season. Most retailers will generate 15–35 percent of their annual sales between Thanksgiving and Christmas. In many areas of the United States, this holiday period is also the snow season. In the North, it may snow as early as October, with periodic snowfalls continuing through April.

The property manager must develop and implement a snow-removal program that allows for safe and convenient access to the shopping center and is cost effective. If snow removal is ineffective, the parking lot will be unsafe; traffic to the shopping center will be reduced, and sales will be lost. After the first substantial snowfall, the tenants will know just how effective the snow removal plan is.

The first step in developing a snow removal plan is deciding who will remove the snow. On-site personnel are usually responsible for keeping the sidewalks and mall entrances clear of snow and ice. To do this effectively, they will need the proper equipment—snow shovels, a snowblower, and possibly salt or other chemicals. If on-site staff have access to a pickup truck with a blade, they may be able to move light snow out of prime parking areas.

A contractor may be hired to augment the work of the on-site staff or to handle all the snow removal. Parking lot sweeping companies often provide snow removal service, and some highway and road construction contractors use their equipment for snow removal in winter. Before entering into a contract for snow removal, the contractor's references should be checked. The contractor should also be asked to provide a list of equipment the company has available, indicating whether it is owned, leased, or rented on an as-needed basis. (Rented equipment may not be available to the contractor during heavy snowfalls.) Once a contract is agreed to, the property manager should walk the parking lot with the contractor and the drivers of the equipment to point out features such as curbs, signs, and speed bumps that may be hidden by snow later on. During this inspection, the current condition of the parking lot should be noted so that when the snow season is over, the contractor will not be held responsible (or billed) for pre-existing damage.

It is not always necessary to remove snow from the parking lot completely. During months when sales are slow (e.g., January and February) snow may simply be moved to areas of the parking lot that are not being used. When snow removal is absolutely necessary, however, it may be possible to arrange with the owner of a nearby vacant lot to pile snow there. It is usually necessary to keep the entire lot clear during December.

Each time snow removal is required, the contractor must be told which areas are to be cleared of snow and where the snow is to be taken—to another area of the parking lot or off the property. Snow moved to the perimeter of the parking lot must not be piled too high because it can reduce the center's visibility from the street. Also, such an accumulation may not melt for months, and eventually it will become an unsightly mass of dirty snow and debris.

Throughout the snow season, sand and hot gravel may be laid down in the parking lot to improve vehicle traction and reduce slickness from ice buildup. Salt or other chemicals may be used on sidewalks to eliminate ice and minimize slippery areas. Care should be taken in using any of these methods, however. Chemicals may be tracked into the mall area or the stores, and the residue can damage the flooring or floor coverings. The residues are also harmful to grass and landscaping. When the snow season is over, the parking lot should be thoroughly cleaned. Often it will take several sweepings to remove all the sand and debris.

In northern states, snow removal is usually budgeted as a separate line item, and the expense is based on slightly more than a year's average snowfall. Weather information published in local newspapers and historical data available from the United States Weather Bureau will help increase the accuracy of the budget projections. In a year of heavy snowfall, the annual snow removal budget may be exceeded in a period of one or two months. The budget may also be exceeded when additional snow removal is necessary to provide for shoppers' convenience and safety and to maintain strong tenant sales.

Pavement Repairs.　The majority of parking lots are constructed of asphalt pavement. Because it is installed during the final phase of shopping center construction, the parking lot may become a victim of spending cutbacks. As the final phase approaches, the developer may determine that construction costs are over budget and attempt to make up for it by laying down too thin a pavement or skimping on the preparation of the underlayment. The result will be an inadequate parking lot.

Improper thickness of the asphalt pavement is one of the major causes of parking lot failures, but the primary cause of asphalt failure is water underneath it. Proper drainage is essential to a well-maintained asphalt parking lot. Excessive moisture underneath the pavement weakens the foundation layers and reduces the ability of the soil to absorb traffic-induced stress. Water enters through cracks and other breaks in the pavement. When the water freezes, it expands, eventually cracking the asphalt and breaking it apart. Once this occurs, the deterioration will continue until the area is properly repaired—or the pavement is replaced.

Asphalt pavement in need of repair or maintenance will usually exhibit one or more of the following characteristics.

- *Raveling* is the undoing of the texture of the pavement due to a progressive separation of aggregate particles. The most common cause of this is lack of proper compaction during construction, but it can also be caused by disintegrating aggregate or poor mix design.
- *Shrinkage cracks* are interconnected breaks in the pavement that form a series of large blocks, usually with sharp angles. They are caused by volume changes in the base or subgrade of the pavement, and sometimes they can be repaired by simply filling the cracks. If the problem is severe, the pavement must be replaced.
- *Alligator cracks* are also interconnected, but they form a series of small blocks that resemble alligator skin or chicken wire. The remedy is similar to that for shrinkage cracks.
- *Potholes* (or chuck holes) are common and easy to recognize. They are often the result of neglect of other types of pavement distress. The remedy is usually replacement of an area that extends beyond the borders of the "hole."
- *Upheaval* is the upward displacement of a pavement area due to swelling of either the subgrade or some portion of the pavement structure. In colder climates, upheaval is commonly caused by expansion of ice in the lower courses of the pavement or the subgrade, and replacement of the area may be the best and only remedy.
- *Grade depressions,* also known as birdbaths, are localized sunken areas of limited size that may or may not be accompanied by cracking. They are usually caused by settling of the lower pavement layers, poor construction methods, or heavier traffic than that for which the pavement was designed. The remedy is either to build up the asphalt paving to support the load levels or to replace it.

Seal coating is an important, cost-effective treatment in the preventive maintenance of asphalt parking lots. A seal coat is a thin layer of asphalt or coal tar sealant applied to the surface to waterproof it, stop oxidation and pavement deterioration, and improve the texture of the asphalt surface. Seal coating protects the pavement from the effects of water, traffic, fuel spills, chemicals, and weather. There are two types of sealers—emulsified asphalt (derived from crude oil) and coal tar—and one application usually can last 3–5 years.

OPERATIONS

The operation of a shopping center goes beyond maintenance of specific areas and equipment. The property manager's operational responsibilities include provision of security to protect the property and the people on it (tenants and shoppers), development of procedures for rapid (and appropriate) responses to emergency situations, disposal of trash and waste materials generated on the property, and conservation of energy by controlling its consumption at the site.

Security

Customers need to feel safe while they are shopping and when they are walking to and from their vehicles. The security needs of a particular shopping center will depend on its size, type, and location. Small strip centers seldom if ever have security personnel, while super regional malls have full-time security forces. When reviewing the security needs of a shopping center, the property manager should meet with the police to collect data on criminal incidents in the area and maintain a log of security-related incidents at the shopping center. The latter will indicate if any area of the shopping center is particularly vulnerable and whether a pattern of crime is developing.

Neighborhood and community strip centers usually do not need on-site security guards. Any incidents are more likely to occur between midafternoon (after school lets out) and late evening, and any necessary security can be provided by a patrol that drives through the shopping center periodically during that time. If on-site security is needed, a guard can be in attendance from midafternoon until the shopping center closes. Sometimes the guard may be needed for only a month or two to address a temporary situation. If security concerns warrant the presence of a full-time guard, a round-the-clock security program should be implemented.

Enclosed community malls usually do not need security 24 hours a day, but part-time security may be warranted. The schedule might provide for an on-site guard Monday through Friday from 3:00 P.M. until one-half hour after the mall closes and during all the hours the mall is open on Saturdays and Sundays. The workdays of maintenance, janitorial, and security personnel may be scheduled so that at least one person is on site at any given hour of the day or night.

Regional and super regional malls typically have security personnel on site either all the hours the mall is open or 24 hours a day. Usually several guards are on duty during the hours the mall is open, with one or two guards assigned to the parking areas while others are inside the mall. Additional security personnel are needed during special promotions and the Christmas season—and on Halloween and New Year's Eve.

Security can be provided by a proprietary (on-site) force or a contracted service. There are advantages and disadvantages to both, and these are spelled out in exhibits 6.4 and 6.5. As with any contracted service, it is important to know the types and extent of insurance coverages carried by the contractor. Ideally, the contractor's insurance will act as a liability buffer for the owner of the property where security services are provided.

A proprietary security program should include specific training of security personnel and development and distribution of a security handbook that outlines their duties. Periodic refresher sessions should be held to review procedures, discuss recent incidents and problems, and obtain feedback and suggestions.

Guards at a shopping center may or may not wear uniforms. If security officers are to maintain a low profile and serve in a public relations role, it is better if they are outfitted in a blazer and contrasting slacks. If high visibility is necessary, a police-type uniform may be worn (provided there are no objections from the local police). "Uniform" expenses (cleaning, repairs, replacement) may be a consideration in the employment or contract discussions.

It is rarely necessary for shopping center security personnel to be armed. An unarmed guard can usually handle most situations. When a gun is necessary, the police should be brought in to handle the incident. Because catching criminals is not the primary responsibility of the security force at a shopping center, a guard carrying a gun sends a message to the public that the center may be an unsafe place to shop.

Representatives of the police department may be invited to speak at security training sessions. Such interaction develops rapport with people in the police department and facilitates good communication and respect between the guards at the shopping center and the police. Some malls offer the police free space, which they can use as a substation where officers patroling the area can make telephone calls, write reports, and take coffee or meal breaks. Also, off-duty police officers can be prime candidates to serve on the property's security force. Police departments in some cities have programs under which a property manager can contract with the city government for the services of uniformed police officers.

If security is needed at a shopping center, it must be implemented regardless of whether it was budgeted. A shopping center cannot afford to have

EXHIBIT   6.4

Advantages and Disadvantages of Contracted Security Services

Advantages of Contract Security Services

1. **Selectivity**—Employer retains only those persons personally approved.
2. **Flexibility**—More or fewer personnel, as required.
3. **Absenteeism**—Replacement of absentees on short notice.
4. **Supervision**—Supplied at no additional cost to the client.
5. **Training**—Supplied at no additional cost to client; may be superior to in-house training program.
6. **Objectivity**—Judgment not clouded by personalities.
7. **Cost**—Generally 20 percent less than in-house, not counting administrative savings (e.g., insurance, retirement pension, social security, medical care).
8. **Quality**—May be of higher caliber than an in-house officer.
9. **Administration and Budgeting**—Brunt borne by security company.
10. **Variety of Services and Equipment**—Security company may be specialists in various criminal justice skills or provide expensive equipment unavailable to home security.
11. **Hiring and Screening Costs**—Borne by security company.
12. **Better Local Law Enforcement Contacts**—May know more law enforcement personnel.
13. **Sharing Expertise and Knowledge**—May have developed security skills, as a result of many jobs, that can be shared with a client.

Disadvantages of Contract Security Services

1. **Turnover**—Extremely high industry-wide.
2. **Divided Loyalties**—Serving-two-masters quandary.
3. **Moonlighting**—Low salary for officers may force them into secondary jobs, resulting in tired and unalert personnel.
4. **Reassignment**—Some agencies send in the best men at inception of contract and then replace with others as new contracts open.
5. **Screening Standards**—May be inadequate.
6. **Insurance**—Determine liability and ensure individual officers are bonded and insured.

The preceding are conclusions drawn following a nationwide survey by a task force funded by the federal government.

---

inadequate security. A well-planned security program is comprehensive and anticipates possible problems. As part of its execution, every guard should be required to fill out a daily or workshift report. (A seemingly unimportant incident may be the lead in solving a crime.) An important component is a review and upgrade, if necessary, of parking lot lighting. A well-lighted parking lot is a deterrent to criminal activity. As an added precautionary measure, especially when employee parking is in a remote section of the lot or off site, a guard may be assigned to walk employees to their vehicles after the mall is closed.

EXHIBIT 6.5

Advantages and Disadvantages of Proprietary Security Forces

Advantages of Proprietary Security Forces

1. **Loyalty**—A positive quality.
2. **Incentive**—Promotion possibilities within the entire company structure.
3. **Knowledge**—Of operation, products, personnel of the company because of permanent employment.
4. **Tenure**—Less turnover than contract officers.
5. **Control**—Stays inside company structure.
6. **Supervision**—Stays inside company structure.
7. **Training**—Can be specifically geared to the job performed.
8. **Company Image**—May become a status symbol.
9. **Morale**—A hoped-for state maintained by security manager.
10. **Courtesy**—Can render courtesies to VIPs because of familiarity with company personnel.
11. **Better Law Enforcement Liaison**—Security manager can informally develop law enforcement liaison with less conflict.
12. **Selection**—Company selection procedures apply.
13. **Better Communication**—More direct.

Disadvantages of Proprietary Security Forces

1. **Familiarity**—May become too familiar with personnel to be effective on job.
2. **Cost**—Expensive (salary, benefits, workmen's compensation, social security, liability insurance, work space, equipment, training).
3. **Flexibility**—Hard to replace absent personnel.
4. **Administrative Burdens**—Must develop an upper-level staff to handle these personnel.

The preceding are conclusions drawn following a nationwide survey by a task force funded by the federal government.

When guards are not available, employees should be encouraged to implement a buddy system and never go to their vehicles alone.

Emergency Procedures

Development and implementation of emergency procedures is a major responsibility of the property manager. Natural disasters and manmade emergencies can occur at any time. Shopping centers, especially enclosed malls, present unique challenges in this regard. Unlike office buildings or industrial properties where the same groups of people are present everyday, most of the people in a shopping center at any one time are shoppers, and they cannot be trained to respond to an emergency. In addition, many of the shoppers will be young children and elderly adults, making evacuation or even simple crowd control more challenging.

The property manager should develop an emergency procedures plan that is tailored to the shopping center. The first step is to determine the likelihood of particular natural disasters or manmade emergencies occurring there and find out the most appropriate responses to them.

The United States Weather Bureau can provide information on weather-related natural disasters (tornados, floods); the U.S. Geological Survey should be able to indicate the possibility of earthquakes. If an area is susceptible to these types of phenomena, the plan should include specific responses to them. A good basic plan can easily be adapted for a particular emergency if it was not anticipated in the first place.

Manmade situations—arson (fires), theft, assaults, bomb threats, vandalism, hostage taking, random shooting, medical emergencies—are not limited by geography. The sociopolitical climate of an area may make it a more likely target for bomb threats and acts of violence. Local police and fire departments can provide assistance in developing responses to these situations. Professional organizations that focus on educating the public about fire safety, hazardous spills, first aid responses, etc., are other possible resources. Consultation with insurance professionals can provide valuable insights and minimize liability and problems with insurance claims.

To assure the most appropriate response to a particular emergency, the property manager should designate two emergency teams—a primary team whose members are assigned specific responsibilities based on the type of emergency and a support team to provide assistance in specific situations.

If the shopping center has an on-site staff, all management, administrative, marketing, maintenance, and security personnel should be members of the primary response team. In a strip center that has no on-site personnel, staff from the property management company should be expected to provide the primary response to emergencies, and they should be trained to handle a variety of emergency situations. Members of the support team include the local police and fire departments, service contractors, and utility company representatives, in addition to the insurance agent and the attorney for the property. In some situations, tenants may also function as part of the support team.

The plan should be designed so that the teams are prepared to handle every *likely* emergency; for any particular situation, each member of the primary team would have a specific task to perform. For instance, if a mall received a bomb threat, the receptionist would call the police; the janitor would check the restrooms; maintenance personnel would inspect the corridors for foreign objects, etc. If the threat was received by a tenant, the store manager would be assisted in conducting a search of the premises while maintenance personnel inspected the mall areas. The property manager would have to decide whether to evacuate the mall—in which case, an announcement should be made over the public address system. (To avoid possible panic, the stated reason for evacuation should be something other than a bomb threat—e.g., the mall is losing electrical power.) The security guard would then direct shoppers into the parking lot, and the marketing director would respond to any media inquiries about the evacuation. Practice sessions should be held for the primary team, and local police and fire departments may be invited to assist in this training.

The property manager should meet with the store managers to review the emergency procedures section of the tenant kit and encourage them to go over that information with their employees. If asked to do so by the store manager, the property manager should arrange a time to meet with a tenant's employees. In multilevel malls where it is more difficult to respond to emergencies, it may be necessary to provide employee training sessions for all tenants and their staffs. However, the emergency procedures for tenants to follow will be less extensive than those for the primary and support teams, but they should suggest ways for the tenants themselves to respond to such emergencies as fires, bomb threats, assaults, and natural disasters (e.g., earthquakes). Training seminars for tenants and their employees would also be less comprehensive. (It will be difficult to train tenants' work forces adequately because of the large numbers of seasonal and part-time workers—and the high rate of turnover among retail workers in general.)

Emergency Procedures Manual.   The responses to particular types of incidents should be written down and collected into an emergency procedures manual. The manual may not address every possible emergency situation, but it should address the ones most likely to occur. Periodic evaluation of established procedures, in particular their applicability to specific incidents that have occurred, will indicate the strengths and weaknesses of the program and provide an opportunity to update the manual.

The manual should include a list of emergency contacts with the names and telephone numbers of all the members of the primary and support teams plus the same information for the tenants. The latter may have to include both home and business numbers for store owners. A plot plan showing locations of fire extinguishers and fire hydrants as well as fire department call boxes will expedite the response to a fire.

The manual should also include a plan for restoration of the property after a disaster. Equipment needed to respond to an emergency should be located on site or readily available from a local rental company. A list of specialized equipment and services, and sources for them, should be a part of the manual as well. The list for an enclosed mall will be more extensive than that for a small strip center.

Disasters and emergencies are usually reported by the media, so an emergency public relations program should also be developed. Its objective is to provide accurate and timely information to the press, the tenants, and the community. Only one person should be authorized to talk to the media. This may be the marketing director rather than the property manager or, if a public relations firm is employed, their assigned spokesperson. Everyone else should refer media inquiries to the spokesperson. Needless to say, hiding information from the media will raise concerns and can lead to unnecessary (and sometimes potentially harmful) investigation. The sooner precise information can be provided to the media, the more likely the incident will be reported accurately and promptly, and the sooner the incident will be over. Care should be taken, however, that information given to the media will not impede a fire or police department investigation.

After the emergency, the property manager (and any other staff members involved) should evaluate the response to the incident and write a report on it. Copies of the report should be sent to the owner and retained in the property files. (Insurance claims for property damage or loss may require additional information.)

Waste Management

Waste management is often overlooked in managing a shopping center, yet it is an important part of center operations. An effective waste collection system should be properly designed into the shopping center in the first place because location and design of trash disposal areas will affect the aesthetics of the property. Dumpsters are unsightly and, if set in the parking lot, will create additional litter. Dumpsters or compactors should be conveniently located, easily accessed by the tenants, and shielded from public view. In small shopping centers, dumpsters are often located behind the shops, with each tenant required to contract separately for waste disposal. Alternatively, the landlord may contract for trash removal for the entire site and include the cost in the common area charges the tenants pay or bill tenants individually based on the size of their dumpsters.

Larger shopping centers often purchase or lease trash compactors. They offer many advantages over dumpsters, the most important one being a reduction in the volume of waste to be disposed. (Lower volume means fewer pickups and lower transportation and disposal costs.) Compactors are totally enclosed and lockable, and their use reduces or eliminates such negative conditions as offensive odors and vermin. In fact, they may contain odor- and insect-control chemicals or devices. Because they are enclosed, unauthorized disposal at the site is precluded. Access can be controlled by a special key or card that activates compaction. Such a card-activated system may also record each tenant's usage, thus permitting more equitable tenant billings. Otherwise, tenants may be billed for waste disposal on a pro rata basis (i.e., based on their square footage). The compactor can be equipped with a fill gauge so the property manager need only call for a pickup when the compactor is full. This eliminates regularly scheduled pickups of less-than-full containers and reduces the cost to the tenants.

Recycling.   Disposal of solid waste has become a priority issue as landfill sites throughout the United States reach capacity and limitations are imposed on the volume and composition of wastes disposed in them. The State of Washington, Department of Ecology, reported the following percentages by weight of business "wastes": office and other types of paper—25.1 percent; organic waste—22 percent; cardboard—15.7 percent; plastics—9.4 percent; glass—4.5 percent; aluminum and tin cans—1.3 percent; other metals—10.6 percent; and other materials—11.4 percent.

To reduce the impact of these volumes of waste on landfill sites, municipalities across the country are gradually requiring residents and businesses to separate their wastes for recycling. Paper, glass, aluminum cans, and various types of plastic containers are among the many items that can be reprocessed into usable products. At the beginning of the 1990s, thirty states had some type of recycling law; by the end of the 1990s, most states and municipalities will have mandatory recycling.

There are several reasons why a shopping center should have a recycling program.

1. Businesses are major generators of waste materials, and as such, they have a responsibility to control the wastes they generate and minimize their impact on landfills.
2. As the numbers and capacities of landfill sites dwindle, the cost of disposing solid wastes keeps rising.
3. Recycling conserves natural resources and energy and lowers the cost of waste removal and disposal.
4. Recycling creates good will in the community and boosts employee morale.

The first step in developing a recycling program for a shopping center is to determine which specific wastes generated there are recyclable, and in what volumes and how rapidly they are being generated. For example, corrugated cardboard from shipping cartons accumulates in large volumes very quickly at shopping centers. If food vendors sell beverages in aluminum cans or glass bottles, these items are candidates for recycling. Other recyclable materials include batteries, metallic items (e.g., steel and tin cans), cooking grease, paper, motor oil, and paper and polystyrene packing materials. There are many federal, state, and county agencies as well as nonprofit organizations that can be called on for assistance in developing a recycling program.

Granted that recycling is desirable and that sufficiently large volumes of specific recyclable materials warrant their separation, the planning process must address storage space and the costs and logistics of a recycling program. A place must be selected to store the recyclable materials, and separate containers must be provided for glass, metals, paper, etc. A contractor is then selected to remove the recyclable wastes. The volumes of specific materials and their value for recycling will determine the cost of the program. The shopping center may be paid by the recycler for some waste materials and charged to have others hauled away. The recycler may provide a dumpster or other container, or the manager may have to arrange for a container. The specific contractual arrangements will depend on the types of waste materials, their volumes and quality, and the facilities available locally for their recycling.

In some communities, for example, there are firms that will provide a large container for accumulation and storage of cardboard. At the shopping center, cardboard may be placed in the container by the tenants themselves or by someone on the maintenance staff. The accumulated cardboard may be hauled away on a regular schedule, or the hauler may be called to remove the container when it is full. To prevent unauthorized dumping of trash in the container, it should be kept locked when not in use. Some major tenants have participated in cardboard recycling programs for many years, and they often have their own balers to compact and tie the cardboard. The volume of cardboard generated by all the tenants at a shopping center would determine whether a baler or compactor for cardboard only is warranted and, if so, whether such equipment should be purchased or leased.

Once a recycling program is planned, the tenants must participate in the program for it to be successful. Containers for collection of recyclable materials must be conveniently located and easily accessed by the tenants. If the containers are too far away from the tenants' premises, they may balk at participating. Tenants will better appreciate their role and responsibility in the program once they are educated to the benefits of recycling. A well-planned program should reduce the volume of waste for disposal and thus lower the amount tenants pay toward this expense item. Some recyclables may generate income for the center, and those funds may be appropriately used for the common good of the tenants. Conversely, if there is a charge for removal of a recyclable material, appropriate proration of that expense may mean that only the generators of a waste pay for its removal (i.e., food vendors who sell beverages in bottles may have to bear the expense of glass recycling). Because volume and quality affect the costs of recycling, costs may also affect individual tenant participation. Once a program is established, however, participation may be mandated by modifying the lease provision covering waste disposal or adding a separate provision to cover recycling.

To effectively execute the recycling program for a regional mall, a member of the management staff may be assigned the role of "recycling coordinator." This person may be responsible for launching the program, educating the tenants and their employees, and encouraging active participation by everyone at the mall. The tenant education program may include a recycling kick-off event, one-on-one discussion with the manager of each store, a regular newsletter for tenants, and publicity for those stores that participate fully.

The community at large may also be invited to participate, and therefore the recycling program should be publicized in the community. Large metal containers for collection of paper, glass, and aluminum can be placed in a side or back area of the parking lot.

Some counties have a mobile unit for pickup of household hazardous waste. It travels to different areas of the county and stays for 3–5 days at a time to collect household paints, motor oil, and hobby chemicals. Such a mobile unit may be permitted to set up in a remote area of a shopping center parking lot. As a safeguard against liability, however, it may be necessary or appropriate to post a special security guard during the hours the unit is closed to ensure that residents do not drop off or spill hazardous wastes at the site. Residents bringing wastes during those off hours must be encouraged to return when the unit is open.

To complete the cycle, so to speak, the program should encourage tenants and others to purchase and use recycled materials. Bags and printed items that utilize recycled paper and boxes made from recycled cardboard are the most obvious examples.

Energy Conservation

Shopping centers are relatively energy efficient—a study conducted by ICSC in the 1970s found that shopping centers consumed less energy than factories and manufacturing plants of comparable size. Even though shopping centers are not major energy users, energy conservation should be one of the design considerations in the development of a new shopping center. (Energy efficiency is often considered equatable with cost effectiveness.) The ideal time to plan for and install energy-efficient lighting and mechanical systems and to meter each tenant separately for both electricity and gas (as well as water) is during development. Tenants have an additional incentive to conserve energy when they are aware of their own usage and pay for it directly.

For an established center, evaluation of energy use should be part of management takeover, and the astute property manager will develop, implement, and monitor an appropriate energy conservation program as part of the center's operations. The goals of such a program should include substantial permanent reduction in energy usage. The first step is to involve representatives of the utility companies in the conduct of an energy audit and development of a chart of energy consumption that covers a period of years. (Some information should be readily available to the manager because utility bills state amounts of electricity and gas used.) The charting process will reveal trends that can be used by the utility representative to compare the energy consumption of similar shopping centers. The utility representatives should walk the shopping center with the property manager to identify specific causes of energy wastage. The property manager should conduct a similar energy audit periodically, perhaps including it in the periodic inspection of the property as a whole.

At a shopping center, the two areas with the greatest potential for energy savings are the HVAC system and the lighting. A service contractor can determine whether the HVAC system is operating at maximum efficiency. As an item of preventive maintenance, frequent filter changes are necessary for HVAC units to operate efficiently. However, the most obvious consumption of energy is for lighting. Lighting in the parking lot and the common areas of the mall is one of the most costly energy uses in a shopping center. However, specific conservation of energy used for lighting must be weighed against the need to maintain adequate levels of lighting for security purposes. Security certainly takes precedence over a reduction of lighting levels in the parking lot. The possibility of replacing existing lamps with more efficient lighting sources should be investigated. Lighting that is strictly decorative may be a candidate for replacement or removal.

Some specific energy-conserving procedures for a shopping center are listed below.

- Whenever possible, use fluorescent rather than incandescent lighting.
- Use light-colored paint on center walls to increase reflected light.
- When practical, schedule mall cleaning and maintenance work during the hours the mall is open.
- Avoid changing thermostat settings. (Frequent changes increase heating costs in winter and cooling costs in summer.)
- Keep fans and coils clean and in good condition, and change filters often.
- If possible, turn off HVAC in storage rooms and unoccupied spaces, or reduce it substantially.

The property manager has a responsibility to the property owner (to maximize the property's NOI), to the tenants (to operate the common areas as cost-effectively as possible), and to the community (to minimize energy usage on the property). An effective energy conservation program should be publicized to the community and the tenants. The tenants, in particular, should be kept informed of the progress the shopping center is making in conserving energy. In fact, the tenants should be actively involved in the energy conservation program. The property manager can arrange meetings between the tenants and representatives of the utility companies, and tenants should be given a list of things they can do to conserve energy in their stores. The cost savings that result from everyone's efforts should lower their prorated CAM charges.

OTHER CONSIDERATIONS

Shopping center leases commonly provide for improvements to the tenants' leased spaces so that they can conduct their business effectively. Most such construction is to be done at the tenants' expense, but the shopping center manager must oversee the work to assure that it does not cause problems for the other tenants or inconvenience shoppers. In order to draw shoppers to the center in the first place, the center must be promoted to them. Once shoppers are in the center, it is often desirable and appropriate to provide additional attractions for this captive audience. Both tenant improvements and promotional activities require the guidance of shopping center management personnel. Maintenance staff members are the workers most likely to be called on to assist the marketing director in preparing centerwide promotions.

Tenant Improvements

In shopping centers, unlike in office buildings, tenants are usually allowed to construct their own "improvements" to their store spaces, finishing the interiors and installing display fixtures. The primary reason for this is that retail tenants' improvements seldom have direct impact on the structural components and mechanical systems in the building. In a new strip center, space is usually leased for the first time as a "shell," which typically includes a storefront, demising walls, a dropped ceiling, a restroom, and HVAC. The tenant is responsible for installation of wall and floor coverings, and a divider wall (partition) may be constructed in the back of the store, along with necessary decorative platforms and dressing rooms. Build-out of a coin-operated laundry, a hair salon, or a restaurant would also require extensive plumbing and electrical work.

Space in an enclosed mall may also be leased in a similar shell state or with only stud demising walls and a dirt floor. The tenant must build out and finish the store proper. Because most mall tenants are sophisticated retailers with the expertise to coordinate extensive tenant improvements, such an unfinished state is preferred, and when spaces are re-leased, most new tenants usually do only minor remodeling.

Whether the shopping center has leased a shell or a previously built-out space, the lease will require that the tenant submit a construction or remodeling plan for the landlord's written approval before improvements can be made. These plans will be reviewed by the property manager, the construction manager, or the shopping center architect. Particular attention must be paid to such items as changes to the storefront, adequate electrical capacity for the tenant's equipment, grease traps in the drains if the tenant serves food, proposed openings in bearing or sheer walls, and changes to the coverage by the fire sprinklers.

The tenant's contractor should be required to have appropriate insurance coverages, and the property owner and the property management firm should be listed as additional named insured parties for the work being done. The tenant may also be required to purchase a performance bond to assure that the contractor will be paid and that the improvements will be completed. The amount of such a performance bond is often one and one-half times the estimated cost of the improvements. Subcontractor lien waivers may be provided to the landlord in addition to or instead of a performance bond.

The property manager should assign specific areas for placement of a construction dumpster (usually behind the leased space) and parking of construction vehicles. To minimize problems and inconvenience to other tenants and shoppers at the center, some specific policies or rules for construction of improvements should be established.

- Construction vehicles must park in the assigned area.
- Construction activity that may be disruptive to other tenants and shoppers (e.g., core drilling) must be performed before the shopping center opens—usually not a problem because most shopping centers open at 10:00 A.M.
- The property manager or an on-site maintenance worker should be present during any penetration of the roof (e.g., by an antenna or other equipment) to assure that the penetration is properly repaired and sealed.
- The installation of tenants' improvements and fixtures should be reviewed by the property manager to assure that the integrity of the building is not violated.

Assistance for the Marketing Director

Marketing directors often work alone, or they may have an administrative assistant. They rarely have their own staff of laborers. However, to assure that promotional events run smoothly, and especially to expedite assembling and dismantling of promotional displays, the marketing director will require assistance in the form of physical labor. Workers can be hired from temporary employment agencies, or maintenance personnel can be assigned to assist the marketing director (provided their work schedules can be adjusted). Center staff being familiar with the property is an advantage that makes the second option desirable. This works best, however, when people's duties are well-planned.

The marketing director should give the property manager an advance schedule of the dates of each month's events and the amount of time necessary to set up and take down the equipment and decorations for each promotion. A particular promotion may require building a stage and setting up chairs, as well as placement of props and decorations. Once the promotion is over, all of the equipment and decorations must be dismantled immediately. Additional security personnel may be necessary to guard the props, control crowds, or direct traffic. The cost of temporary labor and extra security guards should be charged to the marketing fund or merchants' association budget, along with the rental or purchase of equipment or props.

Christmas Decorations.   Family visits to Santa on the mall and the attendant excitement of seeing the mall decorated for Christmas continue to be a holiday tradition throughout the United States. Prior to the energy crisis in the mid-1970s, it was also common to decorate shopping center parking lots for the Christmas season. Garlands were strung along the building canopy or soffits, holiday wreaths and figurines were attached to light poles, and Christmas lights were strung along building eaves and soffits and around light poles. Since then, however, decoration of parking lots has been reduced substantially, and any decorating done today is much less extensive. On the other hand, mall interiors were and continue to be decorated elaborately, often including animated and talking mannequins so that they resemble a Hollywood movie scene. In strip centers, minilights are often used around store windows to draw attention to the stores and their displays.

The focal point of the Christmas displays at most malls is Santa Claus and his special area. Being photographed with Santa is a Christmas tradition for children that dates back to the turn of the century. For years, Santa's arrival at downtown stores or in a parade through the shopping district was the event that started the Christmas season in many cities and towns. When malls became the focus of retailing, they tried to outdo each other in the manner of Santa's arrival. Santa has arrived by helicopter, on the back of a fire engine, as a skydiver, via a hot-air balloon, on a motorcycle, and the old-fashioned way—on a sled drawn by a team of reindeer led by Rudolph. Since the mid-1980s, however, Santa's arrival has not been quite the spectacle it once was. Many malls now start the holiday shopping season with Santa already installed in the Christmas House.

Christmas decorations for a shopping center may be purchased outright or leased. A particular display may be used for three or four years and then replaced with a new and different one, or decorations may be added each year to continually change the scene. Some malls sell or trade those parts of their Christmas displays and decorations that they no longer use.

Installation of an extensive Christmas display requires a well-coordinated plan. Traditionally, Christmas decorations were put on display the Friday after Thanksgiving; for many years, this was the start of the Christmas selling season. However, beginning in the early 1980s, many retailers—especially large department stores—started their Christmas selling seasons earlier and earlier each year, so that some stores now begin showing Christmas decorations in early November or even before Halloween, while others still maintain the traditional later start of the holiday season. In a mall, the ideal situation would be for all retailers' own decorations to be on display concurrently with those in the mall itself. However, this may not always be possible or practical.

In order to create a spectacular and impressive kick-off to the holiday season, decorations in the mall are installed all at once. One day there are no decorations, and the next day the mall is fully decorated. This achievement requires careful planning and a large amount of labor. The decorations are installed while the mall is closed, so if the mall closes at 9:00 P.M., the property manager has until 10:00 A.M. the next day to install the entire array of Christmas decorations. If the holiday season is to begin the Friday after Thanksgiving, decorations are installed overnight Wednesday evening and into the early afternoon of Thanksgiving Day. The work force is divided into crews, and each crew leader is assigned responsibility for a work crew decorating a specific area or setting up an individual scene.

When Christmas is over, the decorations must be taken down immediately. Shoppers get a poor impression of a mall that still has its holiday displays in place after Christmas. Christmas decorations are usually elaborate and expensive, and they must be stored in a dry, safe place when not in use. Older malls often have mezzanine areas for such storage, while newer malls may be designed to include special storage areas, often above the maintenance workshop. If storage facilities are not available at the mall, it may be wise to rent a miniwarehouse or self-storage space so that decorative display elements can be stored intact.

7

Interacting with Tenants

Tenant relations is one of those obscure concepts that everyone in the industry talks about and thinks they understand. Yet the relationship between the landlord and the tenant is one that is both complex and misunderstood.

There has always been a lack of trust between landlord and tenant. The owner of a large property—the landlord—traditionally has been perceived as trying to maximize the return on his or her investment with little or no regard for tenants or their problems. While this perception may fit some landlords, it is more likely that landlords do care about the tenants and their problems, only they do so in a larger context. When the landlord's broader considerations and consequent decisions have had a negative effect on the tenant's immediate needs or desires, it is easy to see why a tenant may think the landlord is uncaring. Regardless of the positions of landlord and tenant on a particular issue, it is incumbent on the landlord to be as understanding as possible of the individual tenant's situation and to approach all tenants' problems with empathy and consideration.

In a shopping center, the property manager represents the property owner in the role of landlord. For their part, most shopping center managers feel that they are quite sensitive to their tenants and their tenants' needs and that when there are problems between landlord and tenant, it is the tenant's fault. On the other hand, there is little feeling among tenants that the landlord, in the generic sense, has any understanding or cares about their position. Obviously, something is being lost in translation.

ESTABLISHING RELATIONS WITH TENANTS

Good tenant relations are the responsibility of the shopping center manager. Although franchise operators and major retailers have their own established systems and procedures, many other retail tenants are comparatively naive and may not understand the complexity of the shopping center environment. What is required is an active program of education and communication directed toward the tenants. The tenants must understand how the shopping center operates and what the center's operations mean in terms of their businesses. For example, the hours the center is open for business are the store hours the tenant must keep. The tenant must also be made aware of operational changes and other events or management decisions that will affect the center as a whole and the businesses of individual tenants. For example, if construction or repair work will require barricades that alter the flow of traffic in some parts of the center, tenants should be given advance notice of the work and advised of specific efforts on the part of management to avert or at least minimize business losses while the work goes on.

The nature of tenant relations demands that the shopping center manager must have superior communication and interpersonal skills. The tenants in a shopping center may have differing levels of sophistication and retailing expertise. The perceptions and needs of local entrepreneurs starting new businesses are substantially different from those of established retailers; the person hired to manage a store that is part of a franchise or chain will differ from the owner of a business. The problems and concerns of a store owner will be personal challenges; those of a hired manager may relate to the store location being far away from the decisionmakers in the corporate headquarters. It is important for the shopping center manager to know not only who the tenant is but whether the store operator is the owner of the business or an employee of the owner. This chapter addresses the manager's relationship with those who are operating the individual stores in the center.

In truth, good tenant relations are like the "golden rule": The manager should treat the tenants as he or she would like to be treated. Each merchant should be dealt with everyday as though his or her lease is about to expire. The tenant is both a customer and a client to the shopping center manager. Whenever a tenant's behavior seems unbearable, the manager should consider the alternative—a mortgage cannot be paid without rental income, and a shopping center cannot operate without tenants.

The Basics of Good Tenant Relations

The success of a shopping center depends on the success of all its tenants—measurable in dollars and sales volumes. Every aspect of the shopping center must be planned to maximize sales and minimize the physical and procedural obstacles to achieving that goal. A good working relationship between manager (landlord) and tenant is prerequisite to success.

Tenant relations begin when the shopping center project is conceived. After selecting the proper site, a well-thought-out plan for the center is the first critical step toward good tenant relations. The developer must create the proper physical plant and understand exactly how the center is to be run before the first lease is signed. The operation of the center must be considered in detail during the planning stage in order to avert problems later.

Examples of problems abound. Imagine the merchant who moves a business into a new center and is paying a share of the common area maintenance (CAM) expenses. That merchant may well become disenchanted with the CAM charges if maintenance people are repeatedly observed hauling out a 300-foot hose to wash down the outside walkways because there are no water faucets next to the walks. The merchant can correctly conclude that the maintenance requirements of the center were not well thought out at the design stage.

To prevent such disenchantment, and the complaints that can result, the shopping center planners should create and follow a checklist of the specific details that have to be included in the design. The following list identifies only a few examples of the types of *operating details* that can lead to problems.

- If a major tenant wants some lights on in the parking lot all night, arrangements should be made for separate circuits and, perhaps, separate meters for those lights.
- If a common collection point is to be designated for trash disposal, its location should be convenient to the tenants' spaces.
- Receptacles for disposal of trash by customers should be convenient for shoppers but not block walkways. Size, use, and labeling of the receptacles are other considerations.
- If bicycle racks are to be provided, they should be accessible to bike riders but not intrude on automobile or pedestrian rights of way.
- Trees and other landscaping elements must not block tenants' or center signage.
- Provision should be made for extra electrical outlets for Christmas and other seasonal or holiday decorations.

Careful planning and management review can avert future problems and allow the tenants to concentrate on their business objective, which is sales.

The *lease* document also must be carefully planned in advance, and shopping center operations will be an important consideration in its contents. In particular, allocation of operating expenses and the method of their proration to the tenants must be appropriate and fair. Common area maintenance expenses, utilities, and taxes are among the items most commonly passed through to the tenants. If roof repairs are to be part of CAM charges, the lease should state whether the costs of such repairs are to be allocated building by building or if the whole center will be the basis for their proration. The number of discrete structures that comprise the center may be a determining factor in the allocation of major repairs. If utilities are master metered, the lease must state the method of allocating them to the individual tenants. Taxes may be allocated for the entire center or parcel by parcel. Ownership and values of multiple parcels of land may be the determining factor here. In centers where there are pad or outlot tenants, it may be unfair to include the pads in computing the in-line shop prorations for some tenant charges. A carefully crafted lease will take all of these issues into consideration.

Another important document that applies to all tenants and must therefore be carefully thought out is the landlord's *workletter*. This becomes a part of the lease, usually as an exhibit. With all the confusion that goes along with moving in, the new tenant who discovers that the promised telephone conduit was not installed will be very unhappy. Most landlords would rectify such a problem eventually, but in the meantime, the tenant's move-in is off schedule and the tenant is aggravated. Because such problems can and do occur, the landlord's workletter must be compared to the construction documents to assure that the tenant is getting everything that is promised.

Also important in a newly constructed center are tenant *punch list* items and responsive follow-up on them after the tenant moves in. This is a management responsibility because quite often the general contractor is from another city. When the job is done, the contractor and the construction crew go home, and there is no one in the local market to take care of the one-year warranty and pick-up items. Often problems arise in relation to maintenance of operating equipment. For example, most tenants do not think it is reasonable to wait three days to have the air conditioner checked, especially when the temperature is 102 degrees.

The Role of the Shopping Center Manager

The shopping center manager must understand that the responsibility for the relationship with the tenants over the long term rests with him or her. It is the manager who must reach out to the tenant and make the effort to establish and preserve the landlord-tenant relationship. The argument that the owner of a regional shopping center has no need to worry about getting along with a specific tenant because the tenant needs the landlord more than he or she needs the tenant sidesteps the issue. Getting along with tenants does not mean giving in to their every request, but rather creating a sound, well-managed environment in which the retailer can operate and having a management philosophy that recognizes and is responsive to the needs of both the property and the tenants. Tenants are more likely to have a positive attitude when the shopping center in which they are located is well run, and their attitude will create a more pleasant shopping environment for the customers. As a result, both landlord and tenant will benefit. In the business of shopping center management, the best management philosophy is one that is "firm but fair." While the manager must make every effort to protect the owner's economic interest in the property and its operation, he or she must also establish a good relationship with the tenants because that, too, is in the long-range economic interest of the owner.

The Role of the Leasing Agent

The leasing agent must be thoroughly familiar with both the lease document and the method of management of the shopping center as it will affect the tenant through the lease. It is not enough to know the size of the rental spaces and the rental rate per square foot. The leasing agent must also know how common area charges will be prorated and passed through, when taxes will be billed, and how much they are expected to be. New tenants will want to know where to pay the rent and whom to call if they have a problem. It is critical that the leasing agent fully understands the lease document and the tenant's obligations under the lease. A shopping center lease is very complex, and the tenants must understand what they are required to do. It is the leasing agent's responsibility to communicate the lease terms and requirements to prospective tenants.

The leasing agent's job is to prospect for tenants and acquire signed leases. Once a space is leased, however, the agent should move on to the next prospect. Overseeing tenant improvements or working on management problems is a waste of a good leasing agent's time. For this reason, it is important for the manager to be available to the tenant once the lease is signed. A good way to make this transition is to have the leasing agent introduce the tenant to the shopping center manager.

When a lease is signed, the leasing agent should deliver a copy of the lease to the new tenant along with a *letter of introduction* that identifies the shopping center manager and sets forth the particulars of the turnover of the premises—e.g., the move-in date, when the first rent payment is due, and the contractors to contact for tenant improvement construction. A copy of the letter should be sent to the manager. The ideal next step is for the leasing agent to introduce the tenant to the manager face to face. However, this may not be possible, and the letter accompanying the lease may have to suffice.

When the Manager Takes Over

Upon receiving the copy of the introductory letter to the tenant, the manager should send the tenant a personal *letter of welcome* along with a tenant kit. The letter should include an offer to be of help if needed. The *tenant kit* should include basic information on the center's operations and a detailed list of resources. At the very least it should list utility providers—whom to call for telephone installation, start-up of electricity billing, delivery of heating oil—and emergency (fire, police) services, and include information on such things as garbage pickup, the center's marketing fund, employee parking, operation of heating and air-conditioning equipment, and mail box keys or combinations (see exhibit 5.1). It may also be appropriate to include a statement of "house rules" (proper use of plumbing, disposal of hazardous substances, fees for late payment of rents, etc.) that apply to all tenants and aid in maintaining the shopping center as a special place to shop.

The contents of the tenant kit as outlined here and in chapter 5 are important for all tenants. If the "tenant" is represented by a store manager, that individual may have little or no knowledge of the details of the lease agreement. In the absence of a copy of the lease, the tenant kit may be the store manager's sole guideline for operating in the shopping center.

A *telephone call* from the manager to the new tenant is also a good idea. This will establish a more personal communication link. Often the manager will be called upon to serve as liaison between contractors and tenants. Moving a business into a shopping center, especially a newly built center, is usually a totally new experience for tenants, and they really need assistance to get through the process. During construction of the tenant's space, it is helpful if the manager stops by or calls to see if everything is working out according to plan. The manager should keep in mind that the shopping center owner has a vested interest in opening a tenant's store as soon as possible, so working with the tenant benefits both the tenant and the landlord.

An especially nice touch on the manager's part is a *letter of congratulations* to the tenant on opening day. This may be accompanied by a token gift such as a plant or flowers. Ideally, the manager should visit the store in person, but it is often difficult to do so. Time constraints and a management office removed from the site can preclude a manager attending each new tenant's opening.

Opening day may present an opportunity for the manager to catch up on any lease details not communicated to the tenant by the leasing agent. A separate letter spelling out the lease commencement and ending dates, when and how to make rental payments, and a statement of charges accrued to date may accompany the letter of congratulations or follow in a day or two.

A goodwill gesture on the part of the shopping center owner can go a long way toward setting the tone of the landlord-tenant relationship. An example is an ad in the local newspaper, designed and paid for by the landlord. The same ad can be used for all tenants if it includes a heading such as "Welcoming the Newest Merchant" and closes with the name and address (and logo) of the center. The middle area of the ad should be for the tenant's use—an announcement of the tenant's opening or promotion of a special sale item. Regardless of its content, such an ad is a nice welcome for the tenant that also promotes the center.

MAINTAINING RELATIONS WITH TENANTS

Once the manager has welcomed a new tenant and that tenant's business, an effort should be made to maintain the relationship established with the tenant—i.e., the store owner or manager. The keys to successful tenant relations are based on lines of communication and prompt responses to tenants' problems and concerns.

Use of first names fosters a more personalized relationship, which can be enhanced in each conversation or meeting with the tenant by asking, "How are you today?" or "How is business?" Other questions such as, "How can I help you?" or "What can we do for you?" let the tenant know that the manager is ready to respond to the tenant's problems and wants to help. These questions are most likely to encourage complaints, as indicated in later sections of this chapter. They are also likely to elicit requests from tenants that cannot be fulfilled. When that is the case, instead of just saying no, the manager can provide some explanation: "I am really sorry, but we cannot agree to . . . because . . . ." Although the result is the same, the manager has both expressed concern about the tenant's request and explained why it was denied.

Communicating with Tenants

The shopping center manager has many opportunities to communicate with individual tenants, and these communications will take many different forms. There is a genuine need for personal contact, and that may best be done in the form of personal visits. However, telephone calls and letters are the most likely methods the tenants will use. This is especially true if the manager is not present at the shopping center every day. Perhaps the most important point to be emphasized is the need to be responsive to the tenants because their efforts to communicate will most likely relate to specific problems they are having. Its nice to hear from them when things are going well, but that is less likely.

Personal Visits.   Once a tenant has moved in, it is a good idea for the manager to visit the tenant's store regularly. At the very least, these visits should take place once a month. However, while the shopping center is very new or if there are problems in its start-up, visits every two weeks or more often may be appropriate. Once most of the tenants are in place and the center is operating smoothly, the visits can be less frequent.

The manager's purpose in these visits is to listen. Tenants are likely to have questioms about the status of lease-up and about other tenants' sales. To answer these questions, the manager should be prepared with as much positive information as possible. The manager should also be prepared when tenants complain about problems or make suggestions. Each new tenant may want to make the manager aware of "things to be done"—for example, installation of additional signage. The manager has probably heard similar comments as every other new tenant was installed. However, the newest one may be "seeing" the center from a tenant's perspective for the first time and is probably just trying to be helpful. Patience and knowledge are needed by the manager in this situation. An explanation—in this instance, that additional signage may be a nice idea, but city ordinances preclude it—will go far in sustaining tenant relations. A disparaging remark that reflects the manager's frustration with these repetitious recommendations will do the opposite. The manager should keep in mind that tenants often have very good ideas, and that makes it worthwhile to keep the lines of communication open.

Often the tenant is aware of problems in the center but does not take the time to call the manager. The personal visits are the perfect time for the manager to gather that information. No matter the complaint, the manager's response should be as positive as possible, but it should not promise what cannot be. If management has decided not to do something the tenant asks, it is not enough to just say no; referring to a lease clause is not sufficient either. There is always a reason why the clause is in the lease, and that is what should be stated. The tenant has a right to a courteous explanation, and the rationale can be further supported by the lease clause, if necessary.

Every visit to a tenant's store may result in a list of things that need attention, so the first calls the manager makes on return to the office should be to take care of the tenant's problems. Tenants can spend 70 to 80 hours in their stores each week, and that allows them to observe day after day the items that have been called to the manager's attention and not remedied. Because of this, it is a good idea to tell a tenant when work is in progress. Letting the tenant know a problem is being addressed but will not be completely corrected for a few weeks will put the tenant's mind at ease. Some types of problems, on the other hand, demand immediate attention—for example, if the parking lot lights are not working at all. Routine maintenance and repairs in a shopping center usually can be handled within 48 hours, and follow-up calls to tenants are not required. However, the manager must be sensitive to possible tenant reaction to an apparent delayed response to a complaint and make an effort to assure the tenant that the work will be done promptly.

Sometimes the tenant will not be in the store when the manager visits. When that is the case, the manager should leave a business card with a handwritten note (e.g., "I stopped by to see how things are going"). The card will let the tenant know of your visit, and the note will indicate a personal interest.

Telephone Calls. Tenants' telephone calls should always be returned. Even though the shopping center manager is very busy, there is no excuse for not returning a phone call. If the manager cannot respond directly to the tenant for a few days, the secretary should let the tenant know that the manager will call as soon as possible and extend an offer to help personally.

In many situations, the management office is located some distance from the retail property, and shop tenants may be reluctant to make a long-distance call. One solution is for the management office to accept collect calls, but that can be very expensive. It is more desirable to have a policy of not accepting collect long-distance phone calls and allow office staff to be somewhat flexible on this issue. Adhering to a firm policy could lead to problems. A caller may be trying to report an emergency in a managed property.

Another, better, solution is to arrange for off-premises phone extensions in the cities where the remote properties are located. The extension is assigned a local telephone number, and all calls to that number are forwarded to the management office. The tenants make a local phone call that rings at the management office, and the management firm pays for the toll portion of the forwarded call.

Still another option is a custom 800 number. It is now possible to obtain an 800 number that covers only the area codes from which the company is willing to accept calls. No additional phone lines are required, and a local 800 number can be comparatively inexpensive. It also is a great convenience for tenants and local contractors who work with the management firm.

Letters.   From time to time, shopping center managers receive letters of complaint from tenants. A letter from an irate tenant should not be responded to in kind. The manager should be sure to have all the facts and understand the situation before a response is made, and that response is better as a telephone call. The tenant's approach to a problem may not be rational, but it is important for the manager to respond rationally. Even if the manager is not going to do anything to resolve the tenant's problem, a sympathetic approach will do more to preserve the relationship than an angry response will. The manager will have to work with the tenant in the future, so it is important to keep the lines of communication open.

Communication goes both ways, and there are cautions for using letters to deal with problems in the center. A letter should not be sent to all tenants if only one or two tenants are causing a problem. For example, receipt of two NSF (not sufficient funds) checks the same day should not be the basis for a letter to all tenants threatening dire consequences if another NSF check is received. The manager will have communicated—but only his or her frustration. No consideration will have been given to how the tenants might react, especially those who have never had a check bounce. In such a situation, the tenant who caused the problem should be contacted specifically. In fact, the most likely reason to write to a specific tenant is in regard to something in the lease, and NSF checks should have been addressed in the lease. A letter related to the lease should show the tenant's proper name, spelled correctly, and be sent to the address specified in the lease or requested by the tenant. (Many tenants have offices away from the center and do not wish to have their business arrangements known to all store personnel.) When it is necessary (or appropriate) to direct a mailing to all tenants, the letters should be addressed to "all merchants" or "all occupants" (to avert negative connotations inherent in the word tenant).

Support from Management

The *merchants' association* can be a very positive part of the landlord-tenant relationship in a shopping center. Alternatively, this association can become a group of tenants who use it as a forum against the landlord. If there is a merchants' association, the landlord should contribute to it—in most cases, the landlord's portion represents about 25 percent of the dues collected from the tenants (about 20 percent of the total). An effort should be made to involve all of the merchants in the activities of the association, and the landlord (manager) should attend all meetings or have a management representative there. The landlord should be supportive of the association's activities and a positive influence at the meetings. To keep the association meetings focused on marketing and avert their becoming gripe sessions, the manager should handle tenants' problems on a regular and timely basis. Then the tenants will not feel a need to bring up their problems at merchants' association meetings.

The landlord (manager) can also be a source of shopping center industry information that can be helpful to the merchants. Often there are positive reports on retailing in the newspaper. These can be cut out and mailed to some or all of the tenants—depending on topics and suitability—with a note saying, "I thought this might be of interest." Beyond the local newspaper are national resources. The International Council of Shopping Centers (ICSC) publishes *The Retail Challenge,* which is distributed quarterly and provides very specific tips on retailing. Some developers subscribe to multiple copies of this publication for their tenants, at no cost to them. Reprints of articles are also useful tools. An excellent article on the benefits of Sunday and evening store hours was published by ICSC, and a number of developers bought extra copies to distribute to their tenants. Anything related to retailing that comes to the attention of the landlord or manager is worth sharing with those tenants who could benefit from the information. Some national and regional chain store operators prefer not to receive such information because they have very strong ideas about how to run their stores. However, most of the tenants in the smaller shop spaces can benefit from timely tips and additional information on retailing, and the landlord or manager is a logical source for them.

Competition being what it is, the shopping center manager can easily find opportunities to be supportive toward tenants. Every visit to a tenant's store is an opportunity to observe the business in operation. Some things to look for specifically are the physical appearance of the store (neatness, cleanliness, utilization of the space), merchandise presentation (appropriate displays, inventory levels, pricing), customer relations, store employees, and store management. Over time, the manager can monitor a tenant's advertising and promotions—and levels of sales. All of these aspects can provide clues to the ongoing success or potential failure of a particular store. As indicated in chapter 5, it is appropriate for the shopping center manager to foster the tenants' success through education and training in better retailing practices. To be able to recognize potential problems and provide appropriate encouragement and support, the manager must understand the basics of retailing (see appendix A).

Because of the nature of the landlord-tenant relationship, managers seem to focus largely on its negative aspects. However, acknowledgment of positive actions on the part of the tenants is also important. If a tenant places a nice ad in the local paper, the manager should cut it out and send it to the tenant with a note of thanks. A thank you letter should also be sent to the merchant who is especially helpful in working with the merchants' association. Sometimes more than "thank you" is appropriate. The manager of a shopping center in a distant location benefited from the efforts of a merchant who voluntarily watched over the common areas. The merchant informed the manager when the center was not swept on schedule or if parking lot lights were not working. Later, when the merchant's store required a repair that would have been a tenant responsibility, management absorbed the cost in appreciation for the merchant's attentiveness. The dollar investment was small, and it made the merchant even more attentive.

Solving Problems

Common area maintenance is the source of many tenant problems and complaints. The maintenance itself is a management responsibility; the tenants' problems relate predominantly to their prorations for the costs. Contractors working on the common areas can pose problems for tenants, and the manager will have to work with both parties to resolve them. Other specific sources of difficulty in tenant relations are maintenance of the tenants' premises and violations of the lease.

Common Area Expense Bills.   Many of the shop tenants do not really understand the allocation of CAM expenses, but with a little extra effort, this can be resolved. The first step is a clearly understandable clause in the lease that sets forth what the tenant will pay, how the amount is computed, and when payment is to be made. In addition, the tenant's bills for CAM expenses should be sufficiently detailed so that the tenant can see the total amount of the expense and understand how the proration was determined (see chapter 12, Administration). It is unreasonable for the manager to expect the tenant to accept whatever is billed, without explanation, and a bill that shows only the amount the tenant is expected to pay is not appropriate. When a tenant calls with a question, the manager should take the time to explain the billing computation.

If monthly billings are based on an estimate of the annual costs, the year-end adjustment statement should provide a comparable level of detail. If there were extraordinary expenses, these should be explained in an accompanying letter. Management may know all the details of a larger-than-budgeted expense, but the tenant cannot be expected to remember it and may not have known about it at all. When a year-end adjustment is much larger than expected, it may be appropriate to allow additional time for payment as well. It may be difficult for some tenants to pay an additional $700 or $800 for an unexpected adjustment, and they may challenge the amount to delay payment. The extra time allowance will avert most tenants' need to challenge the billing.

Some national chains and major retailers may require copies of the invoices for common area expenses and will negotiate this into their leases. In general, however, it is recommended that copies of invoices *not* be provided unless this is mandated by the lease. A tenant can use the invoices as a way to delay payment by arguing for more time to review them. Tenants do have the right to audit common area expenses in the management office, and it is appropriate to provide a copy of an invoice for a single item that is a problem. However, sending copies of all invoices to all tenants becomes very expensive. The cost would have to be borne by the tenants, and this is an expense most tenants would prefer not to have. The best policy is to permit inspection of all invoices in the management office only.

Common Area Contractors.   The common area contractors can cause problems for tenants, and those problems will come back to the manager. Because of this, contracts for work in the common areas require special attention. First, the manager's relations with contractors should be at a distance. Contractors should not be relatives or captive companies unless they are clearly the best and least expensive (or only) providers of a service within the area. Having all contracted work bid to specifications assures cost effectiveness and efficiency. All contracts should include a cancellation clause and state a specific time period in which this can occur (e.g., 7 days). A week may seem like a short time, but when a contractor is just not getting the job done, 30 days is too long to let the situation continue. Contractors should also be required to provide proof of insurance in case there are claims resulting from defects in the work or delays in completing it.

Contract workers often do not realize that their activities are disruptive. For example, a roofer barricaded a walkway to do work overhead. The worker needed some boards for the roof deck and left to get them. It took three days to get the boards, and meanwhile the barricade was in place while no work was being done. The tenant whose access was blocked was rightly unhappy about the incident. Other problems may be less obvious—for example, material stacked in a prominent parking space, workers' behavior on the job (listening to loud radios, sitting in front of stores eating, generally fooling around), etc., are disruptive for the tenants and can become big problems for the manager if they are not resolved quickly. Often a few words with the contract workers ahead of time can prevent such occurrences. Indeed, the contractors who employ those workers must know that the shopping center is an operating entity and that all efforts must be made to do their jobs with minimal disruption of tenants' businesses. This can be stated in the contract itself or in a cover letter, but it must be emphasized. The contractors have to be told that their bills are ultimately paid by the tenants, and that the tenants must be considered when the contractors are working. If a contractor's work will be disruptive to one or more tenants, the contractor or the manager should talk with the affected tenants. The tenants should be advised of what is going to happen and when. They should also be assured that the contractor and the manager will do what they can within reason to minimize the disruption and keep all tenants open for business.

Courtesy on the part of the contractors should be encouraged. If work is being done where it cannot be seen (e.g., a roof repair), the contractor should let the tenant know when the work has been started and completed or if the work will be discontinued for a few days. This provides assurance to the tenant that something is in fact being done, perhaps in response to a complaint the tenant had made. Often repairs and other work are completed out of sight and during off hours, and the tenant who does not see anyone may assume that nothing has been done. If there is a complaint about contracted work, the manager may be able to resolve it by arranging a meeting between the contractor and the tenant. A face-to-face meeting usually will clear the air; however, if the situation is volatile, it may be a good idea for the manager to be present at such meetings.

Maintenance of Leased Premises. One difficult area of landlord-tenant relations is responsibility for maintenance of the leased premises, especially if the warranty on an item has just expired or if responsibility for the item to be maintained or repaired is questionable (e.g., a sewer pipe that serves the premises only but is located 20 feet outside the premises). Some leases are very clear on these issues, but many are not; usually it is the tenants' responsibility to maintain their premises. However, in questionable situations, it may be appropriate to advise the tenant that management will have their contractor investigate the problem and, if the repair is the tenant's responsibility, the contractor will bill the tenant. Sometimes a problem involves more than one tenant. An example is three restaurants that were located side by side in a center, and all had a continuing mouse infestation. Each blamed the other two tenants, and the problem was not being resolved. Management stepped in, with agreement from all three tenants, and hired a pest control company to exterminate the mice. Each tenant was then billed by the exterminator on a pro rata basis. This resolved the problem and the expense was borne by the tenants. However, it is important to note that the manager acted *with the consent of the tenants.*

While there is little doubt that the manager's first responsibility is to the owner who has retained his or her services, the manager also has an obligation to be fair and reasonable with the tenants. While the owner signs the lease as the landlord and makes a financial decision based on the economics of the deal, situations can arise that require an exception to the lease agreement. A major tenant, whose employees are sophisticated and understand the ramifications of taking over existing space, is usually in a position to take care of the leased premises. A problem discovered after move-in is not likely to create sympathy for a major tenant or to change the economics of the deal. The tenant in a small shop space, however, is in a different situation. An interior decorator who has never taken space in a shopping center before may lease an existing store. The space is leased "as is" and, within a month, the water heater fails completely and has to be replaced. This situation may require the manager to exercise his or her judgment. It may be questionable whether the tenant should pay for the replacement under the circumstances. If the manager made a very low rent deal and the "as is" situation was pointed out, making the tenant aware of the risks, then replacement should be the tenant's expense. However, if the deal was for market rent and little attention was paid to the "as is" portion of the lease, it may be more reasonable for the landlord to pay for the replacement. While the landlord should be fair and reasonable regardless of the lease requirements, the lease also represents an economic deal with the tenant, and the basis of that deal will be eroded if the landlord assumes responsibility for what is rightly a tenant's expense. The manager in this situation has dual responsibilities—furthering the landlord's interest and preserving the landlord-tenant relationship.

Lease Violations.   Violations of the lease terms by the tenants require close attention and careful handling. Tenants typically favor a strong lease because it provides a desirable environment for their business. However, most tenants also think their individual needs should be more important than the lease requirements. Violation of the lease requires diplomacy and firmness. An explanation of the violation and why it cannot continue is imperative. As with other items in a lease, the lease clause itself should not be the stated reason for the manager's position. Rather, the reasons behind the lease clause should be explained. For example, a clause in the lease may state that tenants are prohibited from parking in front of their stores, but it is more effective to indicate the importance of the parking space in terms of customer convenience and what that means to the particular tenant and all the other merchants in the center. (Lease administration, as such, is discussed in more detail in chapters 5 and 12.)

LEASE RENEWAL AND TENANT RETENTION

Lease renewal is another critical time in the landlord-tenant relationship. The professional manager keeps abreast of the latest lease terms and conditions; the typical shop tenant usually does not. The merchant may be focused on his or her business to the exclusion of the leasing market. Then, sooner than the tenant expected, the lease term will end. Suddenly, the manager is telling the tenant that rents are 50 percent higher, the new lease will be triple net, and the term will be only three years with no options to renew—and the manager needs to know right now if the tenant is going to renew.

Obviously lease renewals require forethought. Management must decide first of all whether the tenant should be retained. The use may no longer be a good one for the center—e.g., fish and chips shops were popular a few years ago but not now, and stores selling green plants were once the rage but today are few and far between. The second decision is the terms under which the tenant will be retained. An increase in the rental rate is most likely, but other terms of the lease should be reviewed as well. Percentage rents, prorations of pass-through expenses, and the length (duration) of the lease term should be considered carefully.

The renewal process should be started with the tenant approximately six months prior to the expiration date in the lease. This gives the tenant some time to think about the renewal terms and allows the manager time to educate the tenant regarding current market conditions. If the renewal discussion is put off till the last minute, the tenant may become frustrated and leave. Both manager and tenant can lose if that happens. If the rent is going to be raised dramatically, the manager should know what is being charged at other shopping centers so that these figures can be quoted for comparison. Factors that contributed to specific escalations in rent and other payments required under the lease should be identified and explained. Here again, tenant relations are key. The manager may have no choice but to hold out for the new rent and conditions dictated by the market. However, that is no reason he or she cannot be understanding and show compassion for a tenant's frustration with the changes in the new lease. The manager should bear in mind that having empathy for the tenant's predicament does not mean he or she will make economic concessions to the tenant.

Creating the Tenant Mix

The mix of retailers at a shopping center—and the types of merchandise and services they provide—is critical to its success. The tenant mix of a shopping center should be the result of careful analysis and planning, with the objective of providing the broadest range of goods and services consistent with the buying habits and income levels of the people in its trade area. The key elements in establishing an optimum tenant mix are the demographic profile of the trade area population, the competition already established in the trade area, and the size and location of individual store spaces in the center. An exception to this rule is the specialty use center where all tenants are focused on a particular market niche (e.g., an automotive center whose tenants provide a wide range of products and services related to car care). The various types of shopping centers were described in detail in chapter 1.

SPECIFIC CONSIDERATIONS

The concept of tenant mix is more important for shopping centers than for any other type of commercial property. Only in shopping centers is success measured in terms of sales volume, and this is expressed in dollars per square foot of GLA. The only way to generate high levels of sales is by targeting the buyers in the trade area. The more goods and services are tailored to meet the needs of area consumers, the more likely the center (and most of the stores that comprise its tenant mix) will be shopped by those consumers.

Tailoring the tenant mix requires consideration of many factors. Age and family or household composition are critical concerns for some types of re-tailers. Toy stores or children's clothing stores need families with young children in order to thrive; they cannot be expected to do well where the population is predominantly adult professionals. Conversely, women's fashion stores whose major lines are tailored suits will not do well if most women in the trade area are homemakers. Family or household income—and the buying power that it indicates—is even more critical. While high-end fashion stores thrive in affluence, discount stores depend on a need to minimize spending. The former would not survive in a low- to moderate-income area while the latter would thrive there. Home improvement stores are more likely to suc-ceed and sales of major appliances and furniture will be higher in areas where homeownership dominates over renting. Stores selling sporting goods (e.g., skis, golf clubs, and related apparel) will do best where the population has ample discretionary (excess) income to support such expensive hobbies.

It is also important to find the right use for a particular space and the best merchant to operate it. The size and configuration of the store space are im-portant considerations in this regard. Also important is its location—in the center itself and in relation to other tenants. A 2,000-square-foot store may be ample for a card or gift store but too small for a jeans shop. A record store will do well in a similar space, especially next to a stereo store. A women's shoe store can thrive in less space and will do best if it is near or adjacent to a shop selling women's apparel. The key objective is to create a synergy among the tenants and maximize it such that the center as a whole will generate the type of traffic that will benefit most, if not all, of the merchants—i.e., the whole should be greater than the sum of its parts. Often this requires the shopping center manager to work with individual merchants to maximize their sales, not only for their own success but also to benefit surrounding merchants and, of course, the shopping center owner. (Working with retailers is discussed in chapters 5 and 7 and appendix A.)

The success of individual tenants is highly desirable from many perspec-tives. Space in the center can command higher rents if average sales are high—$300 per square foot per year as compared to $150—and successful merchants are candidates for lease renewal. Successful tenants are also less likely to be sources of complaints or collection problems. Most shopping cen-ter leases include provisions for payment of percentage rent, and high sales levels increase the opportunities for collecting percentage rent. Last but not least, the more traffic and sales generated by one store in a center, the greater the likelihood that other stores will benefit from its traffic draw and the po-tential for cross-shopping.

Demographic Factors

Establishing a good tenant mix is as much an art as it is a science. The key is to be realistic in determining the size of the trade area. It is not realistic in most situations to assume that a neighborhood shopping center will draw customers from a ten-mile radius or that customers will drive past two other comparable centers to shop there. Once a realistic trade area is identified, the people in it must be counted and their characteristics analyzed. There are three key elements to be considered when conducting such market research.

1. There must be sufficient population to support the center.
2. The population must have sufficient income.
3. The competition must be analyzed to ascertain that there is sufficient capacity in the market to support the square footage proposed.

In this regard, it is appropriate to look in part to growth in the area, as long as that growth projection is realistic. Trends in population size, age, and income distribution can be determined from current and prior census data.

Income levels of the area population are a very important consideration in planning a tenant mix. In very high income areas, Saks Fifth Avenue, Gucci, and similar shops will do well. In lower income areas, Kmart is a more likely tenant. This does not mean that one tenant is "better" than another, only that shopping center tenants must serve the trade area if the center is to be successful.

The source of people's income is also a consideration. It is not enough to know that a family's income is $35,000; how that money is earned becomes a determining factor because blue-collar and white-color workers generally spend their money in different ways. Also key is the amount of "disposable" income they have. Homeowners have different types of expenses than do apartment renters. People who are in debt often have little money available for niceties (e.g., eating out) after they have paid for the necessities.

The age range of people in the area is also important. For young married couples with both husband and wife working, price is often a primary consideration. The young upwardly mobile population is accumulating goods but must keep an eye on the family budget. They are also very much interested in personal services—they have little time to do things for themselves because they spend so much of their time working. This population will likely be served by value-oriented retailers.

As people attain some degree of success, they want better things and can afford to pay for them. If the population is mostly middle-aged adult professionals working at white-collar jobs, the trade area is more likely to support better quality, higher priced merchandise and a large variety of services. Jeans shops, Mexican restaurants, and "junior" fashions are less likely to be found in retirement communities because older people are less likely to patronize stores selling "young" fashions and restaurants that serve spicy foods.

Tenant mix will also be sensitive to ethnic considerations. In Southern California, for example, 25 percent of the population is Mexican-American. The retailer that ignores this fact will miss one-fourth of the potential market for its store. Supermarkets are one type of retailer that will evaluate the ethnic composition of an area and then carry specialty foods to serve those segments of the market. Many areas of the United States have diverse ethnic populations, and the impact of ethnicity on people's wants and needs should be carefully considered when the tenant and merchandise mix for a shopping center is being planned. It may also be important for retailers (and center managers) to hire personnel with language skills that will facilitate accommodation of ethnic diversity, both within the trade area and among visitors to the trade area (i.e., tourists).

Once the population in the trade area is understood, the competition in the area should be evaluated. In particular, the shopping center manager wants to know which merchants are already in the trade area and which of these are especially successful—or unsuccessful—and why. A merchant who is doing poorly may have poor business skills in general or poor retailing skills in particular. That merchant may not be one the manager would want in his or her shopping center. However, if the reason a merchant is not doing well in a competing center is because of a poor location, that merchant may be successful in the manager's center as well as enhance the center's tenant mix. Also to be considered are the goods and services that could do well in the trade area but are not already there. Often the trade area population changes over time but the merchants do not, and that fact creates an opportunity for the manager to change or broaden a tenant mix.

Market Factors

Information about consumer buying power is available from many sources. Various governmental agencies (e.g., the U.S. Department of Commerce, Bureau of the Census) and numerous private commercial marketing research firms (see appendix E, References and Resources) compile such statistical data for defined geographic areas. *Sales and Marketing Management's Annual Survey of Buying Power,* published in August and October each year, details how people in every major metropolitan area of the United States spend their money. *Dollars & Cents of Shopping Centers* includes information on each type of retailer's sales in dollars per square foot. Once the buying power of a given area is established—i.e., how much is spent per capita on specific types of merchandise—and the sales volumes of specific types of retail tenants are known, an estimate can be made of the square footage of each type of store space that can be supported in the trade area. As an example, suppose a shopping center manager is interested in leasing to a drugstore tenant.

The *Annual Survey of Buying Power* indicates that 1989 drugstore sales in the manager's county were $299,628,000. The county population is 635,000, so each consumer in the county spends an average of $472 per year on drugstore items.

Analysis of the shopping center's trade area reveals a population of 35,000. Multiplying the population count by the average per capita purchases, potential drugstore sales in the trade area amount to $16,520,000. According to *Dollars & Cents of Shopping Centers: 1990,* drugstore sales average $181 per square foot per year. Based on these figures, the manager calculates that the trade area will support more than 91,000 square feet of drugstore space. If the area already has 70,000 square feet of drugstore space occupied, there is room for approximately 21,000 more. (See example calculations in exhibit 8.1.) If it is known that the amount of drugstore space adjacent to the trade area is 40,000 square feet, the impact of that amount of space on the potential expansion in the manager's county will have to be evaluated.

Many factors affect the potential for additional drugstore space. If the current drugstores are doing well, strong customer loyalty to them could make it difficult for a new drugstore to enter the market. On the other hand, the existing drugstores may be operated very poorly, and that could be an open invitation for a good drugstore operation to enter the market and succeed. This type of analysis generally can be done for every category of merchandise found in a shopping center. However, there may be exceptions that cannot be analyzed because an item or a potential retail operation cannot be adequately categorized. As an example, per capita spending on hobbies and hobby store sales figures may be available, but these are very broad classifications and a shop specializing in a very narrow hobby (e.g., military models and supplies) may defy adequate analysis for a firm decision.

Managers of regional and super regional centers will use this method to determine market support for specific stores, and the results will be very accurate because these centers draw customers from a very large trade area population and have fairly predictable market support. For other centers, it is increasingly difficult to pinpoint specific tenant types and square footages that can be supported as center size diminishes, but the exercise is still worthwhile.

Trade Area Factors

The appropriateness of particular tenants to the tenant mix of a given shopping center will vary as the characteristics of the trade area change over time. New single-family residential development is likely to attract more families with young children. If the population of the area had been dominated by unmarried professionals living in apartments, the influx of families will be a significant change. If a large manufacturing plant that employed local workers closed, the unemployment would mean reduced income and could force people to move out of the area. Construction of new retail space or rehabilitation of an old center can change the character of the competition. Any or all of these types of events can occur in an area served by a shopping center. Such

EXHIBIT 8.1

Buying Power, Store Sales, and Store Size

Given the Following information

Drugstore sales = $299,628,000/year
County population = 635,000
Trade area population = 35,000
Drugstores in trade area = 70,000 square feet of GLA
Average drugstore sales = $181 per square foot per year

Calculate per capita purchases

Drugstore sales per year ÷ county population = per capita drugstore purchases (per year).

$299,628,000 ÷ 635,000 = $472

Calculate potential sales volume

Per capita drugstore purchases × trade area population = potential drugstore sales volume in trade area per year.

$472 × 35,000 = $16,520,000

Calculate square footage of store

Potential drugstore sales volume ÷ average drugstore sales = potential square footage of drugstore county will support.

$16,520,000 ÷ $181 = more than 91,000

---

changes will affect the tenant mix of the center, at least to the extent that individual merchants there are affected. The population served by the shopping center and its direct competition are the most important features of the trade area. (The trade area is discussed in the context of market analysis and development of a management plan in chapter 4, and use of a market survey to identify and characterize the competition is discussed in chapter 9.)

The concept of trade area also has geographic limitations. The trade area of a given center can be divided into three zones—a primary zone from which up to 70–75 percent of its regular customers will be derived, a secondary zone that represents another 20–25 percent of its customers, and a tertiary zone that will account for the remainder. The size of the trade area and its respective zones will vary with the size and type of shopping center.

- *Strip centers* have upwards of 50,000 square feet of GLA, a convenience market anchor (when there is one), and a few small shops (2–10 stores). The trade area comprises the immediate neighborhood of the site and the traffic on the adjacent main street (minimum population: 1,000–2,500).

- *Neighborhood centers* have 50,000–200,000 square feet of GLA, a supermarket (plus drugstore) anchor, and 15–25 small shops. The trade area has a radius of 2–4 miles and a minimum population of 5,000–40,000.
- *Community centers* have 200,000–400,000 square feet of GLA, are anchored by a junior or discount department store (but may include a supermarket and a drugstore), and usually have 25–40 small shops. The trade area has a radius of 5–7 miles and a minimum population of 100,000–150,000.
- *Regional centers* range between 400,000 and one million square feet of GLA, with one to three department store anchors and 50–100 small shops. The trade area has a radius of 7–10 miles and a minimum population of 150,000–300,000.
- *Super regional centers* occupy more than one million and up to three million square feet of GLA, with four or more department store anchors and 100–150 small shops. The trade area has a radius of 10–20 miles and a population in excess of 300,000.
- *Specialty shopping centers* in tourist areas can be as small as 50,000 and as large as 200,000 square feet of GLA, with or without anchor tenants, and have as few as 20 to as many as 100 small shops. They are typically part of the tourist attraction and usually require a minimum local population of 150,000 to survive.
- *Specialty use centers* vary in size (25,000–70,000 square feet of GLA) and usually have no specific anchor tenant. Their main attraction is their specificity and, therefore, their uniqueness. The trade area is defined by the specific use and may extend beyond the radiuses usually associated with centers of this size. Restaurants and entertainment facilities may draw from larger areas than, say, automotive services.
- *Value-oriented centers* vary in size. They may include outlet, off-price, and discount merchants and attract customers from a radius of 20 miles to as far away as several hundred miles. Traditionally they required a minimum population of 150,000.
- *Power centers* have between 200,000 and 600,000 square feet of GLA, with most of the space occupied by several large, strong, high-volume, heavy-advertising retailers and very few small shops. The trade area may extend up to 30 miles, depending on local competition; otherwise, they need a minimum population of 150,000.

The characteristics of shopping centers as noted here are representative of typical examples from statistical compilations (e.g., by The Urban Land Institute). Their characteristics will vary with their specific locations and the trade areas they serve. The neighborhood center that is the *only* shopping center within a 20-mile radius will likely offer more soft goods (e.g., clothing), have a broader range of goods and services generally, and draw customers from a much larger area than would a typical neighborhood center. Conversely, a regional shopping center in a heavily developed area such as Southern California will have a much smaller-than-normal trade area—because there are so many regional centers in the area, they are closer together and limit each other's customer draw.

Matching Merchants and Store Spaces

During development of a new shopping center, consideration of specific tenant mix precedes construction of the store spaces. The sizes of the spaces to be built and the placement of the retailers in relation to each other in the center are the next issues to be resolved.

Store Size.   Often the desire is to build large stores, and this can create a number of leasing problems. As the size (area) of stores is increased, it is natural for them to be deeper, and the added depth makes them more difficult to merchandise. Also as store size increases, the number of prospective tenants for a particular space diminishes. Few retailers need (and lease) very large spaces. Smaller spaces command higher rents per square foot, and generally there are more prospective tenants for them. The ratio of store frontage to store depth should be approximately 1:3 or 1:4—i.e., one foot of frontage to, at most, three or four feet of depth. Representative store sizes are 15 × 60 (900 square feet), 20 × 80 (1,600 square feet), etc. Data published in *Dollars & Cents of Shopping Centers* indicate the ranges of store sizes leased by specific types of merchants in different shopping centers. Indications in recent editions of *Dollars & Cents* are that many types of stores are downsizing. (Store size and problems related to it are discussed in chapter 2, Development and Rehabilitation.)

Tenant Placement.   In regional and super regional shopping centers, there have been two schools of thought on tenant placement. The first was to group types of merchandise together to foster cross-shopping. The shopper would find dress shops together, shoe stores together, etc. The second school of thought, and the one most popular in the early 1990s, was to spread out the different retailers so the shopper would be exposed to many types of merchandise during a stroll along the mall. Food courts are the exception; and apart from customer convenience, grouping food vendors together provides cafeteria-like service and selection with a common seating area, optimizing the seating available for each vendor. It also optimizes control of food wastes and general sanitation of the area. Apart from spreading out other types of merchants, there are some juxtapositions to avoid. In particular, a business that generates unpleasant odors (e.g., a pet store or a beauty salon) should not be adjacent to a food vendor or a noisy business (video arcade, music store) next to a quiet one (e.g., a bookstore). On the positive side, some aromas are very pleasant, and a cookie or muffin shop, a tobacconist, or a candle store can emit inviting aromas that will attract people to them. To maximize the benefits of such nice aromas, these businesses should be placed where their odors will not conflict with each other.

The placement of an individual merchant can be critical to that store's success. Jewelry stores usually seek prominent locations and willingly pay a premium rent to obtain them. A barber shop, on the other hand, normally does not need a "prime" location; the volume of sales in this type of service business generally is not indicative of high rental income for the space. Tenants placed *between the anchor tenants* generally do well because of their exposure to a large volume of traffic.

In some strip centers, there are store spaces that do not have "front" exposure. Businesses in such side locations are not exposed to the traffic generated by an anchor tenant. However, dry cleaners, coin laundries, beauty salons, barber shops, insurance offices, etc., can do well in those spaces. Such *destination services* are sought out by their customers specifically, and heavy pedestrian (or street) traffic is not critical for their success.

Controlling the Merchandise Mix

Once the appropriate tenant mix for a shopping center is determined, that plan must be carried out in the actual leasing. The most effective means of controlling the mix of goods and services is the lease document. In particular, the *use clause* must be specific as to what the tenant is permitted to sell. An example of such a use is "to sell women's shoes and for no other purpose." Great care should be taken with the wording of the clause. Such phraseology as "and accessories" or "such items as carried in tenant's other locations" allows too much latitude.

An effective use clause will allow the tenant to carry the specific merchandise lines necessary to its business while preventing a broadening of those lines or a total change of merchandise to capitalize on a fad. For example, a restaurant use clause for operation of "a sit-down restaurant" is much too broad. More likely the clause will be specific: "to operate a sit-down restaurant specializing in Italian foods and selling beer and wine only, and for no other purpose." When it is so specific, a tenant wanting to change the use clause in the future would have to obtain the landlord's approval. That approval would be subject to consideration and would depend on the other uses in the center at the time and the effect the proposed change by the one tenant might have on the tenant mix overall.

When anchor tenants are negotiating their leases, they often seek restrictions on the tenant mix. Sometimes the restrictions are to minimize competition, but they address other concerns as well—e.g., maximizing available parking. Supermarket tenants provide examples of both types of restrictions.

To reduce competition, a supermarket lease may prevent the landlord from leasing space to a delicatessen or a liquor store. To protect parking, the same lease might prohibit leasing to a bowling alley or a theater.

Another mechanism sought by prospective tenants as a way to minimize competition is inclusion in their leases of an *exclusive use* clause. Landlords should be wary of granting exclusives because they can severely limit future flexibility. If a tenant's "use" is to operate a "shoe store," granting that tenant an exclusive could limit the landlord's ability to lease other spaces if the prospective tenants for them wanted to sell children's shoes or athletic shoes. It is reasonable to allow an exclusive for a limited time to help a new business get started, but that is a rare exception. If an exclusive is granted, the lease should state the conditions under which it applies. An exclusive should be allowed for the initial tenant only and not applicable to any assignees or subtenants; it should be in effect only until such time as the tenant's sales reach an agreed upon level and only so long as the tenant is not in default of the lease. The clause should be worded carefully. The exclusive, as granted, should permit other merchants to carry limited amounts of the protected goods without being in default of the exclusive holder's clause. These issues are addressed more specifically in the discussion of the lease document in chapter 10.

A good tenant mix creates a shopping environment in which the whole is greater than the sum of its parts. The resulting *synergism* among the various merchants will allow each of them to achieve higher levels of sales in the shopping center than they would in scattered downtown locations without the support of the other merchants. The manager who achieves this will have done his or her job well.

Retenanting a Shopping Center

One of the most difficult tasks of the shopping center manager is retenanting. During lease-up of a new center, there are no existing leases that can hinder the creation of the right tenant mix. However, it is not unusual for an older center to begin to decline as one merchant and then another closes its doors, yet a few merchants will remain because the location works well for them.

Changing the image of such a declining center is very difficult. Sometimes the only way to turn it around is to replace some or all of the established tenants and create a completely new tenant mix. Such change must be approached with caution. In particular, the leases have to be carefully controlled. It is important for every new store to enhance the new image of the center, and every reasonable effort must be made to convince the remaining established merchants that they must change their individual images to match that of the renewed center. Often the services of a retailing consultant can be helpful in this regard.

Sometimes the only incentive for a merchant to make such an image change is a financial one. The landlord may have to convince the merchant that a new image will lead to greater success; this can be approached using demographic and other information the tenant may not have immediately available. Unfortunately, it is sometimes necessary to buy out a tenant's existing lease, especially when a store does not fit the new plan. (These considerations are presented in more detail in chapter 9.)

Changes to the tenant mix of an established shopping center must be made cautiously and only after extensive planning and evaluation. Before making any attempt to retenant a shopping center, the manager must have a clear understanding of why a new tenant mix is necessary and how the existing tenants may or may not fit the intended image. It is also important to know how flexible the individual tenants may be and whether they are likely to agree to change. It is usually better to do one's homework first and wait to make any changes, rather than create a plan, begin to implement it, and then have to stop after considerable money has been invested.

BASES FOR COMPARISON

The mix of goods and services varies with the type of center, although some types of tenants are found in more than one type of center, and some (e.g., drugstores, radio/video/stereo stores) are common to all. *Dollars & Cents of Shopping Centers* provides an analysis of the tenant mixes at all types of shopping centers throughout the United States. The shopping center manager can gain a better understanding of what works well in particular shopping centers by studying the analyses of dominant uses and the tabulations of merchandise categories with the highest sales volumes. Another important factor is the specific anchor tenant because it sets the tone for the whole shopping center in terms of dominant merchandise types, amount of GLA devoted to specific merchandise categories, and pricing.

Dominant Uses

The mix of tenants found in community shopping centers is a good example to review as a starting point in establishing the mix for any given center. Review of the other types of centers analyzed in *Dollars & Cents* provides further basis for comparison.

Community Shopping Centers.   The most common use in community shopping centers is sales of women's wear (exhibit 8.2), and the average size of these shops is 3,000 square feet of GLA. Fashion has always been a staple of this type of center, as there is typically a junior or discount department store in the center, and the women's wear shops will benefit from the traffic that

E X H I B I T   8.2

Most Frequently Found Tenants in U.S. Community Shopping Centers

Tenant	Rank	GLA	Sales*	Rent†
General Merchandise				
Junior department store	12	35,390	110.29	3.55
Discount department store	15	59,537	133.24	3.38
Food				
Superstore	13	37,430	346.95	4.48
Food Service				
Restaurant (without liquor)	8	2,807	135.12	10.00
Restaurant (with liquor)	2	3,537	138.28	10.57
Fast food/carry out	3	1,500	200.00	12.73
Clothing and Accessories				
Women's specialty	9	1,600	153.91	12.00
Women's ready-to-wear	1	3,000	124.87	8.75
Shoes				
Family shoes	5	3,000	118.88	9.00
Home Appliances/Music				
Radio, video, stereo (≤10,000 sq ft)	14	2,222	191.86	9.00
Gifts/Specialty				
Cards and gifts	7	2,600	101.30	10.00
Books	17	2,400	144.74	9.70
Jewelry				
Jewelry	6	1,260	265.25	14.20
Drugs				
Super drugstore	19	14,600	172.46	4.88
Drugstore	20	7,532	182.48	6.18
Personal Services				
Beauty	4	1,300	96.94	10.59
Cleaner and dyer	11	1,600	86.42	11.34
Unisex hair	18	1,217	125.49	12.00
Video tape rentals	16	2,000	83.51	9.73
Financial				
Banks	10	2,955	3,356.22	11.80

All values are medians.

*Sales volume in dollars per square foot of gross leasable area (GLA).

†Rent in dollars per square foot of GLA.

Reproduced with permission from *Dollars & Cents of Shopping Centers: 1990* (Washington, D.C.: ULI—The Urban Land Institute, 1990).

anchor draws as well as provide opportunities for comparison shopping. In the past, women's wear stores were also found in neighborhood centers. Then there was a period when women's wear stores would only locate in the larger centers to benefit from their customers' tendency to comparison shop. However, as more women opted to hold jobs in addition to being home-makers, women's wear stores began to be seen in neighborhood centers again because those locations provide convenience shopping.

The second most common use found in community centers is the full-service (sit-down) restaurant with liquor. At the beginning of the 1990s, more families were eating out more frequently and, for many consumers, shopping is a family outing that often includes a meal. The third most common use is fast food, which offers two attractions—convenience and lower cost.

Fourth is the beauty salon, and it is a rare traditional shopping center of any size that does not include one. A more recent adaptation is the unisex hair salon, which ranked eighteenth but has become quite popular; this type of store is expected to rank higher in future surveys. Fifth is family shoes, which is to be expected. Where there are clothing stores, one usually also finds shoe stores.

Jewelry is the sixth-ranked use, and these stores are fairly small (1,260 square feet, on average) though usually prominently located and often paying high rents. Typically, the jeweler in a community center is an independent operation or a regional chain. National jewelry chains preferentially locate in regional and super regional centers.

Seventh-ranked is the card and gift store, with an average store size of 2,600 square feet. Depending on the region and the demographic profile, it may be a national chain or a local operation. The success of this use may be marginal, however, if the supermarket or drugstore in the center also carries a large assortment of cards.

The restaurant without liquor ranks eighth, but its rank is likely to change in the future. The trend has been toward much less consumption of hard li-quor and, in some areas, less wine as well. The result is that a lack of alcoholic beverages in a restaurant is becoming less important. In this same vein, res-taurant menus are being changed in response to changing food preferences (salad bars) as well as dietary recommendations ("light" foods, low-salt items).

Ninth-ranked is the women's specialty shop—maternity clothes, fashion accessories, etc. Banks and financial institutions are also very popular (tenth-ranked) tenants. Like most other tenants, banks are downsizing—from 5,000 square feet in the mid-1980s to less than 3,000 in 1990.

Dry cleaning (the cleaner and dyer) ranked eleventh, and the success of this use in a particular location depends on the demographic profile. In a blue-collar neighborhood, the cleaner may be smaller in size or only a pick-up station. The actual cleaning is done at a separate plant. When polyester became popular, the dry cleaning business suffered, but natural fibers and fabrics began regaining prominence in the late 1980s, and dry cleaning increased in popularity again.

Junior department stores (twelfth-ranked) and discount department stores (fifteenth-ranked) remain typical anchors of community shopping centers. However, the retailing industry was changing at a rapid pace in the early 1990s, and there was a whole new line-up of anchor tenants for this type of center. Typically there used to be one junior or discount department store tenant, but seldom more. The supermarket (thirteenth-ranked) is found in community centers at about the same frequency as in neighborhood centers, and it is one of the staple attractions of both types of centers.

Modest-sized (less than 10,000 square feet) radio/video/stereo stores ranked fourteenth and had a much smaller average area (2,222 square feet). The large stores of this type usually do not fit well into a neighborhood center; they need a larger draw than that size center provides. Video tape rentals (sixteenth-ranked) are still somewhat new but very popular; almost every community center has one. They are located in neighborhood centers, too, because the business is a "convenience." (In some areas, supermarkets and drugstores also offered video rentals on a small scale.) The trend has been toward much larger stores that can more readily provide the selection and ease of service demanded by the video rental customer. The next survey for *Dollars & Cents* will likely show this type of store at a higher rank and with a larger store area.

Bookstores remain popular (ranked seventeenth) but difficult to acquire as tenants. If the economics of bookstores were more favorable, there would likely be more of them and they would rank higher on the tenant list.

The super drugstore has moved up in rank (nineteenth) while the small independent drugstore has moved down (twentieth) and will likely be gone from the community center in the future. It is very difficult for an independent drugstore to survive in what has become a very competitive marketplace. The large chains can underprice the independents because they buy wholesale in large quantities, and they carry a broader range of drugstore merchandise. It is also not unusual to find this same type of merchandise in a supermarket.

Depending on the trade area, there are many other lines of merchandise that will be found in a community center. These include liquor and/or wine shops, bicycle shops, optometrists' offices, shoe repairs, pets and pet supplies, computer stores, automotive parts stores, beauty supplies, coin laundries, movie theaters, and art "galleries."

Other Types of Shopping Centers. For each type of shopping center, there are special considerations regarding tenant mix. The strip center is one of the most difficult to predetermine. The available space is limited, and the trade area is difficult to define. Some chains of the 3,000–4,000-square-foot convenience markets will locate two of their stores within sight of each other at a major intersection. The rationales for this are (1) that the population base for each store will support that store or (2) that the traffic at each location will support the store despite its proximity to the other store.

The tenant mix at a neighborhood center will usually be focused on the population base and the anchor tenant. It will be influenced by what is already in the trade area and will likely include numerous services. It is not unusual for the tenant mix of a neighborhood center to be changed over a period of years as the population in the area around it changes. It is for this reason that the center manager must be up-to-date at all times with the status of the trade area.

High Sales Volumes

It is also interesting to note how the tenant mix has changed at the different types of centers over the last half of the 1980s. A comparison of the tenants with the highest sales volumes in 1984 and 1990 at community, regional, and neighborhood centers can be made from data published in *Dollars & Cents of Shopping Centers*.

In *community shopping centers* (exhibit 8.3), supermarkets had high sales volumes in both years. However, the 1990 ranking indicates addition of the superstore, which is a very large supermarket (70,000–100,000 square feet of GLA) but with a broader array of merchandise. Supermarkets have been expanding their merchandise mix to better serve their customers and improve their profit margins. The convenience market is not listed for 1990, perhaps because it has become an anchor for the strip center or can survive as a freestanding store. These markets are still strong tenants, but they do not fit the community center mix as well as they once did. The cookie shop is another food-related tenant that was big in 1984 but is no longer a high-volume tenant in the community center. These shops thrive in the larger regional, super regional, and specialty centers where the volume of traffic is heavier.

Tobacco was a high-volume tenant in 1984 but not in 1990. This change is likely a reflection of two different phenomena: First, fewer people smoke nowadays and, second, these stores tend to be more successful in the larger shopping centers where there is more traffic. Liquor and wine shops were also high-volume tenants in 1984 but not listed for 1990. Here, again, the change is likely a reflection of people's changing habits.

Jewelry stores are listed for both years, but the credit jeweler did not carry forward to 1990. In this case, it is likely that slim profit margins made it impossible for these types of merchants to survive in the higher-rent community center and they have been relocating to the discount center.

Camera stores were very popular in 1984 but not listed for 1990. These,

E X H I B I T   8.3

**Highest Sales Volume Tenants in U.S. Community
Shopping Centers, 1984 and 1990**

1984	$*	1990	$*
Supermarket	265.13	Superstore	346.95
Tobacco	256.00	Telephone store	305.35
Credit jewelry	239.97	Supermarket	266.92
Liquor and wine	200.96	Jewelry	265.25
Film processing store	200.00	Specialty food	242.45
Cookie shop	191.02	Computer/software	233.43
Convenience market	188.16	Athletic footwear	212.19
Jewelry	185.35	Interior decorator	210.33
Cameras	179.32	Fast food/carry out	200.00
Fast food/carry out	146.04	Film processing store	196.08

*Median sales volume per square foot of gross leasable area (GLA).

Reproduced with permission from *Dollars & Cents of Shopping Centers: 1984, 1990* (Washington, D.C.: ULI—The Urban Land Institute, 1984, 1990).

too, seem to be moving to the larger centers where there is more traffic. Despite this fact, picture-taking continues to be very popular, and film processing is shown for both years. Fast food was a high-volume tenant in both years, presumably because of convenience and low price.

New additions to the list in 1990 provide insight into how consumers spend their money. Telephone stores reflect the consequences of the 1982 court-ordered dismantling of the Bell System; that breakup spawned a whole new approach to telephone services and their marketing. Computer stores have become quite popular and, because computers are high-priced items, their sales volumes are good. Athletic footwear, once a small line in a traditional shoe store, has become a big seller. Interior decorating services are becoming standard tenants in community centers and doing a good volume of business.

A review of the *regional shopping centers* (exhibit 8.4) reveals some changes there also, but they are not quite as dramatic as those in the community center. High-volume tenants in both years include cameras, jewelry, computers, and leather stores. Tenants missing from the 1990 list include the specialty meat store (meat, poultry, fish), key shop, pretzel shop, costume and credit jewelry stores and supermarkets. It is likely that the trend for specialty meats and supermarkets is away from location in the larger centers where they do not really fit the mix. Key shops may have difficulty generating sufficient income to meet the rent in the larger centers, and credit jewelers are more likely to be found in discount centers. While pretzel shops and costume

E X H I B I T   8.4

Highest Sales Volume Tenants in U.S. Regional Shopping Centers, 1984 and 1990

1984	$*	1990	$*
Cameras	458.27	Cameras	546.58
Meat, poultry, fish	448.29	Jewelry	452.33
Key shop	330.20	Leather shop	313.75
Pretzel shop	327.07	Computer/software	302.73
Costume jewelry	303.25	Film processing store	301.41
Credit jewelry	296.77	Athletic footwear	285.56
Computer/calculator (retail)	279.39	Telephone store	278.85
Supermarket	264.49	Tobacco	274.42
Jewelry	264.19	Candy and nuts	270.74
Leather shop	243.12	Fast food/carry out	264.82

*Median sales volume per square foot of gross leasable area (GLA).

Reproduced with permission from *Dollars & Cents of Shopping Centers: 1984, 1990* (Washington, D.C.: ULI—The Urban Land Institute, 1984, 1990).

jewelers are still tenants in regional centers, their sales have been eclipsed by those of higher volume merchants. New entries into the high-volume list for regional centers in 1990 include film processing, athletic footwear, telephone stores, tobacco, fast food, and candy and nuts. These trends reflect what is happening in the other types of centers as the buying habits of the trade area population change.

Finally, a glance at the high-volume tenants in *neighborhood shopping centers* (exhibit 8.5) confirms much of what has already been stated. Supermarkets remained high-volume tenants in both years, but the superstore is a new addition here as well as in the community center. The convenience market made a strong showing in both years; their popularity depends on "convenience"—customers can park close to the store, run in and pick up a few items, and be on their way quickly. The donut shop and the liquor and wine shop may have been dropped off the high-volume list because their sales are down due to people's changed eating habits. Records and tapes, film processing, cameras, and computer stores are likely being moved into the larger (community, regional) centers. Fast food restaurants are still very popular in neighborhood centers, but their sales volumes are surpassed by those of other merchants. New entries on the high-volume list in 1990 include specialty meat (meat, poultry, fish), jewelry, delicatessen, and home accessories stores, and drugstores and super drugstores. Both jewelry and women's wear are returning to the smaller centers to provide more convenient shopping for working women. Drugstores have become mini-department stores, also in an effort to provide shopping convenience.

**Highest Sales Volume Tenants in U.S. Neighborhood
Shopping Centers, 1984 and 1990**

1984	$*	1990	$*
Supermarket	271.46	Superstore	322.75
Credit jewelry	185.70	Convenience market	302.22
Liquor and wine	177.89	Supermarket	278.48
Cameras	155.95	Meat, poultry, fish	249.08
Convenience market	152.96	Jewelry	212.29
Fast food/carry out	150.59	Delicatessen	207.65
Computer/calculator (retail)	142.85	Home accessories	193.70
Doughnut shop	141.49	Photocopy/fast print	189.68
Film processing store	137.15	Drugs	175.40
Records and tapes	133.74	Super drug	169.44

*Median sales volume per square foot of gross leasable area (GLA).

Reproduced with permission from *Dollars & Cents of Shopping Centers: 1984, 1990* (Washington, D.C.: ULI—The Urban Land Institute, 1984, 1990).

Anchor Tenants

The tenant mix in a shopping center will generally follow the lead of the anchor tenants. If they are value-oriented, the pricing in the shops will follow the same pattern. According to *Dollars & Cents of Shopping Centers: 1990,* the GLA of community centers is distributed among the various types of tenants as follows: general merchandise, 33.1 percent; food, 15.5 percent; clothing and accessories (mostly women's apparel), 7.5 percent; food service, 6.1 percent; drugstore, 5.1 percent; personal services, 4.6 percent; and other types of stores, less than 3.5 percent each. While the distribution of GLA among tenant categories in individual centers may vary dramatically from these percentages, the numbers shown here offer a good starting point for evaluating the mix of a particular center.

The tenant mixes in regional and super regional centers are designed not only to meet the needs of the shoppers in their trade areas (i.e., based on demographic profile) but also to provide a reasonably large spectrum of offerings (goods and services) within the designated range. For example, if the market would support 180,000 square feet of women's wear shops, that amount of GLA will be distributed among a variety of retailers whose merchandise offerings cover a range of prices consistent with the income levels of the population, including a variety of fashion accessories and other related items. The 1990 edition of *Dollars & Cents* indicates that regional centers have 23.5 percent of their GLA devoted to clothing and accessories, with the remainder of the GLA utilized as follows: general merchandise, 22.4 percent;

food service, 6.5 percent; shoes, 6.3 percent; gifts and specialty items, 5.3 percent; recreation and community services, 5.3 percent; hobby and special interests, 4.8 percent; and the remaining tenants occupy less than 4.5 percent each.

Specialty centers have a completely different set of criteria for their tenant mixes, particularly because there are different subsets of specialty centers. Those that are tourist-oriented are often dominated by entertainment and food services, having several restaurants in particular. For many such as those located on or near a waterfront (e.g., Faneuil Hall Marketplace in Boston, Ghirardelli Square in San Francisco), the location is part of their overall attraction. For others, location may be the inspiration for an architectural theme based on the prior use of the site (e.g., Trolley Square in Salt Lake City). Internally, the restaurants themselves are often the attraction, bringing local people to the center primarily to eat and secondarily to shop. The tenants in specialty centers often have unique offerings of an exclusive type of merchandise—e.g., teddy bears, music boxes, handblown glass, Christmas decorations, left-handed implements, make-your-own wine and beer, movie memorabilia, etc. Center management may try to balance the merchandise mix so it will appeal to local shoppers as well as tourists—i.e., by including traditional shops and merchandise—but that usually proves to be very difficult.

Another variant of the specialty center is the special use center (e.g., merchandise and services devoted to automobile care). These are described in detail in chapter 1. The range of merchandise offered at discount, outlet, and off-price centers was covered elsewhere in this chapter and in chapter 1. The trend among these types of centers is away from their original austerity toward inclusion of shopping amenities (attractive decor, landscaping, seating, food services) so that these value-oriented centers are becoming tourist attractions in their own right. Large-scale discounters of all types are also being accepted as tenants in traditional centers, often as anchors. Another type of center that has a unique array of tenants is the power center with multiple anchors and only a few small shops.

NEGATIVE CONSIDERATIONS

While the emphasis throughout this chapter has been on the "do's" of creating a tenant mix, it is also appropriate to discuss a few of the "don'ts." The desirability of particular types of tenants and the acquisition of the perfect tenant for a specific space are often wonderful intellectual exercises. However, in the real world, the manager often has to contend with one or more vacant spaces, regular mortgage payments that must be made, and the only prospect for a particular space being somewhat less than perfect. There may be times when it is possible to hold out for the perfect tenant. However, there are also times when this cannot be done; in fact, it may be prudent not to wait at all because of declining economic conditions. When this is the case, it is best to be sure the prospective tenant will not be harmful to the tenant mix or to shoppers' perceptions of the center. It is also prudent to write that tenant's lease for the shortest term possible so the tenant mix can be improved as soon as the market will allow.

For example, most managers would not include a dealer in used merchandise (second-hand store) in a traditional center. The perception of used merchandise is that it is rarely compatible with the typical shopping center mix. There are exceptions, of course, and one of the authors can testify to that fact—e.g., a used book store that works well in a traditional center; a used dress store that presents itself just like a traditional dress shop (comparable fixtures and merchandising techniques) and provides customer appeal without adversely affecting the other merchants.

A number of tenant types do seem to present problems in traditional centers. Beer bars and video game rooms are not problems in themselves but rather in the behavior exhibited by their patrons after they leave these establishments. Some prospective tenants prove undesirable when they are being evaluated. Retailers that have poor reputations and poor housekeeping—i.e., those that operate dirty stores or restaurants—will give the center a bad name through "guilt by association." Along this same line, the merchant who advertises specials that are not really special can affect the reputation of the center as a whole and all the other merchants. The merchant who fails to keep regular store hours in a current location is likely to follow the same pattern in a new one. This situation poses a problem for the other merchants in the center because, here again, shoppers may come to assume they are all unreliable, and they will shop elsewhere.

From this discussion, it should be apparent that there are many factors to be considered when creating the tenant mix for a center. Evaluation of the population to be served and the competition in the area should help the manager identify the best types of tenants for a particular center. Within the categories of tenants that are desirable, it is then best to approach those that are most likely to lease a space. The marketing of the center to acquire the best possible tenants and negotiate satisfactory leases with them is discussed in the next chapter.

9

Leasing

Shopping centers are marketed to two groups—consumers and tenants. Marketing to consumers is intended to build customer awareness and loyalty and to generate sales. A key component in this effort is the shopping center's tenant mix. Marketing to tenants is intended to create the right tenant mix and to maintain 100-percent occupancy at the shopping center. Both marketing programs are interrelated to the extent that, without the appropriate tenant mix for the community, the marketing, advertising, and promotional programs directed to consumers will not be successful. If the community does not support the shopping center, the marketing and leasing program directed to prospective tenants will not be successful. Marketing the shopping center to the consumer is discussed in chapter 11; this chapter will focus on development of a marketing and leasing program for a shopping center. The principles discussed here apply to all shopping centers regardless of their size or type.

DEVELOPING A MARKETING AND LEASING PROGRAM

Shopping center marketing and leasing is unlike the marketing and leasing of any other type of real estate. Changing trends—in fashions, tastes, fads, and merchandising techniques—affect both consumers and merchants and, ultimately, the shopping center. The leasing of all other types of real estate is primarily concerned with filling a rent roll. Which space is leased to which particular tenant is of little importance. In a shopping center, however, every tenant has an impact on the tenant mix. Not only the type of merchandise (athletic versus dress shoes) but also its price range (discount or popular price versus "designer") will affect the tenant mix. The property manager must consider what impact each prospective tenant will have on the other tenants and the tenant mix.

Another concern is whether the tenant will be accepted by the community. In any other type of property, selecting the wrong tenant may result in a defaulted lease and the probability of lost rent and remodeling expenses, but none of the other tenants in the building will be particularly affected by that defaulted lease. Community awareness of specific "tenant failures" in offices is usually minimal; awareness of residential lease defaults may be nonexistent. However, the failure of a shopping center tenant has broad implications. Loss of a tenant from a shopping center weakens the tenant mix—assuming the store was appropriate to the tenant mix in the first place—because it eliminates a product or service and thus reduces the synergism of the tenant mix. Tenants in adjacent spaces suffer from the loss of traffic that had been generated by the former tenant. The community has one less choice of merchandise or service. It should also be remembered that a tenant may be wrong for a center even though it can be successful there. Specifically, a tenant whose merchandise or pricing is inappropriate for the trade area will be detrimental to the tenant mix. For all of these reasons, tenant selection is critical. (Tenant mix is discussed in chapter 8.)

The first steps in developing the marketing and leasing program are to determine who will be on the leasing team, whether the brokerage community will be involved, and how members of the leasing team will be compensated. The next steps are to define and analyze the shopping center's trade area to determine the size and characteristics of its customer base. The shopping center must also be analyzed to determine its desirability as a retail location and the types of tenants that are likely to lease space there. The existing tenant mix must be evaluated to identify prospective tenants that will complement and enhance it. The range of market rental rates for the shopping center and the rental rate for each space must also be determined. It must be understood by the leasing team that the leasing process is ultimately one of give and take. The landlord's objective is to maximize rental income; the tenant's is to minimize occupancy costs. During the negotiations, both parties will compromise to reach agreement and, at some point, that may mean agreeing to concessions.

Before beginning to prospect for tenants, the property manager should prepare a leasing information package that promotes the unique features of the shopping center and consider which prospecting techniques are most likely to be successful. Once prospects are found, the manager must assess their ability to fulfill the lease obligations and their merchandising skills.

When it is determined that a prospective tenant is right for the shopping center, a lease is negotiated. If these negotiations involve lease (or rent) concessions, the cost of each concession must be calculated to determine its impact on the cash flow and the value of the shopping center.

Shopping centers offer a multitude of leasing opportunities. In addition to anchor tenants and in-line shops, there may be pad or outlot parcels and food court spaces (booths) to lease, as well as temporary tenancies (e.g., carts, kiosks, wall shops) to consider. Renewing leases and replacing tenants (e.g., lease buy-outs) are other opportunities. Once a space has been leased, the property manager must establish administrative procedures to ensure that the tenants and the landlord fulfill their lease obligations. (Lease administration is discussed in chapters 5 and 12.)

Assemble the Leasing Team

Selecting the right leasing team is one of the most important decisions of a property owner. The leasing team must understand the property owner's objectives, which can vary from maximizing the cash flow of the shopping center during the next few years to maximizing long-term appreciation of its value. In the latter situation, a property owner is usually willing to provide lease concessions to attract the best merchants and buy out the leases of poor performers. The leasing team also has to understand the trade area of the shopping center and the characteristics of its population (demographic and psychographic profiles). They must analyze the shopping center and compare it to competing centers to determine its relative strengths and weaknesses. It is also important to understand trends in the retailing community and be aware of which established retailers are expanding within the area and which new ones are coming into the area for the first time. Such understanding and awareness will maximize the results of the leasing team's efforts and minimize the time it takes to lease a space. Finally, each member of the leasing team must have an understanding and appreciation of the roles of the other team members. They must work together well and avoid dissension when differences of opinion arise.

Members of the Team.   The members of the leasing team will vary depending on several factors, most importantly the amount of space to be leased. Some property owners and property management firms employ a full-time leasing staff. These personnel may be responsible for leasing multiple properties (i.e., several different shopping centers), for leasing and re-leasing a single major shopping center (e.g., a regional mall), or for the lease-up of a brand-new shopping center. The leasing team may consist of some or all of the following: the property manager, the leasing agent, the marketing and promotions director, members of the brokerage community, and, of course, the property owner.

The *property manager* should always be on the leasing team. The property manager may lead the team, supervise the leasing agent (as the owner's representative), or support the team's activities. In the role of team leader, the property manager is responsible for developing the marketing and leasing program and selecting and directing each team member. When the property manager serves as the owner's representative and supervises the leasing agent, the leasing agent reports to the property manager, and the manager is responsible for negotiating the business terms and lease provisions on behalf of the property owner. As a support member of the leasing team, the property manager advises the leasing agent and actively analyzes and discusses the merits of each proposed lease.

Depending on the amount of space to be leased, the property manager may have direct responsibility for leasing some or all of the vacancies. When only a few vacancies exist, the property manager may be able to lease them more effectively than a leasing agent can. The property manager can take the time to lease those few spaces while the leasing agent devotes time and effort to properties with numerous vacancies and, therefore, greater commission opportunities. However, if the shopping center has several vacancies, it is unlikely that the property manager will have sufficient time to prospect for tenants while also fulfilling management responsibilities. In this situation, it usually is more effective to assign the leasing responsibilities to a *leasing agent* who is either a full-time employee of the property management firm or affiliated with one of the local brokerage firms.

When more than one person is prospecting for tenants, each leasing agent is assigned specific categories of tenants to pursue. This eliminates duplication of effort—i.e., the same prospects will not be contacted several times and others not at all. In a new regional mall, for example, the leasing team may consist of four leasing agents. One may be the team captain, but each team member will contact and negotiate leases with specific categories of tenants. The team captain may be assigned food court tenants and other specialty food categories such as candy and nut stores. Another leasing agent will be responsible for jewelry, gifts, and miscellaneous merchandise categories, and the other two will pursue fashion tenants—one assigned to women's wear and accessories and the other to children's and men's clothing and shoe stores.

The role of the *marketing and promotions director* is essentially advisory. This person is expected to understand the strengths and weaknesses of each tenant individually and of the shopping center as a whole. Other requirements of this person include being familiar with the competition and knowing which tenants there are successful, and therefore likely prospects for the center being leased, as well as being active in the retailing community and aware of new retailers entering the market.

The *brokerage community* may be involved directly or indirectly. Often a brokerage firm will be given an exclusive authorization to lease the shopping center. Depending on the amount of space to be leased, one or more leasing agents from the brokerage firm will be assigned to lease a particular shopping center, and they will report directly to the property owner or the property manager.

Although one brokerage firm may be the exclusive leasing agent, the entire brokerage community should be encouraged to present prospective tenants for the shopping center. The marketing and leasing program should actively "work" the brokerage community—i.e., all commercial leasing agents and their firms should be informed about the shopping center, the space available, and general parameters of the lease terms. Leasing agents from brokerage firms are compensated solely by commissions, so they must also know the commission schedule, the commission split, and how their position in the deal can be protected when they present a prospective tenant.

The final member of the leasing team is the *property owner*—the person who will ultimately approve or reject each prospective tenant. The property owner must understand the shopping center's position in the market and the market rent for each space. If the property owner has an unrealistic view of the rental value of the spaces, good deals may be rejected, and this can discourage the leasing team and the brokerage community from working the property. It is the responsibility of the property manager and the leasing agent to keep the property owner informed of the market conditions, the rental rates in the area, and the market rates for the shopping center. The owner's understanding of the market will be reflected in his or her ability and willingness to expedite approval of a proposed lease. Every day that a prospective tenant waits for lease approval is an opportunity for that prospect to have a change of mind and withdraw the offer.

Action may also be delayed when multiple discussions of deal points by the leasing team and the property owner are required during a lease negotiation. To minimize such delays, the leasing team should be authorized to negotiate a lease within certain predetermined parameters. The following are examples of *lease term parameters* for shop spaces.

- Minimum rent is $15 per square foot per year.
- Annual minimum rent increases 50 cents per square foot per year, or adjustment is to be based on the CPI increase.
- Free rent offered is not to exceed one free month for each two years of the lease.
- The lease term is to be no shorter than three years and no longer than seven years.
- The tenant improvement allowance should not exceed $2.00 per square foot.

- The lease should include provision for percentage rent at the appropriate rate.
- The leased space should not exceed 10,000 square feet.

Such parameters allow the leasing team the flexibility to negotiate a sound market deal as expeditiously as possible.

Leasing meetings are held to report on the status of each prospective tenant, identify new prospects to be contacted, and review the ongoing publicity and advertising campaigns. At each leasing meeting, the leasing agent or the captain of the leasing team submits a report that tabulates the status of the leasing activity with specific prospects (exhibit 9.1). *Leasing reports* are necessary to track the progress of the marketing and leasing program. Regular leasing meetings and reports can accomplish several objectives:

1. Inform the property owner about the leasing team's activities.
2. Make the property owner aware of changes in rental rates in the market.
3. Allow the property owner and members of the leasing team to adjust rental rates and concessions to reflect changes in the market.
4. Review marketing and leasing progress since the previous leasing meeting.
5. Review prospects listed in the leasing report.
6. Review proposals and counterproposals (negotiations).

Leasing meetings are usually scheduled every two to four weeks. Meetings held too frequently take up time that can be better used pursuing prospective tenants. Less frequent meetings can lead to communication breakdowns. At these meetings, it should be readily apparent whether the leasing agents are diligently pursuing the marketing plan and actively prospecting for tenants.

Ideally, the property owner will be available to attend each meeting. In the case of absentee ownership or when ownership is represented by an asset manager who visits the shopping center infrequently, attendance at leasing meetings is unlikely. To keep ownership informed appropriately, the property manager should include a thorough leasing report in the monthly management report.

The activity of the leasing team should be monitored not only to measure its success but also to determine when changes are necessary. Every member of the leasing team should have the common goal of leasing the shopping center as quickly as possible on the best rental terms. However, it is not uncommon for leasing agents from a brokerage firm that is leasing several shopping centers to devote more time to the properties with the most numerous opportunities to make deals. Often they will try to maintain the listing even after leasing slows at a location. They do this because they do not want to give

E X H I B I T   9.1

Example Leasing Prospects Report Form

Project Name _____
Month _____

Date Prepared _____
Prepared by _____

Suite No.	Usable Sq Ft	Date Shown Space	Prospective Tenant (Co.)	Type of Business	Name of Contact	Current Location	Phone No.	Term Yrs	Rent Quoted	TI Work (est)	Broker Comm	Status/Remarks

Status Legend

0 = Lease completed
1 = Lease out for signatures
2 = Lease under negotiation
3 = General terms discussion
4 = Preliminary project talks
5 = Problem in talks
6 = Dead deal

Source Legend

(How prospect found out about building)

A = Drive-by
B = Newspaper advertising
C = Cold call by property staff
D = Direct mailing
E = Broker
F = Other

Reprinted with permission from Alexander, Alan A., and Muhlebach, Richard F.: *Managing and Leasing Commercial Properties* (New York: John Wiley & Sons, Inc., 1990).

up and let the property owner down or because they know if a leasing agent from another firm presents a prospective tenant, they will earn at least a partial commission. When the leasing agents have exhausted all their contacts and leasing activity slows, it is best for the property manager to suggest to the owner that another firm be given the leasing responsibility. Even in the absence of any suggestion for change, the property owner will soon detect the lack of activity, terminate the leasing agreement, and hire another leasing agent.

Leasing Commissions.   Leasing agents from brokerage firms receive no salary; they are paid only when a lease is executed, and their compensation is a commission. Though property managers usually receive a salary, commissions can be a significant source of income for them as well. Leasing agents who are employees of the property owner usually receive a salary; however, the greater part of their compensation may be commissions. Because commissions are the driving force behind all leasing activities, the commission structure should provide more than sufficient incentive for the leasing agent or the property manager. Commissions are a small price for the property owner to pay for a properly leased shopping center.

Commission rates are always negotiable; there is no standard commission. Commissions are based on a multitude of factors—the difficulty of the assignment, the size of each space to be leased, the brokerage firm's or property management company's cost to do business, how important the leasing assignment is to them, and what the property owner is willing to offer. Commissions are usually calculated either as a percentage of the income during all or part of the lease term or as a rate-per-square-foot dollar amount.

Commissions based on the income may be a percentage of the gross income (i.e., base rent and pass-through charges), or of base rent only. Once the income basis is agreed to, the percentage rate must be determined. The rate may be a fixed percentage that is applied to the income for the entire term of the lease or for only a portion of the lease term. In other words, a 6-percent commission may apply to all twenty years of a lease or, say, only the first ten. Alternatively, the percentage rate may decline over the life of the lease: A ten-year lease may be commissioned at 7 percent of the first year's income, 6 percent the second year, 5 percent the third year, 4 percent the fourth year, and 3 percent the fifth year, and 2 percent for each of the remaining five years). Another approach to a declining percentage commission is shown in exhibit 9.2.

The other method of calculating commissions is based on a rate per square foot. The commission schedule may be $4 per square foot for all leases in excess of three years (exhibit 9.3), with the rate prorated for a lease term of less than three years. Some property owners prefer to use a rate per square foot because they prefer shorter lease terms, and they believe the leas-

E X H I B I T   9.2

Commissions Based on a Percentage of the Rent

A commission will be earned for all executed leases based on 6% of the base rent for the first 5 years, 3% for the next 5 years, and no commission for any term beyond 10 years.

Store Size: 1,200 sq ft
Term: 7 years
Rent: $15 for 2 yrs; $16 for 3 yrs; $17 for 2 yrs

Year	Sq Ft × Rate	Rent	Commission Percentage Rate	Commission
1	1,200 × $15	$18,000	6%	$1,080
2	1,200 × $15	$18,000	6%	$1,080
3	1,200 × $16	$19,200	6%	$1,152
4	1,200 × $16	$19,200	6%	$1,152
5	1,200 × $16	$19,200	6%	$1,152
6	1,200 × $17	$20,400	3%	$ 612
7	1,200 × $17	$20,400	3%	$ 612
			Total Commission	$6,840

ing agent may encourage a longer lease term if the commission is based on a percentage of the rent received over the entire term of the lease.

An additional commission may be offered as an incentive for leasing a problem shopping center, to encourage extra effort on the part of the leasing agent, or to achieve a specific leasing goal. Because a leasing agent may not negotiate the best terms if the incentive is based on just one factor (e.g., percentage of space leased within a specific period), the incentive should be based on multiple factors. The additional incentive may be stated: An additional $1.00 per square foot of leased space will be paid if 30,000 square feet are leased within nine months at an average effective rate of $16 per square foot per year.

After the commission rate is negotiated, the commission payment schedule must be negotiated. The size of the payments and their timing can vary substantially. Half the commission may be paid when the lease is executed and half when the tenant opens for business and minimum rent commences. Alternatively, commissions may be paid over the term of the lease—if the commission rate is 5 percent of the collected income, 5 percent of the rent is paid each month during the term of the lease. Multiple payments help the property owner regulate cash flow. Sometimes the property owner or the leasing agent will negotiate an early payoff of the commission based on discounting the total commission earned.

A commission may also be negotiated for lease renewals. These, too, may be approached in several ways—a full commission, a partial (say, one-half) commission, a percentage of the increased rent, or a fixed fee. Because com-

E X H I B I T   9.3

Commissions Based on a Rate Per Square Foot

A commission will be earned for all executed leases based on $4.00 per square foot for all lease terms 3 years or longer. How much commission would be earned on a 1,850 square foot space leased at $17.25 per square foot for 3 years?

Term:	3 years
Store Size:	1,850 sq ft
Commission Rate:	$4.00/sq ft
Commission Amount:	$7,400 (1,850 sq ft × $4)

missions are an important incentive to those who do the leasing, the commission schedule should be commensurate with both the assignment and the competition in the market.

Analyze the Trade Area

One of the first concerns of a prospective tenant is whether its customer base is represented in the shopping center's trade area. When opening a store in a shopping center, a retailer must be confident that the demographic profile of the trade area is representative of its typical customer and that consumers will patronize the new store in sufficient numbers for it to be successful. Before they commit millions of dollars to a location as an anchor tenant, entering into the purchase of a parcel of land and building on it or entering into a long-term building lease, department stores, supermarkets, and super drug stores will conduct extensive surveys of an area. National retailers that lease shop spaces will also survey a market before penetrating it. However, local retailers usually do not conduct sophisticated surveys but rely on basic demographic information provided by the leasing agent.

The leasing agent must understand the shopping center's trade area before prospective tenants are approached. Understanding the trade area will enable the leasing agent to identify which retailers are likely candidates for the shopping center and to contact only those that have a high probability of leasing space in the center and being successful there. The knowledgeable leasing agent will not waste time pursuing prospects whose customer base is not represented in the shopping center's trade area or whose store in the center would likely fail.

Defining the Trade Area.   First the boundaries of the trade area are defined, and the population and competition within the trade area are analyzed. This information will be used to determine which categories of merchants are over- and under-represented in the trade area. It will also assist in positioning the shopping center in the marketplace. From this information base, it is possible to determine a tenant mix, solicit categories of retailers, and identify specific prospective tenants.

A shopping center's trade area is the geographic area where most of its customers live, work, or play. The customers for a video rental store will live in the immediate neighborhood. The trade area of a delicatessen in a downtown office building may be within a radius of only a few blocks because its primary customers work there. The customers of an ice cream store in a specialty shopping center or in a resort community are tourists and visitors to the area. The majority of the customers in the trade area of a typical suburban shopping center live in that area. A rule of thumb for determining trade area is to draw a circle around the shopping center. The radius of the circle for a neighborhood center would be two to five miles, while the radius for a regional mall would be eight to ten miles. This is only a guideline, however; the actual boundaries of the trade area for a particular shopping center must be determined from a specific investigation.

The boundaries of a trade area may be defined by natural and manmade barriers that may prevent, hinder, or delay a person from traveling to the shopping center. An example of a *natural barrier* is a river that can only be crossed at a bridge several miles from the shopping center. That distant crossing may discourage people on the other side of the river from patronizing the shopping center. *Manmade barriers,* on the other hand, may be more difficult to pinpoint—for example, a change of property types. A large industrial development a mile from the shopping center may be a detriment because consumers living on the other side of the industrial park may not want to drive through a busy industrial area to get to a shopping center.

The primary barrier that defines a trade area, however, is the location of the competition. If two shopping centers having similar anchor and shop tenants are located two miles apart, one boundary of their respective trade areas will be approximately midway between the two centers. A neighborhood shopping center anchored by a supermarket and a super drug store in a heavily populated suburb may have a trade area of two to three miles in all directions while the trade area for a similar shopping center in a small rural community may extend 10 to 20 miles. The trade area for a regional mall in Orange County may extend less than five miles in some directions because of overlapping trade areas due to the proliferation of malls in the county, while that for a regional mall in a rural location in the Midwest may extend more than 100 miles.

A shopping center may have different trade areas, especially if it has different types of anchors. A supermarket with multiple competitors in the area may draw customers from an area within only four miles from the shopping center, while the trade area of a home improvement center with fewer competitors may extend eight miles from the shopping center. Small shop tenants will have different trade areas, too. A drycleaner's trade area may extend three miles while the trade area for a sporting goods store may have a radius of 10 miles. The trade area of a shopping center may be defined in terms of the center's sales and divided into three zones. The primary zone will account for 70–75 percent of the center's sales, and the secondary zone for 20–25 percent; the tertiary trade area zone, which is the most difficult area to define, will account for the remaining sales.

Creating a Demographic Profile. A demographic analysis of the primary, secondary, and tertiary trade area zones usually includes the following data.

- *Population size* and a projection of future growth or decline. Changes over the preceding twenty years may indicate future trends that need to be studied.
- *Family or household composition* including its size and the ages of its members. The racial and ethnic composition of the area are also included.
- *Homeownership* as compared to rental housing. The number of owners versus the number of renters is an important consideration for many retailers, especially those dealing in furniture and housewares (e.g., carpets and draperies). The cost of housing may be an indicator of relative affluence and availability of disposable income.
- *Household income,* which is a critical consideration because most retailers market to a specific income level. Household income is the primary indicator of disposable income.
- *Employment data* including types of employment and specific employers. Buying habits can be related to type of employment, which is also related to income. The primary source of employment and the kinds of jobs available are important, as is dominance by a single company or a single industry.

Specific demographic information for very small geographic areas can be obtained from commercial sources (see appendix E, References and Resources). In addition, it is sometimes necessary or appropriate to evaluate the psychographic profile of the trade area. For a large center (e.g., a regional mall), the psychological outlook of the population of shoppers can be a negative factor. If the population is older and affluent, shoppers may be less interested in fashion trends, or area residents may have a very strong allegiance to established stores or to a smaller (e.g., community) shopping center. The data on population size, income, etc., may support a particular size center, but the numbers mean nothing if most of the potential customers will not shop at the new center.

Analyze the Shopping Center

Critical to the development and successful execution of the marketing and leasing plan is understanding of the strengths and weaknesses of the shopping center. The property manager and the leasing agent must know how the shopping center measures up to its competition. They also must understand which features of the shopping center meet the needs of prospective tenants, which areas of the shopping center are deficient, and which of those deficiencies can be corrected. This analysis should include a review of the location and design of the shopping center and an assessment of the desirability of each space, as well as traffic counts, lease restrictions, and the tenant mix.

A well-known axiom is that the three most important things in real estate are location, location, and location. This applies directly to the success of shopping centers. There are three key components to a good shopping center location—demographic profile, visibility, and accessibility. (All three of these factors of location have been described in detail elsewhere in this book.) Visibility and accessibility are also design criteria. Traffic counts are a measure of the viability of a location and a factor that permits comparison of different shopping centers. They are also related to visibility and access.

Traffic counts are estimated in two ways—from the number of automobiles driving by the shopping center and from the number of people visiting the shopping center. Strip centers usually rely primarily on the number of automobiles that pass the shopping center each day. Comparison figures should be available from a local governmental agency. Most municipalities count traffic on their main thoroughfares fairly regularly, at least every two years. At some malls the number of automobiles entering the parking lot is counted each day. If the average number of people in an automobile entering the parking lot is known, the number of people visiting the mall each day, each week, and each month can be calculated.

When the numbers of automobiles passing by the shopping center and its competition are known, the shopping center can be compared to the competition. Another variable related to traffic is ease of entry into the parking lot. If traffic is passing at high speed or if left turns are not allowed, it may not be convenient to enter the parking lot from that thoroughfare.

Layout and design are considered next. In a strip center, visibility from the street is critical. A high traffic count may be meaningless if the stores are not visible from the street. When a shopping center is built on sloping land, the parking lot may be on higher ground than the buildings in the back area. If the buildings are several feet below street level, they may not be visible from the street. Visibility is also restricted when a shopping center is built perpendicular to the street. The ideal layout for a strip center is to have all of the stores facing the street. The layout and design of the shopping center must not impede visibility of or access to the tenants' spaces. Visibility in an enclosed mall is related to the mall walkways or corridors and any setbacks or obstacles that are present. Temporary booths or kiosks and interior landscaping elements (skylights above planters filled with tall trees or shrubbery) can reduce visibility of individual shop spaces.

An important part of visibility is signage. The shopping center's sign criteria must provide for tenants to display signs that are easily seen from both the parking lot and the street or from the walkway in a mall. The shopping center itself should have an identification sign that is easy to read and creates an image for the whole.

Each store space, especially those that are vacant, should be evaluated for its location, size, frontage, and depth to determine which categories of tenants are probable candidates to lease it.

The first consideration with respect to store location is visibility—from the street, from the parking lot, from the mall corridor, from wherever the majority of the center's customers spend most of their time while at the shopping center. The next consideration is the amount of traffic that walks by the space—whether the space is next to an anchor tenant (a major traffic draw) or in a low traffic area. The third consideration, accessibility, will be defined by the presence of any actual or perceived barriers. In a strip shopping center, a "No Parking" zone in the immediate area would severely limit access.

Store size is one of the primary criteria of leasability from a tenant's perspective. Each type of retail business has a size range in which it can operate successfully. Doughnut and muffin shops usually average 1,164 square feet of GLA in a range of 980 to 1,620 square feet. The typical card and gift shop may have 1,200 square feet of GLA and range from 839 to 3,280 square feet, while a barber shop may have 898 square feet of GLA and range from 494 to 1,393 square feet. The size of a space will indicate which types of tenants can occupy it and which cannot.

The next consideration is store frontage. Tenants want as much frontage as possible—for visibility. As a rule of thumb, the ratio of the frontage (width) to the depth of the store should be one to three (1:3); a store 20 feet wide should have a depth of 60 feet (20:60 = 1:3). This ratio has been reduced continually since the 1960s, when the typical store depth was 100 feet, and the ratio was one to five (1:5). In the late 1970s and the 1980s, the ideal store depth was thought to be 80 feet—a ratio of one to four (1:4). The change in the ratio of width to depth has resulted from most categories of retailers downsizing their stores. These merchants discovered that they could generate equivalent or greater levels of sales in smaller-sized stores. Such downsizing results in a lower occupancy cost and a more efficient store operation. Part of the reduction in size comes from the fact that merchants no longer need large storage rooms; most, if not all, of their merchandise is displayed on the sales floor, and computerized control of store inventories allows for frequent deliveries of merchandise as it is needed. In addition, many retailers now merchandise their entire cube—floor, walls, and ceiling—while in the past, only the floor area was merchandised.

A few categories of stores have increased in size, however. A notable example is the supermarket. While the typical supermarket of the 1960s and 1970s was smaller than 30,000 square feet of GLA, the state-of-the-art supermarket of the 1990s occupies more than 50,000 square feet. A shop tenant that has increased in size is the video rental store. In the early 1980s, they were typically 1,200–1,500 square feet of GLA; in the 1990s, they are as large as 7,500 square feet.

It is notable that, in downsizing, retailers want the same amount of front-age but less depth. In strip centers, stores more than 75 feet deep have lim-ited prospective tenants. The ideal store size in a strip center is 20–25 feet wide and 55–70 feet deep. Most tenants in a strip center will occupy less than 2,000 square feet of GLA.

Next in importance is store configuration. The ideal shape is a rectangle; other configurations can create problems in store layout and merchandising. In particular, pie-shaped and L-shaped stores have limited tenant prospects.

When evaluating the size and configuration of store spaces, opportunities should be sought to change those spaces that are undesirable. In particular, larger spaces can be subdivided—e.g., a 3,600-square-foot space may be more easily leased if it can be divided into two 1,800-square-foot spaces. If a variety store operator in a 10,000-square-foot space wants to downsize to 6,500 square feet, the remainder may be more leasable as two spaces (one 1,500- and one 2,000-square-foot store).

In many shopping centers, lease restrictions may prevent leasing to spe-cific categories of tenants. A restaurant's exclusive may preclude leasing to another restaurant. An anchor tenant's lease may restrict specific uses within a stated distance from its premises. For example, a supermarket will not want long-term parkers in its parking areas, and its restrictions may preclude leas-ing to such tenant types as offices, movie theaters, bowling alleys, billiards halls, and health spas. A department store may restrict kiosk tenants within 100 feet of its mall entrance. In addition to lease restrictions, the shopping center may have to comply with municipal zoning restrictions that prohibit certain categories of tenants.

Analyze the Tenant Mix

The last item to evaluate is the shopping center's tenant mix. This analysis will indicate the shopping center's weaknesses—which tenants or categories of tenants no longer fit and which areas or portions of the shopping center are having problems. The importance of compatibility with other tenants and with the center's image is discussed in chapter 8. In this chapter, analysis of tenant mix is focused on measurement of tenants' success.

A useful approach to evaluating individual tenants is analysis of their sales per square foot. Each tenant's sales should be compared to the national aver-ages and to the sales levels of other tenants in the same retailing category for the type of center. A good source for this information is *Dollars & Cents of Shopping Centers,* which is issued every three years by the Urban Land Insti-tute and provides data on sales per square foot for hundreds of categories of tenants (along with other specific types of tenant information) that lease space in neighborhood, community, regional, and super regional shopping centers. (The information shown in exhibit 9.4 is derived from that publica-tion.) Separate reports are included for both the United States and Canada.

Other ULI publications that compile data on specialty centers are listed in appendix E, References and Resources.

When each tenant's sales are compared to the national average for the category, sales that are significantly below the national averages may be interpreted several ways. There may be too many similar stores in the shopping center—or in the area generally—or there may not be a sustained demand for the particular merchandise. Another possibility is that the tenant may not be reporting its sales accurately. However, the most likely explanation is that the tenant is a poor merchant.

When there are several tenants in a category, each tenant's sales should be compared to those of similar tenants in the center. From this information, a ranking based on sales per square foot can be developed, and the total sales per square foot for the category can be determined. This is another indicator of which tenants are performing well and which are not. If all the tenants' sales are substantially above the national average, this may indicate the potential for one or more additional tenants in this category. For instance, if the sales for the three jewelers in a regional mall range from $635 to $1,050 per square foot, and the category average for the mall is $870 compared to a national average of $452.33, there is probably sufficient sales potential to support an additional jewelry store. Conversely, if the furniture store sales in a community shopping center are $63.50 per square foot and the national average is $102.87, either there is limited demand for furniture or the tenant is a poor merchant. When the sales analysis indicates there is limited or no demand for specific merchandise or there are too many similar stores in the shopping center or area, retailers in these categories should not be approached as part of the prospecting.

An analysis of tenants' sales in different portions of the shopping center will indicate areas where traffic may be limited, merchants are not competent in selling their merchandise, or the wrong types of merchants are in place. If a mall has an unanchored wing that receives considerably less traffic than the other areas of the mall, most retail tenants located there will not do well. The best tenants for such areas are destination tenants—e.g., tuxedo or formal wear rentals, specialty restaurants, travel agents.

The strengths and weaknesses in the tenant mix will be important factors in seeking lease renewals. Lease renewals should be planned in advance, and to do so, each tenant's lease term must be reviewed. It is often helpful to list each tenant's lease expiration date and options next to the individual space on a plot plan of the shopping center. Notes on the plot plan should also indicate those spaces where tenants are not expected to renew, the landlord will not offer a lease renewal, or there are vacancies. Tenants whose sales are poor can be approached for an early lease termination or buy-out provided their space is readily leasable. Certainly, each shop tenant whose lease is expiring within a year should be contacted. (Lease renewals and buy-outs are discussed in more detail later in this chapter.)

E X H I B I T   9.4

Example Sales Data for Community Shopping Centers*

Tenant Classification (Food, Food Service)	GLA in Sq Ft			Sales per Sq Ft†		
	Lower Decile	Median	Upper Decile	Top Ten Percent	Median	Top Ten Percent
Bakery	492	1,358	2,484	378.82	189.47	638.26
National Chain						
Local Chain		1,283			197.15	
Independent	469	1,300	2,706	414.91	182.66	716.03
Candy and Nuts	409	900	1,836	356.20	165.11	465.87
National Chain		738			207.09	
Local Chain	606	992	2,207		165.11	
Independent		624			142.20	
Health Food	1,041	1,658	2,160	245.18	132.00	356.89
National Chain	1,201	1,679	2,042		110.12	
Local Chain	229	1,658	2,000		151.36	
Independent	1,212	1,734	2,481	269.66	170.97	330.54
Supermarket	15,009	23,828	28,455	479.08	266.92	656.88
National Chain	19,600	25,000	29,000	470.64	282.83	552.38
Local Chain	17,580	25,385	27,980	450.34	266.92	797.43
Independent		12,824			237.99	
Superstore	32,000	37,430	52,114	562.14	346.95	743.55
National Chain	32,036	36,617	52,184	590.60	330.49	842.75
Local Chain	32,554	39,795	47,178	520.19	365.06	552.11
Independent						
Restaurant (no liquor)	1,220	2,807	6,060	258.09	135.12	350.27
National Chain	2,308	3,900	6,080	299.40	176.22	398.45
Local Chain	1,270	2,475	6,291	272.21	135.02	305.27
Independent	1,200	2,400	5,466	241.93	111.98	286.40
Restaurant (liquor)	1,750	3,537	7,321	317.51	138.28	501.99
National Chain	2,921	5,000	9,240	411.92	163.26	478.37
Local Chain	1,800	3,500	6,571	281.21	153.00	314.56
Independent	1,614	3,150	6,375	257.48	126.66	561.53

*Medians are the items midway between the highest and lowest reported values; lower and upper deciles are values between which 80% of all values fall.

†Sales per square foot for the top 10% and top 2% of tenants reporting are shown in addition to the median.

From data reported in *Dollars and Cents of Shopping Centers: 1990* (Washington, D.C.: ULI—the Urban Land Institute, 1990). Used with permission.

Establish Market Rental Rates

Real estate is leased at a market rental rate, which is the most probable rent a property owner can expect to receive for a vacant space exposed to the open market. Market rent is similar to fair market value. The property manager or leasing agent must determine the range of market rental rates for the shopping center. Once the range of rates is determined, each space can be priced on the basis of its location within the shopping center and its size, depth, configuration, and visibility. Other factors to be considered are adjacent merchants and design-related features that may enhance or detract from the perceived value of a particular space.

The market rental rate range is determined by comparing the shopping center to its competition. Each competitive shopping center should be visited and a list of its features compiled. Use of a survey form (exhibit 9.5) will expedite collection of the necessary comparison data.

The form used should provide spaces for information on the size of the shopping center, a list of anchor tenants, the number of shop spaces, existing vacancies, asking and deal-making rental rates, tenant or pass-through charges, and the condition of the shopping center. In exhibit 9.5, the information on the subject shopping center would be shown on the top line, and information on the competition would follow. Notes regarding location may be listed under the heading "Comments." The location of each shopping center in the survey should also be indicated on a map of the area and the map attached to the survey form.

Some data can be gathered easily, merely by observation. The person conducting the survey should drive through the area looking for competing shopping centers. Once located, each competing center should be inspected. The sizes of vacant stores can be estimated by pacing off the front of the store (width) and counting the rows of ceiling tiles (depth). If there is no "For Lease" sign or the name of the property management company is not shown, one of the tenants can be visited and asked for this information. While touring the area, all "For Lease" signs with "Shopping Center Coming Soon" messages should be noted. The property manager can also inquire at the local building department whether any shopping center plans have been submitted for approval.

The leasing agent or the property manager at each property on the survey list and each proposed shopping center should be contacted by telephone to arrange personal visits. The best way to obtain desired information about the competitor is to introduce oneself, state the purpose of the call or visit, and then share rental information on the subject property. The following is an example.

"The asking rate at my shopping center is $18 per square foot; we're making deals between $16.50 and $17.25 per square foot; we've been giving one month free

E X H I B I T   9.5

Example Shopping Center Survey Form

Center Data				Majors		Vacancy	Asking Rts	Deal-making Rts	Rental Info							Condition					Tenants	Comments
Center	Age	Number Shops	Sq.Ft.	PK Lot	Majors				%	Tax	Ins	CAM	CPI	HVAC	Other	P/L	Bldg	Area	Access			

Reprinted with permission from Alexander, Alan A., and Muhlebach, Richard F.: *Managing and Leasing Commercial Properties* (New York: John Wiley & Sons, Inc., 1990).

rent for each year of the lease, not to exceed three months free; and we have an annual CPI adjustment, a percentage rate, and tenant charges of $2.85 per square foot per year."

Asking and deal-making rents, standard concessions, and other specifics—examples of the information being sought—should be readily available. When information is provided up front, the other person is more likely to share reciprocal information. In this context, it is important to distinguish between asking and deal-making rates. If only one rate is stated, it is usually the asking rate. It is also important to find out the sizes of the spaces to which the quoted rates apply.

When the survey is completed, the information should be analyzed and the subject property compared to the competition. Two of the most important features to be compared are the locations and the anchor tenants. Analysis of comparable rents is an art, not a science. There are many variables that can affect rental rates—e.g., access to the shopping center, visibility of small shops, overall condition (maintenance), and the location, size, and configuration of each vacancy—and these can only be discovered by visiting the shopping center. The first time a market survey is conducted, it may take several days. Once the locations and leasing agents of all the competing shopping centers are known, subsequent surveys can usually be conducted in less than a day.

After the shopping center has been compared to the competition, a range of market rental rates should be apparent. Each space in the subject center is then priced within the market rental rate range based on its location, visibility, size, depth, and configuration.

PROSPECTING FOR TENANTS

The main activity of the marketing and leasing program is prospecting for tenants. This activity will consume more of the leasing agent's time than any other. It is the critical element that will determine the success of the marketing and leasing program.

Leasing Information Package

In order for prospective tenants to decide whether or not to lease specific space, they will need to know certain facts about the shopping center, its trade area, and its tenant mix. This can best be provided in a leasing information package. All the materials should be professionally prepared in a manner that will reflect the quality of the shopping center and the professionalism of the leasing agent. Following is a list of several items to consider for a leasing package, bearing in mind that not every shopping center will require all of them.

- Letter
- Brochure
- Layout
- Tenant list
- Aerial photo
- Map
- Demographic profile
- Traffic counts
- Sales information
- Calendar of promotional events
- Unique features

One particularly useful item is a letter that will catch the attention of the prospect. It should be tailored to the prospect's business and focus on the issues that prospect considers important. For example, letters sent to all the ice cream parlors in the area may focus on the proximity of the center to schools, emphasizing the numbers of children and young families in the trade area. The letter may be an announcement of space availability or a more specific invitation to visit the center. Given today's computer and word-processing technology, any such letter can be personalized and focused specifically.

A brochure can be elaborate, with several pages including photographs and printed in color, or it can be a simple one-page handout printed in only two colors. Usually only large malls need elaborate brochures; a handout is adequate for most strip centers. The brochure should include a rendering or photograph of the shopping center, along with demographic and traffic count information, an indication of current tenants, and a layout showing comparative store sizes. A locator map is also a nice touch. It may be advisable to provide a separate scale-drawing layout of the shopping center that shows the size and location of vacant spaces in relation to the anchor tenant, other tenants, and the street.

So that prospects can determine whether they are compatible with the present tenant mix—and vice versa—a list of anchor and shop tenants should be provided. If leases for specific spaces have not been signed at the time the promotional materials are being prepared, an indication of the merchandise category (e.g., supermarket, national chain jeweler) is best substituted for a specific tenant's name.

An aerial photo is a great leasing tool because it vividly shows the access to the shopping center and the relationship of the shopping center to major arterial roads and freeways. It also shows the density of houses and apartment buildings in the immediate area.

For prospective tenants who are not familiar with the location of the shopping center, a map showing freeways, major streets, and other major buildings in the area can be extremely helpful. It not only serves to locate the property but also gives a perspective on the trade area and the competition— or lack of it.

The most critical information to aid a prospective tenant's decision to lease space at a shopping center is a demographic profile of the trade area. Typically, information provided on the residents within a three-, a four-, and a ten-mile radius of the shopping center includes the total population of the area (broken down statistically into age, sex, and ethnic groups), the average family or household size and income level, and the percentage of single-family homeownership. Demographic information can be purchased from research firms, and the source should be included with the information in the leasing package. (This was discussed in analysis of the trade area earlier in this chapter.)

The number of automobiles passing by and the number of people visiting the shopping center are important indicators of business (retail sales) potential. Local governmental agencies and chambers of commerce are possible sources for such traffic counts, although specific counts may have to be done by direct observation. (Traffic counts were discussed earlier in this chapter in the context of shopping center analysis.)

A retailer considers a location based on the potential sales that can be generated there. If the shopping center's sales are strong, they should be included in the leasing package. Figures should be listed for the entire shopping center and for specific categories of tenants that are present in multiples (e.g., five shoe stores in a regional center), but individual tenants' sales should never be indicated.

A calendar of promotional activities sponsored by the merchants' association or marketing fund should be included. Photos of successful merchandising, sales, and promotional events show that the landlord is interested in aggressively marketing the shopping center. Copies of newspaper articles about the center or its events, especially those containing endorsements by prominent citizens or community officials, are good additions, too.

It is also a good selling point to identify specific benefits of locating in the shopping center. Any unique features such as a bus stop in front of the property, or a major employer or a school being within walking distance of the shopping center, should be included in the leasing information package.

Individual components of the leasing package will vary in how long they will be accurate and, therefore, useful. As some protection against liability for erroneous information, it is wise to include a disclaimer on such items as brochures, layouts, tenant lists, etc. A simple statement—i.e., information subject to change—is usually adequate. Legal counsel can advise on the need for specific disclaimers and provide appropriate language.

How to "package" this leasing information should also be given some thought. A promotional package for lease-up of a new regional center may warrant special design and packaging by an advertising or marketing firm. For a less-intensive program (e.g., limited turnover in an established center of any size), a folder with pockets or an envelope may be used. The packaging will depend on the number of component items and their size—and the funds available to spend on them. On the other hand, it may be desirable to provide only some basic information on the first visit to a prospective tenant, and if the prospect is interested, present the remainder as a follow-up package. This allows the manager or leasing agent to better tailor the leasing information to the prospect's needs. It goes without saying that the leasing agent's business card should be provided to all prospects, regardless of whether they receive a comprehensive leasing package.

Choose the Best Method

Prospecting—generating interest on the part of prospective tenants—may take several forms, including canvassing, advertising, working the brokerage community, and using various leasing directories. A direct approach can be used once a specific prospect has been identified; however, identifying prospects may require indirect approaches.

Canvassing. Direct contact with prospective tenants is called canvassing. Cold calling is time-consuming but often very effective. Not every retail business in the community is a prospective tenant; the leasing agent should canvass only those categories of tenants that are needed in the shopping center. Although more people can be contacted by phone, telephone canvassing is generally not as effective as personal contact but is often used as follow-up to a direct-mail campaign.

Current tenants in the shopping center should be canvassed first. One or more of them may be interested in expanding or in opening another type of business. They or their associates and colleagues may know other merchants who are looking for space in a shopping center. Competing shopping centers are always canvassing others' tenants; leasing agents should not forget to canvass their own.

Advertising. Advertising is an indirect approach to prospecting because it will reach a wide range of audiences, not all of which include prospective tenants. However, successful advertising will bring prospects to the center. In reaching out to "all retailers," it has the potential to connect with specific merchants who might not have been anticipated as prospects. Advertising as such may take many different forms.

- *Signage* is one of the most effective leasing tools because thousands of people pass by a shopping center each day, and some of them will be retailers and service providers. *On-site leasing signs* should be prominently displayed near the street. Large paper or posterboard "For Lease" signs can be installed inside the window of each vacancy. The name and phone number of the leasing agent is the most important information on these signs. *Billboards* or very large signs are usually used only for new shopping centers or those soon to be under construction. A simple presentation focused on center identification and inclusion of the leasing agent's name and phone number is best. *Project signs* are often placed on site prior to and during construction and may be incorporated in the materials forming the protective enclosure. Such signage usually includes a rendering of the shopping center, a list of the anchor tenants, and the names of the project participants—lender, developer, architect, general contractor—as well as the leasing agent's name and phone number prominently displayed.

- *Direct mailing* of a flyer (e.g., the one-page 8½-by-11-inch brochure already mentioned) to selected categories of tenants is often an effective way to market a shopping center. Flyers can be mailed to different categories of tenants each day or each week. A response rate of 1–2 percent is considered good in direct-mail campaigns.
- *Radio and television ads* are seldom effective in advertising retail space for lease. However, if the merchants' association or marketing fund is using radio or television spot ads, inclusion of a space-available tag in some of the ads is a possibility.
- *Print advertising* can be very effective. Leasing agents report mixed results from *classified ads* in newspapers. When they are used, it is best to be very specific about the location of the shopping center and the size of the space available. *Display advertising* in a trade magazine (e.g., *Women's Wear Daily*) may be effective for targeting a specific merchandise category. There is a trade or professional organization for just about every category in retailing, and most of these organizations publish a magazine. The local public library may have copies of the resources used by advertising agencies; retailers may be willing to share copies of their trade publications for examination.

Other methods to include in a leasing marketing program are publicity and public relations. While publicity is not paid advertising, it does serve to advertise the shopping center. A shopping center has numerous publicity stories throughout the development process as well as after operations are established. Local and trade media representatives can be invited to attend occasions or they can be sent announcements (before) or reports (after) the events. In particular, press releases can announce:

- Plans for the new development (or rehabilitation)
- Ground breaking
- Signing of anchor leases

- Grand opening (or re-opening) festivities
- New tenancies
- Changes in management personnel

The manager should also plan to take photographs of any ground-breaking or grand-opening ceremonies. These can be duplicated inexpensively and sent along with the press release describing the event.

The manager should also monitor retail advertising by paying attention to retailer's advertisements when reading the newspaper, listening to the radio, or watching television. Monitoring advertising is one way the leasing agent may become aware of prospective tenants in the area. Aggressive local advertisers may be looking for additional locations; others may be seeking opportunities to expand into the area.

Working the Brokerage Community.   The property manager and leasing agent should keep the brokerage community aware of the shopping center and encourage brokers to bring prospective tenants to the shopping center. Many retailers are represented by leasing agents, and they may prefer to approach the brokerage community. The property manager and the leasing agent should take retail brokers out to breakfast or lunch regularly to discuss the shopping center. Periodically mailing a flyer to brokers will keep them informed about vacancies, new tenants, marketing activities, and tenants' success stories.

Other Methods of Prospecting.   In addition to advertising and working with brokers, the leasing team should explore other resources. During its annual convention in May, the International Council of Shopping Centers (ICSC) conducts a three-day deal-making session during which retailers, developers, and property owners meet to discuss leasing deals. In addition, there are several directories of retail tenants that are excellent resources for direct-mail campaigns or telephone canvassing. The retailers are commonly listed by category, and the listings include a variety of information—e.g., the tenant's name, address, and telephone number; the number of locations already established; the type of shopping center preferred and geographic areas sought, and the name of the leasing representative. *Leasing Opportunities,* published annually by ICSC, is just one example. Several other, similar tenant directories are listed in appendix E, References and Resources.

Locally, telephone directory Yellow Pages and the chamber of commerce should be useful sources. Retail trade suppliers (e.g., coin laundry and restaurant equipment vendors; merchandise wholesalers) are other possible resources. In particular, they are likely to know which businesses are successful and which ones are interested in expanding.

Successful merchants often want to establish additional locations. Personal networking with property managers and leasing agents from other shopping centers can be a source for those types of leads. Such contacts can be established and reinforced at meetings of professional organizations— local chapters of the Institute of Real Estate Management usually meet monthly; ICSC idea exchange sessions are held periodically.

Leasing agents should be encouraged to maintain their own files of tenant prospects, preferably organizing them by merchandise categories. Even though a prospect may not be interested in locating at or appropriate for the tenant mix of a particular center when approached initially, that merchant may be an ideal prospect for the same center at another time or for a different center.

EVALUATING PROSPECTIVE TENANTS

The objective of prospecting is to identify and negotiate leases with merchants who will succeed in the shopping center. One way to help assure any tenant's success is to be selective in the *qualification* process in the first place. A prospective tenant for any type of property is evaluated to determine its ability to fulfill the terms of the lease, especially the payment of rent and other charges. Retail tenants are also evaluated on their ability as merchants and their potential to benefit the shopping center.

Usually when a tenant moves out during a lease term, it is because its business has failed. The failure may be due to a lack of sufficient capital, or because the merchant did not have the necessary business experience. The tenant that fails usually owes back rent. If the tenant files for bankruptcy or has no assets, the delinquent rent will not be recoverable. A tenant's failure is costly to the landlord, not only because of the rent lost on the broken lease, but also because of the rental income lost while the space is vacant and the extra expenses incurred for re-leasing. *Downtime*—the period a space is vacant until another tenant takes occupancy and commences paying rent—can range from a few weeks to many months. Re-leasing expenses include commissions in addition to the cost to clean the premises and, possibly, the costs to demolish the prior tenant's improvements or to construct new ones.

The first concern in the evaluation of a prospective tenant is its financial strength. The property manager must be assured that the prospect has sufficient capital to start business at a new location. This includes proper inventory levels, funds for advertising and promotions, and a reserve to carry the business until it is profitable. If the prospect is part of a chain or a franchisee, there may be additional resources available. However, many novice retailers believe their stores will be successful from the day they open for business, and that is not realistic. In fact, it can take between one and three years for a new business to become successful. Often the owner of a new business may be unable to draw a salary during the first year of operation.

The prospect that is a new business must have sufficient capital to support both personal needs and business operations until the business is profitable.

The prospect should be asked to submit a *financial statement* for the business. If the company is new or has a weak financial statement, the manager should request a personal financial statement from the owner or owners. Two important items on a financial statement are liquid assets and monthly obligations. A personal financial statement may show a fairly good net worth, but the assets may consist solely of the value of a residence and selected items of personal property, neither of which is easily convertible to cash. It is important for a prospect to have sufficient liquid assets (e.g., bank savings accounts, stocks, bonds, etc.) to adequately support the business.

A *credit report* should be obtained on the company; these are available from Dun and Bradstreet. In the case of a new business, a credit report should be obtained on the owner as well. Credit references listed by the prospect should always be checked.

Once the prospect's financial capability has been verified, the owner's efficacy as a merchant is evaluated. This assessment should be based on such things as merchandise type and price, sales figures—total volume, dollars per square foot, trends—and present operation (store appearance, efficiency, and reputation; management procedures, and advertising plan).

A tenant's *sales volume* will indicate its ability to draw traffic to the shopping center, operate successfully, and pay rent—and whether it will pay percentage rent. The sales volume at the prospect's current store should be evaluated; if the prospect operates other stores, the sales volumes from those stores should be reviewed, too. However, sales volumes alone can be misleading. Sales should also be evaluated based on *dollars per square foot*. A $500,000 sales volume may be good or poor, depending on the size of the store. In a 2,000-square-foot store, annual sales of a half million dollars is an acceptable level equal to $250 per square foot. In a 20,000-square-foot store, the same annual sales volume would be very weak at $25 per square foot. For a new business, there will be no sales volume to evaluate, so the prospect should be requested to provide a sales projection. The prospect's projected annual sales volume should be calculated as dollars per square foot and compared to the national averages in *Dollars & Cents of Shopping Centers* (see exhibit 9.4). If the projected sales are significantly below the national average for the category, the prospect has little chance to succeed; if the projected sales are significantly above the national average, they may reflect unrealistic expectations.

The next consideration is the *merchandise* itself. So-called trendy merchandise can have been very popular the past year or two and still be just a passing fad. The classic boom-and-bust fad item was the hula hoop in the 1950s. Examples from the 1980s include take-and-bake pizza, video arcades, and tanning salons, which were popular for only a few years in some parts of the United States.

A visit to the prospect's present store (multiple stores if the prospect is a chain) should yield answers to other questions about the prospect's business. In a shopping center, each store's *appearance* reflects on the center as a whole. The manager should observe how merchandise is displayed and how the store fixtures are arranged. An important consideration is *efficiency* of operation because that is a measure of success. In the case of a new business, the prospect's design plans for the store should be reviewed. (If the prospect is not sure how the store should be designed, visits to similar stores that are successful should be encouraged.)

Few retailers have a poor *reputation* overall; those that acquire a negative image usually do not stay in business long. However, some stores have a specific reputation for service, quality, or value. For example, Nordstrom, a Seattle-based specialty department store, is nationally known for its customer service and quality of merchandise. Wal-mart and Target stores are known for value pricing; McDonald's is known for consistent quality. The reputation of the store will be reflected on the reputation of the shopping center.

The property manager should also review the prospect's *management* and *advertising* plans, including proposed inventory levels, sales policies, sales projections, operating expenses, staffing, and an advertising schedule and budget. This review should reveal whether the merchant understands the proposed business and has realistic expectations for its success.

Finally, the prospect's business must be appropriate to and compatible with the shopping center's tenant mix (e.g., a tavern is not compatible with the tenant mix of a fashion shopping center; a discount shoe store is not an appropriate tenant in a high-fashion mall). Appropriateness and compatibility should be addressed in the earliest stages of planning the tenant mix. That process determines which categories of merchants will be approached (see also chapters 2 and 8).

In order to evaluate prospective tenants properly, the property manager must understand the fundamentals of retailing. Merchandise must be priced to be profitable, and it must be displayed to be sold. For different categories of merchandise there are differing approaches to doing business. The successful retailer will do business the right way for its particular merchandise and its particular market. Thus, the store owner's or manager's retailing experience will be an important factor. The property manager must also understand the how and why of retailing to be able to judge a prospect's potential to succeed. The most important considerations in this regard are addressed in appendix A, Retailing Basics.

NEGOTIATING THE LEASE

The prospecting and qualification processes naturally lead into lease negotiations. The lease provides tenant and landlord with specific rights and obligations. The standard form lease the owner (landlord) offers is just a starting point because every provision in the lease is negotiable. However, most of the items that are negotiated specifically are provisions that affect the net operating income (NOI) of the shopping center (e.g., rental rates and pass-through charges) or modify payments made by the tenant (e.g., payback of a tenant improvement allowance). The size of the space and the nature of the prospect (strong national retailer, unique local shop retailer, new business) will determine the amount of compromise required from both parties.

The discussion that follows covers some general points about lease negotiations as they apply to most shopping center tenants—i.e., the numerous shop tenants. There are only a few anchor tenants in a shopping center—sometimes only one—and negotiations with prospective anchor tenants require a more sophisticated approach. In particular, anchor tenants will be sought prior to development of a new shopping center because their commitment to a lease will help expedite construction financing. Pads and outlot parcels are common in large shopping centers, and the leasing arrangements for them require special consideration. When a food court is included in a new shopping center or added to an old one, there are additional considerations. The food vendors may pay two types of CAM charges—one for the food court common area and one for the common area of the center—and their operations may be subject to constraints related to public health issues. Their rents and other charges are also calculated differently than those for regular (non-food) tenants elsewhere in the center. Many shopping centers rent space to temporary tenants, and the rules regarding their leasing agreements are somewhat different because of the short lease terms and the small amounts of space involved. Many of these differences are pointed out specifically in the sections that follow.

Monetary Concessions

The lease document (see chapter 10) usually includes separate provisions for payment of minimum or base rent and percentage rent, proration of pass-through expenses, payment for improvements to the tenant's leased space, and any other amounts that are to be paid by the tenant to the landlord. When the lease term is longer than one year—retail leases in shopping centers are usually for several years—the lease commonly includes a provision to increase the base rent over the term of the lease. Although a specific percentage may be stated, it is also common to tie the increase in base rent to an economic indicator such as the Consumer Price Index (CPI). It is these provisions that are negotiable within the leasing parameters established by the landlord as discussed earlier in this chapter. Negotiation requires agreement and compromise. Often the compromise is in fact a concession on the part of the landlord. Every leasing concession has a cost, and many specific concessions will reduce the amount of income (NOI) generated by the property. Because any reduction in NOI affects estimated market value (see chapter 4), the costs and benefits of each concession must be evaluated—not only for their impact on the deal being negotiated but also for their long-term effects on the shopping center's cash flow and value.

The leasing agent must calculate the financial impact of the specific lease terms that will be offered and any concessions that may be made *before* they are actually negotiated. What follows is a review of some of these cost calculations.

Minimum Rent. The cost of concessions provided in the minimum or *base rent* is easy to calculate. If a desirable prospect is provided with a reduction in base rent to secure the tenancy, the cost of the concession is determined by subtracting the actual rental rate from the projected rental rate. If the base rent is quoted as a monthly rate, it is multiplied by twelve to compute the annual cost (loss). If the rate applies throughout successive years of a long lease term, multiplication by the number of years will yield the "total cost." Often the benefit to the shopping center from having the prospect as a tenant will outweigh the cost of the concession. For example, a successful and well-respected merchant whose business is a major traffic draw will often attract other retailers as tenants, and many of them will pay a higher rental rate. In such a situation, the rent achieved from being able to lease vacant spaces sooner can offset the concession granted to the major draw.

Free Rent. The cost of free rent is the amount of rent *not* received during the free-rent period.

Free Pass-Through Charges. The amount paid by a tenant for specific operating expenses that are commonly passed through to tenants is negotiable. Pass-through charges include but are not limited to taxes, insurance, and common area maintenance. These may also be called *tenant charges* or *billback items*. Often when free rent is provided, the tenant is also not required to pay pass-through charges for that same period. It may be necessary to provide this concession to make a particular deal. When it is granted, the cost of this concession is the monthly amount of each tenant charge waived, multiplied by the number of months the tenant does not pay it.

Cap on Pass-Through Charges. A cap (also called ceiling or lid) may be placed on one or all of the charges passed through to the tenant to limit the amount of the tenant's contribution. This concession may be stated: "The tenant will pay its pro rata share of the common area maintenance expenses not to exceed a certain dollar amount (e.g., $2.00) per square foot per year." An example calculation is shown in exhibit 9.6.

E X H I B I T   9.6

Sample Computation of a Cap on CAM Charges

Suppose a tenant rents a 4,500-square-foot space that was difficult to lease. Common area maintenance (CAM) costs are currently passed through to tenants at $1.80 per square foot per year and are expected to increase 10% per year. What is the estimated cost of a cap at $2.00 per square foot over the five-year term of the lease?

Year	CAM Cost $/Sq Ft/Yr*	Cap	Tenant's Pro Rata Share (×4,500)	Tenant's Actual CAM Cost (×4,500)	Annual Cost of the Concession
1	$1.80	$2.00	$ 8,100	$8,100	–0–
2	$1.98	$2.00	$ 8,910	$8,910	–0–
3	$2.18	$2.00	$ 9,810	$9,000	$ 810
4	$2.40	$2.00	$10,800	$9,000	$1,800
5	$2.64	$2.00	$11,880	$9,000	$2,880
					$5,490

*Pro rata share rounded to nearest whole cent.

The total cost of the cap on CAM over the five-year term of the lease is estimated at $5,490 based on present value. This concession lowered the CAM payment 24¢ per square foot per year of the lease ($5,490 ÷ 4,500 sq ft = $1.22/sq ft ÷ 5 years = 24¢/sq ft/year).

Cap on CPI Adjustments. A tenant may negotiate a cap on the CPI adjustment (rent escalation). For instance, the lease may state that the minimum rent will be adjusted each year based on the increase in the CPI, but in any year the increase from the preceding year shall not be greater than 5 percent. Though the future years' CPI adjustments are not known, the property manager can use a historical rate increase to factor a projected percentage increase over each of the years during the term of the lease. The format of the calculation is similar to that for the cost of the cap on CAM charges (see exhibit 9.6).

Percentage Rate Reduction. When a typical percentage rate and a range of percentage rates are indicated for a retail or service tenant category in *Dollars & Cents of Shopping Centers,* these are national figures. Percentage rates may vary with the type of center and the geographic region in which it is located. Although it is not particularly commonplace, occasionally a landlord will accept a less-than-typical percentage rate. A waiver of percentage rent or a reduction of the percentage rate may be conceded as a way to encourage a new business or secure a long-term lease. An example of the cost of a 25-percent reduction in a percentage rate is shown in exhibit 9.7.

E X H I B I T 9.7

Sample Computation of the Cost of a Lower Breakpoint

Suppose the typical percentage rate for a jewelry store in a community shopping center is 6% and the range is 3.0%–7.3%. If a landlord negotiated for a percentage rate of 6% but accepted (conceded) a 4.5% rate, what is the cost of this concession?

First compute the tenant's breakpoint, then estimate the tenant's sales and their annual growth. Assume the tenant's rent is $24,000 a year for a 2,000-square-foot store ($12/sq ft/yr), fixed for the first 5 years and increased 10% beginning in the sixth year of a 10-year lease. The tenant estimates its sales will be $400,000 the first year and grow at an annual rate of 8%.

Year	Rent	Annual Sales	Breakpoint @ 4.5%	Percentage Rent Owed	Breakpoint @ 6%	Percentage Rent Owed	Difference
1	$24,000	$400,000	$533,333	–0–	$400,000	–0–	–0–
2	$24,000	$432,000	$533,333	–0–	$400,000	$ 1,920	$ 1,920
3	$24,000	$466,560	$533,333	–0–	$400,000	$ 3,994	$ 3,994
4	$24,000	$503,885	$533,333	–0–	$400,000	$ 6,233	$ 6,233
5	$24,000	$544,196	$533,333	$ 489	$400,000	$ 8,652	$ 8,163
6	$26,400	$587,732	$586,667	$ 48	$440,000	$ 8,864	$ 8,816
7	$26,400	$634,751	$586,667	$ 2,164	$440,000	$11,685	$ 9,521
8	$26,400	$685,531	$586,667	$ 4,449	$440,000	$14,732	$10,283
9	$26,400	$740,373	$586,667	$ 6,917	$440,000	$18,022	$11,105
10	$26,400	$799,603	$586,667	$ 9,582	$440,000	$21,576	$11,994
				$23,649		$95,678	$72,029

The estimated cost of agreeing to lower the percentage rate from 6% to 4.5% is $72,029 ($95,678 – $23,649) in percentage rent over the 10-year term of the lease (based on present value).

Negotiated Sales Breakpoint. Percentage rent is usually paid as *overage*—i.e., the amount that sales exceed a specific dollar volume. This *natural breakpoint* in a tenant's sales is determined by dividing the percentage rate into the rent.

$$\frac{\text{Total Annual Rent}}{\text{Percentage Rate}} = \text{Natural Breakpoint}; \frac{\$20,000}{.05} = \$400,000$$

At a fixed percentage rate, the breakpoint increases as the rent increases. A negotiated breakpoint is an agreed-upon sales breakpoint that has no relationship to the above formula. If a desirable tenant expects to generate high sales volume, it may attempt to negotiate an *artificial breakpoint* above the natural breakpoint to lower the amount of percentage rent due. The calculation of the cost of this concession is similar to that used for the lower percentage rate concession (see exhibit 9.7), except that the comparison is between a fixed, artificial breakpoint and the possible percentage rent achievable at a standard percentage rate and a natural breakpoint.

Recapture of Tenant Charges. A prospect may seek to reduce occupancy costs by negotiating to recapture previously paid pass-through charges from percentage rent. This means that the tenant may deduct amounts previously paid toward CAM, taxes, and/or insurance charges from the amount of percentage rent owed. This concession effectively reduces the amount of percentage rent paid but does not alter the actual pass-through prorations.

Tenant Improvements. The landlord may contribute a set dollar amount per square foot toward improvements to the leased space, in which case the cost of the concession would be the rate times the number of square feet. If, instead, the landlord will refurbish the premises, the property manager must obtain firm bids for the cost of the work, and the specific cost will be the amount of the contractor's bill. Sometimes the cost of improvements to the leased space may be paid by the landlord, but the tenant will be expected to reimburse part or all of the landlord's investment by paying additional rent. This may be prorated over the entire term of the lease.

Anchor Tenants

In lease negotiations between a developer or a property manager and a prospective anchor tenant, all parties need to know each other's strengths and weaknesses. It is also important to know the concerns of major retailers in general, because these may become issues in a lease negotiation. An anchor tenant makes a long-term investment in its location and its store space, and consequently its representatives want every possible assurance that nothing will be done to the shopping center that will be detrimental to its sales and profitability.

The real estate deal with an anchor tenant may take one of several forms. In a *build-to-suit* arrangement, the landlord builds the store to the tenant's specifications, and the store and the land beneath it are leased to the tenant on a long-term lease with multiple options. Another approach is a *ground lease* in which a parcel of land is leased to the anchor tenant for its building and required parking, and the tenant builds and owns its building. A third alternative is *outright sale*—the anchor tenant buys a portion of the site and builds its own building, and the tenant owns its building and the land underneath it, plus the land for its required parking. The terms of the sale are usually very favorable to the tenant-buyer. The land may be sold at *par value* (the developer's cost), and par value may also be used to determine the anchor tenant's leasehold rent. The rental rate would be stepped up periodically— usually every 3–5 years. A ground lease or land sale option usually results when the anchor tenant is able to obtain better financing terms than the developer can, or if the anchor tenant wants to own its own building. To raise capital, the anchor tenant that owns its own building may package several of its holdings into a sale-leaseback (sell its buildings to an investor and lease them back).

In an effort to induce department stores to become anchor tenants, some regional and super regional mall developers have given the land to the anchor tenants. This emphasizes the importance of the department store to the feasibility and successful development of a mall.

Whichever type of real estate deal is negotiated, it is usually on very favorable terms for the anchor tenant and often considered a "sweetheart" deal. The type of deal—build-to-suit, ground lease, or land sale—will in large part determine the specific terms of any lease that is negotiated. A lease will always cover occupancy of the premises and the financial arrangements related to occupancy. Other considerations that are important to the prospective tenant—visibility, access, etc.—may be negotiated and stated in the lease, but not necessarily in a direct manner. For example, issues related to visibility may take the form of limitations on other tenants (to be stated in their leases as well).

Occupancy Issues.   The anchor tenant's first concern is its *occupancy costs*—specifically, base rent, percentage rate, and pass-through charges and any upward adjustments to them. Since the early 1970s, all shopping center tenants have been expected to pay their full pro rata share of the real estate taxes and the insurance for their premises and the common areas. Other expenses that are passed through to tenants include management and administrative fees and contributions to common promotional funds.

Major retailers know that there are few prospects available to anchor a proposed shopping center and that anchor tenants are indispensable to the development. Consequently, they are able to negotiate a very favorable *base or minimum rental rate*. Because many major retailers build and own their own buildings, they know the developer's approximate land cost and the cost to build and finance their store areas. With this information, they can easily calculate the developer's cost to amortize the loan for their portions of the center site and building, and they will use that information in negotiating base rent. The rental rate an anchor pays for the initial term of its lease, or the first five years of a longer-term lease, is seldom more than the cost to service the developer's loan for the anchor's building and site.

One element in the landlord's favor is the possibility of *percentage rent* from the anchor tenant. When anchor tenants agree to a percentage rent clause in their leases, the typical percentage rate for a department store is 2 percent, and the range is from 1.5 to 3 percent. The typical percentage rate for a supermarket is 1–1.25 percent with a range from 1 to 1.5 percent. Anchor tenants often negotiate a declining percentage rate, in which case the percentage rate for a supermarket may be 1.5 percent on the first $15 million of annual sales, 1.25 percent on the next $7.5 million of sales, and 1 percent on all remaining sales.

The anchor tenant will want a long *lease term* because it is investing millions of dollars into its store. The typical lease with a supermarket or department store is twenty or thirty years with multiple five-year options. The developer is usually able to negotiate several increases in the rental rate during the initial term of the lease—for instance, a fixed rental increase every five years and at the beginning of each option.

Anchor tenants will agree to pay their pro rata share of most of the center's *common area maintenance (CAM) expenses* although they sometimes attempt to negotiate a cap or lid on these expenses. An expense cap limits the amount of one or more of the charges passed through to the tenant and can be a fixed dollar amount. For example, the anchor lease may state: "The tenant will pay its pro rata share of CAM expenses not to exceed $3.00 per square foot per year" (see also exhibit 9.6). Alternatively, the cap may be based on the tenant's sales: "The pro rata share of CAM expenses shall not exceed one-fourth of one percent of the tenant's sales."

A well-maintained and adequate-sized parking lot is also important, and anchor tenants will usually agree to pay their pro rata share of the *parking lot CAM costs.* Parking lot expenses include maintenance, lighting, and insurance. On the other hand, the anchor tenant may attempt to negotiate not paying for a particular parking lot expense such as security.

While anchor tenants in enclosed malls may agree to pay their pro rata share of parking lot CAM expenses, they often negotiate *not* to pay any CAM expenses for the enclosed mall. Their rationale is that the parking lot is needed for their customers, but they can operate without the benefit of the enclosed mall area. Many anchor tenants negotiate to pay either a nominal charge—far less than their pro rata share—or to not pay any enclosed mall CAM expenses. Mall developers and owners frequently succumb to this request. In centers where anchor tenants own their stores—and sometimes the land beneath them as well—payment of CAM charges will be negotiated carefully on both sides.

When an anchor tenant does not pay enclosed mall CAM expenses, the leases with the other tenants will usually state that the denominator for calculating their pro rata shares of enclosed mall CAM expenses will *exclude* the GLA of the anchor tenants. As a result, the tenants in the small shops pay the anchor tenant's share of the enclosed mall CAM expenses. Conversely, if the leases for the shop spaces state that the denominator will include the GLA of *all* tenants in the mall (thus including anchor tenants), the anchor tenant's share is borne by the landlord.

One part of the CAM charge that becomes a negotiable issue with anchor tenants is the *CAM administrative fee.* Most shopping center leases allow the landlord to add to the common area expenses a 10–15 percent fee for administration of the common areas. While tenants in the smaller shops may accept this charge, anchor tenants will negotiate either to pay no CAM administrative fee or to pay only a nominal fee (e.g., 5 percent). In recent years, however, landlords have been successful in negotiating a CAM administrative fee from many anchor tenants, though it is seldom as high as the fee paid by the shop tenants.

In the late 1980s, some developers included the shopping center's *management fee* in the CAM expenses. The reason for this was to bring the shopping center lease closer to a pure *triple-net lease*. Although shop tenants have accepted this change, anchor tenants inevitably negotiate the management fee out of their CAM charges. Other specific expense items that are negotiated with anchors are real estate taxes, insurance, and merchants' association or marketing fund dues.

In the early years of shopping center development, all of the tenants paid their pro rata shares of the *increase* in real estate taxes and insurance above the amounts for these expenses for the year they took possession of their premises, but *not* the full amounts of those expenses for the first year itself. Since the mid-1970s, tenants have been paying their full pro rata shares of these expenses (including any increases that apply). However, anchor tenants may seek to negotiate which types of *insurance coverage* they will pay and to limit the cost increases that can be passed through to them. For instance, an anchor tenant may attempt to negotiate not to pay for earthquake coverage or for the landlord's rent loss (business income interruption) insurance. The anchor tenant may also attempt to negotiate a limit to the amount of liability coverage charged back—it may offer to pay its pro rata share of only $1 million or $5 million worth of liability insurance. Usually the landlord has liability insurance far in excess of either of these amounts, so the basis for pass through of this expense becomes a negotiable issue between the landlord and the anchor tenant. There is no industry standard as to which party should prevail.

The anchor tenant may seek to include a provision in its lease that allows recapture of some or all of its CAM, taxes, or insurance charges from percentage rent paid or owed. If the anchor tenant owes $25,000 in percentage or overage rent and the lease permits recapture of CAM charges, its $18,000 pro rata share of the CAM charges would be subtracted from the $25,000 percentage rent owed, and the amount of percentage or overage rent paid to the landlord would be only $7,000. A recapture provision was common in many anchor tenants' leases during the mid-1970s, and some anchor tenants still have this provision in their leases. Since then, however, most landlords have been able to negotiate a lease with an anchor tenant that does not include a recapture provision.

The final expense item to negotiate is *merchants' association or marketing fund dues*. Historically, the landlord has not been successful in negotiating this issue with anchor prospects. The anchor tenant's position is that it is spending millions of dollars to promote its store; it does not need the promotions and advertising of the merchants' association or marketing fund. The usual outcome is that the anchor tenant either does not contribute to these organizations or makes only a nominal monthly contribution.

Other Considerations.   The anchor tenant has concerns that go beyond rental terms and clause negotiations. One consideration is how the anchor tenant will be positioned in the shopping center in relation to the other anchor tenants and shop tenants. Other concerns are accessibility of the center, parking, and visibility of the anchor store.

The anchor tenant is rightly concerned about good visibility from the street. To achieve it, the tenant seeks to eliminate or limit the number of pad or outlot tenants in the parking area around its premises. In an enclosed mall, it may not be possible to place each anchor tenant so that it has visibility from the street. In this situation, anchor tenants without street visibility may require a sign either on the side of the building that faces the street or on the shopping center's identity sign. Inside an enclosed mall, an anchor tenant will usually prohibit a kiosk within a certain distance from its mall entrance.

An anchor tenant is also concerned that the shopping center has adequate parking, particularly at its end of the shopping center. Anchor tenants fully understand the need for convenient customer parking and may negotiate for the shopping center to maintain a minimum parking index or ratio or a minimum number of parking stalls. For instance, a supermarket may require the shopping center to maintain a parking index of no less than 5.5 stalls per 1,000 square feet of GLA. On this basis, a shopping center with 130,000 square feet of GLA would have to have 715 parking stalls. (Parking requirements are detailed in chapter 2.)

Anchor tenants are also concerned about the impact other tenants may have on their customers' parking. It is not unusual for neighborhood and community center anchors to restrict the placement of some other tenants in the center. They do not want shops adjacent to their buildings leased to tenants whose customers park for long periods of time. A supermarket lease may restrict such uses as bowling alleys, offices, theaters, and governmental agencies within 100 feet of its premises to assure availability of parking for supermarket customers.

Because the anchor tenant has a long-term lease and special requirements, it is concerned with the impact that changes to the shopping center may have on its sales. Anchor tenants will negotiate for—and frequently obtain—the right to approve any and all remodeling and expansion of the shopping center and changes to the parking lot.

Expansion of the anchor store space is another concern. Supermarkets have grown in size from 25,000 square feet in the 1960s to 30,000–35,000 square feet in 1970 and more than 40,000 square feet in the 1980s and 1990s. Anticipating growth, the anchor tenant may attempt to negotiate the right to expand its store. This right is seldom granted, however. Most developers build the maximum GLA the site can accommodate; there is rarely "extra space" to accommodate anchor expansion. In addition, if an anchor store wanted to expand into an area that was built as small shop space, its rent for this area would be significantly higher than the rent on its original premises. When an expansion right is granted, it usually is based on providing a small area either behind or alongside the anchor's premises which will not otherwise be utilized. An expansion right may be granted more readily when a shopping center is built in phases because anchor space could be expanded when the next phase is developed.

The negotiations between a shopping center developer and an anchor tenant will include negotiating an agreement that will establish how the common areas will be maintained and who will be responsible for their management. The anchor tenant making a major financial commitment and entering into a long-term lease with the developer wants assurance that the shopping center will not be operated in a manner that could have a negative impact on its business. The form and documentation of the agreement depend on the ownership (leasing) arrangements between the developer and the anchor tenant.

A *common area agreement* conveys rights and obligations to both parties. It will set the standard for maintenance, state how each party will be billed for the CAM expenses, and indicate the method for removing the common area manager for nonperformance. The agreement may prohibit the landlord from making changes to the common areas—relocating entrances, adding a pad or outlot building—without the written approval of each signatory to the agreement.

When the shopping center is not under one ownership, a *reciprocal easement agreement (REA)* is often used to state parking rights. The REA is a cross-easement whereby each party has the right to use the other party's parking area for customer parking. If anchor tenants own their buildings and land—or if different people own separate buildings in the shopping center—there must be an agreement to provide for mutual access to each owner's portion of the parking lot and for maintenance of the parking areas. Usually one of the parties to the REA will be assigned as the manager of all the parking area. The REA may include several of the issues found in a common area agreement.

When changes to a shopping center are being considered—expansion or remodeling, especially as they result in changes to the parking areas—the property manager must review these operating agreements. If the anchor tenants have approval rights, the approvals must be obtained before work commences. Violating an anchor tenant's rights can be very costly to the property owner and possibly to the property management firm.

Two major issues to be negotiated with anchor tenants are a *continuous operating covenant* (also known as a "go dark provision") and a *right of assignment*. For many years, anchor retailers have not been willing to sign a continuous operating covenant; they have wanted the sole right to close their stores and cease operations at will. When an anchor tenant "goes dark," it may close all its stores in an area or only the unprofitable ones. An example is when a supermarket chain closes one of its smaller stores and opens a larger state-of-the-art store just a few blocks away.

An anchor tenant that closes or goes dark may sublease its premises. Often the rent received from the subtenant is greater than the rent it paid to the landlord, and the anchor tenant makes a profit on the sublease. If it is operating another store in the immediate area, however, it usually will not sublease to its same use. In other words, a supermarket is not likely to sublease to another supermarket; it is more likely to sublease to a large space user that is not a competitor—e.g., an auto supply store, a furniture store, or a fabric store.

The results can be devastating to a shopping center. Seldom does the sublessee have the customer drawing power of the original anchor tenant, and the traffic to the shopping center will be significantly reduced. Retailers in the small shops may fail, rental rates for existing vacancies may be reduced, and renewal rents may be reduced or only slightly increased. As a result, the shopping center's net operating income will be reduced, and there will be a corresponding reduction in the shopping center's value. The value of many shopping centers around the country dropped radically when a major tenant vacated in the past. Since the 1980s, however, landlords have attempted to negotiate a provision that would prevent this from occurring. Rarely will an anchor tenant agree to a continuous operating covenant, but many developers have negotiated the right to cancel the anchor tenant's lease if it vacates its premises or proposes to sublease its space or assign its lease to another business. If the landlord cannot negotiate such a right to cancel the anchor tenant's lease, the right to approve any sublease or assignment by the anchor or an agreement that limits any sublease or assignment to the same use as that of the original tenant should be sought. Landlords have successfully negotiated one or more of these provisions by contending that they are giving the anchor tenant a "sweetheart" deal because of its customer drawing power. If the anchor's customer draw is lost to the shopping center, the landlord will be burdened with an unfavorable lease with a replacement tenant that is not equal to the original tenant.

Before a major retailer will negotiate with a developer for an anchor space in a proposed shopping center, it wants to be certain that the developer has the ability to execute the project—i.e., whether the developer controls the site, has the ability to obtain financing, and can build the shopping center on time. When negotiating with a major space user, the developer or property owner must assess both its own and the prospective anchor tenant's negotiating positions. Usually, the prospective tenant is in a stronger negotiating position than the landlord. The landlord does not have to capitulate on every issue, however, and many issues can be negotiated in the landlord's favor.

Pad and Outlot Spaces

Pad and outlot buildings can generate high rents, add to the draw of the shopping center, and provide a unique product or service to the tenant mix. A pad or outlot is a parcel of land in a high-visibility, high-traffic area of the shopping center parking lot. The arrangements with the tenant are sometimes similar to those negotiated with anchor tenants—i.e., build-to-suit or ground leases. Alternatively, the owner may build a shop building on the parcel and lease it to one or more tenants. Landlords often prefer a ground lease arrangement for the pad or outlot because their expenses may then be limited to the cost to legally create a separate parcel of land and (possibly) the cost to bring in the utilities. In a build-to-suit lease, the property owner invests in and constructs a building to the specifications of the tenant. However, if the original tenant fails, the building may require major modifications to suit a replacement tenant. Because build-to-suit leases are risky ventures, they are usually not offered to prospects that are *not* triple-A rated (AAA credit rating, as from Dun & Bradstreet). The two most common pad or outlot uses are restaurants and banks, both of which require long-term leases (typically 20–30 years, with one or two 5-year options).

If a shopping center does not presently include a pad or outlot parcel—or if it is desirable to add such space—the property manager should investigate whether creating new pad or outlot space is feasible and if it is permissible. The primary consideration here is the shopping center parking index and whether the property will still meet municipal requirements if some parking stalls are eliminated to make room for the pad or outlot space. (The municipal parking index was discussed in chapter 2.) Review of established leases and common area agreements will reveal any other prohibitions. Because anchor tenants are concerned with a building in the parking lot blocking their visibility or taking away parking area, their leases often contain a required parking index or prohibit a pad or outlot building in any area of the shopping center. Some shop tenants' leases and existing common area agreements may include similar restrictions.

Food Court Tenants

Food courts have been popular components of enclosed malls since the early 1980s, although some malls developed in the early 1960s included them. A food court will not reach its full potential if it is placed in a secondary location; it should always be prominent. Some of the best locations are adjacent to movie theaters or other entertainment facilities (e.g., an ice skating rink) or next to one of the entrances to the mall.

Food courts normally have two customer bases—shoppers and store employees. If there are office buildings nearby, lunchtime business from office workers on weekdays can be significant. Food courts are gathering places for both casual eating and impulse buying. Results of the 1990 Centermation Systems, Inc., Specialty Food Court Survey published in *CarlsonReport* indicate (for those shopping centers reporting) that the typical sales per square foot for the food court is three times that of the rest of the shopping center. According to that report, the following statistics typify food courts:

- 10 to 11 units per food court.
- Average size is 625 square feet per unit.
- Minimum seating area of one seat for every square foot of food court GLA.
- If tenant mix includes both national and local vendors, nationals significantly outperform locals.

Food vendors that appear in more than half of the top revenue-producing food courts are listed below (in descending order).

Pizza	96%
Hot dogs	88%
Sandwiches	83%
Oriental	75%
Ice cream	67%
Hamburgers	67%
Yogurt	58%
Mexican	54%

Food choices change with trends and promotion of health consciousness, so the tenant mix of a food court must be adjusted periodically to accommodate consumers' changing eating habits.

Food court spaces may be leased individually, or the food court may be operated as a concession, in which case the concessionnaire (as the lessee) negotiates arrangements with individual food vendors. As with any food service operations, special care must be taken in locating the food court area and the individual vendors. Food courts thrive on a tenant mix that includes both national and local vendors. The lease document for food court tenants should follow the requirements imposed on any other type of food vendor with respect to operations and compliance with local health codes. According to statistics published in *Dollars & Cents of Shopping Centers,* food court tenants operate in spaces ranging in size from somewhat less than 300 to little more than 1,000 square feet of GLA, and few of these tenants have sales less than $200 per square foot. Total rent per square foot tends to be substantially higher than what other tenants pay, although specific percentage rent may not be paid (because the sales breakpoint is so high). Many also pay prorated pass-through operating expenses (including property taxes and insurance), and many pay special CAM charges encompassing common areas of both the food court and the shopping center as a whole. It should be pointed out that food "fads" are as common (or more so) as so-called fads in fashions, and these fads can make or break individual vendors.

Temporary Tenants

Once a marketing director's afterthought, the pushcarts and kiosks of temporary tenants are becoming an integral part of the marketing and merchandising strategies of many regional shopping centers. Temporary tenants can add a unique element to a shopping center's tenant mix and enhance its drawing power. A temporary tenant program provides a shopping center the unique opportunity to utilize otherwise nonproductive space. Temporary tenants are such an important component of marketing and leasing programs for malls that ICSC presents an annual two-day event—conference, trade exposition, and deal-making session—on temporary tenants.

More specifically, temporary tenants provide additional income and amenities to the shopping center, and most centers have several possibilities for locating them. The obvious place in all types of shopping centers is vacant space. In strip centers, temporary tenants may be located in the parking lot or on the sidewalk; in a mall, they may be placed in the mall corridor, against a vacant space (or inside it), underneath the stairs or escalator to the second level, or along a blank wall.

Most temporary spaces are provided by the landlord. The landlord will have carts or kiosks designed and built to conform to the architecture of the shopping center. Occasionally the tenant will want to use its own kiosk or cart or will offer to build one to the landlord's specifications. (This often occurs when a tenant offers to lease space and place its kiosk in the parking lot.)

The advantages of a temporary tenant program are numerous. First and foremost, temporary tenants are an additional source of revenue, the amount of which can range each year from a few hundred dollars from Christmas tree sales in the parking lot to more than $100,000 from a year-round temporary tenant program in a regional mall. Temporary tenants can fill a void in the shopping center's merchandise mix. Short-term, small-space tenancies can provide an opportunity for entrepreneurs to test new products and concepts. They add a sense of newness that attracts shoppers. Temporary tenancies offer landlords opportunitues to evaluate new merchants without committing to a long-term lease, and some temporary tenants may become permanent occupants of in-line spaces as a result. Temporary tenancies are also a way to eliminate the unsightly appearance of vacant space.

Leasing to temporary tenants is not without problems. Two potential problems that must be resolved *before* a temporary tenant program can be established are existing restrictions and future conflicts. Common area agreements may include restrictions against leasing any portion of the common areas or use of the common areas for selling merchandise. Established leases may include similar restrictions. If such restrictions exist, they are most likely to be found in anchor tenants' leases, but shop tenants' leases should be checked regardless. Anchor leases may restrict use of the common areas within a specified distance from their premises or within a defined area of the shopping center. The lease for a department store may restrict placement of kiosks and carts within 100 feet of its mall entrance; that for a supermarket may prohibit displays in the area of the parking lot in front of its premises. Another restriction that must be honored is that imposed by a tenant's exclusive use clause. The merchandise sold by any temporary tenants must not violate any other tenant's exclusive.

Conflict may arise between the landlord and the permanent tenants regarding direct competition from temporary tenants. The property manager must be sensitive to the concerns of the permanent tenants. Because permanent tenants pay rent 12 months a year, including the months with slow sales, they may rightly object to merchants occupying space only during the best selling periods and taking business away from them. For this reason, temporary tenants should complement and not compete directly with existing tenants. They should sell merchandise (handcrafted items, specialty foods) or provide a service (key duplication, engraving) that is not typically found in the other stores in order to be more readily accepted. Often it is possible to include in their leases the right for the landlord to relocate the temporary tenant or terminate the lease if there is a dispute with a permanent tenant that cannot be resolved satisfactorily otherwise.

The rental arrangements with a temporary tenant may take the form of either a lease or a license agreement. Because temporary tenants use space for a short time—typically one week to two months—many landlords prefer to use a license agreement which does not offer the tenant the same rights as are found in a lease. In some centers, the licensing fees may be paid to the merchants' association, and the funds used to buy more advertising. Permanent tenants may not object to a temporary tenant program when that is the case. Whichever form is used. the rental agreement should include a very specific use restriction. As an example, a temporary tenant may be tempted to sell different types of merchandise in the course of a week in an effort to find the one item that will be a best seller. If the agreement states that the use of the space is to sell handmade wooden toys, sale of any other item would be a violation. In addition to use restrictions, the agreement should state the term (duration), rental rate, frequency of rent payment, and other specific provisions.

- *Term.* The length of time of the temporary tenancy should be stated and include specific opening and closing dates. If the agreement is for the holiday season, the commencement date and the date the tenant opens for business should be between November 1 and one week before Thanksgiving. This will provide sufficient time for the tenant to organize and set up. In addition, the tenant should be required to remain open through December 31 to accommodate returns and refunds.

- *Rent.* The rent charged temporary tenants is seldom based on dollars per square foot. Rent is determined by the amount of traffic that will be in the mall during the time the tenant occupies the space and is directly related to its potential sales volume. Higher rent can be charged for a kiosk or a 1,000-square-foot vacancy during the holiday season (Thanksgiving through Christmas) than at any other time of the year. Kiosks and carts should be located in high traffic areas. A mall kiosk, which typically ranges in size from 75 to 150 square feet, can command $1,000–$3,000 per month in base (or minimum) rent.
- *Percentage rent.* In addition to base rent, temporary tenants should be required to pay percentage rent. Typically, the percentage rate is higher than that for a similar tenant in a permanent location. For instance, if a permanent gift shop pays 5 percent, the percentage rate for a temporary gift shop may be 10 percent. Temporary tenants pay a premium base rent and percentage rate because they are usually brought into the shopping center only during the best selling periods, and they do not experience the slow sales periods.

  Sometimes escalating rates can be negotiated for a holiday season (e.g., 10 percent on sales up to $20,000; then 12 percent up to $30,000, and 15 percent thereafter) to encourage the landlord to provide the best possible location and least possible competition while the tenant has basically the same overhead at any volume of sales. However, it is often difficult to audit their reported sales volumes, and it is therefore appropriate to remind temporary tenants that participation in future programs will depend heavily on their reported sales as well as their compliance with other provisions of the lease or license.
- *Payment of rent.* Temporary tenants can be in one day and gone the next, so it is important that they pay rent often and on time. Percentage rent should be paid for the same period that minimum rent is paid, and sales reports that support it should be submitted no less frequently than monthly. It is also prudent to collect a *security deposit* as a guarantee of performance of the agreement. The schedule for payment of minimum rent may be once a week, every two weeks, or once a month.
- *Other provisions.* The temporary tenant should be required to *pay merchants' association or marketing fund dues.* Because the tenancy is short term and the space may be very small, the dues should be a fixed amount rather than a proration based on square footage. Temporary tenants should be required to *advertise* in the vehicle used by the shopping center for distribution to shoppers on site. This may be an advertising section in a newspaper or tabloid or a weekly flyer (newspaper stuffer). If an in-line space is occupied, the *utilities* should be billed in the tenant's name. Other important provisions of the agree-

ment relate to the temporary tenant's operations. There should be stringent guidelines for and required landlord approval of the *design* of the space, design and use of *signage* (specific signage criteria must be developed for temporary tenants), and the *manner in which merchandise is displayed* (merchandise not professionally displayed creates a flea-market image).

Kiosks.   Enclosed mall space is ideal for kiosks. It provides a weather-protected environment, after-hours security, and high-volume pedestrian traffic. Kiosks can be leased for one month, one year, or several years. Most kiosk tenancies are under short-term leases, usually for one year. The specific advantage of a kiosk is being able to merchandise and sell from all four of its sides, a feature that is attractive to merchants who sell impulse items such as prepackaged food (candy, nuts, dry fruit, popcorn, and specialty cheeses and jellies) or food prepared on site (pretzels, cookies, hot dogs). Sales of hand-crafted items, small electronic gifts and gadgets, leather goods, rubber stamps, keys, stuffed animals, jewelry, and tickets are other typical uses. Actually, one of the first kiosks was Photomat—drop-off and pick-up photo processing—located in shopping center parking lots near the street. In the early 1990s, drive-through espresso kiosks became common in parking lots in some areas of the country.

Carts.   Carts became popular during the late 1980s. They can turn small amounts of previously unused space into money-making opportunities, and they offer many advantages over kiosks because they are more attractive and can have a unique charm. Carts also take up less space than kiosks, and they can be moved easily to accommodate mall promotions or stationed in front of a vacancy or a blank wall. They can be removed and stored when not in use. The term of the agreement between landlord and tenant is often as short as one week or one month. When a mall has several carts, weekly rotation of merchants from one cart to another provides each merchant the opportunity to have the best location. Merchandise sold from carts is typically impulse items at low to medium prices.

Wall Shops.   Often department stores in shopping centers have blank walls between their entrances and their display windows. Building wall shops eight to ten feet deep in front of these walls provides space for both temporary and permanent tenants. Wall shops also eliminate the barren appearance of a blank wall and create an area filled with merchandise and activity, drawing traffic to the entrances of the department stores.

In-Line Spaces.   When temporary tenants occupy in-line spaces, they may merchandise the entire space or only the front portion (one-fourth to one-half) of the premises. If they occupy only part of the space, it may be necessary to build a partial back wall (backing). Usually the tenant will paint the walls. In-line spaces are good locations for service tenants or those who sell bulky or large items or offer several types of goods. A tax preparation service is a common use during the early months of the year; a photo studio is a good seasonal use—Christmas and Easter holidays and the weeks preceding Mother's Day and Father's Day.

Parking Lots.   Parking lots were locations for so-called temporary tenants long before there was such a concept. Three of the most common uses are fireworks stands the week before Independence Day (July 4), pumpkin patches the last week of October, and Christmas tree lots from mid-November through Christmas Eve. Areas for such uses should be roped off, and safety walkways should be clearly marked. Specific uses may be limited by state and local laws (e.g., sales of fireworks are prohibited in some states).

Lease Renewals

Lease renewals can be the easiest or the most difficult deals to negotiate. If the tenant is doing well and understands the current rental market, renewal negotiation can be easy. However, if a tenant's rent is significantly below the market rate, the tenant is unaware of market rates, and there are several vacancies in the shopping center and no replacement tenant available, lease renewal can be difficult. Regardless of the situation, there are several factors to consider when a tenant's lease is expiring.

1. Should the lease be renewed?
2. How successful is the tenant?
3. How well does the tenant fit the current tenant mix?
4. Does the tenant benefit the shopping center?
5. What is the current market situation?

Also to be taken into account are whether rent payments and sales reports have been submitted on time, whether the tenant's store size is still appropriate and, if so, whether the space should be remodeled.

The decision to renew a particular lease is not automatic—the desirability of renewing that lease must first be ascertained. The tenant's success in the shopping center will be a key factor. If there is any doubt about the tenant's capability as a merchant, comprehensive evaluation is required. This should include the tenant's sales volume, how the store is merchandised, how customers are treated, the store's reputation in the community, and whether or not the tenant is a draw for the shopping center.

Even more important is whether the tenant still fits the shopping center's tenant mix. If not, the availability of a replacement tenant should be explored. There may not be an equivalent or better prospect for the location. Another consideration is whether the tenant has contributed to the success of the shopping center or been a chronic problem. Regular advertising in the shopping center's promotional flyers and participation in merchandising events and promotions are measures of a tenant's contribution to the center. Difficulties with rent collection or late submission of sales reports and percentage rent payments, especially on a recurrent basis, signal problems that may caution against renewal. Finally, market conditions and the number of vacancies in the shopping center must be taken into account. A marginal tenant may be offered a lease renewal because there is no other prospective tenant for the space.

Lease renewal negotiations for shop tenants should begin no later than six months before the lease expires; those for anchor tenants should begin at least one year (and possibly two years) before the lease expires. If a tenant has regularly violated one or more lease provisions, the new lease should address those particular issues. As an example, if a tenant routinely submits its sales reports *after* the due date, the new lease may provide for the payment of a penalty (e.g., $100 every time the sales report is late or $10 for each day it is late). If a tenant has been a chronic problem, its renewal lease may be for a shorter term than is usually offered. If a shop tenant has not agreed to a lease renewal 90 days before the current one expires, the property manager should start to market the store.

Most lease renewals are cost-effective deals. There is no downtime, and there are seldom any tenant improvement or concession costs. Also, the commission is typically less than would be paid for a replacement tenant.

Lease Buy-Out

Property managers should always be looking for opportunities to improve the shopping center's tenant mix and to increase the net operating income. Replacing a retail store that no longer contributes to the success of the shopping center is a way to enhance the center's image and its value. There are three opportunities to replace a tenant: (1) when the lease expires (nonrenewal), (2) when a tenant fails and moves out (replacement as necessity), and (3) when a tenant's problems would be solved by a lease buy-out (replacement by choice).

Every month, the property manager should analyze each tenant's sales and the timing of its rent payment. A tenant is a possible candidate for a lease buy-out—

1. If its sales are significantly below the national average.
2. If its sales volume has been regularly declining.
3. If it has trouble paying rent on time.
4. If it has a low rental rate (below current market).
5. If it provides a product or service that is no longer in demand.

It goes without saying that a buy-out should be considered if the tenant no longer fits the center's tenant mix.

It should not always be assumed that the landlord will pay the tenant to buy out the lease. The lease may be canceled by mutual agreement, or the tenant may pay the landlord to terminate the lease early. An example situation is that of a regional shopping center on the West Coast that was being converted from an open to an enclosed mall. A shoe store occupied a prime center court space the landlord wanted to recapture and divide into two spaces. Prior to offering the tenant a $50,000 buy-out, the property manager asked the tenant if it would be willing to pay a fee to terminate its lease. The tenant offered—and the manager accepted—a $25,000 fee for an early termination.

There is no rule of thumb on how much either party should offer to pay to terminate a lease. However, there are some factors that can guide a property manager in deciding the amount of a buy-out. First and foremost is the amount of additional rent another tenant will pay and how much additional value will be created. This assumption is based on the probability that the space can be leased at a higher rental rate and in a relatively short time. Many sophisticated tenants know this and will negotiate for a favorable buy-out; other tenants are happy to be paid to close a marginal or unsuccessful business.

Improving the tenant mix is a major consideration in a lease buy-out. An existing tenant's ability to operate successfully is another. If it is likely that a tenant will struggle with its rent payment for the remainder of its lease term, it may be better to negotiate a lease buy-out or mutual cancellation. The time remaining in the lease term will determine whether and how much to offer as a buy-out. A tenant whose lease term has several years remaining may be able to negotiate a higher buy-out payment.

Once the amount of the buy-out has been agreed on, the next decision is how payment will be made. The buy-out can be paid in a lump sum when the lease is terminated or in installments. The latter may be paid monthly over the remaining term of the cancelled lease or over the term of the replacement tenant's lease.

Before negotiating a buy-out, the property manager should have approached several prospective replacement tenants and identified one or two who are interested in leasing the space when it becomes available. However, it is not advisable (or necessary) to tell prospective tenants that a particular tenant will be approached for a mutual lease termination or buy-out because that would place the replacement prospect in a stronger negotiating position.

Store Split. Sometimes a tenant that can generate an equivalent sales volume in less space would be happy to give up part of its leased space in order to reduce its occupancy expenses. As an example, a 10,000-square-foot variety or fabric store may be able to do the same level of business in 7,500 square feet of GLA. The 2,500 square feet that it gives up may be divisible into two 1,250-square-foot spaces. If so, the rent for these two smaller spaces is likely to be twice the rate per square foot that the larger user had been paying for the area, and two new merchants will be added to the shopping center's tenant mix. A reduction in the amount of space leased may or may not be compensated specifically. Such a store split may be negotiated as part of a lease renewal, with the large tenant paying a higher rent per square foot for the space retained. However, if the store split is arranged during an ongoing lease term, the exchange of funds (from landlord to tenant or vice versa) may amount to a partial lease buy-out.

Lease buy-outs and store splits are unique opportunities for shopping centers to increase NOI, cash flow, and the value of the property.

Documenting the Lease Terms

The lease establishes the relationship between the landlord (*lessor*) and the tenant (*lessee*). It is a legal document that conveys the rights, obligations, and duties of each party. In particular, the *shopping center lease* states the parameters within which the tenant must operate its business. It will state the specific type of business the tenant may operate (the use) along with hours of operation, advertising requirements, occupancy costs (rent, pass-through expenses), insurance requirements, and other obligations that can have a significant impact on a tenant's business. Each lease is similarly important to the landlord because of the impact it has on the property's cash flow and value.

Leases are essential documents in the development and purchase of shopping centers as well as in their management. An investor's primary criterion for purchasing a property is its income stream and the resultant net operating income (NOI). An investor's due diligence (investigation of a commercial property prior to purchase) includes a thorough analysis of each tenant's lease. Similarly, a lender will analyze the strength and reliability of a property's income stream prior to making a loan. The ratio of NOI to debt service is a major component in the lender's evaluation of a proposed loan— i.e., can the property's income support the required mortgage payments. The leases are the basic documents that establish a property's NOI.

Every lease provision will have an impact on the property's NOI and value, either directly or indirectly. Lease provisions that directly affect the property's NOI include minimum rent, percentage rent, Consumer Price Index (CPI) adjustments to rent, and pass-through operating expenses. Lease provisions that affect the property's NOI indirectly include sales reporting, landlord's auditing rights, hours of operation, merchants' association or marketing fund dues, assignment and subletting, radius restrictions, and exclusives. Roof repairs, legal fees, and other types of specific expenses addressed in a lease can also affect NOI.

In no other property are the tenants more dependent on one another for their success or the success of the property more dependent on how the tenants operate their businesses. Because the daily operations of the shopping center and of each tenant's business are central to the success of both tenants and shopping center, a properly drafted and negotiated lease document is critical.

THE LEASE FORM

The lease form should be developed by or in consultation with the landlord's attorney and designed to protect the landlord's interest in the property. It provides the basis for negotiation of the business terms of the arrangement. A strong lease document can protect the landlord if there is ever a dispute with a tenant.

As a result of negotiating with tenants, operating shopping centers, and dealing with landlord-tenant issues over a period of years, landlords' lease forms have evolved into 12–20-page documents. Every time there was a dispute with a tenant, another provision was added to the lease—either to prevent such a dispute from occurring in the future or to address and resolve the dispute if it recurs.

A landlord is usually willing to negotiate and compromise on numerous lease points with a strong regional or national tenant but will negotiate only a few items with a local merchant. It is not uncommon for 50 to 75 lease questions to be raised for discussion or negotiation in a lease with a national shop tenant (e.g., Kinney Shoes, Radio Shack), while a local merchant may be granted only three or four changes to the lease. There are several reasons for this. National shop tenants usually have good credit ratings, are strong advertisers, and have an established identity in the community. They have excellent reputations and appeal to the general public. They are in high demand as tenants because of the volume of traffic they draw. National tenants rarely violate any lease clauses, and consequently landlords tend to have fewer disputes with them. National tenants almost always pay their rent and other occupancy expenses on time. In addition, their approach to merchandising and the business aspects of their operations is normally very professional. National shop tenants generally abide by the store hours established for the shopping center and support management's enforcement of employee parking restrictions. They are also less likely to violate any shopping center rule, regulation, or lease provision. The landlord's willingness to compromise and make concessions is directly related to the strengths and weaknesses of its negotiating position and that of the tenant.

Anchor tenants (supermarkets, department stores, etc.) will insist that their own lease forms be used. Recognizing their importance in the development of the shopping center (securing financing, attracting other tenants), anchor tenants usually negotiate from a position of strength. Thus it is the anchor's lease form that becomes the basis for negotiations between the landlord and the anchor tenant. (The importance of negotiating with anchor tenants prior to development is discussed in chapter 2; specific aspects of these negotiations are covered in chapter 9.)

The specifics of a lease are generally negotiable, and negotiations should result in a compromise between the landlord and the tenant such that the landlord's position in the property is protected and the tenant has the opportunity to operate a successful business without unnecessary encumbrances. Although the property owner is the landlord, it is the property manager who conducts most lease negotiations on the landlord's behalf. To negotiate leases successfully, the property manager must have a thorough understanding of the impact of each lease provision on the operations, cash flow, NOI, and value of the shopping center. Astute property managers are able to negotiate leases successfully with local merchants, national shop tenants, and anchor tenants; they know when to stand firm and when to compromise. Understanding of the lease coupled with the ability to compromise through negotiation is what distinguishes the deal-maker from the deal-breaker. The ultimate goal is not just to make the deal but to make a good deal for both the landlord and the tenant.

Requirements of a Valid Lease

The six requirements of a valid lease describe and define in very specific language (1) the parties to the lease, (2) the term (duration) of the lease, (3) the leased premises, (4) the tenant's use of the premises, (5) the consideration to be paid to the landlord, and (6) the rights and obligations of both parties.

Identification of the Parties.   The lease must include the correct names and signatures of legally competent parties. If a lease is signed by a minor, it is voidable. The age of majority (usually between 18 and 21 years) varies from state to state, and an underage signatory may void the lease. Mental capacity is another criterion of legal competence. If a signatory of a lease is senile or insane, the lease is also voidable.

It is important to establish the authority of the individual representing a business entity. An entrepreneur signs the lease for a business as its owner. In the case of a corporation, an officer of the company may be a signatory on behalf of the corporation. However, the authority of that officer to commit the corporation to the lease should be documented officially. In fact, the landlord should require a corporate resolution authorizing the corporate officer to sign the lease.

Term or Duration of the Lease.   A lease must have a finite term with fixed starting (commencement) and ending (termination) dates—e.g., "The term of this lease shall be five years, beginning on November 1, 1992, and ending on October 31, 1997." The lease should not have an open expiration date—e.g., a date "to be agreed upon in the future." Also, it is best not to have all of the leases in a shopping center expire on the same date. The expiration dates should be staggered over several months and several years.

Regardless of the number of years involved, many landlords prefer a lease to be extended through the Christmas holidays. The extension gives the tenant an additional Christmas selling period and provides a greater opportunity for the tenant to pay percentage rent during the last year of the lease. (Most retailers do 20–30 percent of their annual sales volumes between Thanksgiving and Christmas.) A five-year lease that commences on September 1, and would normally expire on August 31, may be written for a term of five years and four months so it will expire on December 31.

National shop tenants typically negotiate for a lease term between nine and eleven years. However, most leases with local tenants are for terms of three to five years. Landlords prefer a short lease term so the rent can be adjusted upward more frequently. Also, if a tenant's sales are poor, it can be replaced with a stronger merchant sooner than would be possible under a longer term lease. An exception to this is a tenant whose build-out costs are high (e.g., a restaurant). Such a tenant needs a longer lease term to amortize the cost of the fixtures. Besides, the loan to finance purchase of the equipment may be for a period longer than five years. To accommodate these factors, this type of tenant may also be granted a short-term option (to extend the lease). In this case, the lease term might be 10–20 years with one 5–10-year option. Leases for pad and outlot tenants are typically for terms of 20–30 years, also with options. These tenants often build their own buildings and therefore need a longer term to support their investment. Anchor tenant lease terms are generally 30 years with multiple 5-year options. As a general practice, however, it is not in the interest of the landlord to grant such options to shop tenants because the tenant is the only one who benefits from them.

When a lease is entered into before or during the construction of a shopping center, it may not be possible to determine the exact commencement date until the shopping center is complete. In that case, the lease may state: "The commencement date shall be 60 days after the landlord turns the premises over to the tenant, or the date the tenant opens for business, whichever occurs first." (A lease with an uncertain commencement date should also provide that landlord and tenant will sign a letter that ratifies the actual commencement date.) In most situations, the landlord turns the premises over to the tenant while the common areas of the shopping center are being completed and approximately 60 days before the shopping center opens. A retailer entering into a lease will need time to finish the premises (or remodel a previously occupied space), move in its fixtures and inventory, and set up merchandise displays. The tenant is typically given 30–60 days to ready the store to open for business; however, the tenant may be able to accomplish this in less time than that allowed.

As another alternative, the lease may state that the commencement date will be either the day the tenant opens for business, or a specific date, whichever occurs first. If the lease states a date of April 1 and the tenant opens for business *after* April 1, the lease term and payment of rent would commence on April 1. If the lease will commence on a date other than April 1, the property manager should send the tenant a letter (written notice) that states the actual commencement date and the expiration date. To avoid any dispute over this date, the letter should provide a space for the tenant to sign it (in acknowledgment) and, being sent to the tenant in duplicate, request return of a signed copy.

In rare instances, the landlord may not be able to deliver the premises to the tenant on the agreed-upon lease commencement date. The usual cause for this is a delay in construction of a new shopping center or move-out of the existing tenant in the premises. Because the landlord does not want to lose the new tenant, the lease will provide for the landlord's failure to deliver the premises, such that the lease will remain in force, the landlord cannot be held liable for any loss or damage, and the minimum rent and all tenant charges will be waived until such time as the landlord delivers possession of the premises to the tenant and the tenant has utilized the allotted time for start-up of the business (usually 60 days). In negotiating the lease term, the tenant may request that any delay in possession should extend the term of the lease an amount of time equal to the period of delay. In fact, the tenant may insist that, if the delay extends beyond so many days or weeks, it should have the right to cancel the lease. Neither of these requests is unreasonable. Regardless of when the tenant actually occupies the leased space, rent should be paid from the scheduled commencement date unless other arrangements have been made.

Description of the Leased Premises.   The lease must include a readily identifiable description of the leased premises. Usually this takes several different forms—e.g., a street address, a description of the space covered by the lease, the legal description of the property. A site plan showing the layout of the building is usually attached to the lease as an exhibit (discussed later in this chapter), and the leased premises are identified on it (cross-hatched, outlined in red, or otherwise delineated). A ground lease may include a metes and bounds description of the land parcel. A disclaimer should be included on the site plan and in the body of the lease stating that the site plan is not drawn to scale and that the landlord has the sole right to alter the site plan without the tenant's approval. This disclaimer is very important in case the landlord wants to expand the shopping center by extending or adding a building, create a separate parcel in the parking lot for a pad or outlot tenant, or remodel or rehabilitate the property.

In addition, the lease will state the landlord's reserved rights with regard to the property as a whole.

- The landlord has the right to change the size, layout, and dimensions of the shopping center and the parking areas and to modify the number and location of the buildings on the property.
- The landlord makes no representation or warranty with respect to the occupancy of any tenant or tenants (including anchor tenants). This is intended to prevent a tenant from claiming the right to cancel the lease or sue for monetary damages if a particular tenant moves out or never takes possession of its premises.
- The landlord has the right to lease space in the shopping center to any tenant for any purpose including retail, office, medical, governmental, and nonretail uses, and that the shopping center may not be used exclusively or primarily for retail purposes. Most shopping centers, regardless of their size, will have some service and/or office tenants. This provision is to prevent the tenant from claiming the right to cancel the lease or seeking monetary damages if the shopping center is not occupied entirely by retail tenants. Sometimes a tenant may consider suing the landlord as a last resort to solve its financial problems. In that case, the tenant may claim that the landlord breached either a written covenant or an oral agreement. To assure that there is no cause for such a claim, the shopping center's brochure should also refer to "retail, service, and office space" being available for lease rather than "retail space" only.
- The landlord reserves to itself the exterior walls and the roof and any installations in or on them.

Use of the Premises.   The landlord's control over the shopping center's tenant mix is based on the allowable use or uses in each tenant's lease. The lease must state the tenant's use of the premises, and the *use clause* should be very specific about what business the tenant can conduct in the leased premises. Landlords often want to avoid unnecessary duplication of uses in order to enable each tenant to maximize its sales potential, increasing the possibility of percentage rent payment. In particular, a shopping center is likely to have only one of the following: dry cleaner, shoe repair, barber shop, drugstore.

In some situations it is desirable to have more than one tenant with the same use. Regional malls typically include several clothing, gift, and jewelry stores to provide consumers a wide selection of merchandise and opportunities for comparison shopping.

The use clause should limit the type of business the tenant may operate and the products or services that can be sold, without being so restrictive that the tenant cannot operate successfully. Examples of tightly controlled uses are restaurants and shoe stores. If a shopping center has three restaurants, the landlord will not want all three to serve the same type of food. To do so would dilute the sales of each restaurant, limit the variety of selections available to customers, and reduce or eliminate the potential for percentage rent. The likely result would be that one or all of them could go out of business. The use clause in a restaurant lease will state the type of food, whether or not alcoholic beverages (liquor) may be served, and whether the food is eaten in the premises or not (i.e., carried out). Examples of such lease provisions are: "Mexican restaurant with beer and wine for on-site consumption only," or "Chinese restaurant with on-site consumption, take-out and delivery, and no liquor served." Similarly, a landlord will not want every shoe store selling the same type of shoes. A shoe store's "use" may be specified as retail sales of a particular type of shoes—women's, men's, children's, athletic, family.

When a tenant has a broad array of merchandise and the landlord does not want that tenant to dominate a particular product line, the use clause may limit the amount of GLA that can be devoted to a particular—perhaps subsidiary—use. As an example, a book store may be allowed to use only 20 square feet of its premises for the display of greeting cards.

Another way of limiting the use is to state what percentage of the store's entire sales may be represented by a particular product. A landlord, believing that only one candy store can be successful at the shopping center, will be rightly concerned when a lease proposal is received from a card and gift store chain whose national format includes incidental sales of candy. In order to allow the card and gift store to operate its standard store and still protect the sales and potential percentage rent of a candy store, the use clause should limit the percentage of candy sales by the card and gift store. For instance, "Sales of candy may not exceed 15 percent of the tenant's total annual sales volume."

An additional requirement of tenant uses in general is that *the tenant's use must be legal*. If the tenant's use of the premises is illegal—i.e., gambling in a state where gambling is against the law—the lease is voidable, and the landlord may cancel it.

Consideration. The fifth requirement of a valid lease is consideration—what the tenant gives the landlord in return for the use of the premises. (The landlord's consideration to the tenant is the use and possession of the premises.) The consideration in a lease is almost always monetary and is termed *rent*. Rent may be stated as (1) a minimum annual amount (to be divided and paid monthly), (2) a percentage of the tenant's sales, or (3) minimum rent versus percentage rent. Typically, the rent in a shopping center lease is the latter and declared to be *the greater of an annual fixed minimum rent* (paid on a monthly basis) *versus a percentage of the tenant's sales.* This allows the landlord the opportunity to collect more than the minimum rent. The excess rent—the amount above or in addition to the minimum rent—is referred to as *percentage rent* or *overage.* The rationale for "minimum rent versus a percentage of sales" is based on the fact that the landlord has created a unique retailing environment in a good location, with anchor tenants, an appropriate tenant mix, and a uniform design. Under this arrangement, if the tenant benefits from the unique retail environment (i.e., has high sales), the landlord shares in the tenant's success. If the tenant's sales are not greater than they would have been in any other location (outside of that shopping center), the landlord receives only the minimum rent.

Although the great majority of shopping center leases provide for minimum versus percentage rent, some tenants (e.g., banks, governmental agencies, office uses, and professionals such as physicians and dentists) typically do not pay percentage rent. Alternatives to the concept of "overage" rent are requirements to pay *minimum rent only* or *percentage rent only.* When a lease calls for minimum rent only, it usually provides for periodic fixed rental increases. When the lease requires percentage rent only, the tenant pays a monthly rent based only on an agreed upon percentage of sales, with no minimum or base rent due. In this situation, the percentage rate is usually one or two points higher than that used in "minimum rent versus percentage rent."

Rights and Obligations.   The first five requirements of a valid lease are usually found at the beginning of the lease document. The remainder of the lease comprises the rights and obligations of each party. The document concludes by renaming the parties and providing spaces for signatures of authorized representatives. (Because the management firm and the tenant are almost always companies, the authority of those signing should be indicated as well.) If the document was not dated at its beginning, it should be dated at the time of signing. It may also be appropriate to include signatures of witnesses.

Types of Leases

In this context, it is necessary to distinguish among the different types of leases that can be used. The differences are based on the kinds of operating expenses that are passed through to the shopping center tenant on a pro rata basis. In a *gross lease,* the tenant pays base rent only; there are no specific tenant charges. In theory, these charges are included in the base rent. In a *net (or single-net) lease,* the tenant pays base rent plus real estate taxes. In a *net-net (or double-net) lease,* the tenant pays base rent plus real estate taxes and building insurance. In a *net-net-net (or triple-net) lease,* the tenant pays base rent plus real estate taxes, building insurance, and maintenance costs. The latter is also referred to as a *fully net lease*. A useful mnemonic device for remembering the degrees of "net-ness" is the letters (or name) TIM: T = taxes, TI = taxes and insurance, TIM = taxes, insurance, and maintenance.

The foregoing are textbook definitions of gross and net leases. In the real estate industry, some people refer to a triple-net lease as a net lease, while others use the textbook definition. To avoid confusion when the term "net" or "triple-net" is used, it is always best to confirm the intended definition of the term with the other party beforehand, especially if it is not spelled out in the lease.

Most shopping center leases are *modified triple-net leases* under which the landlord may have some maintenance obligations that are not billed back to the tenant (e.g., maintaining the building exterior and the roof). However, since the late 1980s, the shopping center industry has been moving in the direction of true triple-net leases, and by the beginning of the 1990s, many developers and property owners were including roof maintenance, exterior building maintenance, and the management fee as common area expenses in shop tenants' leases. It will be several years before anchor tenants accept these charges as CAM expenses.

SPECIFIC CONTENTS OF THE LEASE

Because of the length and complexity of the retail lease, it usually contains a table of contents preceding the form itself, and those pages are numbered with lower case Roman numerals. The table of contents is included with but not actually a part of the lease. Its purpose is to identify the various provisions (clauses) and indicate the page numbers where they can be found in the lease document.

The first one or two pages of the lease itself provide for a summary of the basic terms and a listing of the parties to the lease. This section includes the business name and address of the landlord, which may be the property owner or the management firm. Also to be listed are the name and address of the tenant—in this case, the address of the leased space—and the tenant's home office when that is appropriate. When the business operated by the tenant is a sole proprietorship, the tenant's home address should be included. When the tenant is a corporation, the address of the corporate headquarters is listed as well.

Also included in this section are spaces to list the tenant's trade name—the assumed (legal) business name—and a description of the permitted uses, the duration of the lease term with its commencement and expiration dates, the amount of minimum rent and when first payment is to be made (rent commencement date), the percentage rent rate, the proration basis for pass-through tenant charges (itemized for operating expenses and common area maintenance), and the amount of the security deposit. If the lease requires a *guarantor*—i.e., another individual (or organization) who promises to assume the tenant's obligations in case of default—the name and address of that party are also included.

Most of the information on the first two pages of the lease will be recorded on the lease summary form used by the management firm to track variations among individual leases (see chapter 12). The sections that follow are intended to indicate the range of provisions in a retail lease, but their presentation is not representative of the sequence in which they would appear. There are many other clauses that apply in particular situations, and specific legal requirements vary in different areas of the United States. Because the economic issues are of utmost importance, they are addressed first.

Tenant's Occupancy Costs

Tenants in shopping centers pay minimum (base) rent, percentage rent, and a pro rata share of real estate taxes, insurance, and common area maintenance (CAM) expenses. All rents and tenant charges are due and payable monthly, concurrent with the payment of minimum rent. Collectively, these payments comprise the tenant's occupancy costs.

Minimum Rent.   The clause states that the tenant will pay to the landlord, without notice or demand and without any deductions, a fixed annual minimum rent to be paid in monthly installments, in advance, on or before the first day of each month of the lease term. If the lease commences on a date other than the first of the month, the monthly minimum rent is prorated for the first month based on a 30-day month.

Minimum Rent Adjustment.   Most leases also provide for periodic increases in minimum rent. The increases may be stated as part of the minimum rent clause or in a separate one. Regardless of its presentation, the provision for increased rent includes several blanks for listing the adjusted (stepped-up) annual and monthly rental rates and the periods they cover. The specific increases may be an agreed-upon fixed amount (e.g., $1.00 per square foot per year).

Cost of Living Adjustment (COLA).   Another approach—one that both landlords and tenants believe to be fair—is based on the rise in the cost of living (i.e., the inflation rate measured in the Consumer Price Index or CPI). The increase in minimum rent is based on the percentage increase in the CPI from one period to another.

Although landlords generally believe that an annual CPI rent adjustment protects the property's value from increased operating expenses and inflation, tenants are usually concerned that the CPI increase may exceed the increase in their sales. For these reasons, minimum rent adjustment based on the CPI is negotiable. In the early 1980s, the CPI was increasing more than 10 percent each year. To prevent a double-digit percentage increase in the minimum rent, tenants attempted to negotiate a ceiling or cap on the CPI increase—a tenant might have agreed to an annual CPI adjustment not to exceed 8 percent. In conceding to a CPI cap, the landlord will want to be assured of receiving no less than an agreed-upon minimum increase and therefore will negotiate for a floor to the CPI. Thus, if the tenant requests an 8-percent ceiling, the landlord may insist on a 4-percent floor. The lease in this situation may state, "The annual rental increase shall be based on the CPI but will be no greater than 8 percent and no less than 4 percent."

When it is agreed that the minimum rent adjustment is to be based on the CPI, there are several specific issues to be resolved and stated in the lease. The first is a definition of the *"base year"*—i.e., the year from which CPI increases will be measured. Usually it is the year the tenant takes occupancy or the first full calendar year during which the tenant occupies the premises. A tenant taking occupancy in November will want the base year to be the following year, but the tenant assuming possession in February should accept as base year the year in which the tenant first occupied the premises.

Along this same line, the next issue to resolve is the date the CPI rent increase is to become effective. CPI increases may commence on the anniversary of the rent commencement date or on January 1 following the rent commencement date. Thus, if a lease commenced July 1, 1990, the base period for rent adjustment would be the first year of the lease—July 1, 1990, to June 30, 1991. However, if the lease stated the CPI adjustment would commence "on January 1 after the lease commencement" (base year as defined above), the first lease adjustment would be for the period January 1, 1992, to December 31, 1992.

A third issue to resolve is which geographic *"price index"* will be used. The CPI—published monthly by the U.S. Department of Labor, Bureau of Labor Statistics—includes the national (U.S. city) average as well as the averages for many (but not all) major metropolitan areas. (The CPI for a few cities is published bimonthly—some in even-numbered months, others in the odd months—or semiannually.) The landlord will not know how to compute the tenant's CPI-related rental increase until the CPI is published. The U.S. city average and the CPIs for those cities that are reported monthly is normally available three to four weeks after the adjusted month—i.e., the CPI for January is published around the end of February. For those metropolitan areas whose CPIs are published semiannually, the report may not be released until three or four months after the period ends. In a major metropolitan area whose CPI is not reported monthly, the landlord may prefer to use the U.S. city average to expedite the adjustment of tenants' minimum rents.

The frequency of minimum rent adjustment is another issue to be resolved. Landlords prefer annual adjustments, while tenants usually negotiate for a less-frequent adjustment (e.g., every three years).

Also to be decided is whether the increase will be based on the full CPI (100 percent) or a part of it. In a partial adjustment, the agreement may be to increase the minimum rent based on a particular percentage of the CPI increase (for example, 67 percent). Thus, if the CPI increase is 6 percent, the rent would be increased 4 percent (6 percent × 67 percent = 4 percent). However, if the change in the CPI is negative—i.e., a decrease from the prior period—the minimum rent would not be reduced.

Percentage Rent.   The typical retail lease provides for payment of whichever is the greater amount, the minimum rent or a percentage of the tenant's sales. The percentage rent clause will state the percentage rate that applies and how often the tenant must provide sales reports. (The percentage rate varies with the type of business, as noted in chapter 9.) Because collecting sales reports and percentage rent can be more difficult than collecting minimum rent, many leases provide for a monetary penalty or fee if tenants do not submit sales reports on time.

Though percentage rent owed is based on annual sales, landlords prefer to receive percentage rent payments on a monthly basis. In fact, small shop tenants are usually required to submit sales reports monthly, typically by the twentieth day of the following month—i.e., January sales figures are due no later than February 20th—but anchor tenants submit sales reports and pay percentage rent annually.

The lease will establish the tenant's annual and monthly breakpoints. When sales exceed the breakpoint, the tenant owes percentage rent. The breakpoint can be natural or artificial. A *natural breakpoint* is derived using a simple mathematical formula: rent ÷ percentage rate = breakpoint. An *artificial breakpoint* is one that has been negotiated. When tenant improvements are very expensive or a tenant's store is being remodeled, the tenant may ask to set an artificial breakpoint *above* the natural breakpoint. This will allow the tenant to offset the cost of the improvements with some of the percentage rent that would otherwise be owed if a natural breakpoint applied. If the shopping center has sales substantially higher than average, the landlord may insist on an artificial breakpoint *below* the natural breakpoint so that percentage rent becomes due earlier. In this situation, the landlord is in a strong negotiating position and can command an advantageous artificial breakpoint. Similarly, the landlord who contributes to the tenant's improvements and wishes to be reimbursed for that contribution expeditiously may insist on an artificial breakpoint *lower* than the natural breakpoint. (Breakpoint calculations are displayed in chapter 9.)

If the tenant pays percentage rent for some months based on monthly calculations, but annual sales ultimately are not sufficient to mandate payment of percentage rent, the landlord is obliged to refund the "excess" percentage rent to the tenant after the first of the year. One type of tenant whose sales fluctuate greatly from month to month is a candy store. Sales may be high during five months of the year because of specific holidays—e.g., Valentine's Day in February, Easter in March or April, Mother's Day in May, Father's Day in June, and Christmas in December—and the store may owe percentage rent for those five months but not for the other months of the year. Individual monthly computations of percentage rent can also result in an accumulated payment that exceeds the amount due for the year. Ultimately, annual sales determine whether or not a tenant receives a refund of percentage rent paid during the year.

The percentage rent clause will also define the *"gross sales"* to which the percentage rate will be applied and list which items, if any, may be excluded from gross sales. Sales tax is one exclusion; refunds and returns may also be deducted. Tenants often seek to exclude discounted sales to their employees, and landlords may be willing to grant this but with limitations—i.e., the lease may refer to "sales to employees at a discount, not to exceed two percent of Tenant's total gross sales." Landlords want to include as many items as possible in the definition of gross sales to maximize the opportunity to collect percentage rent. Obviously, tenants prefer the opposite.

The percentage rent clause will also require the tenant to submit an annual statement of sales signed by an officer of the company. The clause should also state that the payment of percentage rent does not constitute a partnership or joint venture relationship between the landlord and the tenant. The lease generally requires tenants to maintain sales records for a minimum of five years, and grants the landlord the right to audit the tenant's sales. The landlord is responsible for the cost of the audit unless the tenant's reported sales are inaccurate by two percent or more. Some leases permit the landlord to cancel the lease if the tenant deliberately understates its sales.

Note that percentage rent is one of the income components of a shopping center and can have a significant impact on the property's NOI and value. Negotiating the percentage rate determines the landlord's opportunity to collect percentage rent and the amount of percentage rent that will be collected. *Dollars & Cents of Shopping Centers* lists the median percentage rate and the lower and upper decile percentage rates (the typical range) for each tenant category.

Taxes. The real estate taxes and assessments levied by local governments against the shopping center are typically paid by the tenants. A prudent property manager will analyze each successive assessment when it is received. If analysis reveals that the assessment is incorrect, the manager may hire a consultant to appeal the assessment. If the appeal is successful, the savings will be passed on to the tenants—their pro rata shares of the taxes will be lowered. Because the tenants will be the beneficiaries of any tax savings, it is appropri-

E X H I B I T   10.1

Example Lease Clause—Real Estate Taxes

The term "real estate taxes" shall include all real estate taxes and assessments, whether special or general, and including any road improvement districts, water improvement district, if any, and any other utility installation hookup, tie in, or similar charges or assessments that are levied upon and/or assessed against the Premises or the Shopping Center and/or payable during or with respect to the Lease Term, and the costs of professional consultants and/or counsel to analyze tax bills and prosecute any protests, refunds, and appeals, provided that all such payments shall be paid on a cash basis without regard to whether such real estate taxes apply to a period before or after the Lease Term and without regard to whether the Tenant was in possession of the Premises during the time covered by the particular tax statement.

---

ate that they should also pay for the analysis and appeal of the assessment. An example of a typical "real estate taxes" lease clause is shown in exhibit 10.1.

Insurance.   The tenant is responsible for reimbursing the landlord's cost to insure the shopping center. This clause should not limit the type or amount of insurance coverage that may be necessary. The lease may state that "insurance shall include all insurance premiums for fire, liability, rent loss, and any other insurance and endorsement which may include an 'all risk' endorsement or any other insurance that the Landlord or Landlord's lender deems necessary."

Common Area Maintenance (CAM).   The common area maintenance charges include several categories of expense—e.g., maintenance, utilities, insurance, security, and administration. The lease should not limit the expenses included in the CAM charges by stating that the tenant will pay "the following list of expenses." The tenant may interpret this to mean that any expenses incurred but not listed are not CAM expenses. The landlord should have the right to pass through to the tenant all the legitimate expenses of maintaining and operating the common areas of the shopping center. The lease should state the basic CAM expenses and allow for additional CAM items. Representative lease language would be "the common area maintenance expenses shall include but are not limited to the following list," and the clause would include an itemized list of specific components of the CAM charge "and such other related expenses as may be incurred."

The clause should allow for unanticipated expenditures such as a need for temporary or permanent security. Many landlords also pass through as CAM expenses such items as roof repairs, painting of the building exterior, and funding (development of capital reserves) for future maintenance. Alternatively, there may be separate provisions defining these expenses and stating how the tenant's pro rata share is determined. In the late 1980s, some landlords began including the management fee as a CAM expense. (An example of a CAM clause that includes the management fee is shown in exhibit 10.2.) If the management fee is not included as a CAM expense, it is common practice to add an administrative fee for supervision of the common areas. This fee may be 10–15 percent of the actual common area expenses. When the CAM charges include the management fee, it is inappropriate to charge an additional administrative fee.

Enclosed Mall CAM. An enclosed mall will have two CAM budgets, one for the parking lot and exterior areas and one for the enclosed mall common areas. This permits separation of these pass-through expenses for tenant billings. In particular, anchor tenants often negotiate exemption from paying enclosed mall CAM expenses, arguing that their being the major draw and having direct entrances to the parking lot minimizes their specific benefits from the enclosed mall. In that case, the anchor tenant pays only a pro rata share of parking lot and exterior CAM expenses. When the anchor is exempted from paying mall CAM expenses, the landlord usually wants the shop tenants to pay the entire cost of the enclosed mall CAM. Each shop tenant's proration is then based on the square footage of its premises divided by the total square footage occupied by shop tenants whose stores front on the mall. (Store areas of shops in a satellite building and/or pad tenants would not be included.) Thus, if a mall has 800,000 square feet of GLA with 200,000 square feet occupied by shop tenants and 600,000 square feet by anchor tenants, the denominator for the shop tenants' proration formula would be 200,000 square feet. A shop tenant in a 2,000-square-foot space would pay one percent of the enclosed mall CAM costs (2,000 square feet ÷ 200,000 square feet = .01). However, the denominator for parking lot and exterior CAM for all tenants would be 800,000 square feet, and the same shop would pay one-fourth of one percent as its share of these costs (2,000 square feet ÷ 800,000 square feet = .0025). (An example of a clause that provides for exclusion of the anchor tenant's square footage in determining a shop tenant's pro rata share of enclosed mall CAM expenses is shown in exhibit 10.3. This sample provision also includes an administrative fee.)

Note that the sample provision in exhibit 10.2 refers specifically to insurance coverage. In the absence of an itemized list, the reference can be inferred in exhibit 10.3. The insurance included in CAM charges is for property damage to the common areas and liability coverage if someone is injured in those areas. This portion of the insurance premiums is excluded from the building insurance expense that is billed separately to the tenants. The reason for dividing the insurance premiums this way is that some tenants—i.e., those in freestanding buildings—are responsible for providing their own fire, extended coverage, and liability insurance. For example, the landlord would not include a freestanding restaurant in the insurance coverage for the shop-

E X H I B I T   10.2

Example Lease Clause—Common Area Maintenance

1. The term "common areas" refers to all areas within the exterior boundaries of the Shopping Center which are now or hereafter made available for general use, convenience and benefit of Landlord and other persons entitled to occupy space in the Shopping Center, which areas shall include but not be limited to parking areas, driveways, open or enclosed malls, sidewalks, landscaped and planted areas, and roofs.

2. The Landlord shall keep or cause to be kept the common areas in a neat, clean, and orderly condition, properly lighted and landscaped, and shall repair any damage to the facilities thereof, but all expense in connection with the common areas shall be charged and prorated in the manner hereinafter set forth. It is understood and agreed that the terms "common area maintenance charge" and "expenses in connection with the common areas" as used herein shall be construed to include, but not be limited to, all sums expended in connection with the common areas for all general maintenance and repairs; relocation of facilities; resurfacing; painting; striping; restriping; cleaning; snow removal; sweeping and janitorial services; maintenance and repair of sidewalks, curbs and Shopping Center signs, landscaping, irrigation or sprinkling systems; planting and landscaping; lighting and other utilities; directional signs and other markers and bumpers; all roof repairs and maintenance including but not limited to patching, resurfacing and preventive maintenance and painting or renovation of the exterior portion of all or any part of the improvements constructed on the Shopping Center; maintenance and repair of any fire protection systems, lighting systems, storm draining systems and any other utility systems; all cost or expense incurred by reason of any repairs or modifications to the Shopping Center and/or its improvements and/or repair or installation of equipment for energy or safety purposes; personnel to implement such services including, if Landlord deems necessary, the cost of a maintenance supervisor and/or the cost of security guards; all costs and expenses pertaining to a security alarm system for the tenants and/or Shopping Center; reserves for future maintenance and repair work and reserves for replacement of existing capital improvements in the common areas which Tenant hereby authorizes Landlord to use as Landlord deems necessary; personal property taxes on the improvements located on the common areas; fees incurred in managing the Shopping Center and in the performance, management and supervision of the common area maintenance services and obligations and/or administering the accounting, bookkeeping and collection of the expenses in connection with the common areas and Shopping Center; and public liability and property damage insurance covering the common areas in amounts as required by Landlord. Landlord may cause any or all of said services to be provided by an independent contractor or contractors.

3. Should Landlord acquire or make available land not shown as part of the Shopping Center on the Site Plan Exhibit and make the same available for parking or other common area purposes, then said expenses in connection with the common areas shall also include all of the aforementioned expenses incurred and paid in connection with said additional land.

---

ping center, and the restaurant's square footage would be excluded from the denominator used in calculating the other tenants' pro rata shares of the building insurance expense. However, the restaurant tenant would still be obligated to pay a pro rata share of the common area maintenance expenses, including the liability and property damage insurance coverages on the com-

E X H I B I T   10.3

**Example Lease Clause—Enclosed Mall
Common Area Maintenance**

Small shop tenants in the Shopping Center having storefronts on the enclosed mall shall pay their Pro Rata Share of the enclosed mall operation and maintenance expense; Tenant shall pay to Landlord a monthly enclosed mall maintenance charge to defray the enclosed mall operation and maintenance expenses; provided, however, that it is understood and agreed that the area leased by major tenants having storefronts on the enclosed mall shall not be included within the formula used to determine Tenant's Pro Rata Share of mall operation and maintenance expenses. In addition, Tenant shall pay a monthly sum to Landlord for the accounting, bookkeeping and collection of the enclosed mall operation and maintenance expenses in an amount equal to *[specify percentage in words and numbers]* of the total of Tenant's Pro Rata Share of the aforementioned expenses for such year. The amount of the monthly enclosed mall maintenance charge shall be equal to Tenant's Pro Rata Share of the enclosed mall operation and maintenance expense incurred for the prior calendar month, which share shall be determined by multiplying such expense amounts (less the sums, if any, contributed by major tenants for such expenses, under their leases) by the Tenant's percentage of enclosed mall operation and maintenance expenses, which percentage is computed by obtaining a fraction, the numerator of which is the leasable area of the Premises and the denominator of which is the gross leasable floor area of small shops and services located in and fronting on the enclosed mall area.

---

mon areas as already mentioned. By allocating part of the premium for the insurance on the whole shopping center as a CAM expense, the landlord assures that those tenants paying for maintenance of the common area are also paying to insure it. The same situation prevails when an anchor tenant owns and insures its building but pays a pro rata share of CAM expenses.

Tenant's Pro Rata Share.   The tenant's proportionate share of the pass-through expenses is calculated as a percentage based on the relationship between the square footage of the tenant's premises and the leasable area or the leased areas of the shopping center. The distinction here is between "potential" and "actual" leased square footage, and the difference in the resulting payment can be substantial. The *leasable area* includes the square footage of all the buildings in the shopping center, whereas the *leased areas* comprise those spaces in the shopping center that are actually under lease. Shopping center leases typically base the tenants' pro rata shares on the leasable area, which includes all occupied and vacant spaces in the center. Each tenant's pro rata share is computed by multiplying the specific expense (e.g., insurance, taxes, CAM) by a fraction, the numerator of which is the GLA of the tenant's premises and the denominator of which is the GLA of the shopping center.

$$\frac{\text{GLA of tenant's space}}{\text{GLA of shopping center}} = \text{Tenant's pro rata share}$$

E X H I B I T   10.4

Example Lease Clause—Tenant's Pro Rata Share

For the purposes of this Lease with respect to allocations of each Tenant's share of taxes, insurance, common area maintenance expenses and other Tenant charges, the term "Tenant's Pro Rata Share" shall be a fraction, the numerator of which is the gross leasable area of the Premises and the denominator of which is the gross leasable floor area of the buildings constructed within the Shopping Center from time to time. Provided, however, that if any tenants in said buildings have obtained written approval from Landlord to pay their taxes directly to any taxing authority, or to carry their own insurance, or to maintain part of the common area at their own expense, their square footage shall not be deemed a part of the floor area for the purposes of prorating said taxes, or said insurance, or said common area maintenance expenses.

When the formula is based on leased space, the numerator is still the GLA of the tenant's premises, but the denominator is the GLA of the leased spaces only, so that the denominator will change every time a space is vacated or leased. Also, as the value of the denominator gets smaller, the tenant's pro rata share gets larger. For example, a tenant in a 2,000-square-foot space in a shopping center with 100,000 square feet of GLA has a pro rata share of 2 percent based on leasable square footage. However, if the center is only 80 percent occupied, that tenant's pro rata share becomes 2.5 percent when based on the leased space (2,000 ÷ 80,000 = .025). That one-half percent difference becomes more meaningful when applied specifically. If the pass-through tenant charges (CAM, taxes, and insurance) total $300,000, the tenant in the example pays only $6,000 based on leasable area ($300,000 × .02) but would have to pay $7,500 based on the leased area ($300,000 × .025).

It is obvious from this why tenants believe they are being unfairly penalized by having to pay a higher percentage of tenant charges because the landlord is unable to lease the vacant spaces in the shopping center. The landlord's argument for using leased space as the denominator is that those tenants and their visitors are the only ones using the whole of the common areas of the shopping center. Most sophisticated tenants will not accept a pro rata formula based on the leased area, and most shopping center leases use the leasable square footage in the denominator. (An example of a definition of "tenant's pro rata share" based on the leasable area appears in exhibit 10.4.)

Standard shopping center leases require tenants to pay their pro rata shares of tenants' charges (pass-through expenses) each month based on the landlord's estimated budget. After the end of the year, the actual costs are reconciled with the budget. If the total paid out exceeds the budget, the tenants will be billed for their shares of the difference. However, if the budget exceeds the actual costs, the overpayment is returned to the tenants, either as an outright refund or as a credit toward the next month's rent. (See also the discussion of lease administration in chapter 12.)

Tenant's Use of the Leased Premises

A number of clauses spell out requirements related to the tenant's occupancy and use of the leased premises.

Landlord's and Tenant's Work. The lease usually includes a provision that states the condition of the premises when the landlord delivers them to the tenant and that the tenant agrees to accept the premises subject to completion of any landlord's work, which is to be described in the landlord's and tenant's work exhibit (discussed later in this chapter). The exhibit also specifies what work the tenant will provide in its premises.

Typically, when space in an existing shopping center is leased, the tenant assumes the premises in "as is" condition. This usually means that the prior tenant's fixtures have been removed and the space is "broom clean." In general, any painting and replacement of the prior tenant's improvements by the landlord would be wasted because the new tenant usually redesigns the premises for its specific business. Most retailers and service tenants have their own unique store designs and layouts. When a tenant successfully negotiates with the landlord for tenant improvements, the landlord usually provides a monetary allowance and the tenant does the build-out. The allowance is paid *after* the tenant completes the improvements.

New shopping center space is usually leased in "shell" condition to be completed by the tenant. In a strip center, the landlord may provide a concrete floor, unfinished demising walls, a drop ceiling, light fixtures, a restroom, and a storefront. (In other types of centers and in different areas of the United States, what is provided as "shell" space can vary substantially; see also the discussion of tenant improvements in chapter 6.) In these circumstances, either the landlord provides a monetary allowance toward the tenant's build-out expense (e.g., $5 per square foot), or the landlord agrees to provide (build out) some or all of the improvements to the tenant's premises.

Continuous Operation. An element critical to the synergism of a shopping center is uniform hours of operation in all the stores. The continuous operation clause requires the tenant to maintain store hours as designated by the landlord. It also requires the tenant to keep in stock, on the premises, a full and ample line of merchandise and maintain an adequate sales force.

The shopping center is the only property type that requires a continuous operation clause in all leases. The primary reason the landlord requires the tenants to maintain the hours of the shopping center and have adequate stocks of merchandise is to assure that they have ample opportunities to maximize their sales and pay percentage rent. This is also to optimize the tenant mix because all stores are maintaining the same hours. In office buildings and industrial properties, the primary concern is with the tenant paying rent; seldom is there concern whether the tenant occupies the leased premises or

if the tenant is closed periodically, except as these practices may signal financial problems. (Monitoring of store hours is discussed in chapter 5.)

Quiet Enjoyment.   This is one of the few lease provisions that directly
benefits the tenant. "Tenant shall have and quietly enjoy the premises during
the term of the lease, provided that Tenant fully complies with and promptly
performs all of the terms, covenants, and conditions of the lease."

Floor Area—Definition of Measurement.   Unlike the office building
industry, the shopping center industry does not have a standard method for
measuring store areas. This provision of the lease states the method to be
used in measuring the tenant's premises. Typically, measurements are made
from the centers of demising walls (the walls or partitions that separate tenants) and from either the inside or outside of exterior walls. No deductions
from the square footage of the floor area are made for columns, shafts, or any
penetrations of the floor. Mezzanine areas are usually measured and included
in the tenant's GLA.

Tenant's Rights and Obligations

The lease spells out what is required of the tenant in maintaining the leased
premises and operating its business in the shopping center. Many clauses specifically limit the tenant's actions.

Tenant Alterations.   A shopping center is one of the few property types
in which the tenants are responsible for coordinating and contracting for the
improvements to their premises. The lease will state that the tenant cannot
construct any improvement to the premises until the landlord reviews—and
approves in writing—the plans for any alterations, additions, or other improvements in or to the premises. The tenant will be required to provide its
own container for construction debris. In a newly constructed center where
store spaces are leased as "shells," improvements to tenant spaces may be
arranged as part of construction "finishing" and the lease provision regarding
tenant alterations would reflect this.

Tenants are usually prohibited from doing work on the roof, and many
landlords prohibit tenants from core drilling or other construction activities
during normal business hours because of the likelihood they will be disruptive to the other tenants and their customers. At the landlord's request, all
improvements must be removed at the tenant's sole expense when the premises are vacated or the lease expires.

Maintenance of Tenant's Premises.   This clause states that the tenant is
responsible for all repairs and maintenance to the leased premises. It also
states which repair and maintenance items are the landlord's responsibility.
Basically, the tenant is responsible for all maintenance inside the leased

premises, and the landlord performs all maintenance outside the tenant's premises. Typically, the landlord maintains the exterior walls, roof, foundation, and structural portions of the building, and the cost of repairing and maintaining some or all of these items may be included in the CAM charges. If the tenant fails to maintain the premises, the landlord, after written notice, has the option of performing the maintenance or repairs and charging the cost to the tenant. The tenant is expected to repay the landlord promptly for any such maintenance or repairs.

Utilities. This clause requires the tenant to pay, in a timely manner, all utilities that are billed directly to the tenant for its premises. This provision also grants the landlord the right to bill the tenant for a pro rata share of any utility that is not separately metered for each of the premises. Electricity and gas are commonly provided by private utility companies and metered directly, but other arrangements exist. Water is often provided by municipal or other governmental authorities, and charges for sewage disposal are usually based on water consumption. The lease should specify the sources of utility services for the particular shopping center and spell out the formula for allocating costs for the center as a whole. All shopping center tenants will have electricity expenses and, unless their store spaces do not include "washrooms," they will all have some water (and sewer) expenses.

Sometimes an incoming "utility" is on a master meter for the center as a whole. In that situation, when a tenant uses more than its pro rata share, the landlord may charge the tenant for the excess utility usage. Water is a typical example of a master-metered utility for which the landlord bills each tenant on a pro rata basis. However, some tenants (e.g., restaurants, car washes, coin laundries, and hair salons) use very large volumes of water—excessive amounts in comparison to a typical tenant's usage. Because of this, the property manager should estimate the percentage of the total water bill each tenant should pay based on use rather than any other proration formula. A representative from the water company can provide typical water usage data for each category of tenant.

Garbage pickup (trash disposal) may be considered as a "utility" or addressed separately in the lease. Disposal service may be contracted for the entire center or by individual tenants. The expense involved will depend on how that service is provided. Special consideration should be given to the needs of certain tenants whose "garbage" can pose disposal problems—e.g., food wastes from supermarkets and restaurants, animal excrement and other materials from pet stores. Some disposed materials are potentially hazardous (e.g., medical wastes).

Tenant's Insurance. The landlord wants to be certain that if any of the tenant's inventory, fixtures, or equipment is damaged, stolen, or destroyed, the tenant will have the funds to replace these items and continue to operate the business. The insurance clause states that the tenant will carry insurance on the furniture, fixtures, equipment, and inventory of the business in addition to plate glass coverage and liability insurance in a required minimum amount. The tenant is required to provide the landlord with evidence of such insurance and to name the landlord and the landlord's property management company as named insured parties on the policies.

Tenant's Employee Parking.   One criterion of a successful shopping center is convenient parking. The parking stalls that are closest to the stores will turn over six to eight times a day—i.e., six to eight customers may use each of those "convenient" stalls each day. When a tenant's employee parks all day in one of these stalls, one of the most convenient stalls has been taken away from six to eight customers. This clause requires tenants' employees to park in a designated area of the parking lot. It prohibits their use of prime customer parking areas and grants the landlord the right to fine tenants each time one of their employees parks in a nonemployee parking area—usually $10–$20 per violation. The fine is assessed against the tenant, not the employee, because the tenant is a party to the lease. A tenant may ask to be given a warning the first time one of its employees parks in a nonemployee parking area and for the fine to apply to subsequent violations. (See also the discussion of lease administration in chapter 5.)

Signs.   The tenants want to advertise to people walking or driving by the shopping center or their stores, and the landlord wants to control the appearance of the shopping center and prevent it from being gaudy or offensive. To address both parties' desires and concerns, the landlord should develop signage criteria that will limit the types and sizes of tenants' signs while still allowing them to have signage that is representative of their business, easy to read, and visible. Sign criteria should take into account any local laws that may govern the issues of size, materials, and positioning for display.

A signage clause requires tenants to submit plans for their exterior signs for the landlord's approval. The plans must be based on the shopping center's sign criteria, which are included as an exhibit appended to the lease, and the sign must be installed and maintained by the tenant. The tenant usually arranges for a sign contractor to prepare a drawing of the proposed sign— showing details of dimensions, colors, and materials to be used—and submit it to the property manager, who is responsible for approving or denying proposed signs. When a sign is denied, the property manager should tell the tenant why. The most common reasons for denial are excessive size and use of unsatisfactory or inappropriate materials.

Advertising.   The landlord wants all the tenants to advertise and promote their businesses to maximize their sales potential. This clause requires tenants to spend a minimum percentage of their gross sales on advertising (usually 2 percent) and to provide evidence of this expenditure. The advertising provision may require the tenant to advertise in a minimum number of the center's advertising tabloids. If the tenant does not advertise a minimum number of times, the landlord may place an ad giving the tenant's name and address, and the tenant will be responsible for reimbursing the landlord for this cost. This lease provision is more common for an enclosed mall than for a strip center.

Merchants' Association or Marketing Fund. Most enclosed malls and many large strip centers have either a merchants' association or a marketing fund. A specific lease provision requires the tenant to participate in funding this entity, states the minimum payment (per square foot), and provides for an annual increase in funding. Membership in and the requirement to pay dues to a merchants' association—or the requirement to contribute to a marketing fund—should not be contingent on a percentage of all the tenants belonging to or paying for either organization. Older shopping center leases would state that the tenant was required to join the merchants' association only if a specific percentage of the merchants belonged (usually 75 or 80 percent). If the landlord believes that a merchants' association or marketing fund will benefit the shopping center and the tenants, the tenants' participation should be mandatory. As noted elsewhere in this book, anchor tenants will seldom agree to mandatory membership in a merchants' association; however, they will often agree to contribute to the funding of a merchants' association or marketing fund.

Originally, merchants' association dues were based on a tenant's front footage. Since the 1970s, however, dues have been based on tenants' square footage. Sometimes the dues schedule will allow a reduction in the rate per square foot for tenants with larger spaces, or the amount (or rate) of dues will be reduced as store size increases. As an example, annual dues may be 50 cents per square foot for the first 1,500 square feet, 40 cents per square foot for the next 1,000 square feet, 30 cents each for the next 1,000 square feet, and 25 cents each for the remainder. The lease may require minimum dues regardless of the size of a tenant's premises. This will prevent a tenant with very small premises (e.g., a 50–100-square-foot kiosk) from paying only nominal dues. Anchor tenants' contributions may be based on a fixed annual amount or on a formula whereby dues would be less per square foot than those of a shop tenant. All dues are paid monthly.

Because inflation will erode the buying power of the merchants' association or marketing fund if dues are fixed for the term of the lease, the clause may call for an annual increase in dues based on a CPI adjustment. If the shopping center is new, the tenants will be required to pay an additional grand opening assessment, usually a set dollar amount per square foot. In the absence of a specific merchants' association or marketing fund, the lease may require the tenant to pay a monthly promotional fee as "additional rent."

Rules and Regulations. The landlord is responsible for operating the shopping center in a manner that is generally beneficial to both tenants and shoppers. To achieve this, the landlord usually sets rules for tenants and their operations that address issues of conformity and safety. Typically, rules and regulations may specify constraints on such activities as loading and unloading, shipping and deliveries, accumulation of garbage, maintenance of the shopping environment (store temperature, use of loudspeakers, etc.), employee parking, and general housekeeping.

The provision requires the tenant to comply with the rules and regulations that the landlord may promulgate or modify. It also states that the landlord is not responsible to the tenant for the nonperformance of any rules and regulations by any other tenant and that the rules and regulations will apply and be enforced uniformly.

Liens and Encumbrances. If the tenant does not pay its contractor for tenant improvements or maintenance, that contractor may place a lien on the leased premises or on the shopping center itself. Such an encumbrance can delay or prevent the sale or refinancing of the shopping center. To protect the landlord's interests, this clause requires the tenant to keep the premises and the shopping center free from any liens arising out of any work performed or contracted by the tenant. It also gives the landlord the right to require the tenant to obtain payment and performance bonds in an amount equal to one and one-half times the estimated cost of such work, materials, labor, and supplies.

Auction and Sale. Because "going-out-of-business" signs, sales, or auctions can give the impression that the shopping center itself is failing, landlords include in the lease a provision stating that the tenant may not conduct a bankruptcy or going-out-business sale or auction—or post signs announcing such activities—without the prior written consent of the landlord.

Landlord's Rights and Obligations

A number of lease clauses specifically protect the landlord's rights in the property, including the right and opportunity to collect percentage rent.

Security Deposit. A security deposit is an amount paid by the tenant to the landlord to guarantee the tenant's faithful performance of all the terms, covenants, and conditions of the lease. It is not intended to be the last month's rent. If the tenant does not pay the rent or other payments due— including rental adjustments, pass-through expenses, merchants' association dues or marketing fund contributions, or late charges—the security deposit may be used to cure the nonpayment. The security deposit also may be used to undertake repairs or maintenance as required of the tenant under the lease but that the tenant refuses to perform. (Because the tenant in a shopping center is usually responsible for finishing the interior of the store, a security deposit may be less critical for this type of property.) The security deposit clause should require the tenant to reimburse (or restore) the full amount of the security deposit held by the landlord if the deposit is used to correct a default by the tenant.

Anchor tenants and national shop tenants typically have established credit ratings, and they will negotiate to omit the provision for a security deposit. On the other hand, local and regional merchants will sometimes agree to pay a security deposit. In lieu of a specific deposit, the lease can require the tenant to provide a letter of credit valued at a certain amount.

The amount of the security deposit is typically one month's rent. However, if the tenant's business is new or financially weak, the equivalent of two or even three months' rent as a security deposit may be necessary or appropriate. A financially strong local or regional tenant with a successful business may negotiate for an early refund of the security deposit. For example, the landlord may agree to credit the security deposit to the rent for the twenty-fifth month if the tenant's rent has always been paid every month by the first of the month and the tenant was never in default of the lease during the first two years.

Another approach is to make an early refund contingent on the tenant's sales exceeding an agreed-upon dollar volume or the payment of percentage rent. This might read, "If Tenant's sales exceed $200 per square foot during the second calendar year of the lease, and if Tenant's rent has always been paid on or before the first of the month and Tenant was never in default of the lease, the security deposit will be credited to the twenty-fifth month's rent." A reverse approach would require no security deposit unless the tenant's net worth falls below an agreed-upon amount; however, this approach is more difficult to monitor.

The security deposit clause usually concludes by stating that the landlord will return the security deposit to the tenant without interest and within 30 to 60 days after the expiration of the lease term if the tenant has faithfully performed each provision of the lease.

Late Charge.   If a tenant does not pay the rent on time, the landlord has two primary means of recourse—eviction or assessment of a late charge. The lease gives the landlord the right to assess a late charge if the tenant does not pay the rent by a predetermined date.

The clause may require the landlord to give the tenant written notice that the rent has not been received and to grant a grace period before the late charge will be assessed. Alternatively, the lease may state that if the rent is not received on the date it is due, the landlord may automatically assess a late charge. The amount of the late charge should also be stated (e.g., 12 percent of the amount past due); in no event should the percentage rate be more than the legal maximum allowed. If the landlord uses the services of an attorney to collect delinquent rent, the attorney's fees are a tenant expense.

Store Hours.   This clause is included to protect the landlord's opportunity to collect percentage rent. Landlords want all tenants to maintain necessary and reasonable hours to maximize their sales. This lease provision is unique to retail properties and has evolved over many years. Originally, the retail lease stated that shop tenants would maintain the same hours as the anchor tenant. When anchor tenants—namely supermarkets—extended their hours, it became impractical to require shop tenants to maintain the same hours as the anchor tenants. The next phase was a period when the lease required the tenant to maintain the hours established by the merchants' association. This was basically inappropriate. The merchants' association should never be given the responsibility to determine any shopping center management or operating policy. The merchants often cannot agree on issues, and some of their decisions may not be in the landlord's best interests. Still another approach was to require the tenant to maintain the hours of similar businesses in the community. This allowed an outside influence to determine the merchant's hours of operation.

The most effective approach to store hours is to state the basic daily hours of operation in the lease and allow the landlord to change them when necessary or appropriate. Frequently, the basic hours are stated to be Monday through Friday from 10:00 A.M. to 9:00 P.M., Saturday from 10:00 A.M. to 6:00 P.M., and Sunday from 11:00 A.M. to 6:00 P.M., and the landlord extends the hours during the Christmas season.

A store hours clause may also state which days, if any, the shopping center will be closed—usually specific holidays: New Year's Day, Easter, Independence Day (July 4), Thanksgiving, and Christmas. This particular stipulation is only needed in leases for enclosed malls. Landlords do not want to open a mall if only a few tenants will be open. In an open mall or a strip center, tenants may be open on these days. If the lease states the days the mall will be closed, it should also provide for the landlord to change them.

Radius.   To protect the landlord's opportunity to collect percentage rent, the tenant is prohibited from diverting sales at the shopping center by opening another store nearby. The radius clause either prohibits the tenant from opening a similar store within three to five miles from the shopping center or requires the tenant to add to the sales of its store the sales from any other similar store it operates within three to five miles from the shopping center for the purpose of calculating percentage rent.

HVAC Maintenance.   Originally tenants were responsible for maintaining the HVAC units in their premises, but improper maintenance during occupancy and costly repairs when the premises were vacated led to a requirement for the tenants to submit a copy of their maintenance contracts to the landlord. Use of different contractors, inconsistencies in the quality of service and the specifications in the maintenance contracts, and the added problem of damage to the roof made the situation worse. (HVAC maintenance is discussed in detail in chapter 6.)

The updated HVAC maintenance clause gives the landlord the right to maintain the HVAC unit and makes the tenant responsible for the cost of preventive maintenance, repairs, and replacements. Because all work is contracted to one company, the property manager is usually able to negotiate a discounted service price. This assures that HVAC units will be serviced properly and in good condition at the expiration of the tenant's lease. Also, an efficiently run HVAC unit and a discounted service fee result in direct savings for the tenant, and the life of the equipment is prolonged. In addition, only one service contractor has access to the roof.

Relocation.   A clause granting the landlord the right to relocate the tenant's premises is not often found in shopping center leases. It is usually omitted for two reasons—the importance of location in a shopping center and the differences in the rental rates for particular locations. However, relocation may be an important consideration in a lease with a temporary or seasonal tenant (see chapter 9).

Most sophisticated retail tenants will not accept a relocation clause. However, when this provision is acceptable to a tenant, it has benefits for the landlord. The property manager may have to protect a location for future expansion of a valuable tenant, for combining spaces to attract a large tenant, or to allow the flexibility to recapture a space to expand or remodel the center. In any of these situations, the lease should have a relocation provision. If the tenant agrees to such a provision, the relocation will probably be limited to a particular area in the shopping center and approximately the same size premises as the tenant presently occupies. The landlord is responsible for the tenant's moving expenses and improvements to the relocation space, and rent is usually abated during the time the tenant's business is interrupted.

Assignment and Subletting.   Over the years, the courts have ruled both for and against the landlord's right to deny a tenant's request to assign the lease. Early shopping center leases gave the landlord the right to approve or deny a tenant's request to assign the lease or sublet the premises. Some states have ruled that the landlord must be reasonable in any decision to deny the tenant's request. One version of the assignment provision allows the landlord the right to refuse to consent to an assignment or sublease if, in the landlord's reasonable business judgment, the quality, merchandising experience, or financial worth of the proposed new tenant (assignee or sublessee) is not of the same caliber as the primary tenant or that tenant's guarantor. The assignment clause may allow the landlord to charge the tenant a fee, usually approximately $200, for processing the request for assignment or sublease. The lease should not be silent on this issue.

If the landlord approves an assignment, it should be characterized as an "assignment without release"—i.e., the assignor (the tenant assigning its lease) must fulfill the obligations of the lease if the assignee defaults. An "assignment with release" frees the assignor from all future obligations of the lease; if the assignee defaults, the landlord cannot look to the assignor to cure the default. Default of a lease is usually nonpayment of rent. Under an assignment without release, the landlord can collect from the assignor if the assignee stops paying rent.

Lease Provisions Detrimental to Landlords

Several specific clauses are detrimental to landlords—exclusive use, cotenancy, most favored tenant, and options.

Exclusive Use.   A tenant may seek to negotiate an exclusive use clause that grants the tenant the sole right to sell a specific product or provide a specific service. Because such an exclusive prevents the landlord from bringing in other tenants whose product lines may overlap those of the first tenant, landlords are understandably reluctant to grant a tenant an exclusive. Even if the landlord does not intend to duplicate a use, it is best not to grant an exclusive. The exclusive would be detrimental to the landlord's effort to create the best tenant mix for the shopping center. In an enclosed mall, most uses can and must be duplicated to provide the consumer with a wide variety of merchandise and opportunities for comparison shopping. In neighborhood and community centers many uses can be duplicated without harm to any of the merchants.

It may be possible to grant an exclusive that may not fully satisfy the tenant but will be less burdensome for the landlord. If an exclusive must be granted in a lease for a shop tenant, the following restrictions (exemptions) to it should be considered.

1. It should not apply to the anchor tenant or its assignees or sublessees. Anchor tenant use provisions have few, if any, restrictions. The anchor tenant will add new lines of merchandise during its lease term, and some of this merchandise may conflict with a shop tenant's exclusive.
2. It should not apply to any existing tenants. It is possible that one or more existing tenants' use clauses may not prohibit them from selling a product that a new tenant has an exclusive right to sell. (An exclusive can apply to future time and subsequent tenants but not to past time or prior tenants.)
3. It should not apply to the tenant's assignee or sublessee. (The tenant cannot transfer the exclusive to others.)
4. It should be very limited—i.e., an exclusive use to operate a beauty parlor should not include the exclusive right to sell beauty products because several other types of stores sell such products.
5. It should exclude the incidental sale of the product by other tenants.

6. It may be limited to a particular area—e.g., the north wing of the shopping center.
7. It should be contingent on payment of percentage rent. (If the tenant does not pay percentage rent, it loses the right to the exclusive.)

Exclusives, once granted, must be monitored and enforced by the landlord. They must be taken into account whenever new tenants are being considered. The purpose of an exclusive is to exclude others from operating the same type of business or selling the same product within the center. This limitation on competition between tenants or product lines constitutes a restraint of trade, which may be problematic on a different level. Federal antitrust legislation prohibits certain kinds of actions in restraint of trade.

Cotenancy. It is not uncommon for a national shop tenant to sign a lease for space in a shopping center because of the presence of a specific major tenant or combination of tenants. That tenant may ask for a lease provision that would allow it to either pay percentage rent only or, worse yet, cancel the lease, if the major tenant—or another specific tenant—went dark (closed its store) or its lease was terminated. Most shopping center managers hope to avoid tenants going dark by including a *continuous operation* clause in the lease. Store closings and other efforts by tenants to terminate leases can have a disastrous effect on the shopping center. A cotenancy clause making one tenant's rights or obligations dependent on another tenant's presence or operations should be avoided. Seldom are cotenancy rights included in a tenant's lease, not even an anchor tenant's lease. However, if an important tenant is in the balance, one may not have a choice. If a cotenancy is granted, the provision should allow the landlord six months to one year to replace the vacating tenant before that tenant may cancel its lease.

Most Favored Tenant. The most favored tenant provision—also known as a "favored nation" clause—derives its name and function from the favored nation trade advantages that one country gives another. Such a provision grants to a tenant all the concessions that other tenants are or have been granted. For example, if one tenant has a cap on real estate taxes and another does not pay CAM charges, a tenant whose lease includes a "most favored tenant" provision is granted these same privileges. Often this provision is sought by tenants whose leases are negotiated early in the lease-up period of a new shopping center. The first tenant to lease space may be told it is receiving the "best" deal any tenant will be offered. To assure itself that it is getting the "best" deal, that tenant asks for a most favored tenant provision.

This particular lease provision is another one to be avoided. It is more likely to appear in a lease form generated by a tenant. Occasionally a national shop tenant will include this provision in its standard form lease, usually toward the end of the form. However, at the landlord's insistence, the tenant will usually delete it.

Options. Several different "options" can be incorporated into a retail lease, and they are usually granted by the landlord as specific concessions. The option or options granted in a particular lease may relate to the lease term (extension or renewal of the lease), the premises (expansion of the tenant's space), or the lease itself (cancellation by the tenant). Because options favor the tenant at the landlord's expense, it is understandable why landlords are reluctant to grant them.

. An *option to extend* grants the tenant the right to extend the lease term without interruption; this provides a benefit to the tenant and creates an obligation for the landlord. Most landlords prefer not to grant this option because there are so many factors that can work to the landlord's detriment during the term of the lease—e.g., a tenant's sales may be low, rent may not be paid on time, or a tenant may be a poor merchant. Seldom should a landlord have to agree to an option to extend, but there are situations that call for it, as noted earlier in the discusion of the lease term. If an option to extend the lease must be provided, it should be contingent on several criteria, including those listed below.

1. The tenant must not be in default of the lease on the date the option is exercised and the lease is extended.
2. The tenant must provide notice of its intention to exercise the option within a specific time frame in relation to the lease termination—e.g., no later than 120 days and no sooner than 180 days before the lease expires.
3. The option right should be canceled if the tenant assigns the lease or subleases the premises.
4. If possible, the option should be contingent on the tenant paying percentage rent during the last two years of the lease.

The rent for the option period can be stated as a predetermined amount, as the market rate, or as an increase based on the CPI; however, it should be no less than the rate paid during the last month of the prior lease term. The latter should be stated specifically. If the rent is to be based on the current market rate and that market rate is less than what the tenant is already paying, setting such a minimum will protect the landlord from undue financial loss.

An *option to expand* the tenant's leased space may be stated as such and related to specific space designated on a plan of the shopping center. However, a landlord is more likely to grant a *right of first refusal* to lease additional (usually contiguous) space, based on the lease terms the landlord would offer to another prospective tenant for that space, and the tenant is given a limited time (usually three to five days) to accept the landlord's offer. Alternatively, some landlords will offer a *first right to negotiate* which gives the tenant the opportunity to negotiate for additional space before the landlord negotiates with any other prospective tenant. When this provision is used, it should state that if the landlord and tenant are unable to agree on the terms of the lease for the additional space within a specific time period (e.g., ten days), the landlord may negotiate and enter into a lease with another tenant. Neither of these "first rights" provisions is common in shopping center leases.

Occasionally, a tenant may request an *option (right) to cancel* its lease. The landlord should avoid granting this, but such an option may be a necessary concession in order to have a lease with a good tenant in a distressed shopping center. If an option to cancel is granted, the lease should be very clear on the conditions under which it can be exercised.

- The right or option to cancel should be contingent on the tenant's failure to achieve a predetermined sales volume within a specified period of time. (The tenant must have had sufficient time to achieve the stated sales volume.)
- The option should be granted as a one-time right and require the tenant to provide sufficient advance notice (a specific period of notice may be stated): "If, in the second calendar year of the lease term, Tenant's sales volume does not exceed $300,000, Tenant may cancel this lease by providing Landlord with written notice of cancellation during the month of January following the second calendar lease year. Tenant's lease shall be canceled 90 days after Landlord has received written notice from Tenant."
- Whenever possible, the landlord should attempt to obtain a cancellation fee, and the right to cancel should be a mutual right of the tenant and the landlord.

It is also appropriate for a lease to include options that favor the landlord. The landlord should have the right to terminate the lease if the tenant does not achieve agreed-upon sales objectives, which may be stated as total dollars or dollars per square foot, within a certain time period. The lease may also be cancelable if the tenant has not generated overage (percentage rent) within a prescribed period. Retail leases for anchors and national shop tenants are commonly negotiated for terms of ten or more years while those for shop tenants generally are for three to five years or longer, and it may be prudent for the landlord to be able to terminate a lease early if the tenant's space is needed for other purposes (e.g., planned expansion of another tenant's space, a major rehabilitation of the shopping center, etc.).

Other Specific Clauses

Standard lease forms usually include additional provisions that address rights and obligations of both parties and anticipate particular kinds of problems.

Broker's Commission.   Occasionally, more than one broker or leasing agent will claim to represent the same tenant. A dispute can arise if it is not clear who represents the tenant, and the landlord may be forced to pay a double commission or incur legal expenses, or both. To protect against this, the lease provides a blank for the tenant's broker's name and requires the tenant to represent and warrant that no other broker is authorized to represent the tenant.

Estoppel Certificate.   The lease will include a clause requiring the tenant to execute an estoppel certificate on the landlord's request (usually within ten days afterward). If a tenant does not respond to the landlord's request, the landlord is empowered to act as the tenant's attorney-in-fact in executing the estoppel certificate.

A prospective buyer of income-producing property or a lender of financing for it will want to know the status of each tenant's lease and to verify the information provided by the landlord. An *estoppel certificate*—a statement by the tenant of the status of its lease—will include the following information: the term of the lease, the rental charges, the amount of the security deposit, whether any rent is delinquent or prepaid, whether any option exists, and whether the tenant is in default of the lease. It also states that the lease is in full force and effect, and it should include the date to which rents and other charges have been paid.

Holdover.   This clause has important economic implications for both parties. Any holdover by the tenant after the expiration or termination of the lease is construed to be a month-to-month tenancy subject to all the terms and conditions set forth in the lease. However, the minimum rent is increased for the holdover period—usually in an amount equal to one and one-half to four times the minimum rent due for the last month of the lease term. The greater the rent increase during the holdover period, the greater the likelihood that the tenant will agree to a lease renewal or vacate the premises. A large rental increase can motivate the departure of a tenant considering a delay in vacating the premises (past the lease termination date). This is especially helpful when the premises are already leased to another tenant expecting to take occupancy.

Condemnation and Eminent Domain.   This clause addresses the government's right to take property for public use upon the payment of just compensation. Such a provision cancels the lease if all the premises are taken by eminent domain. In case of a partial taking, the landlord and the tenant have a right to cancel the lease if more than a specific percentage (e.g., 15 percent of the premises or common area) is taken by eminent domain. The clause will reserve to the landlord all rights to the entire damages awarded or the total payment for any taking by eminent domain. The tenant is allowed to claim from the condemning authority all compensation that may be recoverable because of any loss incurred by the tenant in removing its merchandise, furniture, trade fixtures, and equipment or damage to the tenant's business. The landlord wants to reserve to itself its claim for the taking of the shopping center as a whole, separate from the tenant's claim for any loss of business and equipment.

Force Majeure.   This clause relieves the landlord of liability or responsibility if the landlord is delayed, hindered in, or prevented from performing any act or obligation required by the lease because of strikes, lockouts, acts of God, riots, failure of power, governmental laws or regulation, war, or other causes beyond the landlord's reasonable control. Any obligation so delayed is extended for a period equivalent to the period of the delay. The most likely delay on the landlord's part is during construction of the shopping center or the tenant's improvements. Tenants will usually negotiate for the same right.

Hazardous Substances.   It is very costly to clean up a hazardous spill. In addition, a buyer may delay the sale of a property or a lender may delay the financing or refinancing of a property until the hazardous substance is removed. However, some tenants must use hazardous materials in the operation of their businesses—photo processors, dry cleaners, automobile repair shops and service stations are obvious examples—and their activities must be closely monitored. The landlord's main concerns are illegal use and disposal of hazardous materials.

Beginning in the 1980s, a hazardous substances clause was added to commercial leases to prohibit tenants from illegally using or disposing of hazardous substances in or on the premises or the common areas of the shopping center. The tenant is required to (1) comply with all governmental regulations regarding hazardous substances, (2) allow the landlord to inspect the premises, and (3) pay for all cleanup costs, fees, and penalties imposed by any governmental authority.

LEASE EXHIBITS

Attached to and incorporated in the lease are several exhibits. They are usually appended in the order in which they are referenced in the body of the lease, and they are identified as Appendix A, Appendix B, etc. These attachments usually augment or clarify specific aspects of the lease or spell out details that are relevant to that lease alone. The most common lease exhibits are listed below.

- *Site Plan of the Shopping Center.* This exhibit depicts the layout of all the buildings and the boundaries of the shopping center. It is likely that there will be changes to the site plan in the future, the most common being changes to the parking lot to accommodate expansion of the main building, addition of a pad or outlot building, or changes in configuration when the shopping center is remodeled or rehabilitated. The site plan should include a disclaimer of accuracy so that the landlord is allowed to make changes to it. (An example of such a disclaimer appears in exhibit 10.5.) The same statement or one similar to it should be considered for inclusion in the shopping center's brochures if they include a site plan.

- *Demising Plan of Tenant's Premises.* The tenant's premises (store) are marked on a layout of the building where the tenant's leased space is located. It may be outlined in colored ink or cross-hatched in red or blue. The same disclaimer as appears in the Site Plan exhibit should be included in this exhibit.
- *Description of Landlord's and Tenant's Work.* This exhibit, usually a standard form, lists the improvements to the premises that will be provided by the landlord and by the tenant. Usually this document also includes specifications for particular work—e.g., types of doors, widths of partitions, stud placement, construction materials, etc.
- *Corporate Resolution of Tenant.* If the tenant is a corporation, a corporate resolution authorizing one or more individuals to sign the lease should be appended to the lease. The resolution, which should be signed by two officers of the corporation, states that the officers who signed the lease on behalf of the tenant have the authority to bind the corporation to the lease.
- *Guaranty of Lease.* If the landlord thinks that the tenant may not be able to perform its lease obligations, especially those related to rent, the landlord will require one or more individuals to guarantee the lease. If the tenant is an individual with a limited net worth, a friend or relative may guarantee the lease. If a corporation has a limited net worth, the landlord will require that the owner (the officers or principal stockholders) or key employees of the corporation personally guarantee the tenant's performance of the lease.

  The tenant may counter offer a limited guaranty which may be for a specific period (e.g., two years) or limit the amount of money that is guaranteed. The guaranty may be terminated after the tenant's sales exceed a certain sales volume during any calendar period or after the tenant has paid percentage rent. The assumption in this situation is that the tenant's business is prospering and a guarantee is no longer needed.
- *Sign Criteria.* The sign criteria will restrict the size, location, and materials used for fabricating the tenant's sign. All tenants' exterior signs must comply with the sign criteria. This is for the shopping center, to maintain its image.

E X H I B I T   10.5

Example Disclaimer for a Site Plan

Landlord does not make any representation or warranty with respect to any matter shown in this site plan, which is not drawn to scale, and reserves the right to modify this site plan, in whole or in part, to change, add, relocate, eliminate, modify the size, shape, nature or identity of any improvements, buildings or common areas shown herein and/or to modify, add or eliminate the name, nature, or use of any tenancy shown herein.

Landlord shall also have the right to convey its ownership of all or any part of the shopping center to one or more third parties and thereafter the third party shall have the right to remove said conveyed portion from the definition of "shopping center" set forth in this lease.

- *Letter of Credit.* A letter of credit may be agreed to in lieu of a security deposit (or to assure availability of funds for tenant's improvement expenses or other use). The bank issuing such credit will write a letter stating the amount of credit allowed and the terms under which such credit is obtainable.

OTHER CONSIDERATIONS

The foregoing discussions have highlighted many of the specific clauses that are commonly found in retail leases and, hopefully, present a sense of their respective importance to both landlord and tenant. Numerous other issues are covered in a lease form, usually in standardized language and as part of the "standard form." In particular, the landlord should be able to access the leased premises under specific circumstances (e.g., in an emergency) as well as to show them to prospective replacement tenants when the lease nears expiration. Provision for notification of the parties is commonly included, and there may be a separate section with definitions of terminology used in the lease.

The contents and the terms and conditions of a specific lease will depend not only on the parties to it (i.e., landlord and tenant), but also on the type and complexity of the property and the premises being leased. No lease should be entered into without appropriate legal consultation. The lease must comply with all applicable laws promulgated at the local, state, and federal levels.

11

Marketing, Advertising, and Promotions

The shopping center is the only property type in which the landlord provides funds to promote the tenants' businesses. There are several reasons for this, the most important one being the "bottom line." The key to this reasoning and to a shopping center's success is *sales volume*—the volume of sales generated by each tenant and by the center as a whole, measured in both total dollars and in dollars per square foot of GLA. A high sales volume typically translates into overage (percentage rent) paid to the landlord. Thus, it is in the ownership's interest to promote sales in order to improve NOI and enhance the value of the shopping center.

THE RATIONALE FOR COORDINATED PROGRAMS

Sales volume affects all the criteria for measuring success in a shopping center. A retailer considers a particular site based on an evaluation of its sales potential. The retailer's chances of being successful are greater in a shopping center where established tenants have above-average sales volumes, while low sales volumes can indicate that a prospective tenant's potential for profitability may be limited.

Centers with high sales volumes attract the best tenants, those who are willing to pay higher rents to be part of a retailing community where most if not all of the tenants are doing well. Conversely, those shopping centers with low sales volumes have difficulty attracting the best tenants; their tenants tend to be marginal to begin with, and that marginality often becomes self-fulfilling—i.e., such centers typically have higher failure rates. Because tenants' sales volumes are the determining factor in the desirability of a retail location, it is no wonder that sales information is among the most important leasing tools.

Besides influencing a tenant's decision about a location, sales volume affects almost every aspect of shopping center operations and landlord-tenant relations. The projected sales productivity of a particular prospect determines the total rent that the tenant will be able to pay. Thus, anticipated sales is often the basis for structuring the financial "deal" with the tenant. Projected sales are used to negotiate minimum rent, percentage rent, and extra charges and can also serve as justification for landlord-paid tenant construction allowances or other concessions to induce a quality tenant to lease space. On a continuing basis, sales productivity will influence the tenant's ability to meet its financial and other obligations under the lease and thus has direct impact on rent collections, lease renewal, and long-term viability of the tenant.

In deciding whether to locate in a particular shopping center, a prospective tenant will evaluate sales figures for the shopping center as a whole (combining all tenants' sales) and for each category of tenant (combining sales of tenants in the same category—e.g., women's shoes). Important as the center's sales volume is, the sales in dollars per square foot is an even more important yardstick. It provides a basis for comparing occupancy costs because minimum rent and tenant pass-through charges are also computed on a square-foot basis. (Note that these kinds of data are compiled routinely by the shopping center manager and may be made available on request. However, sales figures of a particular tenant should always be regarded as confidential.)

Once the probable sales for a location are determined, an estimate is made of how much rent the retailer can afford to pay. Because base rent is calculated as a percentage of the retailer's anticipated sales, minimum and renewal rental rates are directly affected by the tenant's sales volume. When sales are considerably below projected levels or below the breakeven needed to generate a profit, tenants often find it less costly to close a store and continue to pay minimum rent and tenant charges than to remain open and operate the business at a loss. As the lease expiration date approaches, the tenant's sales volume will determine whether or not it is interested in pursuing a lease renewal and what it can afford to pay as rent.

The amount of percentage rent to be paid is determined from three factors—minimum rent, percentage rate, and sales volume. Minimum rent and percentage rate are negotiated, but sales volume is primarily the result of the tenant's merchandising ability and success in operating its business—as well as consumer market considerations.

Excluding tenant charges, which are reimbursement of the landlord's direct expense of operating the center, sales volume will be the critical factor in determining the income stream of a shopping center. Income is a component of the formulas for determining both NOI and property value, and sales volume determines minimum rent and percentage rent, both of which are components of the property's income. Thus, sales volume has a direct and significant impact on the shopping center's NOI and value. Considering this, it is no wonder that an astute shopping center owner will actively support and participate in a coordinated program to market, advertise, and promote the center. Provision of funds to promote the tenants' businesses is not for altruistic reasons—financial contribution to such a promotional fund is regarded as an investment from which the landlord expects a return in the form of increased cash flow and enhanced property value.

Types of Coordinated Marketing Programs

There are three approaches to marketing, promoting, and advertising a shopping center. The *merchants' association* is a joint effort by the landlord and the tenants to promote the shopping center. The *marketing fund,* also known as a promotions fund or advertising fund, is a landlord-controlled method of marketing the shopping center in which the tenants may have an advisory role. The third method is for the landlord to market the shopping center without any participation from the merchants. The latter is the least effective approach and is not recommended for further consideration.

Merchants' Association.   The merchants' association was the first attempt at organizing tenants at a shopping center to promote both the shopping center and the tenants. Initially, merchants' associations were voluntary organizations. However, as their benefits became apparent, a merchants' association provision was incorporated into the standard lease form. Early lease provisions stated that when a percentage of the tenants (usually 75–80 percent) agreed to form a merchants' association, all tenants would be obligated to become members. Ultimately, the lease provision made membership in the merchants' association mandatory.

The merchants' association is a nonprofit corporation, which must file bylaws and articles of incorporation in the state where it is created. The bylaws establish the purposes, organization, and participation requirements of the merchants' association (see appendix D). Ideally, the bylaws and articles of incorporation are drafted and filed while the shopping center is being developed. This allows the developer to draft bylaws that are in the best interests of the shopping center.

The bylaws will provide for the structure of the merchants' association and for regular, special, and annual meetings. They will state the voting rights of the members and how they can lose this right. Each member may have only one vote or there may be provision for multiple votes based on either the amount of dues paid (e.g., one vote for every $500 of dues), or on the square footage leased. The bylaws will provide for the election of a board of directors and their election of executive officers. Also included are voting procedures for removing an officer and filling a vacancy. Typically, the property owner and the anchor tenants (if they are members of the merchants' association) have permanent seats on the board of directors. The duties of each officer are spelled out, and dues, assessments, and other issues are addressed. The officers are responsible for the day-to-day business of the merchants' association, but they may delegate responsibilities to committees. Typically there are nominating, advertising, promotions, community relations, and social committees, each comprising representatives of the local, regional, and national merchants in the center. The dues may provide the funds to hire a marketing director for the center; otherwise, committees may manage the association's day-to-day business.

Because the association is an organization of the merchants, it is important that they meet periodically. Most merchants' associations meet once a month or quarterly. This provides every member an opportunity to express an opinion, evaluate past programs, and offer suggestions. The officers and board of directors usually meet every month.

Originally, dues were based on either frontage (the number of front feet of the tenant's premises) or area (the square footage of the tenant's store). Eventually, the latter prevailed, and dues were calculated as a rate per square foot. This can be a flat rate (e.g., 50 cents per square foot per year) or a declining rate (e.g., 50 cents a square foot for 1,200 square feet, 40 cents each for an additional 1,200 square feet, and 25 cents each for all square footage in excess of 2,400). When anchor tenants contribute to the merchants' association, their dues are seldom based on square footage. Usually they are negotiated as a fixed annual amount. Dues are computed annually but paid monthly or quarterly. The merchants' association has the right to increase the dues.

One of the disadvantages of a merchants' association is friction among the merchants. Conflicting views, egos, and personalities are among the difficulties that can rise among retailers. Another potential problem is that some tenants will attempt to use the merchants' association as a forum to complain to the landlord about the cost of common area maintenance, the level of maintenance, and vacancies in the center. If meetings are allowed to become gripe sessions, merchants will lose interest and avoid participating. Therefore, it is important to focus the discussion on marketing, advertising, and promotions. At the first meeting of a new association, the merchants should be informed of the purpose of the association and advised that only marketing activities and promotions will be addressed. The property manager should offer to discuss other issues in private after the meeting, either at the tenant's store or in the property management office.

Another common occurrence is the splitting of the tenants into factions—large stores versus small stores, national chains versus local merchants, fashion merchants versus service tenants. These groups frequently have opposing points of view about where to advertise, how many sales events to conduct, and whether or not to increase dues. If dissension grows, many tenants will lose interest in the merchants' association and avoid participation in its activities. Having representatives of the different sizes and categories of merchants serve as directors, officers, and committee members will reduce the likelihood of factions developing among the merchants.

Marketing Fund.   When shopping center owners recognized the possibilities inherent in a coordinated marketing program, they began to search for a method of carrying forward the benefits of the merchants' association and leaving behind its potential for problems. By the mid-1970s, some major regional mall developers had arrived at the conclusion that the merchants' association was not the most effective way to market a shopping center. Understanding the importance of percentage rent to the shopping center's cash flow and value, the developers were no longer willing to rely on groups of tenants to create and direct the marketing programs for their properties. They also recognized the potential for squabbling and differences of opinion among those serving in leadership roles in the merchants' association. Then, too, when landlord and tenants disagreed on the direction of the marketing program, they often became adversaries.

What the developers wanted was a strong and aggressive marketing program that was completely under their control, and the marketing fund concept allows them to do this. In a marketing fund, both tenants and landlord contribute funding, just as they do in a merchants' association. However, there are no bylaws, no required meetings, and no elected officers. The marketing director is compensated from the marketing fund but employed by the shopping center developer or owner.

Once the developers of major malls pioneered the method, other developers, regardless of the sizes of their shopping centers, created marketing funds for their properties. Some tenants, especially national tenants, prefer marketing funds over merchants' associations. They, too, became disenchanted with the frequent squabbling among tenants and wanted a more professional approach to marketing. A side benefit was their store managers no longer having to take time away from managerial duties to serve as officers and committee members.

The marketing fund, like the merchants' association, is covered by a specific lease provision. It requires the tenant to contribute to the marketing fund, provides for an annual increase in funding, appoints an advisory board consisting of representatives of each anchor tenant and the shop tenants (usually only two of the latter), and gives the landlord sole responsibility for developing and implementing the marketing program. (An example is shown in Exhibit 11.1.)

In order to gain the tenants' support, it is critical for the landlord to have good communications with the tenants. This is largely achieved through the efforts of the marketing director and the property manager, and the most effective means of communication is one-on-one meetings with tenants. The advisory board meets with the marketing director and property manager regularly (usually quarterly or semiannually). The board has no control over the activities of the marketing fund; rather, its purpose is to suggest programs, assess proposed plans, and evaluate past events. Usually a newsletter is sent to all the tenants each month informing them of upcoming promotions.

Converting a Merchants' Association to a Marketing Fund.   Since the mid-1970s, a significant percentage of new shopping centers have established marketing funds, and many existing centers have been successfully converted from merchants' associations to marketing funds. When conversion is contemplated, it must be remembered that the merchants' association is a nonprofit corporation that has articles of incorporation and bylaws. Current leases most likely include provisions establishing the merchants' association and requiring the landlord to belong and pay dues. The first step in this direction is to have these documents reviewed by legal counsel to determine appropriate means of dissolving the association before a marketing fund can be created.

The next step is to gain merchant support for a marketing fund. To do this, the marketing director should prepare a formal proposal. The proposal should show the advantages of a marketing fund, answer questions tenants are likely to raise, and indicate how the entity will be managed and funded. A budget for the first year and a marketing plan should be included.

Anchor tenants and national shop tenants are more likely to support a marketing fund, so they should be the first ones approached. After their support has been won, the other tenants should be contacted. Once the proposal is supported by a majority of the tenants, a special meeting should be called to vote on the issue. An attorney should recommend legally (locally) acceptable procedures. It may be possible to convert the merchants' association to a marketing fund directly, or it may be necessary to dissolve the former in order to establish the latter. As part of the process, it may also be necessary for all established tenants to execute a lease amendment canceling the merchants' association provision and replacing it with a marketing fund provision. Subsequently, all new and renewal leases should include the marketing fund provision or a provision allowing the landlord to convert from a merchants' association to a marketing fund (exhibit 11.2).

EXHIBIT   11.1

Example Lease Clause—Advertising and Promotional Service; Marketing Fund

Advertising and Promotional Service. Landlord may, at its option, establish an Advertising and Promotional Service (the "Service") to furnish and maintain professional advertising and sales promotions to benefit all merchants of the Shopping Center. In conjunction with said Service, Landlord shall, in its discretion, hire and supervise all necessary personnel, including but not limited to a marketing director and sufficient secretarial and support services. The salaries, office rent, utilities, supplies, telephone systems, and all other administrative expenses necessary for efficient day-to-day operation of the Service shall be paid from the Marketing Fund, as described below. A committee, composed of a representative of Landlord, the anchor tenants, and two representatives of the shop tenants in the Shopping Center, will be formed to annually review and make recommendations regarding the annual advertising and promotional activities sponsored by the Service. Decisions as to the advertising and promotional activities will be the sole responsibility of Landlord.

Marketing Fund. In the event Landlord elects to establish a promotional service as described above, Tenant agrees to pay Landlord an annual amount equal to *[specify rate]* per square foot of floor area of the Premises per year, or a minimum annual fee of *[specify dollar amount]* per year, whichever is greater ("Tenant's Marketing Fee"), as Tenant's contribution toward the costs of operating the Service. Tenant's Marketing Fee shall be payable by Tenant in twelve (12) equal monthly installments due on the same day as Minimum Rent is due under this Lease. Tenant's Marketing Fee, together with similar fees paid by other tenants of the Shopping Center, shall be collectively referred to as the "Marketing Fund." All monies received by Landlord under this Section shall be used solely for the purpose of conducting advertising and promotional services of the Shopping Center, for payment of the personnel, operational, and administrative expenses of the Service, and for related purposes. Tenant's Marketing Fee shall be increased at the end of each Lease Year in the same proportion that the revised Consumer Price Index—All Urban Consumers—All Items (1982–84 = 100) for the U.S. City Average as published by the United States Department of Labor, Bureau of Labor Statistics, published at the end of each Lease Year, is increased over the same index for the prior Lease Year. Landlord hereby agrees to contribute to the Marketing Fund an annual amount equal to twenty-five percent (25%) of the total amount of the Marketing Fund contributions by Shopping Center tenants for such year. Landlord shall not be obligated to expend more than twenty-five percent (25%) of the Marketing Fund actually collected from Tenants for each such year. In addition to the foregoing, Tenant also agrees to pay Landlord, within ten (10) days of execution of this Lease, an initial assessment of *[specify rate]* per square foot of the floor area of the Premises, or *[specify dollar amount]*, whichever is greater, for pre-opening advertising and promotional activities.

Roles of the Participants

The success of a coordinated marketing program and, ultimately, the success of the shopping center depend on the landlord, the property manager, the tenants, and the marketing director and how they play their respective roles.

Landlord.   An effective program begins with the right attitude on the part of the landlord. The landlord must understand how coordinated marketing,

E X H I B I T   11.2

Example Lease Clause—Pre-Existing Merchants' Association

Notwithstanding the provisions of Section *[specify lease section number(s)]* above, in the event the Shopping Center has a pre-existing Merchants' Association, then, at Landlord's option, the Tenant shall (i) become a member of such Merchants' Association and perform all obligations and pay all fees and charges due as a member of such Merchants' Association, including Tenant's share of advertising events, or (ii) pay the Tenant's Marketing Fee as described in Section *[specify lease section number]* above; provided that the Tenant shall cease participation in the Merchant's Association and commence payment of the Tenant's Marketing Fee at such time as Tenant receives written notice and direction from Landlord.

NOTE: This is representative of the type of clause that might be used in conjunction with the example shown in exhibit 11.1 to facilitate conversion from a merchants' association to a marketing fund.

---

advertising, and promotions benefit the landlord's investment, the shopping center as an entity, the individual tenants, the property manager, the leasing effort, and the community at large. The landlord's support of the program must be evidenced by a specific commitment to the merchants' association or marketing fund. This usually means contributing a portion of the funds for either of these organizations. It also means providing personnel to coordinate the program. It is important for the landlord to set an example for the tenants. Without the landlord's active support, the probability of the program's success is greatly diminished. The scale of the landlord's commitment will depend on the type and size of the shopping center.

Property Manager.   First and foremost, the property manager provides leadership. He or she represents the landlord in developing and implementing the marketing program and interacting with the tenants. Working with the marketing director, the property manager is responsible for starting the merchants' association or marketing fund. For a merchants' association, this means planning the first meeting and attending and representing the landlord at meetings with merchants and committees. For either entity, the manager is responsible for meeting with each tenant to explain the purpose, goals, and benefits of a coordinated marketing program, supervising the activities of the marketing director, and participating in the development of the annual budget and calendar of activities. The property manager should review the financial reports periodically, and he or she may be one of several signatories for the entity's checking account.

The property manager's duties include managing the common areas. This includes reviewing and approving how the common areas will be used for promotional activities. If the property manager believes a promotional activity may cause damage to the property or injuries to customers or tenants' employees, he or she can veto the activity. As an example, a hot-air balloon ride promotion may be vetoed because it presents too great a liability. The property manager seldom vetos a promotional activity, however.

During the life of a merchants' association or marketing fund, there may be times when tenants' interest in it wanes. The property manager, along with the marketing director, is responsible for maintaining tenants' interest and active participation in the marketing program. Though the property manager is a major player in developing and implementing the marketing program, the day-to-day operations of the merchants' association or marketing fund are usually the responsibility of the marketing director.

Tenants.   The benefits the tenants derive from the marketing program are directly related to their levels of active participation. In the ideal situation, the lease will require all tenants to belong to and contribute funding for either a merchants' association or a marketing fund. The tenants collectively provide the bulk of the funds to market, advertise, and promote the shopping center. They also participate in planning the marketing program—in a merchants' association, they serve on the board of directors and on committees; in a marketing fund, they may be appointed to an advisory board.

The effectiveness of specific advertising is directly related to the number of tenants participating in it and the selection and price of the merchandise advertised. The greater the number of tenants who participate in a shopping center's tabloid section or other print or electronic advertising vehicle, the greater its impact and the greater the sales for each store. Tenants must also participate in merchandising events such as fashion shows, and they may be encouraged (or required) to coordinate store windows and possibly apparel worn by store employees with the theme.

When negative attitudes toward the marketing program develop, it is important to provide positive reinforcement and support to the wavering tenants. Such support may come from the marketing director and the property manager and, separately, from the other tenants.

Marketing Director.   This individual is directly responsible for developing and executing the marketing program and for the operation of the merchants' association or marketing fund (see chapter 5). He or she must be creative in developing an effective marketing strategy and successfully executing the advertising and promotional programs. A marketing director must have good communication and "people" skills to gain tenants' confidence and cooperation and motivate them to active participation in a coordinated marketing program.

Though the skills required of a marketing director do not depend on the size of the shopping center, the budget and the extent of the marketing program do. Each year, the marketing director must determine the marketing budget. The anticipated funding will determine the specific programs that can be accomplished. Next, a marketing strategy is developed and, from that, a calendar of activities. The steps and the other participants in the process depend on the promotional entity established for the shopping center. In a merchants' association, the program is developed with the guidance of its officers; after they approve the plan, it is presented to the merchants. Under a marketing fund, the program is submitted to the property manager for approval and then presented to the merchants. The marketing director schedules the meetings with the merchants. In a merchants' association, the bylaws usually require annual meetings of the general membership and provide for regular or special meetings to be scheduled as needed. The board of directors is not required to meet on a specific schedule, but quarterly or even monthly meetings may be appropriate. The president of the association conducts the meetings. Under a marketing fund program, there usually is no requirement for specific tenant meetings, and quarterly meetings of the advisory board may be sufficient. However, quarterly or semiannual meetings may be called to advise the tenants about how the program works and their specific participation in it. The marketing director conducts the marketing fund meetings. In either case, the marketing director prepares the meeting agenda and sends out the notices and reminders. Implementation of the marketing program includes creating, planning, and coordinating advertising, publicity, and promotional events.

The role of the marketing director is characterized in the results of a survey of 173 individuals who hold that position. The survey—published in the September 1990 issue of *Monitor* magazine, a monthly shopping center publication—indicated that (1) shopping center marketing is a young person's career; (2) the field is dominated by women; (3) they work long hours; (4) substantial numbers of marketing directors hold professional designations; and (5) most work at large shopping centers. The following specific statistics were reported.

- 39 percent were between the ages of 20 and 29; 42 percent between 30 and 39.
- 81 percent were women.
- 36 percent worked 40–49 hours a week and 50 percent worked 50–59 hours.
- One in three held the Certified Marketing Director (CMD) designation from ICSC.
- 52 percent worked at regional malls; 24 percent at super regional malls.

In describing what they liked about their jobs, 22 percent listed variety and diversity; 19 percent stated the job was rewarding and satisfying; and 17 percent liked the creativity.

In 1971, ICSC inaugurated a professional designation for marketing directors called the Accredited Shopping Center Promotions Director (ASPD). Later, in recognition that the responsibilities of the job were more extensive than just developing and coordinating promotions, the name of the designation was changed to Certified Marketing Director (CMD). ICSC also offers one-week seminars on marketing shopping centers.

In 1972, ICSC initiated the annual Maxi Awards as a means of recognizing "excellence in marketing" of shopping centers (Maxi derives from "maximum effort"). These awards are additional evidence of the evolution of the role of the marketing director. Maxi Awards are given for nine categories of events:

1. Community relations/service
2. Sales promotions/merchandising
3. Consumer advertising
4. Customer service
5. Grand opening
6. Expansion and renovation
7. Retailer motivation/development
8. Corporate marketing
9. Single property development and/or leasing campaign

These categories are subdivided into six classifications of shopping centers, five based on total GLA and one for combined marketing efforts of two or more shopping centers.

1. Shopping centers of up to 150,000 square feet
2. Shopping centers of 150,001 to 400,000 square feet
3. Shopping centers of 400,001 to 750,000
4. Shopping centers of 750,001 to 1,000,000
5. Shopping centers of 1,000,001 or more square feet
6. Joint shopping center efforts.

Each entry is judged on four criteria:

1. Marketing strategy,
2. Creativity,
3. Execution, and
4. Overall excellence.

CREATING A SUCCESSFUL MARKETING PROGRAM

Shopping center marketing, advertising, and promotions programs are complex. They begin with advance development of an annual marketing plan that is based on anticipated funding. Media advertising and promotional events will comprise most of the budgeted items. For a brand-new center, there will be a grand opening event which will be funded separately and planned while the center is under construction.

The first step in preparing the annual marketing plan is to propose a specific budget. This requires analysis of the available income and evaluation of how it can best be spent. The major sources of income are the respective contributions by the tenants and the landlord. Merchants' contributions are based on their square footage, so the larger the shopping center the bigger the budget. If contributions are not mandatory for the anchor tenants, voluntary contributions should be solicited. While they may agree to monthly or annual cash contributions, the anchors may choose to participate in other ways—e.g., contributing merchandise as prizes for promotional drawings, or contributing funds for Christmas decorations.

The bulk of the funding will come from the so-called shop tenants as mandated in their leases. However, three other variables will affect the amount collected. These are the rate per square foot, whether the anchor tenant contributes (and its rate), and the landlord's percentage contribution. Some leases commit the landlord to a specific financial contribution, or the merchants' association or marketing fund provision will state a formula for the landlord's contribution. Typically, the landlord's contribution is equal to 25 percent of the amount collected from the tenants or 20 percent of the total funding. This makes the landlord the largest contributor. Thus, if the tenants contribute $80,000, the landlord's contribution would be $20,000 ($80,000 × .25), and the funding available would be $100,000. In addition to a specific cash contribution, the landlord may pay the marketing director's salary and contribute office space, equipment, and supplies.

Other sources of revenue should also be explored. Occasionally, merchants located near a shopping center will contribute to its merchants' association or marketing fund so they can participate in the joint advertising and promotions (e.g., an adjacent strip center may "join" with a larger shopping center). Another source of income is revenue-generating promotions. Sales of photos with Santa Claus usually yield a profit for an enclosed mall. Significant income can also result from vendor fees. Many malls charge dealers to display their cars, RVs, or boats during shows, and income from such events (often exceeding $10,000 each) can be used to defray the costs of advertising and promoting the event. Another possibility is cooperative advertising with a manufacturer—a cookie company may donate money or goods for a tie-in to a cookie promotion.

A debatable source of income is rents from temporary tenants occupying space in the common area. Because mall tenants pay for common area maintenance, they may take the position that any income derived from temporary tenants in these areas should go to the marketing fund or merchants' association. (In some centers, temporary tenants may be licensed rather than having them sign formal leases.) Such an arrangement would be subject to any prior restrictions imposed on common areas under anchor tenants' leases or otherwise (see also the discussion of temporary tenants in chapter 9).

The amount of money available for advertising and promotions determines the magnitude of a center's marketing plan. In general, the larger the shopping center, the more extensive the marketing, advertising, and promotions program can be. The opportunities for ancillary income—vendor fees, cooperative advertising, etc.—occur primarily in larger shopping centers. The funding available for marketing a neighborhood strip shopping center over the course of a year is likely to be between $10,000 and $25,000, while that for a regional mall may range from $150,000 to $500,000.

The size of the marketing budget will also determine the size of the marketing staff. A super regional mall will have a marketing director plus an assistant marketing director or a secretary or both. A regional mall will have a marketing director and one other person (e.g., an assistant-secretary), or the marketing director may share a secretary with someone else. At a community mall, there may be a marketing director with no support staff, or the on-site property manager may perform the duties of a marketing director. A neighborhood center usually cannot afford a full-time marketing director; a person may be hired to work a few hours each week coordinating advertising and promotions, or an agency may be employed. Such an "agency" is often the former marketing director of a regional or super regional mall who has started a business that specializes in marketing small shopping centers. Seldom does the property manager serve as the marketing director for a neighborhood shopping center.

The primary expenses of a marketing program are administration, advertising, promotions, and decorations. Administration includes the salary and employee benefits for the marketing director (and other marketing personnel) plus office and general administrative expenses. Advertising expenses have two components—ad costs and agency fees. The agency's fee includes the cost of producing the ad. Most promotional events have no inherent costs other than the expenses to coordinate them—rented equipment (tables, chairs, podium, microphone), decorations, and supplies—although traveling promotions may charge shopping centers a fee. Decorations expenses are primarily for the Christmas shopping season. Some shopping centers add to their Christmas decorations every year while others replace all their decorations every three to five years. The budget should include reserves for unexpected expenses and donations.

Advertising

The purpose of advertising is to appeal to a specific audience—in this instance, so they will visit the shopping center and shop there. The marketing director is responsible for determining the right media mix for the advertising program. Though numerous advertising media are available, the ones used most often for shopping centers are newspapers, direct mail, radio, television, transit signs, and billboards. The media mix will depend on the location of the shopping center, the size of its trade area, the specific audience each medium will reach, and the advertising budget.

Many large shopping centers hire an ad agency to assist in planning ad campaigns, recommend media and negotiate contracts, create and produce the ads, place ads with the different media, and handle the accounting and record keeping. Smaller shopping centers may rely on services provided by the media (their sales representatives or production department). Advertising for strip centers is often scheduled on a regular basis (e.g., a monthly joint advertising section in the local newspaper and a monthly coupon promotion).

Newspapers. Newspaper advertising is primary for most shopping centers. The cost of newspaper ads makes them available to all shopping centers regardless of size. Compared to other vehicles, newspaper ads are relatively inexpensive means of obtaining broad market coverage. A newspaper ad can be viewed any time during the day by several members of the household, and it can be reread and saved.

Rates are usually quoted by the column inch, and volume rates or discounts are offered. When tenants group their ads together, they can achieve a volume rate considerably lower than the open rate (what they would pay to advertise alone). Newspapers also offer one-year contract rates. At the end of the year, if the total space used is less than the amount contracted, the shopping center will be billed a "short rate" (the difference between the contract rate and the rate actually earned).

The marketing director can select the size, placement, and design of an ad and when it will be published. Newspapers serving major metropolitan areas usually have zoned editions, allowing the advertiser to target a specific neighborhood or suburb. For example, if the marketing director at a mall located in Orange County does not want to pay for the entire distribution area of the *Los Angeles Times,* ads can be placed in a zoned edition for Orange County.

Direct Mail. One of the main advantages of direct mail advertising is its flexibility. There are no broadcast schedules or publication deadlines. Mailed pieces can vary in size, shape, color, and texture. They can be inserted in newspapers, mailed separately or with other direct-mail advertisements, or hand-delivered. Mailings can be targeted to specific segments of the market based on postal zip codes, occupations, membership in specific organizations, etc. Mailing lists can be purchased from organizations, created (typed) from directories, or compiled from checks taken in at center stores. Stores that issue their own charge cards have ready-made mailing lists, or names and addresses can be collected during contests or at promotional drawings held at the shopping center. An accurate measure of the effectiveness of a direct mail campaign can be achieved by including a coupon redeemable at the center by a certain date. As a mailing, a collection of coupons from a variety of stores will provide an array of savings opportunities for the consumer. This can lead to multiple purchases, cross-shopping, and repeated shopping trips—all traceable to the one promotional mailing.

There are also some negatives for the marketing director to recognize when creating direct mail advertising campaigns. Postal regulations define dimensions, weights, and degrees of presorting to qualify for the most economical bulk mailing postage rates. These rules should be studied beforehand. Often delivery of third-class mail is not expedited, so extra time must be allowed. Also, while printing costs on a per-piece basis will decrease as the number of printed pieces increases, such items as specialty papers, specified ink color matches, die cutting, and special folds will add to the costs.

Radio.   This is a medium that reaches just about everyone—98 percent of U.S. households have more than one radio, and approximately 95 percent of people in cars listen to the radio. Radio is "live" advertising that is flexible—ads can be changed on short notice.

Every major market has a wide range of "local" radio stations, almost all of which accept advertising. Often the stations in large metropolitan areas serve suburban communities and adjacent rural areas as well. Stations that are part of a national "network" also accept advertising for the local market. This multiplicity of choices allows the marketing director to target a specific audience. Based on the station's format (all news, all talk, sports) or programming (including broadcasts in foreign languages) and the type of music played (rock, oldies, classical), the message can be targeted to a specific audience by age, income, type of work or profession, gender, ethnic group, etc.

Radio is the least-expensive electronic medium and radio advertising is affordable for most shopping centers. Ad rates depend on the number of spots (commercials), the time period specified, and the radio station's share of the total audience. In major metropolitan areas, the advertising day is commonly divided into five time periods or segments:

> Morning drive—6:00 A.M. to 10:00 A.M.
> Daytime—10:00 A.M. to 4:00 P.M.
> Evening drive—4:00 P.M. to 7:00 P.M.
> Evening—7:00 P.M. to midnight
> Nighttime—midnight to 6:00 A.M.

Radio advertising works especially well in smaller communities where the shopping center's trade area encompasses most of the broadcast area and there are few stations. In major metropolitan areas, ads will cost more because the station's broadcast range is wider and the audience is much larger. Actually, regional and super regional shopping centers and malls use this medium to attract shoppers from outside their normal trade areas. For a small strip center, however, radio advertising may not be the most cost-effective medium. The cost of advertising beyond the center's trade area must be weighed against the number of people within the trade area who will receive the message.

Television.   Usually only enclosed malls and very large shopping centers advertise on television—here, again, because of the cost. While radio spots can be read by staff announcers (rather than prerecorded), TV ads must have visual impact (images, motion) to be effective, and therefore the production cost is high compared to such costs for other media. The rate for a television spot ad is based on the time of day, the size of the audience, and the length of the spot. Television time is sold in 10-, 20-, 30-, and 60-second increments, 30-second spots being the most popular. Discounts may apply for multiple spots or extended advertising periods (over days, weeks, or months), and the advertiser may have to contract for a minimum number.

Even though television advertising can be costly, it can also be very effective. Television reaches a large and varied audience. As with radio advertising, specific audiences can be targeted based on time of day and type of show (morning cartoons, afternoon soaps and talk shows, evening news, prime time, sit-coms, adventure series, and late-night talk shows and movies). Many malls budget for television advertising as part of their Christmas media mix and for special events such as boat shows and sidewalk sales. In some markets, cable television advertising may be more affordable than spots on local commercial stations. Both types of television stations should be able to characterize their markets so that advertisers can choose "spots" that will optimize the audiences they reach.

Transit Advertising.   Advertising on mass transit (buses, elevated and subway trains, streetcars or trolleys) is a way of having the shopping center's message seen over a wide area. Advertising space is available on the exteriors and interiors of most such vehicles, including taxis. Some rapid transit districts can ensure that an ad will be on a specific route. The cost is relatively low, and such programs offer flexibility in ad design, use of color, and frequency of message changes.

Billboards.   Billboards can be used to direct people to a shopping center or to promote a major event such as grand opening. Mostly they provide repeated exposure of the message, and the cost per view is measurably lower than for any other medium. However, billboards are seldom used for shopping center advertising because of their limited effectiveness. Though the message can be changed frequently, the changes themselves can be expensive. Billboard ads are prepared as either painted or printed panels, and their showing locations are rented for a minimum of three to six months. The time frame makes them less useful for advertising a specific short-term event.

Publicity.   Publicity is information that is published or aired by the media at no charge to the shopping center. Shopping centers have countless events that an editor of a newspaper or the manager of a radio station might consider reporting, especially if press releases or announcements are received in advance. Stories that feature local residents (prize winners, new local merchants, store or center personnel changes such as promotions and appointments) are of interest to the community at large. Community activities at the center (a Girl Scout exhibit, a health fair, Little League signup) and major activities or unusual promotional events such as a carnival or circus in the parking lot or a bridal fair may bring media people to the center so they can report personally.

The marketing director should always notify the media well in advance of events that are newsworthy. However, there is no guarantee that such information will be published or aired. Selection for publication is based first on space or time available and then on the interest to the community. Copies of press releases should be kept together in a file along with notes or records of their publication. A useful exercise is to calculate what they would have cost if they had been purchased ads.

Mandatory Tenant Advertising

One criterion of a successful advertising program is participation by a majority of the tenants. Regardless of the event being advertised, the greater the number of ads in a shopping center tabloid or advertising section, the greater its impact—and the greater the opportunity for the event to be successful. Not all tenants (local merchants, in particular) understand the importance of and the need for their participation. To assure tenant participation, many landlords will include a mandatory tenant advertising provision in the lease (exhibit 11.3). This provision requires the tenant to participate in a minimum number of advertising events. If the tenant fails to do so, the landlord, through the marketing fund or merchants' association, may submit an ad on behalf of the tenant and bill the cost to the tenant. Such ads would be institutional (image) ads and not show products. Another approach to mandatory advertising is to require tenants to submit evidence that they have spent an agreed-upon minimum percentage of their sales on advertising (usually 2 percent). Lease requirements for mandatory tenant advertising are most common in regional and super regional shopping centers and specialty or theme centers.

Promotional Events

When shopping centers were first developed nationwide during the 1950s and 1960s, the people in charge of marketing were called promotion directors. Their primary responsibility was to generate traffic to the shopping cen-

E X H I B I T   11.3

Example Lease Clause—Tenant Advertising

The Marketing Fund shall schedule and offer regular promotional and advertising events ("Advertising Events") during each calendar year through the local newspaper, direct mail, radio and/or television media to promote the business of tenants in the Shopping Center. Tenant shall, at its own expense, contribute at least six (6) print advertisements for its business during each year. The Marketing Fund shall provide Tenant with a schedule for the Advertising Events. Tenant's advertisements must be submitted to the Marketing Fund or its newspaper advertising representative no later than thirty (30) days prior to the publishing deadline for the advertising events, which deadlines shall be set forth in the schedule. (All advertisements shall be subject to approval of the Marketing Fund.) In the event that Tenant fails to submit six (6) approved advertisements from among the first nine (9) advertising events of each calendar year, the Marketing Fund shall be authorized to include advertisements for Tenant of the Marketing Fund's own choosing and design, in any or all of the last three (3) advertising events of each year, provided that (a) Tenant does not submit approved advertisements bringing to six (6) the number submitted each calendar year by the deadlines stated for those last three (3) advertising events, (b) the Marketing Fund shall not be authorized to require Tenant to have more than six (6) advertisements in any one calendar year, and (c) the cost for any such advertisements added by the Marketing Fund on Tenant's behalf shall be charged to Tenant and shall be due and payable by Tenant upon receipt of a written invoice from the Marketing Fund or the newspaper or other media advertising representative.

---

ter by developing and implementing a calendar of promotional activities. The responsibilities of today's marketing director encompass multiple functions, and promotions are still one of the most effective ways to build traffic at a shopping center.

To be successful, promotions must be well thought out and planned in advance. Savvy marketing directors develop annual calendars of promotions and have them approved two to four months before the start of the year. Many promotions will be supported by advertising, and all such events will be supported by publicity. The number of promotions a shopping center can conduct is directly related to its marketing budget.

To be certain that no other event will detract from promotions planned for the shopping center, the marketing director should check the dates of major activities planned by local authorities, community organizations, and the center's anchor tenants. Often, a shopping center promotion can be coordinated with a promotion by an anchor tenant (e.g., a sidewalk sale the same weekend as the anchor's midsummer clearance sale).

Most promotions require three to six months of preplanning. There are four basic types of promotions.

1. *Sales events* are among the most successful promotions and offer endless possibilities tied to seasons or particular holidays (sidewalk sale, moonlight sale, Presidents' Day sale, after-Christmas sale, anniversary

sale). Sidewalk sales are among the most successful promotions for all types and sizes of shopping centers.

2. *Entertainment activities* are very popular promotions. Traditional examples include arts and crafts, boat, RV, auto, bridal, fashion, and antique shows; photos with Santa Claus at Christmas and special celebrations are others.

3. *Educational promotions* can be coordinated with local agencies and community organizations (e.g., a safety fair cosponsored with local police and fire departments, a health fair with participation by the local hospital).

4. *Community events* allow local groups opportunities to promote their organizations (e.g., a charity bazaar where several groups sell handcrafted items or baked goods).

Whenever possible, merchandising should be related to the promotion. If a mall has a boat show, clothing stores should be encouraged to display summer and beach wear or nautical styles, and sporting goods stores should feature swimming, fishing, and boating equipment.

After each promotion, the marketing director should poll the merchants for their opinions of the event and their sales figures during it. Not every promotion will directly benefit every merchant. A sporting goods store will benefit directly from a boat show but not from a bridal show; however, a bridal show can provide exposure and recognition that will result in sales of sporting goods at a later date.

The situation is somewhat different at strip shopping centers. Their programs will be much less extensive, and so-called community activities may be minimal or nonexistent. Sidewalk sales usually are very successful in smaller centers, and such events may provide opportunities for including community-related activities—an inexpensive way to promote the shopping center. Small centers can become involved in programs coordinated with local charitable organizations (e.g., collection of items to be "recycled" such as used books or old eyeglasses). Sweepstakes and other giveaways (for example, drawings for a turkey during the holidays) are also possibilities. In general, however, strip shopping centers should not try to compete with malls. They have neither the funds nor the space for major promotions.

Grand Opening

Grand opening is a major one-time event in the life of a shopping center. The only similar event likely to occur is a grand reopening after major remodeling, rehabilitation, or expansion at a later date. A grand opening takes months of planning because every aspect of the event must come off like a Hollywood production. Planning and creativity are the keys to a successful grand opening event. Also important are its objectives, which will vary somewhat with the particular needs of the shopping center but usually include the following specific goals.

- To build awareness of the shopping center in the community.
- To position the shopping center as a valuable asset in the community.
- To gain community support.
- To introduce new merchants to the community.
- To capture a share of the retail sales in the community.
- To assist the center's leasing program.

The adage, "you never get a second chance to make a first impression," applies to the objectives of the grand opening. The effort to make that first impression begins long before the actual event. For a strip shopping center, planning for the grand opening is started no later than three months before the event. For a regional shopping center or an enclosed mall, grand opening plans should begin at least six months prior to the event. The steps are the same regardless of the type of center although a larger center will most certainly have a larger budget, more people involved in the planning, more tenants to work with, and larger crowds of visitors. A well-executed, creative event will draw many customers to the shopping center and establish the standard for the ongoing marketing program.

The first thing to be determined is the amount of money available for the event. Review of the leases will indicate each tenant's grand opening assessment and assure accurate billing. Tenants' grand opening assessments typically range from 20 cents to $1.00 per square foot. The anchor tenants may not be obligated to participate; in which case, they should be asked to make a donation. Typically, the landlord's contribution will be 25 percent of the total collected from the tenants although some landlords will provide additional funds to assure a successful opening. (When a shopping center is not fully leased by the grand opening date, the landlord often contributes the amount that would have been collected if the vacancies were occupied. This assures that sufficient funds will be available for all the grand opening activities. As vacant spaces are leased, new tenants may be billed their share of the grand opening expenses up to one year after the event. Even though they were not open at the time, they are benefiting from the grand opening.) The grand opening budget may equal or exceed the budget for a year of advertising and promotions. Grand opening budgets for strip centers usually range from $15,000 to $75,000; those for enclosed regional malls range from $100,000 to $500,000. After the income is projected, an advertising agency is hired.

The next step is to create a schedule of specific deadlines for accomplishing different phases of the grand opening program; this may be developed with the ad agency. A timetable of grand opening events must also be planned. The grand opening itself will be the culmination of a series of events that have already been publicized. The property manager and the marketing director should plan to arrive at the mall several hours before events are scheduled to begin.

Traditionally, grand opening begins with a ribbon-cutting ceremony. Promotional activities and, possibly, giveaways are included. The benefits of the grand opening can be maximized by extending it over three to four days (e.g., beginning on a Thursday and continuing through Sunday).

Often the grand opening of an enclosed mall is preceded by a charitable event—a dinner dance or some other activity on the mall, with proceeds going to a local charity. This will yield additional publicity, as well as bring community leaders to the mall and start the process of positioning the mall as a focal point in the community. For this event, a special guest list must be developed, invitations sent, and arrangements made to rent chairs and tables, etc.

The grand opening should have a theme to help focus the advertising, publicity, and promotional events. Examples are "What's In Store for You" and "A Mall for All Seasons." The theme for the grand reopening of an open-air regional shopping center converted to an enclosed mall was "We've Got You Covered."

As grand opening planning begins, many stores will not have managers appointed yet, or appointed managers may be busy preparing the stores for opening. As a result, tenants usually are not available to participate in the planning. Regular communication with the merchants is essential so they will be kept up to date with the plans and the schedule of events. A meeting should be held with the merchants to present the program and solicit their support. The merchants will need to know the advertising plans and specific ad deadlines.

Numerous other details have to be addressed well in advance. Some specific examples are noted here.

- Develop an advertising schedule that includes preopening, opening, and postopening advertisements—a comprehensive program should consider utilizing newspapers, radio, TV, billboards, and direct mail.
- Develop a press kit for the media representatives.
- Schedule a press conference before the charitable event or before or during the grand opening proper.
- Select decorations and arrange for their installation and removal.
- Prepare an agenda for the ribbon-cutting ceremony.
- Send invitations to community leaders.
- Invite two or three VIPs to speak and cut the ribbon.
- Select and purchase promotional giveaways—balloons, refrigerator magnets, shopping bags, etc., imprinted with the shopping center name and logo.
- Hire extra personnel and select costumes or special apparel for those who will hand out promotional items.

- Design and print a consumer brochure showing the layout of the shopping center and a list of the tenants; arrange to install holders for them near the mall entrances or directories.
- Interview, hire, and schedule entertainers.
- Arrange for catering, music, equipment rentals, etc.
- Hire a photographer to take publicity photos—include dignitaries, entertainers, the ribbon-cutting ceremony, crowds, and the full parking lot—for a follow-up press release and for inclusion in the leasing package.
- Send flowers and a welcoming card to each tenant.
- Schedule cleanup of the mall and parking lot.
- Develop a contingency plan in case anything goes wrong.

In addition, several operational issues must be thoroughly analyzed, planned, and implemented. First, everyone on the management and marketing teams must be briefed on the event and assigned their particular duties. Items such as trash cans, ash urns, planters, benches, etc., must be installed in their proper places. Extra maintenance personnel must be scheduled to work on the mall and in the parking lot. Elevator and escalator service personnel should be on call or at the mall during the beginning of the events.

Security and crowd control are especially important considerations. Additional security personnel should be hired and assigned to the mall proper, the entrances, and the parking lot. Activities in the parking lot can also be observed from the roof. The local police department should be asked to direct traffic in front of the shopping center; security personnel should direct traffic inside the parking lot. Two-way radios should be rented so all security personnel can be in direct communication with the property manager, the marketing director, the management office, and each other. Levels of traffic control and mall patrols should be coordinated with scheduled events.

Preopening Publicity.   Even before the grand opening of a shopping center is planned, a comprehensive publicity program should be developed. In particular, press releases should be sent out announcing specific milestones leading up to the opening.

- Development of the shopping center
- Lease commitments by anchor tenants
- Ground breaking
- Construction progress
- A list of tenants who have signed leases
- The grand opening events

Once the shopping center is open, publicity in the form of periodic press releases should continue. Announcements of new tenants, changes in the operations or management of the center, and special promotional events are all possibilities. An ongoing publicity program can augment purchased advertising and help promotional dollars go further.

BENEFITS OF A COORDINATED PROGRAM

A coordinated marketing, advertising, and promotions program benefits everyone involved in the shopping center—the landlord, the tenants, the property manager, the leasing agent, and the community at large.

For the landlord, coordinated marketing results in increased tenants' sales, which means more successful tenants, higher base rents, and greater opportunities for percentage rent, as well as less tenant turnover and faster lease-up of vacant spaces. All of these are reflected in the shopping center's cash flow and, from that, the property value increases.

For the tenant, a coordinated program provides opportunities for more sales and, therefore, greater success. Specific tenant benefits include:

- A location where most (if not all) of the other merchants are coordinating some of their advertising. This means one tenant can capitalize on a major promotion by another tenant. For example, if a department store anchor is having a seasonal sale, other merchants can plan similar sales for the same period. Department stores do extensive advertising for such events, and if the other tenants use the same media, they can maximize the impact of their ads by association with the department store's ad. Thus, the department store will draw more customer traffic, and shoppers will be looking for additional bargains at the other stores' sales.
- The opportunity to participate in the shopping center's regular advertising pieces—e.g., flyers for on-site distribution, tabloid sections inserted in the local newspaper, etc. The individual tenant's ad has more impact if it is included with other tenants' ads than if it is run by itself in the newspaper. When tenants advertise jointly, it is often possible to negotiate a lower ad rate for each participating tenant.
- Increased traffic flow. Promotional events at the shopping center attract additional visitors, each one a potential customer.

For the property manager, coordinating promotional activities provides an opportunity to develop a rapport with the tenants. The resulting goodwill can help overcome the adversarial relationship that often develops between landlord and tenant on issues related to management, operations, and leasing. Another benefit is that the tenant whose sales are strong is less likely to have financial difficulties and, therefore, less likely to become a rent collection problem. On a more personal level, the property manager's compensation—the property management fee—is typically computed as the greater of two amounts, a minimum fee or a percentage of the property's income. Increased tenant sales increase rental income for the property immediately in the form of overage (percentage rent) payments; subsequent escalations in base rent (at renewal and when spaces are re-leased) boost the property's income further. When the income of the property increases, the management fee increases.

The job of the leasing team is easier when a shopping center's tenants are successful. Nothing sells as well as success, and retail tenants are attracted to shopping centers where the tenants—individually and by categories—have high sales volumes. In fact, such shopping centers become known throughout the retailing community. Consequently, the annual marketing calendar and the specific advertising campaigns and promotional events become effective tools in the leasing agent's discussions with prospective tenants. Prospects can be shown how the center works for its tenants—advertising and promotions bring customers to the center.

Finally, the community as a whole benefits from a shopping center's marketing, advertising, and promotions in several ways.

- Being made aware of new fashions and products—coordinated merchandising programs (e.g., back-to-school and spring fashions) address consumer's needs on a seasonal basis.
- Saving money—periodic centerwide sales events (e.g., Presidents' Day sale, sidewalk and moonlight sales) provide a wide array of merchandise at lower prices.
- Being entertained—promotional events (e.g., arts and crafts festivals, boat shows, Santa's arrival before Christmas) are repeated annually at many malls, often becoming traditions for local shoppers.
- Participating in community-focused activities—use of the center for fundraisers, membership drives, educational displays, etc., benefits particular groups (Girl Scouts, Little League, charitable organizations) as well as the individual shopper.

12

Administration

A key step toward the successful management of a shopping center is control of administrative activities and their attendant paperwork. A good administrative system will assure accurate billing, maintain the property's income stream, and help the manager fulfill the landlord's obligations under established leases and other agreements. It should be pointed out, however, that while the manager is responsible for administration, the day-to-day work may be delegated to personnel hired for that purpose.

ADMINISTRATIVE RECORD KEEPING

Accurate records of collections, payments, and other operational activities at a shopping center are an extremely important part of the administrative function. A good administrative system will include comprehensive policies and specific procedures. An efficient one will minimize the amount of work and the time required to do it yet provide the information needed for day-to-day operations and for reports to the owner.

In any administrative system, there will be a number of different records that list information on all the tenants in the center. The best way to approach such records is to list every space in the shopping center in the order in which it appears on the site plan or other schematic layout. (Visualization of individual spaces will be easier because of the tendency to associate adjacent spaces and tenants with each other.) In a large mall, the list should start at one end or entrance, proceed along one side of the mall concourse to the other end, and then return along the other side of the concourse. Each occupied space should be identified by the tenant's name, and all unoccupied spaces should be identified as vacant. In this way, the manager can be sure that no tenant or store space has been omitted.

In setting up administrative records, it is best to use the store name to identify the tenant; the name of a corporation (or a person) may be difficult to recognize as the tenant in a specific space. However, cross-references are also important. Athletic Express, a tenant in some California centers, is owned by Kinney Shoes. Showing the name as Athletic Express assures that the tenant will be easily recognizable by everyone involved with the property, but accounting records must indicate that checks received from Kinney Shoes are for Athletic Express so that payments will be recorded properly.

In today's high-technology offices, computers are often used to maintain and update the array of property management records and to prepare reports from them. Software available for various types of microcomputers includes numerous property management-specific programs. Accounting and word-processing programs are also extremely useful. Depending on the size of a managed shopping center and the level of detail required in reporting, some managers may find manual systems adequate for their purposes. Because most computerized data manipulations are adaptations or derivations of the manual systems and procedures, discussion here of the latter will provide a basis for understanding what can be done with computers.

Accounting

Accounting for income and expenses is typically done in one of two ways. In *cash-basis accounting,* income is recorded when it is received and expenses are recorded when they are paid. In *accrual-basis accounting,* income and expenses are recorded when they are due—regardless of when they are received or paid. The method used will depend on the need for specific types of information. Because most such information will be incorporated into reports to the owners, it may be appropriate to consult a professional accountant before establishing a particular system or specific accounting procedures.

The accumulation of income and expenses throughout the year is usually recorded in a general ledger, and accounting for specific items is facilitated if a chart of accounts (exhibit 12.1) is used. A chart of accounts establishes a specific distribution of income sources and recurring expenditures. Most categories of income and expense are subdivided to account for specific expenses and items that are likely to represent substantial dollar amounts by themselves. The assignment of numbers to major categories and their respective subcategories facilitates tracking of recurring items because it assures

E X H I B I T   12.1

Example Chart of Accounts—Alphabetical List of Expenses

Administrative—70000 series
Accounting fees 77100
Advertising 71100
Airfare 79100
Automobile expense 74100
Bank charges 76105
Entertainment and promotion 71105
Insurance—life 80115
Insurance—medical/dental 80120
Leasing commissions 77120
Legal fees 77110
Management fees 74810
Merchants' assn contributions 71101
Office supplies 76120
Payroll taxes 80105
Permits 78110
Postage 76125
Real estate tax 78120
Telephone expenses 76135

Building Supplies—83000 series
Alarm 83150
Licenses and permits 83100
Security 83250
Trash removal 83500

Repairs and Maintenance—85000 series
Elevator 85600
Flooring 85200
Landscaping 85400
Parking lot 85800
Roof 85500

Utilities—81000 series
Electricity 81100
Gas 81200
Sewer 81500
Water 81400

This abbreviated listing is intended to suggest the range of items that may be accounted separately. Such an alphabetical list is a handy reference for identifying account numbers for particular types of expenses. A comprehensive chart of accounts will usually include numbers for discrete sources of income, specific assets and liabilities, and capital expenditures—as well as the entire spectrum of operating expenses—displayed in numerical order.

---

they will be handled the same way. Using account codes to identify receipts and expenditures assures consistency of recording and, in turn, makes it easier to develop an accurate budget.

Forms and Files

Accounting and record keeping are by nature detail-oriented activities. In property management, these activities require high levels of precision and accuracy that are typically met by using a variety of forms.

Management Takeover Checklist.   The manager's administrative functions typically begin with takeover of the management account, and the operating records are often received concurrent with the management takeover. The manager should develop a management takeover checklist (exhibit 12.2) to help speed the transfer of specific information and records as well as expedite development of an appropriate administrative system. (It is also a

E X H I B I T   12.2

Example New Account Checklist

Shopping Center _____ Takeover Date _____
Contact _____ Phone Number _____
Company _____ FAX Number _____
Address _____

Administrative

Contract Signed _____ Accounting Notified _____
Obtain Former Budgets _____ Obtain Tenant List _____
Notification of Tenants _____ Notification of Suppliers _____
Copies of All Leases _____ Copies of Project Files _____
Set of Plans (As Built) _____ Keys for Project _____
Copies of Service Contracts _____ Notify Police/Fire _____
Prepare Emergency Lists _____ Notify City Hall _____
Pending Insurance Claims _____ Pending Litigation _____

Accounting

Tenant Ledger Cards _____ CAM Estimates _____
Special Billings _____ Delinquency List _____
Security Deposit List _____ Tickler File _____
Percentage Rent Information _____ Tax Billing Files _____
Bank Accounts _____ Tax ID Numbers _____
Mortgage Information _____ Reporting Formats _____

Site Activity

Site Inspection _____ Vacancies Inspected _____
Safety Inspection _____ Meet Contractors _____
Meet Tenants _____ Verify All Meters _____
Inventory of Personal Property _____ Verify Employees _____

---

good idea to know who managed the shopping center previously because that person or company may be helpful in obtaining needed information.) A suitable form will assure that the manager obtains all pertinent records, notifies all appropriate personnel and agencies, and performs all necessary inspections and other tasks related to the takeover of management. Once all the items on the list have been checked, the checklist can be discarded. However, some managers prefer to note the dates when items were accomplished and retain the forms for future reference.

Lease Summary.   In a shopping center, everything the manager does will stem from the leases. They determine the property's income (base rents, percentage rates), the prorations of operating and CAM expenses passed through to the tenants, and the rules and regulations that govern how the merchants are expected to operate their businesses in the center. However, much of the information in the lease itself is not needed for the day-to-day operation of the property. It is much easier for the manager if the data are compiled on a

E X H I B I T   12.3

Example Tenant Lease Summary Form

Shopping Center _____ Date _____
Prepared By _____
Tenant Trade Name _____ Corporate Name _____
Mailing Address _____
Home Office Contact _____ Phone _____
Store Address _____ Phone _____
Store Manager _____ Phone _____
District Manager _____ Phone _____
Lease Date _____ Commencement _____ Termination _____
Square Footage _____ Security Deposit _____
Lease Term _____ Options _____

Monthly Rental Rate

$_____ for the period _____ to _____
$_____ for the period _____ to _____
$_____ for the period _____ to _____
$_____ for the period _____ to _____
Percentage Rate _____ Breakpoint _____ Reports Due _____

Reimburse Landlord (dollar amounts)*

Common Area Estimate _____ Tax Estimate _____ Insurance Estimate _____
HVAC Maintenance _____ Utilities _____ Supervision Fee _____
Merchants' Assn _____ Roof Maint _____ Environmental Exp _____

Tenant Responsibility

HVAC Maintenance _____ Utilities _____ Liability _____
Fire & EC _____ Plate Glass _____ Boiler _____

Miscellaneous Items _____

_____

*Estimated from CAM Budget

lease summary form. There are many types of forms for this purpose, but one that is four or more pages long tends to defeat the purpose of summation even though it is better than handling a 60-page lease each time information is needed. For most managers' purposes, a one- or two-page lease summary form (exhibit 12.3) will suffice.

Even if the former manager has left lease summaries in the files, those summaries may have been compiled differently or not kept up to date. It is best if a new manager compiles his or her own summaries. The compilation process will help the manager understand the lease document itself and the variances in its specific terms and conditions. Once new summaries have been compiled, they can be compared to earlier records for accuracy, consistency, and completeness, and any discrepancies can be rechecked against the original leases.

The lease summary is normally used only as an internal record, so the summary forms can be completed in pencil (rather than ink). Lease summary data are used to set up records of tenant payments, common area prorations, percentage rent schedules, insurance requirements, and myriad other documents that facilitate analysis and comparison of tenant and lease information. Because the lease summary includes terms and conditions of the particular lease, it also serves as a ready reference regarding restrictions, exclusives, options, etc., when current leases come up for renewal and whenever new leases are negotiated with prospective tenants.

Alternatively, lease information can be entered into a computer, and appropriate software will facilitate searching this data base and compiling specific types of information (e.g., tenant rosters, security deposit reports, rental rates, expiration dates, exclusives).

Tenant Roster.   An important record prepared from the lease summaries is a tenant roster. Typically, it lists each tenant's square footage, the rental rate per month and per square foot, the percentage rate, and the amount of any security deposit. The length of the lease term and the lease commencement and termination dates may also be included, but a tenant roster usually will not show any specific payments made by the tenant. The example shown in exhibit 12.4 is sufficiently comprehensive for most managers' needs. However, some clients may require a more complete roster showing, for example, estimated common area charges, date of next rental increase, breakpoint, number of options (to extend the lease), and terms of the options in addition to the items shown in the exhibit. In fact, each individual client or shopping center owner is likely to have a preferred format for a tenant roster, and it is best to try to accommodate the client. However, the client's roster may not fulfill the manager's information needs, which are generally secondary to those of the client. While the manager may be responsible for only one shopping center, a client who owns several properties must have consistent records for all of them.

The tenant roster is another record that can be computerized. Once this information is in a computer, it is easily resorted to generate vacancy reports, for example. This is helpful because both of these items are included among the regular reports sent to the shopping center owner. Regardless of how a tenant roster is prepared, it should be dated, and the date should be changed each time the roster is revised. That way, the manager can assure that the record being worked with is current.

Expense Prorations.   A list of tenants' prorated operating expenses and CAM charges (sometimes called a "billback analysis" as in exhibit 12.5) is also compiled from the lease summaries. Data to be included are tenant name, store size, the natural proration percentage based on the area of the store

E X H I B I T   12.4

Example Tenant Roster

Heartland Plaza Shopping Center

Date: April 30, 1991

Tenant	GLA Sq Ft	Monthly Rent	Sq Ft Rent*	Deposit	Term	Lease Date	Start Date	End Date	Percent Rate†
Fast Food	1,250	$1,560	1.25	$2,500	5	03-01-91	04-02-91	04-30-96	6.0
Restaurant	4,215	$5,300	1.25	–0–	10	02-11-91	05-06-91	05-31-01	5.0
Dress Store	2,400	$3,120	1.30	$4,000	5	04-03-91	05-01-91	04-30-96	6.0
Computers	1,152	$1,613	1.40	$3,000	3	02-11-91	03-01-91	02-29-94	5.0
Video Rental	4,800	$4,800	1.00	$7,200	5	01-21-91	02-01-91	01-31-96	6.0
Photo Shop	900	$1,350	1.50	$ 900	5	05-01-91	05-01-91	04-30-96	5.0
Shoe Repair	440	$ 770	1.75	$1,000	5	01-12-91	02-01-91	01-31-96	6.0
Insurance	880	$1,452	1.65	$1,800	2	02-12-91	03-01-91	02-28-93	–0–
Realty Office	600	$ 900	1.50	$2,100	3	01-15-91	02-01-91	01-31-94	–0–
Pool Supply	1,460	$1,825	1.25	$1,460	5	03-03-91	04-01-91	03-31-96	5.0
Bicycle Shop	2,230	$2,899	1.30	$2,230	10	09-12-90	03-06-91	03-31-01	6.0
Florist	1,200	$1,680	1.40	$2,400	5	09-30-90	03-27-91	03-31-96	5.0
Travel Agency	1,200	$1,800	1.50	$2,400	5	01-13-91	02-04-91	02-28-96	–0–
Dental Office	1,860	$2,604	1.40	–0–	10	09-10-90	02-01-91	01-31-01	–0–
Pet Store	3,216	$4,020	1.25	$5,000	10	01-27-91	03-16-91	03-31-01	3.0
Totals	27,803	$35,693		$35,990					

*Monthly rate/sq ft (when lease shows $/sq ft/year, divide that rate by 12).

†Based on sales volume; collected as overage.

E X H I B I T   12.5

Example Billback Analysis

Heartland Plaza Shopping Center   Date: January 1, 1991

Tenant	Square Footage	Share	Taxes	Insurance	CAM + Supv	Notes*
Fast Food	1,250	.045	P/R	P/R	P/R + 15%	None
Restaurant	4,215	.152	P/R	P/R	P/R + 10%	None
Dress Store	2,400	.086	P/R	P/R	P/R + –0–	No Trash
Computers	1,152	.041	P/R	P/R	P/R + 15%	None
Video Rental	4,800	.173	P/R	P/R	P/R + 12%	Max .25
Photo Shop	900	.032	P/R	P/R	P/R + 15%	None
Shoe Repair	440	.016	P/R	P/R	P/R + 10%	None
Insurance	880	.032	P/R	P/R	P/R + 15%	None
Realty Office	600	.022	P/R	P/R	P/R + 10%	(1)
Pool Supply	1,460	.053	P/R	P/R	P/R + 15%	(2)
Bicycle Shop	2,230	.080	P/R	P/R	P/R + 15%	None
Florist	1,200	.043	P/R	P/R	P/R + 15%	None
Travel Agency	1,200	.043	P/R	P/R	P/R + 15%	None
Dental Office	1,860	.067	P/R	P/R	P/R + 15%	(3)
Pet Store	3,216	.115	P/R	P/R	P/R + 15%	None
Totals	27,803	1.000				

Analysis is subject to change as tenants move in and out.
P/R = pro rated; Supv indicates supervision or administration fee.

*Dress store arranged own trash pickup; video rental pays 25 cents sq ft max (for all billback charges).
(1) Realty office pays for two reserved stalls in addition to normal CAM.
(2) Pool supply pays additional storage of $180 per quarter.
(3) Dental office pays quarterly on actual.

(square footage), and any variances that may apply to individual tenants. Once the listing is properly prepared, the actual billings are easily computed.

With regard to tenant prorations, it is not unusual for a tenant to have a negotiated percentage instead of the computed rate (e.g., a supermarket may occupy 27 percent of the center's GLA but pay for 25 percent of the operating expenses). Nor is it unusual for a strong retailer to agree to pay prorated common area costs but negotiate a cap on its share (paying a maximum amount per square foot or a maximum total dollar amount) or an offset against percentage rent (deducting CAM charges and real estate taxes from overage due). Many tenants negotiate different administrative or supervision fees, and some may successfully exclude one or more items from the list of operating expenses and CAM charges they will pay. Major repairs, insurance premiums, and taxes are commonly excluded from calculation of administrative fees; usually the administrative fee applies expressly to CAM and related charges. Many national retailers will have specific exclusions in their leases—e.g., security, trash removal, some insurance premiums, etc. If a tenant is exempted from paying a particular prorated expense such as security, that tenant will also be exempt from any administrative charges for that expense. (Lease negotiations are detailed in chapter 9, and administrative fees are discussed in chapter 10.)

The manager must be aware of any rights or privileges granted to major tenants. In particular, the anchor tenant may have negotiated the right to pre-approve large expenditures (e.g., a parking lot pavement repair). All specific rights and exemptions that relate to tenants' payment of operating and CAM expenditures should be noted in the analysis of tenant charges. Failure to make such notes can lead to expensive problems—for example, if the manager proceeds with a large repaving job without obtaining the requisite anchor tenant approval, he or she is risking the tenant's refusal to pay its portion of the bill on the grounds that the manager did not comply with the lease agreement.

Note that the example in exhibit 12.5 includes taxes and insurance. However, if any tenants' leases require them to pay anything different from their store-size proration of taxes or insurance, these two expenses should be analyzed separately. Particular lease terms to be aware of are base year exclusions, caps on taxes or insurance premiums, exclusions on insurance premiums (types of coverages), and any specific agreements regarding administrative fees for these two items.

Security Deposit Register.   One of the greatest accounting difficulties is being certain that security deposits are actually received. When a security deposit is demanded—and agreed to—most center owners require that the deposit accompany the signed lease from the tenant. However, this can lead to the assumption that a deposit was received when in fact it was not. The manager should establish a straightforward policy on security deposits and a precise procedure for their collection. The accountant should maintain a record of all security deposits received (exhibit 12.6), keeping the list current as tenants move in and out. This record is typically included in the report sent to the owner each month.

It is best to keep security deposit funds separate from operating funds because part or all of these monies will be returned to the tenants when they vacate the leased premises. If the deposit is used by the landlord to offset a tenant expense, an accounting of this should be given to the tenant along with a request for reimbursement. As long as a security deposit is required, the full amount should be in the landlord's hands (as discussed in chapter 10).

Tenant Ledger.   Rent payments are recorded on a tenant ledger that is set up from the lease summaries. When a computerized system is used, accounting software will lead the user stepwise through the process. However, it is helpful for the manager to understand the elements of accounting as exem-

E X H I B I T   12.6

Example Security Deposit Register

Heartland Plaza Shopping Center   Date: April 30, 1991

Tenant	Square Footage	Deposit	Date Paid
Fast Food	1,250	$2,500	03-01-91
Restaurant	4,215	–0–	
Dress Store	2,400	$4,000	04-03-91
Computers	1,152	$3,000	02-11-91
Video Rental	4,800	$7,200	01-21-91
Photo Shop	900	$ 900	05-01-91
Shoe Repair	440	$1,000	01-12-91
Insurance	880	$1,800	02-12-91
Realty Office	600	$2,100	01-15-91
Pool Supply	1,460	$1,460	03-03-91
Bicycle Shop	2,230	$2,230	09-12-90
Florist	1,200	$2,400	09-30-90
Travel Agency	1,200	$2,400	01-13-91
Dental Office	1,860	–0–	
Pet Store	3,216	$5,000	01-27-91

NOTE: None of the deposits require interest to be paid, and none are required to be kept in a separate trust account. Security deposits in residential properties are handled differently; their requirements are much stricter.

plified in a manual or hand-posting system (exhibit 12.7 shows a commercially available preprinted tenant ledger card). The top portion of the card showing tenant and lease-specific information is filled in. Then all payments are recorded in the columns below. Note that the sample includes spaces for a total payment and for distribution of the amounts that apply; there is provision for 24 separate entries.

In accounting for tenant payments, some managers enter the rent and pass-through amounts due each month and identify specific payments when the money is received. Others merely enter the amounts received. The advantage of prelisting the amount due is that it provides a check point for what is paid and when it is received.

Tickler File.   One of the most useful administrative systems is a so-called "tickler" file for reminding the manager and others of what has to be done and when. A tickler file can be computerized, but a manual system using 3-by-5-inch file cards will work just as well. In addition to a supply of file cards, a manual system requires a small file box and section dividers for each of the twelve months for several years into the future. Regardless of its level of sophistication, the purpose of the tickler file is to provide a means for the shop-

E X H I B I T   12.7

Example Tenant Ledger Card

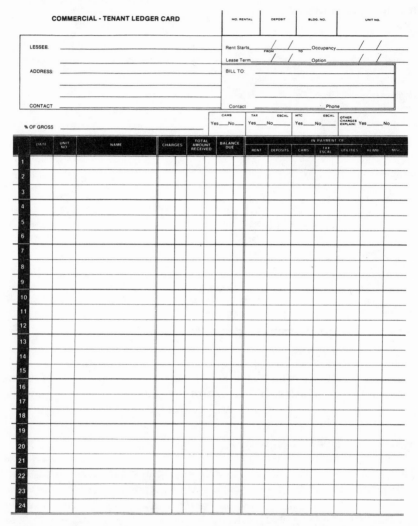

Reprinted with permission from Alexander, Alan A., and Muhlebach, Richard F.: *Managing and Leasing Commercial Properties: Forms and Procedures* (New York: John Wiley & Sons, Inc., 1991).

ping center manager to prepare for specific changes in advance. (The cards for each month are removed from the file on the first day of the month and used to schedule that month's administrative activities.) A tickler file is easy to use and reliable, and it assures that the manager does not miss any important events or activities.

A good way to start a tickler file is to review the lease summaries. From them, such things as rent increases, lease termination dates, and related events can be noted on individual file cards and arranged in the tickler file to appear as advance reminders. Each card should also show the month and year or years in which an activity will take place, the specific change, and the tenant to whom it applies. In a system that covers more than one center, the name of the shopping center would be included as well. Thus, if a tenant's lease calls for an annual CPI rental increase effective April 1 of each successive year of a five-year lease, that information would be recorded appropriately on cards for each of the four future years. The cards would then be filed in the sections for March of those years to remind the manager to calculate the CPI increase in advance of the April 1 due dates. A more compact system might have a single card for the series of rent increases, and the user would note when the current year's increase was computed and billed (check off and date it), then refile the card under March of the next year.

A one-month lead time may be adequate for many items (e.g., scheduled rent increases, as noted above). However, some activities will require more lead time and may need reminders for subsequent follow-up. For example, lease expiration dates may be recorded in duplicate to provide reminders both six months and 60 days prior to the expiration. The extra time is important because the manager must evaluate the tenant's performance of the current lease and, assuming a continued relationship is desirable, determine the terms of a renewal lease. Also, the tenant must be given time to evaluate the new lease and decide whether to sign it. For some tenants, it may be appropriate to set up reminders for 90 days and one year prior to expiration. These time frames should be adequate for most small shop leases. However, anchor lease renewal can require many months and even years of negotiations. The same may apply for some national shop tenants.

The tickler file can also be used to track other lease requirements such as option terms and dates, cancellation rights, and submission of insurance certificates as well as recurring activities for the shopping center as a whole— e.g., property tax assessments, payment of insurance premiums, etc.

General Files. Files are the repositories of specific information on a shopping center's tenants as well as its operations. When a management company is responsible for several shopping centers, there should be a separate set of files for each center. Color coding can be used to distinguish the files of different shopping centers. If the management records are maintained strictly on site, color codes will be helpful in the organization of different types of records. Even more important, the contents of individual file folders should be maintained in chronological order, with the newest material at the front of the folder. Each folder should be labeled to show its contents. In a management company office, folders will show the shopping center name in addition to other specific contents. A separate file folder should be prepared for each tenant, and a copy of the lease, any other pertinent documents, and all correspondence with that tenant should be filed there. In some offices, the lease is attached to one side of the folder and correspondence to the other. In addition to tenant files, there should be separate files for different types of expenses as well as specific management activities and reports (e.g., common area maintenance, property taxes, insurance premiums and certificates, correspondence, service contracts, budgets, monthly reports to ownership, etc.). Separate files should also be created for individual employees and for management personnel employment and payroll records. The numbers of folders and the complexity of the filing system depend on the amount of material to be retained and the size of the shopping center. If more than one person will be using the files, a "file out" card can be inserted to replace a file temporarily, and that will help others track down the file when it is needed. It is also a good practice to have the file name, dates of removal and return, and the name of the person using it logged on a form used for that purpose only.

Reporting to the Owner

A key responsibility of the shopping center manager is to provide the owner with regular reports on the financial status of the property and its operation. These reports may have to be prepared in specific formats, especially if the owner is represented by an asset manager or has complex investments. A standardized format makes it easier to compare the reports for the property over an extended period. It also facilitates the transfer of information about one property to a larger compilation covering several properties. Accuracy of information and on-time submission of reports are critical; delays in reporting or information that is incomplete or incorrect can create problems when data from reports on several properties are merged. Repeated problems with a manager's reports can result in loss of the management account.

Reports are usually prepared and submitted monthly, and the package usually includes several discrete analyses. A key document is the operating statement. This may be accompanied by an analysis of income and expenses that compares actual figures to budget projections—and an explanation of specific variances from budget. A bank account reconciliation is not always a requirement. When it is included, it assures the owner that the bank balance is generally in agreement with the operating statement (except for items in transit). Most of the other reports are statistical in nature. (The tenant roster, security deposit register, and a list of vacancies may not be included with each month's reports unless there have been changes in the tenancy.) Monies not received will be accounted in a delinquency report, and percentage rent income will be supported by a sales analysis. Leasing activity is also covered in a separate report. Accompanying these reports, there should always be a narrative summary of the operating results and other statistics.

Operating Statement. The operating statement shows the current month's income and expenses. It compares actual and budgeted amounts and indicates specific variances. The year-to-date cumulative figures are also compared.

Typically, this is presented as a cash statement, but institutional clients often prefer accrual or modified accrual statements. Some owners want to see copies of bills sent to tenants and invoices for expenses. However, most prefer the manager to retain such backup documentation and have it available for inspection.

Delinquency Report. The month-end delinquency report lists each tenant who owes rent or other payments due the landlord, showing how much is owed and how long it has been delinquent. It should also include a statement of what is being done to expedite collection—e.g., agreement on a payment plan, submission to a collection agency or to an attorney, etc. The owner must be advised of delinquencies and how they affect the shopping center and its income stream.

Sales Analysis. An effective report will include a sales analysis for all tenants comparing this year's sales to last year's for both the current month and the year to date—in total dollars and sales per square foot. The format for display of information will vary from owner to owner. (An example in current use is shown in exhibit 12.8; note that it includes the breakpoint for calculation of percentage rent and an evaluation of the "overage" or percentage rent income.) Here again, computer software will facilitate calculation of variances as well as permit tracking of average sales per square foot. For purposes of comparison to prior year figures, it may be important to include figures for spaces that are presently vacant but whose previous occupants contributed sales figures in the prior year.

Leasing Report. Leasing is a critical component of shopping center operations, and a monthly report on this activity is essential. Usually this will cover tenants that moved in, those that moved out, and leases coming up for renewal. For the latter, it is helpful to indicate the likelihood of renewal.

Narrative Report. This is generally a summary of the specific statistical reports and important changes to them. It should cover such things as occupancy, specific move-ins and move-outs, leases due for renewal, the condition

E X H I B I T   12.8

Example Sales Analysis Form

Center _____   Month/Year _____

MERCHANT	AREA	MONTHLY SALES COMPARISON				YEAR-TO-DATE COMPARISON				BREAK-POINT	OVERAGE POTENTIAL EVALUATION		
		MONTH	MONTH	% CHANGE	$/S.F.	CURRENT YEAR	PREVIOUS YEAR	% CHANGE	$/S.F.		CURRENT MONTH	YEAR-TO-DATE	
											% CHANGE	YEAR-TO-DATE	% CHANGE

Monthly sales comparison reflects total sales dollars and dollars per square foot for current month current year (left) and same month prior year (right). **Year-to-date** figures are total sales dollars and dollars per square foot, January through current month current year (left) and same period prior year (right). **Overage potential** reflects amounts of overage rent due for current month current year versus same month prior year and year-to-date for current year versus prior year.

of the property, capital expenditures in progress, legal issues, marketing activities, and special problems. Detailed explanations of substantial variances from budget are usually reported here as well. When prepared properly, the narrative report will give the owner an overview of the month's activities, identifying particular successes and calling attention to specific problems.

BUDGETING

A budget is necessary to full understanding of the financial status of a property at all times. A property owner may think budgets are unnecessary, but property managers rely on them. A budget can be simple or complex. The best ones project income and expenses on a monthly basis, accounting for several categories of income and dividing (or subdividing) expense categories as appropriate. The important thing to remember is that the budget will be more accurate if it shows specific income amounts in the months when they are expected to be received and expenses in the months when they are expected to be paid. A budget will be easier to use if it is prepared in a format that matches the monthly reports so that variances—both favorable and unfavorable—can be identified more precisely when comparing actual versus budgeted figures for the current month and the year to date.

While budgets can be prepared by hand on columnar pads or preprinted forms, computers have made budgeting comparatively easy. Computer programs allow the user to rely on formulas (e.g., incremental percentage increases of specific items), and they can automatically distribute equal portions among the twelve months. The computer also makes it possible to evaluate different assumptions such as the impact of varying rental increases or the effects of protracted vacancies or changes in the allocation of pass-through expenses. The time invested in programming the formulas will be paid back in flexibility and ease of making changes.

Projecting Income

Preparation of the annual budget begins with a projection of income for the coming year. The primary income of a shopping center is the base rents paid by each tenant. Having recorded the rental rate on a lease summary form, the manager uses those forms as the basis for projecting income. Information for each tenant should be compiled in a budget format that permits itemization for each month as well as the total for the year. If the rent is constant, the same amount is entered for each month; if a CPI increase is scheduled during the year, the percentage increase should be estimated and the higher rent amount recorded for those months in which it will be paid. Scheduled increases should also be recorded in a footnote or noted in the budget explanation because actual CPI increases will not be known until they go into effect.

Vacancies affect the income of the property in a negative way, and for this reason they are a consideration in budgeting. A space that is currently vacant can be listed in the budget in several ways. One approach is to enter the market rent for each month and include a vacancy factor in the budget computations. Another approach is to show no income until occupancy is expected and then enter expected income for the remaining months. Still others do not account for vacant spaces in the budget and omit a line item for a vacancy factor. However, it is advisable for the shopping center budget to show the full potential income stream and an accounting for vacancies. Displaying the "cost" of vacancy serves as a strong reminder that money is being lost each month that a store space is empty.

Having accounted for base rental income (adjusted for vacancies), the manager next records additional sources of revenue. Percentage rent is difficult to estimate accurately. However, if leases call for payment of percentage rent, the amounts should be estimated for the budget but based on very conservative calculations. Percentage rent is more likely to be collected in an established center. Centers that are less than three years old generally are not expected to yield percentage rent although a few tenants (restaurants in particular) may pay overages from the beginning of their leases. In estimating percentage rents, an incremental increase in annual sales is projected from a review of the tenant's sales history. The potential for percentage rent based on the increased annual sales is then estimated, along with any negotiated offsets of tenant charges, and the amount is entered in the budget. Percentage rent should be indicated in the month or months in which it will be paid. If a tenant reports once a year in February, percentage rent payment would be expected in March unless the lease states a different due date. If tenants report and pay each calendar quarter, income would normally be received in the month following the quarter (first quarter—January through March—paid in April). Monthly reports and payments would also be received in following months (January sales reported and percentage paid in February). Percentage rent is always extremely variable; individual tenants may report and pay on very different schedules. While it is important to anticipate this income in budgeting for a shopping center, it must be remembered that percentage rent is not an absolutely reliable source of income.

Also to be considered is income from miscellaneous sources such as bank interest, late fees, and otherwise unscheduled reimbursements from tenants. Other possible income sources are pay telephones and temporary tenant rents and charges. Last year's budget is usually the best source for this information, and estimations of future income should account for operational changes over the past year. In the absence of prior experience or records, it may be best to omit miscellaneous income from the budget. It is better to be surprised with additional funds than to be disappointed because anticipated funds did not materialize.

There is one other major source of income—tenant payments of pass-through expenses. However, this is typically calculated *after* expenses have been budgeted so that the figures will be accurate. Each tenant's payments should be estimated separately—whether prorated on the basis of GLA or computed using an agreed-upon formula. This allows the manager to consider exclusions, caps on CAM payments, differing payment schedules, and other exceptions that will affect the amounts paid. Each tenant's expected payments for different items should be computed, and the amounts for each item from all the tenants can be totaled and entered in the months in which they will be received.

One pass-through expense that poses problems is the CAM administrative or supervision fee. Such a fee is included in the lease to reimburse part of the landlord's expense of administering the maintenance of the common areas, and it is usually stated as a percentage to be added to the CAM proration. Some shopping center owners want these fees shown as part of the budgeted income, but that often distorts the figures—the larger pro rata payments can indicate that the owner is collecting more than 100 percent of the pass-through expenses. However, the CAM administrative fees can be a significant part of the owner's cash flow, so they are worth including despite the potential distortion. In fact, one of the authors is required to show these fees as a separate line item so the owner can see how they offset the monthly management fee.

Ideally, the proration of pass-through expenses will be distributed over the twelve months of the year so tenants can make equal monthly payments. (Adjustments for the difference between estimated and actual expenses are normally made after the year ends.) However, some tenants' leases may call for a different distribution of payments, and those who are permitted to do so may pay for an item when it becomes due (e.g., taxes may be paid twice a year and insurance premiums paid annually). Such exceptions should be noted in the budget summary to explain the significant fluctuations in cash flow that will result.

In centers that have merchants' associations or marketing funds, tenants' leases usually require monthly contributions to fund them. The specific amounts and payment schedules are stated in the leases. Most owners prefer to have this income displayed as a separate line item so it will be easy to track receipts. The total collected from the tenants determines the amount to be contributed by the landlord, and these funds are intended to be used exclusively for promotion of the center.

Estimating Expenses

Once income has been projected, the next step is to estimate expenses. This, too, can be approached in different ways. In its most simplified form, the budget shows each type of expense as a line item, and amounts are entered when they are scheduled to be paid (exhibit 12.9). However, it is not unusual for a

E X H I B I T 12.9

Example Expense Budget

Heartland Plaza Shopping Center   Date: 1991

Description	Jan	Feb	Mar	Apr	May	Jun	Jul	Aug	Sep	Oct	Nov	Dec	Total
Management fee	2,200	2,200	2,250	2,250	2,250	2,400	2,400	2,400	2,300	2,200	2,200	2,600	27,650
Insurance	-0-	6,050	-0-	-0-	-0-	-0-	-0-	6,050	-0-	-0-	-0-	-0-	12,100
Real estate tax	-0-	-0-	-0-	31,600	-0-	-0-	-0-	-0-	-0-	31,600	-0-	-0-	63,200
Licenses	-0-	-0-	-0-	-0-	-0-	-0-	-0-	-0-	70	-0-	-0-	-0-	70
Electricity	7,800	7,700	6,300	5,700	5,000	4,600	4,500	4,500	4,700	5,200	6,400	7,200	69,600
Water/sewer	200	200	250	250	280	280	350	350	360	320	240	200	3,280
Gas	1,500	1,500	1,200	900	800	750	750	750	750	900	1,200	1,400	12,400
Security	300	300	300	300	300	300	300	300	300	300	300	300	3,600
Signs	100	-0-	-0-	200	-0-	-0-	100	100	-0-	-0-	-0-	-0-	500
Supplies	225	225	225	225	225	225	425	225	225	225	225	225	2,900
Trash removal	435	435	435	435	435	435	465	465	465	465	465	465	5,400
Landscaping	450	700	550	550	550	550	550	550	550	450	450	450	6,350
Building repair	150	150	150	150	150	150	150	150	150	150	150	150	1,800
Roof	-0-	-0-	-0-	3,450	-0-	-0-	-0-	-0-	-0-	-0-	200	-0-	3,650
Elevator	350	350	350	350	350	350	350	350	350	350	350	350	4,200
Plumbing	30	30	30	30	30	30	30	30	30	30	30	30	360
Electrical	25	25	25	25	25	25	25	25	25	25	25	25	300
Parking lot	-0-	-0-	-0-	-0-	500	1,500	-0-	-0-	-0-	-0-	-0-	-0-	2,000
Janitorial	3,500	3,500	6,100	3,600	3,600	3,750	6,250	3,750	3,650	3,500	6,000	3,900	51,100
Sweeping	125	125	125	125	125	125	125	125	125	125	125	125	1,500
HVAC	875	875	875	875	875	875	875	875	875	875	875	875	10,500
Total	18,265	24,365	19,165	51,015	15,495	16,345	17,645	20,995	14,925	46,715	19,235	18,295	282,460

NOTE: This example shows only the range of expenses budgeted for the shopping center. The completed budget will include items of income, and total expenses should equal total income to be effective. Other information may be included as well (e.g., account numbers for line items, calculation of dollars per square foot, etc.) along with spaces for indicating date prepared, by whom, and revisions and approvals. A budget can be prepared using a ruled form and filling in the blanks by hand. Alternatively, computer programs can be used to automatically enter amounts in columns and calculate totals. The latter will expedite comparison of actual figures to budget projections and facilitate calculation of variances.

shopping center to have three or four separate sub-budgets that distinguish among owner expenses (those that cannot be passed through to the tenants), common area expenses (those commonly prorated to the tenants), promotional expenses (budgeted separately for a merchants' association or a marketing fund), and capital expenses (tenant improvements, leasing commissions, building repairs). Separation of these types of expenses allows them to be analyzed more readily and precludes a need for separate reporting on them.

Owner's Expenses.   This budget usually consists of the management fee, business licenses, the landlord's contributions to the merchants' association or marketing fund, legal fees, and any business expenses of the shopping center that are not chargeable to the tenants. The fee paid to the property manager (or property management firm) is typically a contractual item and easily calculated. Fees for business licenses are usually fairly stable; last year's actual fees are a good starting point. The landlord's promotional fund contribution is based on lease requirements and can be calculated from the estimated merchants' association or marketing fund income from the tenants. Legal expenses should be based on anticipated problems, and that can be difficult to determine. Some properties have heavy legal fees year after year and others have none. If an attorney is on retainer, that amount can be stated in the budget. The manager's prior experience with legal expenses may be the sole guideline, although past years' actual expenses should also be reviewed.

Common Area Expenses.   The total for common area expenses may be derived from two separate lists of items. Most owners distinguish between site expenses and building expenses because major tenants frequently pay for the former but not the latter. If they own their buildings or are responsible for maintaining them, anchor tenants are often exempted from some CAM expenses.

Such things as sweeping, landscaping, pest control, security, site utilities (e.g., parking lot lighting), liability insurance premiums, etc., are considered *site expenses*. Last year's budget is a good starting point, especially to identify specific items. Last year's actual expenses, if significantly different from the budget, should be the basis for estimating amounts. The total amount spent for an expense should be analyzed to determine whether next year's expense will be higher or lower. Estimates should be distributed across the twelve months as appropriate. In many instances, the amount of an expense will not be the same for each month. For example, landscaping fees vary with the seasons and the climate; fertilization, trimming of excessive growth, removal of dead plants and addition of new ones are all activities that recur—but rarely on a monthly schedule.

If last year's budget is not available, there are other resources the manager can utilize. The Institute of Real Estate Management publishes *Income/*

Expense Analysis: Shopping Centers—Open and Enclosed each year. *Shopping Center Operating Cost Report* from ICSC and *Dollars & Cents of Shopping Centers* from the Urban Land Institute are other sources of such information. Because *Dollars & Cents* is published every three years, care must be taken in extrapolating figures for a budget. However, it does provide a good sense of the proportional relationship of specific expenses. Managers of other shopping centers in the area can help pinpoint local costs, and utility companies, local government, suppliers, and contractors can provide useful information on rates, taxes, materials, and labor expenses, respectively.

In evaluating expenses, each line item should be analyzed separately. It may seem easy—and logical—to just add a percentage to last year's totals, but individual line items can vary dramatically from year to year. This is a reflection of both local and national economic conditions as well as climatic and geographic variables. In some areas, utility rates have increased much more rapidly than the general cost of living. On the other hand, contractors' fees have tended to hold steady because of the competition; most would rather not lose an account because of an increase in their charges. Insurance premiums have varied markedly, and only the owner's insurance agent can provide valid figures for the next year's premium costs. Typically premiums are paid once a year, but large premiums may be paid in installments. Also, different coverages may be paid individually. The budget should show insurance payments in the months they are due.

Specific site expenses often vary with the time of year. Utility rates vary with usage, and parking lot lighting costs less in summer when the days are longer and the lights are on for shorter periods. In areas with heavy snow, there may be a high landscape watering expense in summer and no expense in winter. After each expense has been analyzed, the spread of payments should show amounts in the months they will be paid. If electricity is billed monthly, the amounts should be varied appropriately, remembering that payment follows use.

A similar approach should be taken in evaluating *building expenses*. In this case, utilities will include gas, which is used primarily for providing heat and hot water. In northern states, gas expense will be much higher in the winter months and electricity expense, because of air conditioning, will be very high in the summer months. Maintenance of HVAC systems and elevators or escalators is typically covered by service contracts; last year's expenses and anticipated contractual changes should help the manager budget accurately for these. Union contracts, changing utility rates, and expenses that do not recur monthly are of particular concern.

Promotional Expenses.   These are often estimated separately, especially when there is a merchants' association or a marketing fund. Although the income collected from the merchants and the landlord is intended primarily to pay for advertising, decorations, and centerwide promotional events, the funds may also be used to pay part or all of a marketing director's salary and benefits as well as the related administrative costs. Merchants' association by-laws regulate the collection and disposition of funds, and this should be separate from the shopping center's operations and budget. When there is a marketing fund controlled by the landlord, the income and expenses may well be included in the center budget as separate income and expense items. In this instance, the reason for distinguishing them is to assure that collections will cover expenditures.

Capital Expenses. Major roof repairs, parking lot repaving, and similar kinds of expenses are difficult to classify. Often they are paid out of funds accumulated in reserve for just such a use. Whether or not a reserve fund is used, these major improvements are recorded in a capital budget, not the operating budget.

Sometimes it is difficult to distinguish between capital and operating costs. Leasing commissions and construction of tenant improvements are examples. If the manager is budgeting for a brand-new shopping center, the expenditures for marketing and initial lease-up will be substantial, and leasing commissions and tenant improvements may well be included in that separate early budget. However, for an established center, the manager will budget for rental income beginning when a new tenant takes occupancy of a vacant space, and the lease commission would be due on the rent commencement date. Similarly, tenant improvements are usually provided and paid for when the lease commences. In general, leasing commissions and inexpensive tenant improvements are considered operating costs and included in the operating budget. Very expensive tenant improvements might be included in the capital budget. The manager should consult an accountant when unsure whether an item is an operating or a capital expense.

Debt Service. While not actually an operating expense, debt service is paid out of the income of the property. Most owners do not require the budget to show a breakdown between principal and interest, but they can be separated if desired. Debt service is not considered until all operating expenses have been accounted for; debt service is deducted from the property's net operating income.

Budget Overview

The shopping center budget generally is developed with the intention of estimating potential cash flow—i.e., what the owner will collect as his or her "profit" from the investment. The following flow chart indicates how the budget works.

Gross possible rental income
minus   vacancies and collection losses (actual or factored)
plus   miscellaneous income
plus   percentage rents
plus   collected pass-through items
equals   effective gross income
minus   owner's expenses
minus   site operating expenses
minus   building operating expenses
equals   net operating income (NOI)
minus   debt service (principal and interest) payments
equals   cash flow.

All possible sources of income should be identified and the various operating expenses deducted from them. Merchants' association or marketing fund contributions may be included as income and promotional costs deducted as expenses—as separate line items—if appropriate. Deducting operating expenses from effective gross income yields net operating income (NOI), and it is from NOI that debt service is subtracted to find the actual cash flow. Capital expenditures are funded out of the cash flow.

Budget Explanation

In discussing both income and expenses, reference was made to a "budget explanation." This is a form or narrative statement that indicates the assumptions made in preparing the budget and anticipates the kinds of variables that may be encountered during the budget year. It will help the owner understand the reasoning behind the budget and remind the manager of contingencies when he or she must report actual income and expenses as variances from the budget. For example, if the manager assumed a 6-percent increase in utilities expense based on then-current information but utility regulators actually approved a 9-percent increase, the budget explanation would provide the reason for the discrepancy between budgeted and actual figures.

It is important to realize that budgets are rarely finalized on the first attempt. It is not unusual for a manager to analyze each line item and be satisfied with the individual result only to discover when all the line items are added up that the budget as a whole is not viable. That discovery means adjustments must be made until the budget balances—i.e., there is sufficient income to pay expenses and debt service with money left over (cash flow).

The completed budget should be signed, dated, and forwarded to the owner for approval. Most managers work closely with the shopping center owners during the budgeting process. This helps avert assumptions that the owner cannot or will not accept. When the manager works closely with the owner, major changes in the budget are less likely to be needed. If changes are made, the new version should be identified as "revised" and carry a new date. This will assure that everyone knows which generation of the budget they have. Once the owner approves the budget, it should be marked "approved" and show the approval date.

LEASE ADMINISTRATION

The lease grants both landlord and tenant specific rights; it also imposes specific obligations on both parties. One of the shopping center manager's major responsibilities is monitoring tenants' compliance with the specific terms of their leases. The most important and, perhaps, most difficult task is collection of rents when they are due. In addition to base rent, tenants often are required to pay a percentage of their sales as rent. Tenants are also required to provide proof that they have adequate and appropriate insurance coverage, and if the landlord asks them to do so, they must execute estoppel certificates. There are numerous other lease provisions that must be enforced for the safety and security of both tenants and shoppers and for the maintenance and preservation of the shopping center (see also chapter 6).

Rent Collection

The manager's job is to collect the rent and maintain the owner's cash flow. This can be difficult when tenants do not pay their rent on time or at all. Some managers choose to bill the tenants as a systematic approach to rent collection.

There are two schools of thought on billing tenants for rent and prorated pass-through expenses. One is that billing reminds the tenant that monies are due and states the specific amounts. With a computerized system, such billing is fairly simple and little extra effort is required. There are disadvantages, however. It is expensive to issue bills, and billing gives tenants an excuse for nonpayment (no bill, no payment made). Also, the onus is on the manager to be sure the billing goes out on time and the amounts are accurate.

The other school believes tenants should *not* be billed because they know the amount of rent and when it is due from the leases they signed, and their monthly payments for pass-through expenses are based on budget estimates the prior year. By not billing tenants, the manager saves accounting time and office supplies. However, tenants may complain that they forgot to pay or did not know how much they owed. A study done several years ago comparing two office buildings, one of which billed tenants monthly, found that collection was equally difficult at both properties. There is no industry standard on billing rent or tenant charges, so the choice is usually left to managers' personal preferences.

Regardless of whether tenants are billed for rent, the manager should generally stand firm on issues related to rents and on-time payment. Because effective collection of rents is critical to the owner, the manager is not doing the tenant a favor by allowing delinquencies to occur or permitting them to continue. The amount of a delinquency will grow very quickly and become even more difficult to pay; when that happens, the tenant may just give up.

To encourage tenants to pay their rents on time, the lease should state a specific due date (typically the first of the month). It should also state a definite delinquency date and a penalty for late payment. The amount of the penalty is generally dictated by local practices and the attitude of the courts (when such situations have been prosecuted). A delinquency date of the fifth of the month and a 10-percent penalty for payment after that date are not unusual provisions. (All unpaid rents are reported to the owner each month in a delinquency report.)

The most effective means of collection is to telephone the responsible party. (Mailed or hand-distributed notices are generally not effective, but some leases require written notice and specify a time period for a response.) The tenant should be told that the rent has not been received, and the conversation should not end until an agreement has been reached as to when the rent will be paid. The agreed-upon date should be noted on the delinquency report. If the rent is not received on that date, a follow-up telephone call is warranted.

Diplomacy and tact are required in handling collections, and usually the manager attends to them personally. Regardless of whether the contact is by telephone, personal visit, or written notice, the tenant should be given the benefit of the doubt in the requests for payment. There may be a misunderstanding or extenuating circumstances that have to be addressed. Actual delinquency may provide the context in which a late charge may be used as leverage—the manager may express concern about having to add to the tenant's burden, but this should be accompanied by an affirmation that the manager has no choice but to assess a late charge if the amount due is not received by an agreed-upon date.

The ultimate collection tool, of course, is the threat of eviction, but most managers prefer to avoid this step. Eviction should not be threatened unless the manager intends to follow through with it. Because eviction is a legal proceeding, and the local jurisdiction defines the specific procedure to be followed, the manager should not start an eviction without the express approval of the owner. Advance instructions from the owner may take the form of a specific policy on eviction—i.e., the manager may proceed with eviction only after certain conditions have been met. However, it is often the case that the owner must be consulted on each specific situation. Nonpayment of rent is not the only reason for eviction, and substantial documentation is usually necessary. The services of an attorney may also be required.

Percentage Rents

The shopping center manager should develop a schedule for collecting tenants' sales reports and analyzing them to determine percentage rents due. The system should include a policy and a procedure for auditing tenants' sales records periodically to assure accurate reporting and collection of all monies due the center owner.

To develop an analysis of percentage rents, a list of all tenants should be compiled showing their percentage rates, when reports and payments are due, and any qualifying conditions. If a tenant is not required to report sales or pay percentage rent, that fact should be noted. A tenant may have a split percentage or a cap on the amount to be paid. The lease may also provide for exclusions from gross sales for the purpose of calculating percentage rent. (These elements were considered in detail in chapters 9 and 10.) It is also appropriate to show the breakpoint that applies. Usually this is the natural breakpoint (when sales dollars divided by the percentage rate equals the base rent), but negotiated artificial breakpoints will adjust the figure up or down. The breakpoint can also change as rents are escalated over the term of the lease. The manager will need all of this information in order to complete the analysis.

Sales Reports.   The lease will stipulate "when" sales reports are due, but it will not tell the tenant how to present the information. Major tenants usually provide sales reports in their own formats (on time and without prompting). However, independent merchants usually need instructions and support both to report on time and to present the information accurately and completely. A letter reinforcing the importance of sales reports and encouraging on-time submission should be sent to each new tenant when the lease commences. The entire process can be expedited by providing blank forms for tenants to use; a year's worth of forms (fourteen for those reporting monthly; six for those who report quarterly) can accompany the letter. Then, if reports are not received on time, the manager should call the tenant to request the information informally and ask that the written report follow immediately. (A sample form for tenant use is shown in exhibit 12.10.) When these reports are received in the management office, each tenant's sales are recorded on a cumulative sales volume report (exhibit 12.11, page 328) that permits comparison of the tenant's sales month-to-month over a period of five years.

Sales reports are the basis for payment of percentage rent. The tenant's report should be checked for accuracy and then percentage rent should be calculated. If percentage rent is due but not paid, a bill should be prepared and sent to the tenant. This will assure that all monies due the landlord are

E X H I B I T   12.10

Example Tenant's Sales Report Form

Monthly Sales Report

Date: _____   Reporting Month of: _____

Merchant: _____

A. Gross Receipts for month as
   defined in Lease Agreement   A. $_____

B. Exclusions: Sales tax $_____
                 Other exclusions $_____
   Exclusions Subtotal   B. $_____

C. Sales for Rental Calculation   (A − B)   C. $_____
D. Percentage Rent = C × rate (_____%)   D. $_____
E. Monthly Minimum Rent   E. $_____

F. AMOUNT DUE   (D − E)   F. $_____

I hereby certify that the above is true and correct.
                      By: _____

Please forward, with any monies due, to:
[Management Company Name]
[Street Address]
[City, State, Zip Code]

The same format is used when sales reports are collected quarterly. Note that this format assumes a
natural breakpoint and a single percentage rate applied to all sales.

---

collected in a timely manner. Typically, tenants are required to provide a year-end report in addition to the monthly reports. Analysis of this annual report will determine whether the tenant has overpaid or underpaid percentage rent, and appropriate adjustments can be arranged.

Tenants' individual sales reports are also used for a centerwide sales analysis comparing both total dollars and dollars per square foot. Sales in total dollars and dollars per square foot are also compared to the same period in the prior year. These analyses are reported each month to the owner (see exhibit 12.8). In large centers, merchants are separated into categories (women's wear, shoes, gifts, etc.), and each tenant's sales are compared to those for the category as well as those for the center. Comparisons can also be based on location in the shopping center to help identify a particular area or group of stores where sales are weak.

Ultimately, analysis of tenants' sales assists the manager in evaluating established tenants. A disparate or negative sales report may be an early warning sign that a tenant is having problems or provide insight regarding a tenant that might benefit from relocation or a change of store size. These types of signals can help the manager fine tune the mix of tenants and merchandise as well as provide a partial basis for minimum or base rental rates. Compilations of centerwide sales figures and comparisons within merchandise categories can also be useful in the leasing process. However, sales figures of individual tenants should not be released to other tenants or to prospects. The tenants themselves would consider such information confidential.

Sales Audits.   The sales data used for centerwide analyses must be accurate. If not, the data could be misleading, and decisions based on them could be questionable or invalid. To help eliminate errors and misrepresentations of results, tenants' sales should be audited on a regular and systematic basis. This is also important because the manager has a fiduciary responsibility to assure that all monies due the landlord are collected. In addition to discovering errors, audits should also disclose any cheating that may be going on. The right to do this is typically granted to the landlord in the lease, but that does not mean the property manager must conduct the audit personally. In fact, it is better to have an impartial third party conduct such audits because of their delicate nature. There are companies that provide professional auditing services, and the manager can hire one that is familiar with retail leases and retailing sales records.

Rarely is every tenant audited every year. That is prohibited by the cost of the service. (The cost of an appropriate audit will likely exceed $500—in mid-1991 in California, $600 was an average—but the result is worth it.) The wisest course of action is to establish a specific program for monitoring tenants' sales, auditing some percentage of the tenants in a center each year on a rotating schedule. Ideally, every tenant in the center whose sales volume approaches (or should be exceeding) the breakpoint would be audited at least once within a period of three to four years. Center management should plan to audit all classes of tenants, whether national, regional, or local chains or independents. Underreporting is bound to happen, intentionally or otherwise, so no tenant should be exempt from the process.

Likely candidates for audits are tenants whose reported sales warrant concern—those whose total sales hover just below the breakpoint every year, those who have not shown any increase in sales over a period of two or more years, those who are known to have good traffic but report low sales, and those who have complicated leases with exclusions and other provisions that can lead to erroneous reporting. Other likely candidates include those tenants whose leases require percentage rent only (waivers of base rent), whose reported sales are well below the normal averages (in dollars per square foot), whose sales are running counter to the trend within the center or local area generally, or whose leases will expire within the next six months to one year.

Regardless of the reason a particular tenant is to be audited, it should be a rule of thumb that tenants are not to be audited as a punishment. The audit should be conducted in a business-like manner. If the audit discovers a prob-

E X H I B I T 12.11

Example Sales Volume Report

Percentage ———— M Q A

Monthly Rent ————

Square Footage ————

Base ————

Tenant Name ————

Address ————

Notes:

Project ————

Commencement Date ————

Lease Term ————

Month	1991	1992	1993	1994	1995
January					
February					
March					
April					
May					
June					
July					
August					
September					
October					
November					
December					
Total					

lem, the problem should be discussed with the tenant privately. The manager's approach should be one of seeking a solution to the problem and not an accusation of any wrongdoing. The manager's objective is to collect the monies due the landlord *and* to preserve the relationship with the tenant while doing so.

Prorated Expenses

Each year when the budget has been approved, the tenants' pro rata shares should be estimated. The ratio of the tenant's GLA to the center's GLA is usually the proration basis, and that percentage may be applied to all operating expenses. For example, a tenant occupying 1,000 square feet of GLA in a 100,000-square-foot center would pay one percent of the center expenses. The proration cannot always be so straightforward. Often the size of the "common area" to which a particular expense applies will vary because of tenant exclusions and other lease concessions. When that is the case, individual expense items are divided by a specific number of square feet to calculate a cost per square foot (exhibit 12.12), and that cost is multiplied by the individual tenant's square footage to determine the pro rata share.

Tenants should be notified of their common area and operating expense assessments in advance so they can be paying the correct amounts for the entire year. Most budgets are for a calendar year, so tenants should receive their payment estimates early in December.

Estimates should be presented in considerable detail. Two things should be readily apparent in the statement—what the tenant is paying for and how the tenant's proration was computed. If major or unusual expenses (e.g., roof repairs) are included, it is best to provide an explanation when the estimates are distributed to the tenants. Budget estimates are usually rounded to the nearest whole dollar to minimize bookkeeping problems and make year-end reconciliation easier. (It is not unreasonable to round to the nearest five dollars, especially on large dollar items, but whole-dollar rounding is appropriate and recommended.)

After the end of the year, the actual common area expenses should be calculated and reconciled with the budgeted amounts. Reconciliations should be timely and accurate, and they should be provided in sufficient detail so that the tenant can readily understand the difference between budget and actual—and the reasons why.

Reconciliation of common area expenses can be made easier by segregating invoices as they come in, keeping separate copies of those related to common area items, and recording individual expenses on a thirteen-column work sheet (ledger). After the end of the year—before year-end common area expenses are billed to the tenants—categories can be totaled and checked for accuracy against invoice totals. Having a separate file is also handy if the manager wants to answer an individual tenant's questions. The

EXHIBIT 12.12

Example Statement of Common Area Estimates

Heartland Plaza Shopping Center   Year: 1991

Base CAM	$/Yr	Square Footage	$/Sq Ft /Month
Site Costs			
Landscaping	15,600		
Sweeping	11,400		
Steam cleaning	14,520		
Parking lot repair	2,400		
CAM electricity	3,000		
Liability insurance	1,800		
General repair	2,400		
Subtotal (Site)	51,120	128,293	.0332
Building Costs			
Trash removal	28,800	61,523	.0390
Building insurance	8,000	50,243	.0133
Alarm monitor	3,600	54,023	.0056
Roof repair	4,800	54,023	.0074
Water and sewer	24,000	51,608	.0388
Building electricity	4,800	54,023	.0074
Building repair	4,800	54,023	.0074
Taxes—levies	58,000	131,871	.0367
—building	48,500	71,951	.0562
—site	19,000	98,538	.0161
Subtotal (Building)	201,900		.2279
Total CAM	253,020		.2611*

Merchant _____

Footage _____ †Estimate $_____

*Total including supervision fee rounded to .28.

†NOTE: Square footage × .28 = $/month CAM estimate.

extra effort involved pays off in efficiency and accuracy when the year-end accounting is due. Another point to consider is the handling of large expenditures that are prorated over more than one year. To assure that subsequent years' portions are not forgotten, both the common area file (as noted here) and the tickler file should include reminders to the manager. The expense ledger can also be annotated.

Some tenants will question the reconciliation as a matter of course. Others may ask to see the invoices on which it is based. Unless their leases prohibit it, tenants may be permitted to inspect invoices in the manager's office so they can audit their prorated shares. However, unless their leases provide for them to receive copies of invoices—a right usually only granted to major tenants—none should be given out. It is appropriate to provide a copy of an invoice when that is the only item in question. Many managers have found, however, that demands for copies of all invoices are made by tenants seeking ways to create problems or, at least, to get out of paying their due share.

A tenant who challenges the accuracy of the year-end billing may be signaling a lack of funds to pay for it. Usually this can be resolved fairly readily by meeting directly with the tenant and working out a payment program. Sometimes year-end adjustments can be substantial, and a tenant may find it difficult to accept the difference between budget projections and reality. The manager should monitor expense variances closely and, if warranted, advise the tenants about increases and follow through with them regarding a possible adjustment. Understanding, sympathy, and a time-payment plan will usually assure receipt of the funds due and preserve the landlord-tenant relationship. Adjusting the payments before the end of the year—with tenant agreement—may be even more helpful.

Tenants' concerns over large reconciliation bills are only one reason to strive for accuracy in preparing the budget. Another reason is that a large discrepancy can mean a lack of funds when they are needed. Sometimes the year-end reconciliations do go the other way. A high estimate compared to low actual expenses means the tenant overpaid. When this occurs, the important step is to acknowledge the overpayment. Some owners prefer to pay tenants back directly by check; others prefer to handle it as an accounting exercise—they issue a credit memo and apply the overpayment against the next monies due. Regardless of how the overpayment is handled, the check or the credit memo should always be accompanied by the reconciliation calculations. Otherwise the resulting confusion can create an accounting nightmare.

Insurance Certificates

Tenants are required by their leases to obtain insurance and to list the landlord (the owner of the shopping center and/or the manager or management firm) as an additional named insured party on the policies. Shopping center tenants should be insured against liability for injuries to persons and damage to others' property. Those who employ others are required by law to carry workers' compensation insurance. Anchor tenants and those who own their buildings will likely require fire and other casualty coverages. Crime insurance is important for all retail tenants, as is business interruption insurance. Plate-glass insurance may also be appropriate. Specific coverages may vary with the type of business being operated (see appendix B, Insurance and Risk Management). When insurance is purchased, the insurer will issue a "certificate of insurance" that shows the types of coverages, the names of all insured parties, and the term of the policy (beginning and expiration dates).

To administer tenants' insurance coverage, the manager should prepare a schedule showing the insurance requirements for each tenant. The manager is responsible for collecting certificates of insurance from all the tenants and checking them for completeness. Notes should also be made of expiration dates so that reminders can be sent to the tenants 30 days before their certificates expire. A certificate should be submitted to the manager each time the policy is renewed, and tenants often have to be reminded to submit the current ones.

Although it is spelled out in the lease, the insurance requirement may be reiterated in the tenant kit (distributed at move-in) or in a letter sent to the new tenant. A letter is especially helpful in guiding the new store owner who has no prior experience in a shopping center and may not fully understand the insurance requirements. (The letter can be provided to the tenant in duplicate with a recommendation to forward one copy to the insurance carrier.)

Estoppel Certificates

An estoppel certificate is an affirmation of the lease terms by the tenant. Most leases require the tenant to execute an estoppel certificate if the landlord requests it. Basically, an estoppel states the lease commencement and termination dates, the amount of rent and any deposits paid, and that the landlord is not in default. In the past, this document was a brief paragraph, but this is no longer the case, and tenants may show a reluctance to sign the expanded version of the estoppel certificate.

To assure uniformity and consistency of presentation, the manager usually prepares a form estoppel certificate and hand delivers it. Small shop tenants may have to have the document and its purpose explained; major tenants usually have their legal departments examine estoppel certificates, and this can take a few days. The manager is responsible for collecting the signed certificates and may have to follow up on them repeatedly.

Enforcement of Lease Provisions

Various lease provisions require tenants to do or not do a variety of things, but it is people who make lease contracts in the first place, and it is people who ultimately break them. Chapter 5 addressed issues related to store hours, employee parking, and merchandising beyond the lease line. Other specifics are described in detail in chapter 10. It is the manager's job to assure that violations of the lease contract are corrected. However, he or she must obtain the tenant's compliance without damaging (or destroying) the landlord-tenant relationship. The keys to accomplishing this delicate task are diplomacy, tact, and education.

An informed tenant who understands why something is required is more likely to accept and comply with it. An excellent means of educating tenants is the "tenant kit" described in earlier chapters. It provides an informal reminder of their lease responsibilities without being heavyhanded. However, neither the kit nor the lease itself is a guarantee of perfect performance of all lease obligations. While the tenant should be given the benefit of the doubt on a first-time offense, it is also a good idea to explain the business reasons for having the clause in the lease. The tenant must understand how default of the lease—other than nonpayment of rent—can also lead to eviction.

When the manager becomes aware of a lease infraction, a telephone call or a personal visit is an appropriate way to communicate a sympathetic reminder that an activity is not permitted under the lease. Besides softening the impact of the consequences of a lease violation, such an approach affords an opportunity to generate understanding. The tenant should be given a reasonable time to cure the problem, and when it is cured, the tenant should be thanked for cooperating. However, if the cure is not expedited in a reasonable time, the manager should telephone to remind the tenant of the need for compliance and establish a firm date for a cure. For a problem that persists, a written "notice of default" may be the first step toward official documentation of actions leading to eviction.

Enforcement of lease provisions is an important responsibility. Although at times it may seem easier for the manager to ignore a lease infraction, the usual result of such inaction is further infractions by that tenant and, ultimately, by other tenants who become aware that the lease is not being enforced for the one tenant. Thus, fair play becomes an important consideration; all tenants should be treated as equals. In enforcing lease provisions, it is important to establish an agreed-upon deadline for curing a problem and then to follow up on that deadline. Notes should be made of the problem, the required cure, and the time allowed for the cure. The documentation of the manager's actions may become an important issue if a problem persists and eviction becomes necessary.

Problems relating to the lease are not always defaults by the tenant. Sometimes it is not clear who is responsible for a specific maintenance task, and tenants may well ignore things that are their responsibilities. When such situations arise, the manager should investigate the problem and the cure, with the understanding that if an item is the tenant's responsibility, the expense will have to be paid by the tenant. Often the manager is in a better position to identify and arrange solutions for maintenance problems than a shop tenant is. A major tenant, on the other hand, is likely to investigate the problem and call the manager's attention to the question of responsibility.

Appendixes

NOTE: Forms, documents, and other exhibits in this book are samples only. Because of varying state and local laws, competent advice should be obtained before using any of these published examples.

APPENDIX A

Retailing Basics
by Robert Bearson

The evolution of the shopping center as described in the Introduction to this book is an extension of the history of retailing. Retailing in the United States began with Yankee peddlers selling door-to-door and progressed through a variety of distribution forms, all of which can be seen today.

General stores
Single-line stores
Department stores
Variety stores
Mail-order houses
Chain stores
Discount stores
Catalog stores
Supermarkets
Shopping centers
Automated Retailing
Convenience stores
Warehouse "stores"

Almost every new retailing "method" has been sold to consumers as a way to save money. Each innovation has been based on reduction or elimination of some expense, benefits of bulk purchasing, or savings associated with more-professional management. Only shopping centers, convenience stores, and automated retailing do not claim cost savings as their reason for being. In fact, what the shopping center does offer is (1) variety in a wide assortment of merchandise at one location, (2) breadth of selection based on competing stores, (3) convenience of common and long shopping hours, (4) ready access through proximity of stores, and (5) parking that is convenient—and usually free. However, this also saves the consumer money—one-stop shopping reduces the time invested in shopping and saves the time and expense of traveling among several stores at different locations while providing opportunities for comparison shopping for the best prices.

Property managers should keep in mind that selection and convenience are what make shopping centers successful and invest their efforts in further improving those elements. Also desirable from the viewpoint of the present-day shopper is saving money. This can be met by encouraging off-price or discount operations to locate close to or become tenants in the shopping center.

EVALUATING PROSPECTIVE TENANTS

The most desirable prospects are those who have proven themselves in other retailing environments. The merchant who has done well in one location usually will do equally well in another; if a new location is more favorable, a successful merchant will do even better. Current sales volumes can be used to predict future success in a new location.

Because a shopping center usually includes other complementary shops, it provides an optimum environment for sales growth. In fact, analysis of various locations relating occupancy costs to sales potential and profit projections yields the following order of preference: super regional shopping center > regional shopping center > specialty shopping center > community shopping center > strip shopping center > free-standing store. On the other hand, development of large regional and super regional centers has been curtailed, and the many chain retailers still intending to expand will have to consider locating in smaller centers, the ones they would have passed over previously. As occupancy costs increase at regional and super regional centers, the profit potential will improve at smaller centers—notwithstanding lower sales volumes.

In evaluating prospective tenants, the primary concern is usually the prospect's financial strength—the ability to pay rent and meet other lease obligations. However, the prospect's retailing expertise should also be a consideration, especially if a prospect is starting a new business. This can be addressed by seeking answers to the following questions which address the six essentials for successful specialty store retailing.

1. Is the planned mix of merchandise adequately specialized?
2. Is the store likely to be as good as or better than any in its trade area?
3. Will the merchandise include adequate representation of higher-priced items?
4. Does the retailer's operating plan permit the store to be fully price competitive on identical merchandise?
5. Does the retailer's plan include a specific program to rid the store of past-season, slower-selling merchandise?
6. Will top management (or ownership) of the store be personally involved in daily operations?

Other important considerations are whether the store appeals to women, how its customers are treated, and what efforts are made to promote the store.

Only if the mix of merchandise is narrow can the specialty store be truly outstanding. The smart merchant will have chosen a merchandise category in which the shop can be the very best in the trade area. In a large community with a heterogeneous population, interested customers will find the specialty shop and patronize it.

There will always be more numerous sales of low-priced items compared to high-priced merchandise. However, it is often the case that the larger number of transactions does not bring in the same total dollar volume as the fewer sales of higher-priced items (see accompanying table comparing two gift shops). In store #1, items priced above $25 represented only 14.1 percent of the total number of sales transactions, but they accounted for 68.5 percent of the dollar volume of sales; only 4.7 percent of the transactions were for items priced above $50, yet they represented more than half of the dollar volume of sales. In store #2, 13.2 percent of the transactions were for items priced above $25, and they represented nearly 61 percent of the total dollar volume of sales; the 4.0 percent of transactions that exceeded $50 represented more than 40 percent of the dollar volume. As these data suggest, having a significant

Comparison of Dollar Volume and Transactions

Merchandise Price Range	Gift Shop #1		Gift Shop #2	
	Percent of Transactions	Percent of Dollars	Percent of Transactions	Percent of Dollars
$4.99 or less	40.1	5.4	42.0	8.0
5.00–9.99	21.9	7.6	22.7	9.7
10.00–24.99	23.9	18.5	22.1	21.4
25.00–49.99	9.4	16.0	9.2	19.4
$50.00 or more	4.7	52.5	4.0	41.5

Total each column is 100%.

portion of an inventory in higher-priced items is vital. Often there is a greater profit potential for items that sell at higher prices.

While competitive pricing is important, the shopping center manager must understand that specialty retailers cannot always compete effectively. In highly competitive areas, large-scale discounters have essentially eliminated the opportunity for independent specialty retailers to sell identical brand-name merchandise. The large discounter has a tremendous advantage in buying power, continuous market presence, management expertise, and financial strength. It is just not practical for the single store or small chain operator to maintain a comparable selection and offer the same low prices. Successful discounting requires volume sales. More items must be sold at a lower price to break even—i.e., to recoup the cost of merchandise and operating expenses such as rent, utilities, salaries, etc. Initial pricing (markup) must be adequate for a specialty retailer to break even, let alone make a profit.

Another key point to be considered is whether a store appeals to women shoppers. Because women typically shop for themselves, their homes, *and* their families, it is reasonable to assume that women account for most of the purchases in a shopping center. It is therefore important for retailers and shopping center managers to recognize that women are their predominant customers and that stores and promotions should be designed primarily to appeal to women.

However, as more and more women enter the work force, they have less and less time to shop. Shopping is no longer recreation; it has become a chore. This is borne out by responses to customer surveys conducted at shopping centers. The surveys indicate that most visitors to a shopping center are shopping for a particular item or at a particular store. The stores most frequently shopped are women's apparel stores and department or specialty stores. Most shoppers visit a shopping center twice a month or more and spend one to two hours there. High percentages of shoppers indicate weekends as most convenient days for shopping, and actual sales levels at shopping centers support this: Sunday has the most sales hour for hour and Saturday is the best full day of the week. While evenings are not clearly rated the most convenient time to shop, evening shopping hours contribute more business per hour to shopping centers than do daytime hours. Clearly, shoppers' preferences must be addressed in creating a tenant mix for a shopping center and in establishing centerwide store hours.

Once a customer enters a store, it is important for the customer to feel welcome and important. Customer policies are a major factor in customer satisfaction. Many independent retailers drive customers out of their stores and into their competitors' larger stores because they are unwilling to offer the same liberal customer policies. It is good business practice to follow the adage, "the customer is always right." It is rare that an exception to this has to be made, and the payback is enormous. Liberal policies on acceptance of merchandise returns, cash refunds, exchanges, etc., foster customer goodwill and bring in more business. If a customer can return an item and receive a refund, the store will sell more merchandise. Liberal policies also make sales staff and supervisors more comfortable in their roles.

An unhappy customer, on the other hand, can have tremendous negative impact. This is confirmed by information from Technical Assistance Research Programs, a consulting firm in Washington, D.C. They found that most customers will not complain to management if something goes wrong with a purchase. However, "depending on the severity of the problem, an average customer will tell between 9 and 16 friends and acquaintances of the bad experience. Some 13 percent will tell more than 20 people. More than two out of three customers who received poor service will never buy from the store again and, worse, management will never know why."

Customers are easily discouraged. Many merchants are sensitive to pilferage and react to this by reducing merchandise on open display or preventing handling altogether by locking it in display cases. However, according to a report in *Chain Store Age* (October 1982), while shoplifting represented 25 percent of such loss, employee theft was responsible for much more (40 percent). (Paperwork errors accounted for another 15 percent.) Making it difficult to shop is counterproductive. Preventing merchandise handling is more likely to reduce sales than to preclude pilferage. A reduction in sales of less than 1 percent is approximately equivalent in gross margin dollar loss to a stock shortage in excess of 2 percent.

It is more productive to bring customers into the store and encourage shopping and buying. A store's advertising and promotion should be evaluated. A recommended pattern is for small specialty stores to allocate between 3 percent and 5 percent of projected annual sales to advertising and promotion. First priority should be direct mail advertising to the store's own mailing list. Second priority should be cooperative promotion with other merchants in the center. (If there is a merchants' association or marketing fund, the latter will usually be required by the lease.) Any leftover funds should be used to experiment with other forms of promotion.

Cooperative promotions are effectively limited to seven times during the year.

January—clearance
February/March—sidewalk sale
May—Mother's Day specials
June/July—clearance
September—sidewalk sale
October/November—clearance
December—Christmas specials

Advertising and promotion of the shopping center itself generally are not very important in attracting shoppers. The exceptions to this are announcements of grand opening or grand re-opening. It is the cooperative promotion of all the retailers in the center that is most effective. People come to a shopping center in response to specific merchandise being offered. To effectively stimulate business, a center will do well to schedule sales events in which all merchants offer significant savings.

Retailers should be encouraged to experiment with having something on sale at all times and having a sign at the door announcing it. Placement of a sign may be limited by center policies; if it cannot be outside the door, then it should be just inside. Giveaways, contests, and drawings can be used to attract customers. Names can be drawn from the store's customer mailing list, or business cards can be collected in a fishbowl or forms filled out in the store. The "prizes" need not be expensive to be effective (e.g., a free cup of coffee, a merchandise item, free gift wrapping).

HELPING TENANTS SUCCEED

In a shopping center, it is the first-time retailers that are most likely to have problems and need assistance and encouragement. Failures of "new" businesses can result in vacancies that are difficult to fill. However, business failures are not all that common and not always related to new businesses. They may, in fact, relate more to the type of business and changes in the marketplace. A report on business failures in the early 1980s (from Dun & Bradstreet) indicates that department stores (16/10,000) and drug stores (20/10,000) show very low failure rates while infants' and children's wear stores have a high one (114/10,000). Stores selling durable goods such as furniture have a higher failure rate (84/10,000) than do soft goods such as women's ready-to-wear (61/10,000) and shoes (42/10,000). Specialization also tends to enhance success: Toys and hobby crafts stores (26/10,000) and jewelry stores (24/10,000) also have low failure rates.

While sales of durable goods such as automobiles, furniture, and major appliances are affected by an economic downturn, nondurable goods retailing is relatively immune to recession. Durable goods are "big ticket" items. Often they are replacements for things that are still functional, so their purchase can be postponed. In recessionary times, they are. On the other hand, it is normal for sales of nondurable goods to grow during such times. When newspapers and other media report that retail sales for the past month were down, the comparison is often to the prior month rather than the same month a year ago. Government statistics indicate that total retail sales—durable *and* nondurable goods—almost always exceed the total for the same month in the prior year. This was true even during the recessionary period of 1980–1982. Between 1984 and the end of 1990, only three months' total sales were reportedly lower than the same month a year earlier—January, September, and December 1987—and then the difference was very slight. Part of the reason that most nondurable goods sales endure is that children do not stop growing, and birthdays, anniversaries, and other events are recurring occasions for celebration. Regardless of the economy, consumers continue to purchase clothing and gift items. Nondurable goods are the mainstay of shopping centers. In general, most such retailers are not much affected by recession, so a poor economy is usually not an acceptable explanation for poor sales performance.

Many small shops in retailing centers are struggling, however. In particular, they have difficulty recruiting salespeople. Sales jobs are relatively low paying, so they do not normally attract highly motivated, formally trained personnel. Retail selling is often sought as an interim job or a means of supplementing a regular income, and large numbers of teenagers are hired for part-time and seasonal jobs. Management personnel in retail stores may be so occupied with buying and administrative activities that they have little time for training and supervision of sales workers.

Given the property manager's role in making the shopping center successful, it is both practical and appropriate for the manager to offer assistance and promote sales training and professionalism to the managers of tenant stores. Store owners and managers who are new to retailing can benefit from seminars and workshops relating to internal business operations, merchandise presentation, and motivation. Sales techniques are another important area for training. Newsletters can be an economical means of reminding all tenants of merchandising opportunities and fostering good retailing practices.

Helping tenants succeed does not mean the manager has to be better at retailing than the tenants. It does mean the manager must be a keen observer of what makes retailers successful and have the ability to communicate those observations to other retailers effectively and in a manner that will earn the retailers' respect. In situations where the manager observes a problem but is unable to communicate it effectively (or with authority), it may be more appropriate to bring in a consultant (i.e., a respected retailing expert) with whom the merchant can work directly.

Merchandise Presentation

One of the things a shopping center manager should evaluate is the retailer's merchandise presentation. This can be accomplished by answering some specific questions regarding the store.

- *Initial impact*—Do the windows, entrance area, approach to the store, and area immediately inside the entrance help the customer quickly identify what the shop is all about?
- *Merchandise suggestions*—Are merchandise displays shown at every opportunity (in the aisles, hanging from the ceiling, on the walls, on the ends of fixtures)?
- *Idea presentation*—Does each display and display area convey only one idea?
- *Use of color*—Is the impact of single-color families carried throughout the store (e.g., windows, wall displays, area displays, each merchandise presentation)?
- *Vertical stocking*—Is merchandise stocked vertically to allow more categories to be represented at eye level (using available sources such as shelving, wall areas, etc.)?
- *Categorization*—Is merchandise categorized by use, product, sex, age, interest?
- *Service desk*—Is the service desk being used to sell? Does it call attention to items that (1) deserve to be talked about; (2) are new, timely, or higher priced; (3) can be pointed out to a customer; (4) can be demonstrated?
- *Sampling or demonstration*—Is merchandise shown voluntarily or on request?
- *Price marking*—Is the price easily available to the customer for each item and each price-reduced item?
- *Gift suggestion*—Is gift giving suggested by presenting reminders such as wrapped packages, bows, gift certificates, signs announcing gift-giving occasions (e.g., graduations in June, weddings, birthdays and anniversaries all year round, and less-traditional but often promoted occasions such as Secretary's Day, Sweetest Day in October)?
- *Signage*—Do signs appropriately announce such things as sales, specials, pricing, price guarantees, store policies, and store hours?

The shopping center manager is in a unique position to evaluate the effectiveness of merchandising techniques. The manager can help a struggling retailer understand the importance of merchandising by pointing out examples of successful presentations by other stores in the center and suggesting things the retailer can do to achieve comparable results.

Sales Training

In a shopping center environment, the property manager can play a key role in encouraging store managers to train their sales personnel to give more personal service. By observing sales transactions, the shopping center manager can identify areas that can be improved by application of professional selling techniques.

A retail sales transaction can be divided into the following elements.

- *Preplanning*—The salesperson should know the merchandise and the store's policies and procedures so that he or she can provide accurate information to customers.
- *Greeting*—Customers should be greeted warmly as soon after entering the store as possible—within one minute—to assure them that the salesperson is ready to be of help.
- *Identification of customer's interest*—Often it is possible to establish an area of customer interest by observation (an item the customer looks at or touches, comments to a companion, etc.).
- *Approach*—Personal selling means the salesperson engages the customer in conversation, commenting about a merchandise item on display or an expressed need that was overheard, etc. (Assistance may be offered, but not with the words, "May I help you?")
- *Merchandise presentation*—The customer should be encouraged to handle merchandise, to try on clothing. This is an opportune time to present information about the item (features, special care required) and demonstrate its use if appropriate. Observing what the customer takes into the fitting room provides opportunities to bring additional items to the customer's attention.
- *Countering objections*—The salesperson should listen to what the customer is saying and be prepared to counter a customer's stated objections with facts about the merchandise—or alternatives to consider. Having presented an item's features (preceding step), it is appropriate to describe its benefits (i.e., how those features will help the customer personally). In the ideal situation, the customer will be choosing between two items to buy rather than deciding whether or not to buy only one.
- *Closing*—The salesperson should encourage the customer to finalize the transaction by asking how it will be paid for or if it is a gift. This is the step in which store policies regarding guaranteed pricing, merchandise returns, and layaways can be explained.

A shopper entering a store is interested in the merchandise and may be looking for a specific item. The customer entering a specialty store is most likely looking for whatever is that store's unique offering. The decision to buy is usually made while in the store, and the customer will generally do the "selling." What is needed is help in locating merchandise. While it is important to point out items that are on sale, it is a disservice to show only those with low prices—the merchandise that is unique to a store is likely to be higher priced. For the customer, having found and bought a particular item provides more satisfaction than savings alone.

The role of the salesperson should be that of a helper. It is more important to show merchandise to the customer than to sell it. Interaction with the customer is key. Salespeople who become involved with their customers derive greater satisfaction from their work. When customers are engaged in conversation, they are likely to remain in the store longer. Such interactions provide the salesperson opportunities to respond to questions and to counter objections. By demonstrating competence, knowledge, and professionalism, the salesperson can inspire customer confidence. The longer the customer stays, the more items the customer can be shown and the more items that will be considered and bought.

By applying the guidelines outlined in this appendix, store management can anticipate a significant increase in customer satisfaction, dramatic improvement in staff feelings of professionalism, and a substantial percentage increase in sales.

RETAILING FUNDAMENTALS

The key to helping retailers succeed is understanding, and that means the shopping center manager must learn some of the fundamentals of retailing. The following discussions of basic arithmetic related to retail pricing and inventory and definitions of retailing terms are not intended to be comprehensive.

Retailing Arithmetic

Achievement of adequate sales volumes depends on appropriate pricing which, in turn, depends on merchandise costs and other factors. It is also important to have sufficient merchandise in stock. This means not only replenishing inventory as needed but selling off out-of-season merchandise and replacing it with new. Merchandise is marked up initially to cover operating expenses and achieve a profit. It is marked down later on to make way for new stock.

The terms markup, mark-on, and margin are often used interchangeably to identify the difference between the cost of an item (plus inbound freight) and its selling price. An item that sells for $98 may cost $54 plus $2 freight; the difference is the markup. This can also be expressed as a percentage:

Markup = Selling Price − Cost

Markup Amount = $98 − ($54 + $2) = $98 − $56 = $42

$$\% \text{ Markup} = \frac{\text{Markup}}{\text{Selling Price}} \times 100 = \frac{\$42}{\$98} \times 100 = 42.9\%$$

The term *keystone markup* is used to indicate that the markup is 50 percent (i.e., the selling price is exactly double the cost of the goods).

Markup can be used in checking that an adequate differential between cost and

Sales and End-of-Month Inventory Figures
(Thousands of Dollars)

Month	Sales This Year	Sales Last Year	Stock at End of Month	Stock-to-Sales Ratio	Sales Percent Change
Jan			52.1		
Feb	16.0	15.2	66.7	3.4	5.3
Mar	23.8	20.1	73.7	3.3	18.4
Apr	20.6	20.9	68.0	3.5	<1.4>
May		19.9	75.4	3.3	
Jun		22.0	77.2	3.4	
Jul		23.9	73.6	3.2	
Aug		20.6	84.0	3.6	
Sep		24.3	87.3	3.5	
Oct		28.2	90.0	3.1	
Nov		23.1	94.2	3.9	
Dec		42.5	64.7	2.2	
Jan		21.7	60.3	3.0	
Total	**282.4**		**967.2**		
Average		*23.5*	*74.4*		

selling price is being maintained. It allows the retailer to calculate an appropriate selling price. For example, what price must be used to maintain a markup of 46 percent on an item that costs $38 (+ $2 freight)?

$$\text{Selling Price} = \text{Cost} \times \frac{100}{100 - \text{Markup \%}}$$

$$\text{Selling Price} = (\$38 + \$2) \times \frac{100}{100 - 46\%} = \$40 \times \frac{100}{54\%} = \$74.07$$

Markup also permits calculation of an acceptable invoice cost for an item. How much can be paid (+ $1 freight) for an item selling at $49 if the required markup is 43 percent?

$$\text{Cost} = \text{Selling Price} \times \frac{100 - \text{Markup \%}}{100}$$

$$\text{Cost} = \$49 \times \frac{100 - 43\%}{100} = \$49 \times \frac{57\%}{100} = \$27.93$$

$$\text{Invoice Cost} = \$27.93 - \$1 \text{ freight} = \$26.93$$

The table (top of page) shows the kinds of information that are typically available for sales and end-of-month inventories (in thousands of dollars at retail). These figures will be used to calculate percentage change, stockturn, and stock-to-sales ratios in the following examples.

Percentage change is the difference between this year's and last year's figures, expressed as a percent of last year's figure. The basic formula and its use with the figures for February through April in the table are shown here (in full amounts).

$$\% \ \text{Change} = \frac{\text{This Year} - \text{Last Year}}{\text{Last Year}} \times 100$$

$$\frac{\$16,000 - \$15,200}{\$15,200} \times 100 = 5.3\% \text{ for February}$$

$$\frac{\$23,800 - \$20,100}{\$20,100} \times 100 = 18.4\% \text{ for March}$$

$$\frac{\$20,600 - \$20,900}{\$20,900} \times 100 = -1.4\% \text{ for April}$$

February and March results are favorable; April is unfavorable and would be shown in brackets or parentheses in a tabulation, thus: <1.4>.

Stockturn, also called stock turnover, is the rate at which inventory is sold. It is calculated as net sales dollars divided by the average inventory value at retail. Average inventory is the sum of the first-of-the-year inventory plus the following twelve month-end inventories, divided by thirteen. (Stockturn can also be calculated as the annual cost of goods sold divided by the average inventory at cost.) From the table, total net sales are $282,400; average monthly inventory is $74,400 (13 months' total of $967,200 divided by 13).

$$\text{Stockturn} = \frac{\text{Net Sales}}{\text{Average Inventory}} = \frac{\$282,400}{\$74,400} = 3.8$$

The stock-to-sales ratio is particularly useful in planning inventories. The inventory at the beginning of a month divided by that month's sales shows how many months' worth of inventory is on hand. Using figures from the table, the January end-of-month inventory would be divided by February's sales, as shown below:

$$\text{February Stock-to-Sales Ratio} = \frac{\text{Stock at end of January}}{\text{Sales in February}} = \frac{\$52,100}{\$15,200} = 3.4$$

The stock-to-sales ratio is used to determine the amount of inventory to be kept on hand.

$$\frac{\text{Total Annual Sales}}{12 \text{ months}} = \text{Average Monthly Sales}$$

Using information from the table and a stockturn of 3.8, if average monthly sales are $23,500, stock levels should be maintained at approximately $90,000.

$$\frac{\$282,400}{12} = \$23,533 \text{ (rounded down to } \$23,500)$$

$$\$23,500 \times 3.8 = \$89,300 \text{ (rounded up to } \$90,000)$$

Progressive Markdown Schedule
(Item Priced at $100.00)

Weeks on Sale	In-Season Percent Markdown	New Price
4	25%	$75
8	33%	$66
12	50%	$50
16	+20%	$40
20	+20%	$32

At season's end, it is important for stock levels to be low enough to allow for addition of merchandise for the new season. For months when higher levels of sales are antici- pated, the stock can be increased. However, it is desirable to end the year with a lower inventory—January is usually a slow selling month. (Most retailers close their books January 31, having used "closeout" sales during this normally "slow" month to reduce inventory levels still further.)

Knowing when to mark down prices to sell slow-moving merchandise is extremely important. The retailer must be able to make room for new stock that will bring in new sales. If an inventory is held constant—if reductions are not taken—the stock becomes very uninteresting over time. For this reason, a considerable portion of an inventory is marked down before it is sold—in many businesses, half or more—and the average markdown percent is substantial. The reason for marking down prices need not be poor buying, or competition, but rather a changing marketplace—cus- tomers constantly want new merchandise. To be effective, a pricing program should plan for markdowns after a certain selling period, and merchandise should be dated to implement the program. After the first markdown is taken, repeated markdowns should be taken until all the merchandise is sold. The timing of markdowns is also related to the stockturn. Any item that has not sold in 25 percent more time than the average is not selling acceptably and should be marked down.

$$\text{Acceptable Selling Period} = \frac{\text{Weeks in a Year} \times 1.25}{\text{Stockturn}} = \frac{52 \times 1.25}{3.8} = 17.1 \text{ weeks}$$

If one-half of a group of items has not been sold in one-half of the acceptable selling period, what remains of the group should be marked down ($17.1 \div 2 = 8.5$ weeks). Sales goals for shorter time frames are also related to the acceptable selling period.

$$\frac{\text{Time Available for Sale}}{\text{Acceptable Selling Period}} = \text{Percent of Stock to be Sold}$$

$$\frac{4 \text{ Weeks}}{17.1 \text{ Weeks}} \times 100 = 23.4\%$$

In-season markdowns typically begin at one-fourth off and progress at four-week in- tervals to one-third and one-half off the original price, with subsequent reductions by one-fifth of the reduced sale price. Out-of-season merchandise is usually marked down on a shorter schedule (i.e., 2–3 weeks), with the first reduction being one-third. The table at the top of the page shows a progressive markdown on a single item (using percentages for the fractions).

Retailing Terminology

Although there is little specialized language or jargon in retailing, there are some terms the property manager should know so he or she can understand and participate in conversations with retailing personnel.

Back order Part of an order that the vendor has not filled on time but still intends to ship.

Breakeven point The sales volume at which revenues and costs are equal.

Consignment Merchandise shipped for future sale or other purpose for which title (ownership) remains with the shipper (consignor).

Cumulative mark-on The difference between the total cost and the total original retail value of all goods handled to date.

Free on board (FOB) A shipping term indicating delivery without charge. *FOB destination* means seller pays freight to destination (the buyer); *FOB origin* means buyer pays all freight from point of shipment or other designated place.

Initial markup The difference between the merchandise cost (including freight) and the original retail price placed on the goods expressed as a percentage of the retail value; also called *initial mark-on*.

Loss leader An item sold at a lesser markup than would normally be obtained on that item in order to increase store traffic.

Maintained markup The difference between the cost of goods sold and net sales; also called *maintained mark-on*.

Markdown A reduction in the original or previous retail price of an item stated as a percentage of net sales.

Markup The difference between merchandise cost and the retail price; also called *mark-on* or *margin*.

Markup percentage The difference between cost and retail price expressed as a percentage of retail (or, less commonly, as a percentage of cost).

Net terms Requiring payment for the billed amount of the invoice; no cash discount is allowed.

Stock turnover A measure of how quickly merchandise has been sold; the number of times during a year that the average inventory is sold (also called *stockturn*).

Insurance and Risk Management

Protection against financial loss is what links insurance to risk management, and insurance against many of the hazards that could produce financial loss is essential for the profitability of a shopping center. Although an insurance and risk management program is vital to a successful shopping center, the property manager is not expected to have specific expertise in these matters. However, to manage real property effectively, the property manager must be able to assist the shopping center owner in assessing risks and establishing appropriate insurance coverages for the property.

A well-insured shopping center is one that is prepared for loss. Because shopping centers are generally larger and costlier than many other types of property investments, many shopping center developers and owners are more concerned about protection against major risks on the property than about minor losses. They carry high deductibles in order to pay lower premiums and concentrate on major coverages. Insurance is a major component of a good risk management program.

RISK MANAGEMENT

Broadly defined, risk represents uncertainty, and many uncertainties affect the shopping center each day. In shopping centers, there are hundreds of potential risks or *loss exposures,* ranging from individual tenants' spaces to common areas and the structures themselves. Wherever people gather in one location, as they do in a shopping center, the number of risks increases. A shopper can suffer a *bodily injury* for which the center may be held liable. The common area may be defaced (*vandalism*), or a *windstorm* may blow down a fence surrounding the parking lot. Even a federally imposed guideline can be considered a risk if the owner must abide by it or face litigation. Insurance is one way to protect against economic losses.

Defining Risk Management

Risk management prepares the owner for the financial demands of claims arising from accidents and lawsuits; it gives the center owner, the property manager, and their creditors protection against such claims. Thus, insurance serves as a financial shield against risk. By managing risk, center owners increase their profits both directly and indirectly. Direct protection takes the form of financial support when damage occurs. Indirect protection results from rigorous inspection of the property for loss exposures. A rigorously inspected property will likely be better controlled and managed than one that has not been so scrutinized. Thus, risk management encompasses prevention of and preparation for the financial demands of unexpected accidents or litigation.

An effective risk management program offers peace of mind. With an adequate amount of insurance coverage, the investor may try to reduce the loss from various hazards, insure the remainder, then assume the cost of the lessened risks. Risk management can also improve the quality of investment decisions. After identifying all the potential loss exposures from locating in a region with a high crime rate, and being unable to find reasonable insurance coverage, the developer may ultimately decide that the project is unwise. Risk management is a primary issue that shopping center managers must confront, and insurance is just one of the ways to manage risk.

Insurance in Risk Management

Insurance companies do not prevent losses; they offer financial protection against the consequences of such losses. Insurance is based on the probabilities that events will occur in various climates, regions, areas, or neighborhoods. From a statistical review of many factors, rates are determined for a given exposure. The insurance company pools together the premiums paid to it and thus has the funds to pay for claims as they are made.

Obtaining Insurance. The insurance policy is a legal contract which is prepared by an underwriter and issued by an insurance company. The property owner's insurance agent should negotiate the insurance contract, and the owner's primary concerns are the amounts and types of insurance that should be carried. The amount will depend on the value of the property, the types of stores at the center, and the types of consumers it attracts. The types of coverages will depend on the potential risks.

It is important to find an insurance agent who specializes in writing policies for income properties. Insurance agents act as independents, or they represent a single company as "direct writers" or "exclusive agents." Even more important than this distinction are the credentials, experience, and training of the particular agent. Although there are many professional designations insurance agents can earn, the most prestigious is the CPCU, which stands for Chartered Property Casualty Underwriter. The insurance agent should review the loss exposures at the property with the owner and the manager, offer suggestions, answer questions, review the owner's objectives, and propose a program of appropriate insurance coverages in keeping with the risk management plan.

The person charged with finding insurance coverage for the shopping center should examine the reputations of potential insurers. A proven track record, a wide selection of policies, prompt processing of claims, and thorough service are all considerations in the evaluation of an insurance company. *Best's Insurance Report: Property–Casualty,* published annually by A. M. Best Company in Oldwick, New Jersey, is an independent source for such data. Of particular interest are three activities of an insurance company:

1. *Coverage*—the insurer's ability to provide the appropriate contract for the exposures.
2. *Capacity*—the insurer's ability to offer insurance policies and limits that meet the needs of the buyer.
3. *Claims*—the insurer's capabilities to process claims quickly and efficiently.

Also to be evaluated are the means that the insurer uses to handle sales, underwriting, loss control, policy issuance, claims records, and policy renewals.

As part of the decision-making process, the property owner should assess property values on a replacement-cost basis. When insurance is based on "actual cash value," an amount is deducted for depreciation—the loss of value—based on the age of the insured property. Such a plan may penalize the insured when a loss occurs because it covers only the original cost of the item, and inflation precludes replacement at the same (original) cost. Newer package policies often provide full replacement cost coverage if insurance is at 80 percent of value at the time of loss. In deciding on the amount of coverage to purchase and the type of policy to carry, the owner and the manager must understand the exact coverage provided under each policy being considered. If some coverage will be limited, there could be major effects on the center's profits because a particular loss may not be covered.

Once policies are in effect, the insurance company's performance must be evaluated on a continual basis. Of concern are whether the agent and the insurer are providing the expected services and how quickly claims are processed. Comments of other insured parties may also be taken into account. If there are problems with an insurance carrier and service does not improve, it may be necessary to start the process all over again. Sometimes a simple warning that a policy may be dropped is enough to improve the services provided by the agent and the insurer.

Factors Affecting Rates and Premiums.   Essentially, property insurance rates are based on four factors:

1. *Construction*—the materials used in building the shopping center structure. Interior materials and the layout and design of the center are also evaluated. Of concern are the susceptibility of materials to fire, the presence (or absence) of a fire sprinkler system, and other perils.
2. *Occupancy*—the types of tenants in the center. Most tenants are retailers, but more and more service tenants (doctors' offices, dry cleaners, cinemas) are leasing space in shopping centers. Of importance is the greater exposure of one tenant (a restaurant) compared to another (a women's apparel store); the greater the risk, the higher the premium.
3. *Protection*—actions taken to protect the property and reduce its exposure to loss. Systems such as sprinklers, parapets, fire doors, and fire "divisions," used effectively, ultimately reduce premiums and underwriting problems. Prevention activities such as fire drills, meetings with tenants to discuss fire safety, and periodic store inspections may ultimately reduce both the threat of fire or other losses and insurance rates.
4. *Exposure*—external hazards that increase the dangers to the property. These include vulnerability to physical hazards such as might result from being located near a chemical manufacturing plant (e.g., property damage and potential liability in the event of an explosion) and weather-related perils such as tornados, hurricanes, or hailstorms. Geologic perils such as earthquakes and volcanic eruptions are other possibilities.

When underwriters review a property for coverage, they often look at the losses that similar businesses in the area have suffered. Some plans offer rate credits to those businesses that have active loss-prevention programs.

Coinsurance.   A coinsurance clause requires the insured to carry insurance equal to a specified percentage of the value of the property at the time of the loss to avoid a penalty. If less insurance is carried, the insurer pays for only a part of the loss. Under an 80-percent coinsurance clause, for example, the insured must have coverage equal to 80 percent of the replacement cost of the property at the time of the loss in order to receive 100 percent reimbursement (up to the policy limit)—otherwise, the insured is penalized, and the loss is shared between the insurer and the insured. In essence, the insurer is agreeing to a rate reduction if a coinsurance clause is included. As an example, consider a building worth $100,000 that, because of coinsurance (at 80 percent), must have $80,000 of coverage. As long as the building's value remains at $100,000, 100 percent of losses will be covered (up to the policy limit). However, if the amount of coverage remains at $80,000 and the value of the property increases to $150,000, the insured will have to pay the difference because the amount of insurance required to cover the increased property value is $120,000 ($150,000 × .80 = $120,000). In this case, the insured will receive two-thirds of the value for a partial loss, and only the maximum value of the policy (i.e., 80 percent of the original value) for a total loss. The following equations show how this works.

$$\frac{\text{Amount carried}}{\substack{\text{Amount required at} \\ \text{the time of loss}}} \times \text{Amount of Loss} = \text{Dollar amount received}$$

$$\frac{\$80,000}{\$80,000} \times \$10,000 = \$10,000 \ (100\% \ \text{coverage})$$

$$\frac{\$80,000}{\$120,000} \times \$10,000 = \$6,666 \ (\text{insured must pay the remaining } \$3,334)$$

$$\frac{\$80,000}{\$80,000} \times \$100,000 = \$80,000 \ (\text{because policy limit} = 80\% \ \text{of original value})$$

Another approach is called an *agreed amount endorsement*. In this case, the insurer and the insured agree that the property will be insured for a specific amount for a specific period of time. The insured need not worry about being uninsured so long as the agreed amount of insurance is carried; the insurer will always honor the full amount of the loss up to the face value of the policy. An inflation clause may be included so the amount of insurance is automatically increased by a predetermined percentage periodically during the policy term—e.g., for an annual policy, inflation may be calculated each quarter.

Regardless of the method used to determine the amount of insurance coverage, annual review of all the insurance policies for the property is recommended.

Record Keeping.   A fully qualified insurance agent will handle insurance record keeping and inform the property manager of policy expiration dates, premium payments, inspection reports, and loss history. However, the management agreement usually specifies whether the owner or the manager will maintain insurance records and coverages. In practice, the manager usually obtains and monitors insurance coverage, maintaining a cross-index of renewal and follow-up dates. If the owner obtains and pays for the insurance, the manager may still have responsibility for monitoring the program. In that case, the manager must alert the owner to new risks that arise during the policy term and prepare renewal data for the owner at lease 90 days before the term expires. The manager will likely have to maintain records of losses and inspections as well.

Ultimately, it simplifies matters if the manager handles all insurance matters, including the decision-making process. The manager knows what happens on the property day-to-day and can usually maintain a more thorough and efficient insurance program.

Applying Risk Management Concepts

Risk can be static (pure) or dynamic (speculative). Speculative risks are the uncertainties involved in any business decision resulting in either a financial gain or loss. The decision to buy or build a shopping center is such a risk. Static risks are created by the center's construction, tenancy, maintenance, and location. Static risks create loss or premium costs but no gains other than insurance payments for actual damage claims. Once a buyer becomes an owner, the dynamic risks become static.

Careful planning can minimize loss exposures. Location, design, leasing, and operations may affect the amount of risk at a center, and these are factors that managers can try to control. A risk-management decision-making model can help the manager develop an appropriate program. Risk management has three modes—planning, action, and decision making—and each of these modes has numerous components.

Planning.   This first mode comprises three stages. The first is *identification* of all possible loss exposures on the property. This can be accomplished by studying blueprints of the property and making a comprehensive inspection. This is followed by *analysis* of the probability that an event will actually occur and the frequency at which it may recur. Frequent losses generally have limited financial impact; some exposures can cause severe loss. As an example of the latter, earthquakes are difficult to anticipate, and when a destructive one occurs, many centers are not covered. The third stage is *selection* of the actions to be taken in managing specific risks.

Action.   There are four possible actions for dealing with a specific risk.

1. *Avoidance* is chosen when it is possible to avoid a risk and the cost of avoidance is less than that of assumption. For example, the risks of losses from damage to a building can be avoided by not owning any buildings. However, the money lost because of unwillingness to accept the risks involved in buildng ownership usually will outweigh any benefits of avoiding such ownership. A more appropriate act of avoidance involves elimination of a known risk or employment of methods to control that risk within the context of ownership or operation.
2. *Control* involves taking active steps to reduce loss exposures for both people and things. This includes *loss control* measures to protect customers and employees from injury (e.g., fire drills). It also includes *property preservation* measures such as installation of sprinkler systems and use of fire-resistant materials. Such things are generally under the control of the property owner and his or her representatives. (The property manager must take responsibility to control losses at the shopping center.) Private associations that specialize in loss prevention (e.g., the National Safety Council, insurance companies) can be resources for information and services. The federal government, under the Occupational Safety and Health Act of 1970 (OSHA), establishes standards and provides funding for specific ser-

vices. Some of the OSHA safety standards that affect shopping centers are listed below.

- Walking and working surfaces
- Means of entering and exiting
- Powered platforms, handlifts, and vehicle-mounted work platforms
- Hazardous materials
- Personal protective equipment
- General environmental control
- Medical and first aid
- Fire protection
- Compressed gas and compressed air equipment
- Material handling and storage

If an inspector discovers that the center or a tenant at the center is violating an OSHA requirement, a citation will be issued describing the violation and requiring that the employer or the owner must remove the hazard or correct the condition within a specific time frame.

3. *Retention* can be intentional (active) or unintentional (passive). In an active retention, the risk manager consciously decides that the center owner will pay the consequences of a known exposure. This may be done when the probability of loss is very low and essentially can be ignored. Passive retention is often the result of ignorance because a risk is unknown or unobserved (e.g., an old mine shaft beneath the property).

4. *Transfer* is the action related specifically to insurance. Risk is transferred to a professional risk bearer through property, casualty, life, and health insurance policies. Often such transfer is combined with some form of retention or control. A noninsurance transfer may be effected via a hold-harmless agreement.

Decision Making.   In this mode, the manager reviews the selection criteria and assigns the actions to treat the loss exposure. This may involve convincing the shopping center owner of the effectiveness of the risk management program, especially if it will be costly to implement or if a less-costly insurance plan would reduce the coverage. Because several people may be involved in this decision-making process, the management agreement should set forth the limits of the manager's authority and indicate the approvals needed for major decisions ragarding insurance matters. With selection criteria approved in advance, the manager knows the parameters for planning the program and can implement the program as soon as decisions are made. The *transfer* of risk to the insurance company requires the advice and assistance of the insurance agent. *Control* activities generally require the insurance company employees to work continually with the center staff and tenants. Specific risk *retentions* must be monitored and notes made of various risks to be *avoided* and eliminated.

TYPES OF INSURANCE COVERAGE

There are many factors to consider when insuring a shopping center, including the size and type of the center, the center's location, the center's physical characteristics, and local ordinances, financial institutions, and insurers. Basically there are two types of insurance to be obtained—*property insurance,* which covers damage to the shopping center, and *liability insurance,* which covers injuries to third parties or damage to others' property. Often the two are packaged as a Special Multiperil Policy, which may incorporate other types of coverages as well.

Property Insurance

Basic coverage for property is often established under a fire and extended insurance policy with an extended coverage endorsement that covers not only damage from fire and lightning but also damage caused by windstorms, civil commotions, vehicles, aircraft, hail, explosions, riots, and smoke. Property policies can also cover consequential losses—income losses that occur because of the insured damage—and so-called specialty losses.

Fire Insurance. A standard fire policy offers only limited coverage; it essentially provides the insured with coverage only for damage caused by fire, lightning, and the removal of property from the premises. Claims under a standard fire policy are paid on an *actual cash value (ACV)* basis—the person who handles the claim must determine the replacement cost with materials of "like" kind and quality and subtract an amount for depreciation.

Fire is a constant threat on any type of property, and it is one of the main reasons that property owners buy insurance. Fire kills, and it puts people out of work. It destroys property. All property owners need protection against the financial consequences of fire.

Lightning—a natural electrical charge—strikes properties less frequently than does fire. Nevertheless, when lightning does strike, it can destroy property. Most insurance policies provide coverage for damage to property caused by lightning and consequent fire.

Most states require that specific information be provided in the fire insurance policy.

- Terms of the policy.
- Description of the property.
- Losses covered.
  The standard fire policy protects the center owner from losses caused by fire or lightning. The insured may choose and pay for coverage for other items. No insurance policy covers damages caused by war or nuclear attacks.
- Amounts covered.
  A fire insurance policy is intended to pay the insured for the amount of the damage—no more and no less. The standard fire policy attempts to put the insured back in the same financial position as when the contract was signed or when the loss occurred.
- Suspension.
  The standard fire policy is suspended—not cancelled—when either of the following occurs: (1) a hazard increases in some way, with the insured's control or knowledge; or (2) during any period that the center, for any reason, stands vacant for more than 60 consecutive days.

- Cancellation.
A standard fire insurance policy holds that both the tenant and the landlord have cancellation rights, provided that both parties adhere to the specific guidelines that are stated in the contract.
- Subrogation.
Most insurance companies insist on this clause in their contracts. Basically, the clause states that the insurer assumes all rights to recover amounts paid to the insured for damage caused by a third party.
- Apportionment.
This is the pro rata distribution over several policies held by the same insured.

Extended Coverage. This provides the insured with coverage beyond the perils of fire and lightning—including windstorms, hail, riots, civil commotions, vehicles, explosions, aircraft, and smoke. Intentional, destructive acts of vandalism done to the property can be insured under a *vandalism and malicious mischief (VMM)* endorsement. There are many other property insurance coverages that can be considered to provide as broad protection as is needed.

Crime Insurance. The high cost and limited availability of insurance coverage might prevent many owners from buying crime insurance. Coverage for crime should be tailored to the needs of the center. Shoplifting and theft are major problems, especially in large shopping centers, and insurance companies cannot afford to cover all such losses. Some center owners, or individual tenants in the center, may want to obtain coverage for burglary, robbery, theft, and employee crime. Shopping centers have limited crime exposure, but many tenants have high exposure. Therefore, tenants are generally more concerned with crime insurance than are property owners.

Special Coverage. Shopping center owners can also purchase insurance that covers specific risks in their areas. Flood insurance and earthquake insurance are examples. A flood is an overflow of water that comes from a lake, river, or ocean. Floods can devastate regions and destroy properties. A business located in an area susceptible to such water overflows should have flood insurance and may be required by law to obtain such coverage. Flood insurance is available from the federal government. Earthquakes occur because of movements of the earth's surface. They are possible in almost any region but mainly in those areas located along a geologic fault. Most centers do not carry earthquake insurance because, compared to other risks, the probability of a destructive earthquake occurring is low.

Specialty Contracts. Basically, the shopping center owner and the retailer/tenant should consider four types of specialty policies.

- *Accounts payable* insurance covers risks associated specifically with the destruction of payment records.
- *Valuable papers* insurance covers the loss of important papers such as blueprints or leases.
- *Plate glass* insurance covers accidental glass breakage and the subsequent board-up service. It also insures against possible damage to glass caused by the application of acid or other chemicals.
- *Rent loss* insurance pays the contract rent to the property owner during the restora-

tion of the property. Most leases provide that tenants' rents are abated during restoration of a building that suffers a casualty loss.

Business Interruption Coverage.   One form of this type of insurance covers *indirect damages*—the loss of profits resulting from direct damage. If the operation of the
shopping center is interrupted, tenants would lose business as a result. In that case,
retailers measure their damages in terms of their losses in sales volume. The insurance would cover not only the profits lost but also all of the expenses that have been
incurred because of the interruption of business and the efforts to reduce the loss.

Contingent business interruption results when one supplier's product is so important that interruption of its delivery or availability (because of damage to the supplier)
causes a loss to the distributor. An example would be the loss of business a bakery store
would incur because its bread supplier was burned out.

Extra expense insurance covers extra expenses that are the result of continuing
business in the event of damage. An example would be the cost to fly in parts and the
overtime wages paid to maintenance workers to expedite repairs of a fire-damaged
elevator.

Liability Insurance

An employee's act of negligence that causes injury to a customer or damage to another's property may result in the shopping center being held responsible for monetary damages. Because the person who makes the liability claim is a "third party,"
liability insurance is refered to as "third party insurance." Shopping center owners
carry liability coverage, not only because the cost of paying a legal suit is high, but also
because of the amounts of damages awarded to injured parties by the courts.

Boiler and Machinery Liability.   The extensive heating and cooling systems in
shopping centers are insured under this type of coverage. The policy provides protection for damage to the operating machinery in the building, including air-conditioning
units, generating systems, heating systems, and electrical control panels. Coverage includes repairs to existing units, any costs up to a fixed dollar amount (e.g., $1,000) that
will expedite the repair process, any consequent damage to others' property (for
which the insured is liable), and new equipment (coverage is automatically added, on
installation), but *not* damage caused by wear and tear, corrosion, and erosion.

General Liability Insurance.   A typical general liability policy provides one or
more of the following three coverages: bodily injury liability, property damage liability, and medical payments. A single policy may be used to cover different scheduled
hazards. Specific examples include the following:

- *Owners, Landlords, and Tenants Liability (OLT).* This type of policy provides coverage for problems that arise out of ownership, maintenance, or use of the insured
  premises and all operations necessary and incidental to it.
- *Contractual Liability.* This type of coverage is common in shopping centers because
  of the serious problems raised by contracts which require one party to assume liability for another party's conduct. For example, a lease may include a hold-harmless
  clause that shifts to the tenant the landlord's liability for building defects or for acts
  of negligence by the tenant or by any other person, including the landlord.

- *Medical Payments Insurance.* This type of coverage reimburses medical, hospital, and funeral expenses to members of the public who are injured on the premises—regardless of liability. Medical payments insurance may be added to certain liability policies. It surpasses the medical payments provision in the general liability contract and imposes no prerequisites of negligence on the part of the insured.
- *Personal Injury Liability.* Many shopping center owners choose to add personal injury liability coverage to their general liability policies. This type of insurance is particularly important for shopping centers because of the frequency of incidents of shoplifting and subsequent arrest. Many shopping center tenants also carry this type of coverage. Personal injury includes libel, slander, invasion of privacy, false arrest or imprisonment, and wrongful eviction.
- *Comprehensive General Liability.* This type of policy provides the broadest protection against liability claims. It covers premises/operations, elevators/escalators, products, completed operations, and owners' protective liability. Many separate endorsements can be added to this policy to broaden the coverage even further.

Workers' Compensation.   The theory behind this type of insurance is that an employer must assume responsibility for injuries or illnesses that arise out of or during the course of a worker's employment. Workers' compensation insurance provides unlimited coverage for death benefits, medical expenses, lost wages, and disability payable to the insured—the employee. The premium paid by the employer will depend on payroll size, job classifications, and the claims experience of the insured parties. The shopping center owner, individual retailers, and the merchants' association will all have to carry this type of insurance if they have a certain number of employees—the standards (number of employees) are established by the states.

Adapted with permission from *Managing the Shopping Center* (Chicago: Institute of Real Estate Management, 1983).

Note that insurance as a method of risk management substitutes regular payment of insurance premiums for the unpredictable cost of an economic loss, based on the probability of a particular type of loss occurring.

APPENDIX C

Maintenance Forms

Shopping Center Exterior Inspection Report

PROJECT: _____ DATE: _____

ADDRESS: _____ INSPECTED BY: _____

ITEMS	CONDITION	NEEDS	EST. COST
I. SURROUNDING AREA			
1. Neighborhood			
2. Access to Project			
3. Street Condition			
4.			
5. Comments:			
II. SIGNAGE			
1. Pylon Signs			
2. Entry Signs			
3. Parking Lot Signs			
4. Tenant Signs			
5.			
6. Comments:			
III. PARKING LOT			
1. Driveways			
2. Parking Stalls			
3. Striping			
4. Parking Bumpers			
5. Drainage			
6. Concrete Curbing			
7.			
8. Comments:			
IV. LIGHTING			
1. Pole Mounted			
2. Wall Mounted			
3.			
4. Comments:			
V. LANDSCAPING			
1. General Appearance			
2. Ground Cover			
3. Trees			
4. Shrubs			
5. Sprinklers			
6. Curbing			
7.			
8. Comments:			
VI. OTHER ITEMS			
1. Walls & Fences			
2. Sidewalk & Ramps			
3. Bike Rack			
4. Newspaper Rack			
5. Trash Bins			
6. Loading Docks			
7. Electrical Cabinet			

ITEMS	CONDITION	NEEDS	EST. COST
8. Meters			
9. Sprinklers (Bldg.)			
10.			
11. Comments:			

VII. BUILDING EXTERIOR

ITEMS	CONDITION	NEEDS	EST. COST
1. Walls			
2. Stucco			
3. Wood Siding			
4. Wood Beams & Trim			
5. Columns/Posts			
6. Store Fronts			
7. Doors			
8.			
9. Comments:			

VII. ROOFS

ITEMS	CONDITION	NEEDS	EST. COST
1. Soffit/Overhang			
2. Main Roof			
3. Flashing			
4. Drains/Gutters			
5. Mansand/Decorative			
6.			
7. Comments:			

IX. VACANCIES

ITEMS	CONDITION	NEEDS	EST. COST
1. Store Fronts			
2. Doors			
3. Door Hardware			
4. Flooring			
5. Walls			
6. Base			
7. Ceilings			
8. Sprinklers			
9. Thermostats			
10. H.V.A.C. Vents			
11. Restrooms			
12. Comments:			

X. MISCELLANEOUS

ITEMS	CONDITION	NEEDS	EST. COST
1.			
2.			
3.			

XI. GENERAL COMMENTS:

1. Total Cost of Work Needed: _____

   _____
   _____

2. Capital Expenditure Anticipated: _____

   _____
   _____

3. Special Problems _____

   _____
   _____

4. Comments: _____

   _____
   _____

Shopping Center Interior Inspection Report

PROJECT: _____ DATE: _____
ADDRESS: _____ INSPECTED BY: _____

ITEMS	CONDITION	NEEDS	EST. COST
I. ENTRANCES			
1. Glass			
2. Doors			
3. Door Hardware			
4. Sign (Entry)			
5. Sign (Doors)			
6.			
7. Comments:			
II. VESTIBULE			
1. Glass			
2. Door			
3. Flooring			
4. Walls			
5. Furniture			
6. Lighting			
7.			
8. Comments:			
III. MALL			
1. Carpet			
2. Wood Flooring			
3. Tile			
4. Stairs			
5. Elevator			
6. Escalator			
7. Benches			
8. Walls			
9. Columns			
10. Hand Railings			
11. Fountains/Pools			
12. Drinking Fountains			
13. Telephones			
14. Sand Urns			
15. Trash Bins			
16. Fire Extinguisher			
17. H.V.A.C.			
18. Hose Cabinet			
19. Return Air Vent			
20. Light Fixture			
21. Banners			
22. Windows			
23. Skylights			
24. Ceiling			
25. Fire Detector			
26.			
27.			
28. Comments:			

Shopping Center Interior Inspection Report—(continued)

ITEMS	CONDITION	NEEDS	EST. COST
IV. LANDSCAPING			
1. Planters			
2. Sprinkler			
3. Hose Bibs			
4. Ground Cover			
5. Color			
6. Shrubs			
7. Trees			
8.			
9. Comments:			
V. RESTROOMS (MEN)			
1. Doors			
2. Door Hardware			
3. Floors			
4. Base			
5. Walls			
6. Ceilings			
7. Partitions			
8. Watercloset			
9. Paper Dispenser			
10. Urinal			
11. Counter			
12. Sinks			
13. Mirror			
14. Soap Dispenser			
15. H.V.A.C. Vent			
16. Fire Detector			
17.			
18. Comments:			
VI. RESTROOM (WOMEN)			
1. Doors			
2. Door Hardware			
3. Floors			
4. Base			
5. Walls			
6. Ceilings			
7. Partitions			
8. Watercloset			
9. Paper Dispenser			
10. Vending Machine			
11. Counter			
12. Sinks			
13. Mirror			
14. Soap Dispenser			
15. H.V.A.C. Vent			
16. Fire Detector			
17.			
18. Comments:			

Shopping Center Interior Inspection Report—(continued)

ITEMS	CONDITION	NEEDS	EST. COST
VII. CORRIDORS			
1. Doors			
2. Door Hardware			
3. Floors			
4. Base			
5. Walls			
6. Ceiling			
7. Lighting			
8. Signs			
9. Ventilation			
10. Vents			
11. Fire Detector			
12.			
13. Comments:			
VIII. ELECTRICAL ROOMS			
1. Doors			
2. Door Hardware			
3. Floors			
4. Base			
5. Walls			
6. Ceiling			
7. Lighting			
8. Signs			
9. Ventilation			
10. Vents			
11. Electrical Panels			
12. Fire Detector			
13.			
14. Comments:			
IX. STORAGE ROOM			
1. Doors			
2. Door Hardware			
3. Floors			
4. Base			
5. Walls			
6. Ceiling			
7. Lighting			
8. Signs			
9. Ventilation			
10. Vents			
11. Lockers			
12. Cabinets			
13. Fire Detector			
14.			
15. Comments:			

Shopping Center Interior Inspection Report—(concluded)

ITEMS	CONDITION	NEEDS	EST. COST
X. VACANCIES			
1. Storefront			
2. Doors			
3. Door Hardware			
4. Flooring			
5. Base			
6. Wall			
7. Ceiling			
8. Sprinkler			
9. Thermostat			
10. H.V.A.C. Vents			
11. Restroom			
12. Fire Detector			
13.			
14. Comments:			
XI. OCCUPIER STORE			
1. Storefront			
2. Door			
3. Signs			
4.			
5. Comments			
XII. MISC.			
1.			
2.			
3.			

XIII. GENERAL COMMENTS

1. Total cost of work needed: _____

2. Capital expenditure anticipated: _____

3. Special problem: _____

4. Comments: _____

JANITORIAL SPECIFICATIONS—MALL

Scope

1. *Coverage*—The Contractor shall perform the following specified services throughout the entire premises—including lobbies, corridors, sidewalks, plaza areas, stairways, lavatories, passageways, service and utility areas—if landlord is obligated to maintain such areas. Building mechanical areas are included at discretion of Owner.
2. *Quality*—The intent of this specification is that the Contractor will provide cleaning services of a character customarily provided in first-class buildings, whether such services are included in the specifications or are special services requested by Owner or tenant of Owner. Owner to be sole judge of said quality and required frequency of services to be provided herewith.

General

1. *Schedule*—All nightly cleaning services shall be performed 7 nights per week. Nightly cleaning operations will begin after 9:00 P.M.; all work to be completed by 8:30 A.M.
2. *Supervision*—Contractor shall employ competent supervisory personnel and place a qualified foreman in the building who will be capable of and will provide all reports required by Owner. Contractor will provide easy access to Owner or his foreman 24 hours a day so that Owner may review ongoing work or provide special instructions.
3. *Personnel*—Contractor shall employ on the premises only persons skilled in the work assigned to them. Contractor shall promptly furnish substitute qualified persons for any employees that, in the opinion of Owner, are unsatisfactory. All Contractor personnel shall be bonded, and Contractor shall pay all wages, payroll taxes, and insurance and all payments required by union contracts, if any.
4. *Uniforms and Equipment*—Contractor shall furnish proper cleaning materials, implements, machinery, and uniforms for the satisfactory performance of all services. All Contractor personnel shall be properly uniformed and display identification of the Mall at all times. Landlord shall have right to select and/or approve uniforms worn by personnel in the building. Night personnel shall have at least three uniform changes per week.
5. *Storage*—Owner shall provide Contractor with space on the premises for storage of cleaning materials, implements, and machinery.
6. *Rules*—Contractor shall at all times maintain good order among its employees and shall assure compliance with building rules and regulations.
7. *Security*—While cleaning the building areas, Contractor's personnel will not admit anyone into the building. Lids or seats on all toilets will be left in a raised position. All mop sinks, locker areas, and other service areas will be cleaned thoroughly and all cleaning equipment neatly stored in a central location. The Building Manager or designated Supervisor will be promptly notified of any irregularities.

Exterior Patios and Walks—Nightly

1. *Trash*—During each shift, Contractor will empty trash containers, replace can liners, and pick up any debris on the sidewalk in the vicinity of the main entrance.

Public Areas—Nightly

1. *Carpeted Floors*—All carpeted floors are to be vacuumed and edged with a small broom or edging tool, moving all furniture and accessories as necessary. Baseboards will be wiped with a treated dust cloth after vacuuming. Carpet and baseboards will be spotcleaned where necessary.

2. *Uncarpeted Floors*—All hard-surfaced floors are to be mopped and spray buffed as needed to maintain uniformly bright appearance, with particular attention to edges, corners, and areas behind doors. All spills and stains will be removed with damp mop or cloth. Baseboards will be wiped down with treated dustcloths. All chewing gum will be removed.

3. *Walls*—All walls will be spotcleaned to remove all smudge stains and handmarks, using only clean water (or mild cleaning agent where necessary). When soap or cleaner is used, the wall will be rinsed with clear water and dried. No abrasive cleaner is to be used.

4. *Doors and Jambs*—All doors and jambs will be spotcleaned to remove any handmarks, stains, spills, or smudges. Use only clear water or mild cleaning agent where necessary. Rinse with clear water and dry. Door edges and jambs will be dusted where necessary. When completed, doors and jambs shall have a uniformly clean appearance.

5. *Glass Doors and Partitions*—All glass doors and partitions, including any directory glass, will be spotcleaned to remove any fingermarks, smudges, or stains and will be left in a uniformly bright, clean condition.

6. *Miscellaneous Metalwork*—All metalwork such as mail chutes, door hardware and frames, metal lettering, and other metal accessories will be wiped and polished and left in uniformly clean and bright condition, free of all dust and streaks.

7. *Cigarette Urns*—Clean all cigarette urns, removing all butts and debris, and polish as needed.

8. *Dusting*—Dust all furniture, accessories, ledges, and all other horizontal surfaces, using a treated dustcloth. No feather dusters will be allowed. All surfaces to be left in a clean, dust-free condition. Spotclean as necessary.

9. *Furniture and Miscellaneous*—All furniture is to be wiped using a treated dustcloth, paying particular attention to legs and surfaces near the floor.

Public Areas—Weekly

1. *Uncarpeted Floors*—All hard-surfaced floors will be wetmopped, dried, and spray buffed. All wax and marks will be removed from baseboards. Floors and baseboards to be left in a uniformly bright, clean condition.

2. *Carpeted Floors*—All carpeted floors will be vacuumed, using an approved beater-bar/brush system, to remove all embedded dirt and grit and restore pile to a uniformly upright condition.

Public Areas—Monthly

1. *Uncarpeted Floors*—All hard-surfaced floors are to be stripped (removing all wax or other coating) down to the bare, clean and dry floor surface, removing any marks or stains. Floors will then be refinished and polished and left in a uniformly bright, clean condition. All wax spills and splashes will be completely removed from baseboards, walls, doors, and frames.

2. *Carpeted Floors*—All carpeted floors will be shampooed or steam cleaned at Owner's discretion to remove all dirt and stains. All furniture and accessories will be moved so that when completed, the carpet will have a uniformly clean appearance.
3. *High Dusting*—All high dusting beyond the reach of the normal daily dusting will be accomplished monthly. This will include but not be limited to all ledges, charts, picture frames, graphs, air diffusers, and other horizontal surfaces.
4. *Doors and Jambs*—All painted doors and jambs will be washed down with clean water and dried, leaving no streaks, marks, or smudges.

Public Areas—Annually

1. *Light Lenses*—All light lenses will be removed, washed clean, dried, and reinstalled as often as necessary, but not less often than once a year.

Restrooms—Nightly

1. *Floors and Tiles*—Floors will be swept clean and wetmopped, using a germicidal detergent approved by Owner. The floors will then be mopped dry and all watermarks and stains wiped from the walls and metal partition bases.
2. *Metal Fixtures*—Wash and polish all mirrors, powder shelves, bright work (including exposed piping below wash basins), towel dispensers, trash receptacles, and any other metal accessories. Mirrors will be cleaned and polished. Contractor shall use only approved nonabrasive, nonacidic materials to avoid damage to metal fixtures.
3. *Ceramic Fixtures*—Scour, wash, and disinfect all basins, including faucet handles, bowls, and urinals, including tile walls near urinals, using Owner-approved germicidal detergent solution. Special care must be taken to inspect and clean areas of difficult access, such as the underside of toilet bowl rings and urinals, to prevent buildup of calcium and iron oxide deposits. Wash both sides of toilet seats with approved germicidal solution and wipe dry. Toilet seats to be left in an upright position.
4. *Walls and Metal Partitions*—Damp wipe all metal toilet partitions and tiled walls, using approved germicidal solution. All surfaces are to be wiped dry so that all wipe marks are removed and surface has a uniformly bright appearance. Dust the top edges of all partitions, ledges, and mirror tops. All graffiti to be removed.
5. *General*—It is the intention of this specification to keep lavatories thoroughly clean and not to use disinfectant to mask odors. Odorless disinfectants shall be used.

Remove all waste paper and refuse, including soiled sanitary napkins, to designated area in the building and dispose of same. All waste paper and sanitary napkin receptacles are to be thoroughly cleaned and washed and new liners installed. Fill toilet tissue holders, seat cover containers, soap and hand lotion dispensers, towel dispensers, facial tissue dispensers, and sanitary napkin vending dispensers and maintain operation of same. Paper products to be supplied by Owner. Whenever possible, dispensers are to be filled in sufficient quantity to last the entire business day.

Restrooms—Weekly

1. *Floors*—All restroom floors will be machine scrubbed, using a germicidal solution, detergent, and water. After scrubbing, floors will be rinsed with clear water and

dried. All water marks will be removed from walls, partitions, and fixtures, If directed by Owner, an approved floor finish will be applied and buffed.

2. *Floor Drains*—Clean, disinfect, and fill with water at least weekly.

Restrooms—Monthly

1. *Walls, Metal Partitions, Washable Ceiling*—Wash with water and germicidal solution. Wipe dry and polish to a uniformly bright clean condition.

Restrooms—Quarterly

1. *Light Fixtures and Ceiling Grills*—Remove light lenses and ceiling grills where possible. Wash thoroughly, dry, and replace. This will be done as often as necessary, but not less often than quarterly.

Janitors' Closets and Storage Rooms

All janitors' closets, mop sinks, storage rooms, restrooms, lunchrooms, and work areas provided by Owner for use of Contractor personnel will be kept in a neat, clean, and orderly condition at all times.

Mop sinks and the areas immediately adjacent will be thoroughly cleaned immediately after each shift. Before leaving the premises each night, all of the service areas will be dustmopped, and spotcleaned when necessary but not less often than every sixty days. Concrete floors will be initially sealed, dustmopped nightly, and wetmopped monthly. All doors and walls will be spotcleaned nightly.

Stairwells and Offices—Daily

1. *Mall Offices*—All uncarpeted stairs, offices, kitchens, restrooms, and landings will be swept with a treated dustmop daily, and spotcleaned as necessary, to remove all spills, stains, and litter. All carpeted stairs and offices will be vacuumed and edged. Baseboards and handrails will be wiped with a treated dustcloth.
2. *Spotcleaning*—All doors, jambs, and walls will be spotcleaned daily to remove all fingermarks, smudges, and stains. All office furniture, accessories, ledges, and surfaces will be dusted with a treated dustcloth.

Stairwells and Offices—Monthly

1. *Uncarpeted Stairs and Landings*—All uncarpeted stairs and landings shall be inspected then wetmopped with cleaner, rinsed, and dried, as needed upon request of Owner.
2. *Carpeted Stairs and Offices*—All carpeted surfaces will be shampooed or steam-cleaned at Owner's discretion to remove all dirt and stains. All furniture and accessories will be removed so all surfaces may be cleaned.
3. *Dusting*—All risers, handrails, stringers, baseboards, light fixtures, and all horizontal ledges and surfaces will be wiped with a treated cloth.

Stairwells and Offices—Quarterly

1. *High Dusting*—All high dusting, including but not limited to door closers, and all other surfaces not reached during normal dusting operations, will be dusted or cleaned as necessary, but not less often than quarterly.

Standards

The following standards shall be used in evaluating custodial services:

1. *Dusting*—Surface free of all dirt and dust streaks, lint, and cobwebs.
2. *Plumbing Fixture and Dispenser Cleaning*—Item is free of all deposits and stains so it is left without dust streaks, film, odor, or stains.
3. *Sweeping*—Floor is free of all dirt, dust, grit, lint, and debris except for embedded dirt and grit.
4. *Spotcleaning*—Surface is free of all stains and deposits and substantially free of cleaning marks.
5. *Dampmopping*—Floor is without dirt, dust, marks, film, streaks, debris, or standing water.
6. *Metal Cleaning*—Surfaces are without deposits or tarnish and have a uniformly bright appearance. Cleaner is removed from adjacent surfaces.
7. *Glass Cleaning*—Surfaces are without streaks, film, deposits, and stains, and have a uniformly bright appearance. Adjacent surfaces have been wiped clean.
8. *Wax Removal (Stripping)*—All wax has been removed down to the flooring material; floor is free of all dirt, stains, deposits, debris, cleaning solution, and standing water; and floor has a uniform appearance when dry. Plain water rinse and pickup must follow wax removal operation immediately.
9. *Scrubbing*—All surfaces are without embedded dirt, cleaning solution, film, debris, stains, marks, and standing water, and floor has a uniformly clean appearance. A plain water rinse must follow the scrubbing process immediately.
10. *Light Fixture Cleaning*—All components, including bulbs and tubes, are without insects, dirt, lint, film, and streaks. All lenses removed must be replaced immediately.
11. *Wall Washing*—After cleaning, the surfaces of all walls, ceiling, exposed pipes, and equipment will have a uniformly clean appearance, free from dirt, stains, streaks, lint, and cleaning marks. Painted surfaces must not be unduly damaged. Hard-finished wainscoting or glazed ceramic tile surfaces must be bright and free of film, streaks, and deposits. Cloth wall coverings shall be free of dust, spiderwebs, and spots; covering will be groomed with a stiff brush to give a smooth, consistent grain to fabric.
12. *Buffing of Waxed Surfaces*—Buffed areas have a uniform appearance with maximum gloss and removal of surface dirt.
13. *Carpet Cleaning*—Periodic cleaning of carpets shall be accomplished by steam cleaning or any other method now in use, or which may be developed in the future, as directed by owner.

APPENDIX   D

Merchants' Association Bylaws

ARTICLE I — NAME

The name of this organization shall be *[Shopping Center Name]* Merchants' Association, Inc., a not-for-profit corporation organized in the *[name and classification of local community]* under the laws of the State of *[name of state]*.

ARTICLE II — PURPOSE

Section 1. General. *[Shopping Center Name]* Merchants' Association, Inc., is organized for the purpose of furthering the general business interest of *[Shopping Center Name]*, and all of the merchants in this shopping center, and, in the furtherance of such purpose, to engage in and conduct promotional programs and publicity, special events, decoration, cooperative advertising and other joint endeavors in general interest and for the general benefit of the center and its merchants; to encourage the maintenance of high business standards and a spirit of cooperation among its members; and to compile and distribute business information to its members for their benefit.

Section 2. Nonpartisan/Nonsectarian. The Association shall be at all times conducted as a wholly and completely nonpartisan and nonsectarian entity. The Association shall not at any time or in any way act on behalf of, either directly or indirectly, or in any other way show any partiality to any religious, political, racial, national, ethnic, or gender group or individual of such group. Nor shall it in any way or at any time discriminate against any religious, political, racial, national, ethnic, or gender group or individual of such group.

Section 3. Not for Profit. The Association shall be conducted at all times as a not-for-profit organization which shall not engage in any function, plan, design, or any other activity intended for the profit of the Association, or for any officer, director, or member(s) of the Association.

ARTICLE III — MEMBERSHIP

Section 1. Class. This Association shall have one class of member with equal rights, duties, and privileges. Each tenant in the Shopping Center and the owner, whether individuals, partnerships, co-partnerships, associations, or corporations, shall be entitled to membership in the Merchants' Association. Membership in the Association shall continue so long as the respective members continue as tenants or owners in the center or as otherwise provided herein.

Section 2. Termination. The resignation, withdrawal, or expulsion of a member shall result in termination of membership. The termination of membership shall constitute forfeiture of all interests of the member in and to the property of the Association, and the member shall thereafter have no right thereto or any part thereof.

ARTICLE IV — GENERAL MEMBERSHIP MEETINGS

Section 1. Annual Meeting. Commencing with the year *[19xx]*, the Association shall hold an annual meeting with the general membership on the *[date indicated as a specific day in a specific month]* of each year, or on such other date as may be fixed by the Board of Directors. Said annual meeting shall be for the purpose of election of directors for the ensuing year, and the transaction of any business within the powers of the Association. Any business of the Association may be transacted at an annual meeting without being specifically designated in the notice, except such business as is specifically required by statute or by the charter to be stated in such notice. Failure to hold an annual meeting shall not, however, invalidate the corporate existence of the Association or affect otherwise valid corporate acts.

Section 2. Regular or Special Meetings. At any time in the interval between annual meetings, regular or special meetings of the members may be called by the President whenever it may be considered necessary or desirable or may be called by a majority of the Board of Directors, or may be called by the written request of a majority of the general membership of the Association. This provision shall not affect any of merchant's other obligations pursuant to its respective lease with the owner/developer, its successors and assigns.

Section 3. Notice. Not less than five (5) days before the date of any meeting of the general membership, the Secretary shall give to each member written notice. Said notice shall state the time and place of the meeting, and in the case of a special meeting, the purpose for which the meeting is called. Such notice shall be delivered, either personally or by mail, to the latest address of the members recorded in the books of the Association. Any meeting of the general membership, annual or special, may adjourn from time to time to reconvene at the same or some other place, and no notice need be given of such adjourned meeting other than by announcement.

Section 4. Quorum. A quorum shall consist of a majority of the entire general membership present at the meeting, either in person or by proxy. In the absence of a quorum, the Secretary shall be directed to send notice as herein provided of another meeting, and at said meeting a simple majority of those members in attendance will constitute a quorum.

Section 5. Proxy. Any member may vote either in person or by proxy or by representative designated in writing by such member. All proxies shall be in writing and submitted to the Secretary of the Association prior to any meeting of the general membership.

Section 6. Voting. Each member of the Association shall be entitled to one vote, plus an additional vote for each *[stipulated dollar amount, stated in words (and numbers)]* that such member contributes to the Association in dues. Each member shall have the right to attend and participate in all meetings of the members.

ARTICLE V — BOARD OF DIRECTORS

Section 1. Powers. The business and affairs of the Association shall be managed by its Board of Directors, all of whom shall be members in good standing of the Association. The Board of Directors may exercise all the powers of the Association, except such as are by statute, charter, or bylaws specifically reserved to the membership only.

Section 2. Number of Directors. The number of Directors of the Association shall be *[indicate number in words (and numbers)]*. *[The number of anchor tenants plus one, indicated in words (and numbers)]* of the Directors shall be permanent Directors, namely the manager(s) of *[show name of each anchor tenant store]*, and the manager of *[Shopping Center Name]* or a representative appointed by the owner/developer. The remaining Directors shall be elected by the members for one-year terms.

Section 3. Election of Directors. At each annual meeting, the members shall elect Directors to hold office until the next succeeding annual meeting or until their successors are elected and qualified. The President, not less than thirty (30) days prior to the annual meeting for the election of Directors, shall appoint a nominating committee of three (3) or more members of the Association to nominate from the general membership the Directors to be elected. Said committee shall file a list of the nominees recommended with the Secretary not less than ten (10) days before the election. Other nominations than those recommended by the nominating committee may be made by any member by petition signed by not less than five (5) members of the Association and delivery of said petition to the Secretary not later than five (5) days before the date set for such election.

All voting for the election of Directors shall be by written ballot. Every member shall have the right to cast its vote(s) in person or by proxy, or by representative, for as many members as there are Directors to be elected. The number of nominees corresponding with the number of Directors to be elected who received the highest number of votes, shall be declared elected.

Section 4. Vacancy. Any vacancy occurring on the Board of Directors for any cause, including the transfer of an elected Director, will be filled by a majority of the remaining Directors within ten (10) days after such vacancy occurs. The Directors elected by the Board of Directors to fill any such vacancy shall be elected to hold office until the next annual meeting of the general membership or until their successors are elected and qualified.

Section 5. Meetings. Regular and/or special meetings of the Board of Directors may be called at any time by the President or by the Board of Directors by a vote at a meeting or by a majority of the Directors in writing with or without a meeting and shall be held on such dates and in such places as may be designated by the Board of Directors. The Board of Directors shall keep minutes of its meetings and distribute copies of same to the membership within thirty (30) days following any regular or special meeting of the Board of Directors. The Board may adopt such rules as may be necessary for the proper conduct of the business of the Association.

Section 6. Notice. Not less than five (5) days before the date of any regular or special meeting of the Board of Directors, the Secretary shall give to each Director written or personal notice stating the time and place of the meeting, and in the case of a special meeting, the purpose for which the meeting is called. Such notice shall be delivered or sent by mail to the latest address of the Director recorded in the books of the Association. Any meeting of the Board of Directors, regular or special, may adjourn from time to time to reconvene at the same or some other place, and no notice need be given of such adjourned meeting other than by announcement.

Section 7. Quorum. At all meetings of the Board of Directors, a majority of the entire Board of Directors shall constitute a quorum for the transaction of business. Except in cases in which it is by statute, by the charter, or by the bylaws otherwise provided, the vote of a majority of such quorum at a duly constituted meeting shall be sufficient to elect and pass any measure. In the absence of a quorum, the Secretary shall be directed to send notice as herein provided of another meeting, and at said meeting a simple majority of those in attendance will constitute a quorum.

Section 8. Removal. Any elected Director of the Association may be removed by two-thirds (2/3) of the general membership whenever, in their judgment, the best interests of the Association will be served thereby.

Section 9. Compensation. In no event shall the Directors of the Association receive compensation for their services to the Association.

ARTICLE VI — OFFICERS

Section 1. Executive Officers. The Board of Directors shall elect from among the members of the Board, a President, a Vice President, a Secretary, and a Treasurer, and any other officers as shall be deemed necessary to carry out the affairs and business of the Association. Each officer shall hold office until the first meeting of the Board of Directors after the annual meeting of general members next succeeding the officer's election, or until a successor shall have been duly chosen and qualified, or until the officer shall have resigned or shall have been otherwise removed.

Section 2. Vacancy. Any vacancies in the above offices shall be filled by a member of the Board of Directors for the unexpired portion of the term, elected by a majority of the remaining Board of Directors within ten (10) days after such vacancy occurs.

Section 3. President. The President shall preside at all meetings of the members and of the Board of Directors at which the President shall be present. The President shall have general charge and supervision of the business of the Association. The President shall perform all duties as, from time to time, may be assigned by the Board of Directors. The President shall be an ex officio member of all committees.

Section 4. Vice President. The Vice President, at the request of the President, or in the absence of the President, or should the President be unable to complete the duties and exercise the functions of the job, and when so acting as President shall have the powers of the President. The Vice President shall have such other powers and perform such other duties as may be assigned by the Board of Directors or the President.

Section 5. Secretary. The Secretary shall keep the minutes of the meetings of the members and of the Board of directors in books provided for the purpose, and shall distribute same to the membership as required. The Secretary shall see that all notices are duly given in accordance with the provisions of the bylaws or as required by law and shall be custodian of the records of the Association and in general shall perform all duties incident to the office of a Secretary of a corporation, and such other duties as, from time to time, may be assigned by the Board of Directors or by the President.

Section 6. Treasurer. The Treasurer shall have charge of and be responsible for all funds, receipts, and disbursements of the Association, and shall deposit or cause to be deposited, in the name of the Association, all monies or other valuable effects in such banks or other depositories as shall, from time to time, be selected by the Board of Directors. The Treasurer shall render to the President and to the Board of Directors, and to the membership, whenever requested, an account of the financial condition of the Association, and in general, shall perform all duties incident to the office of a Treasurer of a corporation, and such other duties as may be assigned by the Board of Directors or the President.

Section 7. Executive Committee. The officers of the Association, as herein provided, and the manager of *[Shopping Center Name]* or a representative appointed by the owner/developer shall constitute the Executive Committee, which shall be empowered to act on behalf of the Board of Directors when the Board is not in session.

Section 8. Subordinate Officers. The Board of Directors may from time to time appoint such subordinate officers as it may deem desirable. Each such officer shall hold office for such period and perform such duties as the Board of Directors or the President may prescribe. The Board of Directors may, from time to time, authorize any committee or officer to appoint and remove subordinate officers and prescribe the duties thereof.

Section 9. Removal. Any officer of the Association may be removed by three-fourths (3/4) of the Board of Directors or by two-thirds (2/3) of the general membership whenever, in their judgment, the best interests of the Association will be served thereby.

ARTICLE VII — DUES AND ASSESSMENTS

Section 1. Dues. Regular annual dues shall be paid by each member to the Association as provided by lease or other agreement. The annual dues shall be payable each calendar quarter in advance as billed or as otherwise provided. Payment of dues shall be paid to the Association in care of *[Shopping Center Name]* Merchants' Association, Inc., *[show street address with city, state, and postal zip code]*, which will be responsible for depositing same to the account of the Association.

Section 2. Delinquency. Whenever a member shall be in arrears in payment of dues or assessments for a period of more than thirty (30) days, the member shall be notified in writing by the President or Secretary of the Association that if such dues or assessments or both are not paid within thirty (30) days, the member shall be deemed as delinquent.

Section 3. Suspension. Upon certification by the Treasurer to the Board of Directors that a member is so delinquent, such member may be suspended from membership in the Association by a majority vote of the Board of Directors.

Any member so suspended shall not be entitled to vote, participate in Association affairs, or be a member of the Board of Directors, and in the event such member is a Director or an officer, the member shall be automatically removed from such office upon suspension. Upon certification by the Treasurer to the Board of Directors that a suspended member has cured delinquency, the member shall be automatically reinstated to membership in the Association on the date of such certification. However, such reinstatement shall not entitle such member to regain previous membership on the Board of Directors nor any previous office held prior to the suspension unless re-elected in accordance with the applicable provisions of these bylaws.

Section 4. Expulsion. Members may be expelled by a majority vote of the entire Board of Directors for cause or nonpayment of dues or assessments as provided herein. In the event such member is a Director, or their natural person representative an officer, the member shall be automatically removed from any such office upon expulsion. However, no member may be expelled without opportunity of a hearing before the Board of Directors. An expelled member shall have the right to appeal within thirty (30) days from the date of expulsion by the Board to the entire general membership and, upon written request, must be allowed to make such an appeal at the next annual meeting or at a special meeting called for the purpose within thirty (30) days of such a request.

A member may be reinstated by a majority vote of the general membership. A member so expelled, may, at any time after the expiration of thirty (30) days from the date of expulsion, petition the Association for reinstatement. Said petition shall be in writing and submitted to the Board of Directors. Within thirty (30) days of such a petition the Board of Directors, by a majority vote of the entire Board, shall act upon said petition, subject to ratification by a majority vote of the general membership.

In the event of reinstatement, the member shall not be entitled to regain previous membership on the Board of Directors nor any previous office held prior to the expulsion unless re-elected in accordance with the applicable provisions of these bylaws.

ARTICLE VIII — SUNDRY PROVISIONS

Section 1. Contracts. The Board of Directors may authorize any officer, agent, or employee of the Association to enter into any contract or execute and deliver any instrument in the name of and on behalf of the Association, and such authority may be general or confined to specific instances.

Section 2. Borrowing. The Association shall not make any loans to any member, officer, or Director, either individually or as a group.

Section 3. Deposits, Checks, Drafts, etc. All funds of the Association shall be deposited from time to time to the credit of the Association into a special account to be designated by the Board of Directors; and disbursements of said funds shall be made with the approval of the Board of Directors.

All disbursements shall be made by check, and all checks, drafts, and orders for the payment of money, notes, and other evidences of indebtedness, issued in the name of the Association shall, unless otherwise provided by resolution of the Board of Directors, be signed by the President or Vice President and countersigned by the Secretary or Treasurer, who shall be bonded to the extent deemed necessary by the Board of Directors.

Section 4. Bonds. The Board of Directors may require any officer, agent, or employee of the Association to give a bond to the Association, conditioned upon the faithful discharge of duties, with one or more sureties and in such amount as may be satisfactory to the Board of Directors.

Section 5. Budget. The Board of Directors shall prepare annually, with the commencement of each new fiscal year, an annual operational, promotional, and advertising budget, which shall be presented to the general membership for their approval. Once approved, this budget shall govern the financial affairs of the Association for the fiscal year.

Section 6. Annual Financial Report. There shall be prepared annually, under direction of the Treasurer, a full and correct statement of the financial affairs of the Association, including a Balance Sheet and a Financial Statement of Operations for the preceding fiscal year, which shall be submitted to the general membership.

Section 7. Annual Corporate Report. The Secretary shall cause to be prepared and filed annually any corporate reports required by the laws of the State of *[name of state]* for not-for-profit corporations.

Section 8. Annual Tax Return. The Treasurer of the Association shall cause to be prepared and filed annually any Federal, State, or Municipal tax returns required for not-for-profit corporations.

Section 9. Fiscal Year. The fiscal year of the Association shall be determined and fixed by the Board of Directors.

Section 10. Committees. The Board of Directors shall authorize and define the powers and duties of all committees. All committees so authorized shall be appointed by the President, subject to confirmation by the Board of Directors.

Section 11. Insurance. The Association shall hold harmless and indemnify the center owners from all injury, loss, claims, or damage to any person or persons or property while within or upon the center premises, occasioned by any act, omission, neglect or default by the Association or by any member or group of members while acting for or on behalf of the Association. As a result, the Association shall effect and carry and pay for, and keep in full force and effect, insurance issued by reputable companies authorized and qualified to do business in the State of *[name of state]* which companies are satisfactory to owners, if coverage is not provided in any other insurance policy carried by owner/developer. In addition, the Association shall furnish a certificate issued by the Industrial Board or other appropriate agency in the State of *[name of state]* showing that Workers' Compensation insurance is in full force and effect if said Association has any employees.

ARTICLE IX — AMENDMENTS TO BYLAWS

Any and all provisions of these bylaws may be altered, amended, or repealed, and new bylaws may be adopted, by a two-thirds (2/3) vote of the membership at any annual meeting of the Association without notice, or at any special meeting of the Association, provided that at least ten (10) days written notice is given of intention to alter and amend at such special meeting. Further, any proposed amendments to these bylaws shall be submitted to the Board of Directors thirty (30) days in advance of any meeting at which said amendments may be presented. The Board of Directors shall make available to the membership the proposed changes in said bylaws fifteen (15) days prior to the meeting at which said bylaws will be considered.

APPENDIX   E
References and Resources

The following lists represent potential resources the shopping center manager can consult for additional information. They are not intended to be all-inclusive but rather to identify publications and organizations that may be useful to the shopping center manager. *Books in Print* and *Periodicals in Print,* published annually by R. R. Bowker and available in libraries, list current publications by author, title, and subject.

Books and Articles

Alexander, Alan A., and Muhlebach, Richard F.: *Managing and Leasing Commercial Properties* (New York: John Wiley & Sons, Inc., 1990).

Alexander, Alan A., and Muhlebach, Richard F.: *Managing and Leasing Commercial Properties: Forms and Procedures* (New York: John Wiley & Sons, Inc., 1991).

Before Disaster Strikes: Developing an Emergency Procedures Manual (Chicago: Institute of Real Estate Management, 1990; videotape and book).

Bolton, William D.: Disaster Planning: Insurance for Success, *Journal of Property Management* 54:78–79, July–Aug 1989.

BSCA Floor Care Manual (Fairfax, Va.: Building Service Contractors Association International, 1984).

Calderon, John: Advanced HVAC Management, *Journal of Property Management* 56: 41–43, Jan–Feb 1991.

Casazza, John A., and Spink, Frank H., Jr.: *Shopping Center Development Handbook, Second Edition* (Washington, D.C.: ULI—The Urban Land Institute, 1985).

Doocey, Paul: The Great Roof Warranty Debate, *Shopping Centers Today* July 1989, pp. 21–22.

Eiseman, Robert: Selecting a Roofing System, *Journal of Property Management* 52: 41–44, Nov–Dec 1987.

Evening Openings and Sales Volume (New York: International Council of Shopping Centers, 1969).

Flynn, Robert J. (ed.): *Carpenter's Shopping Center Management: Principles and Practices, Third Edition* (New York: International Council of Shopping Centers, 1984).

Graffiti Removal Manual (Providence, R.I.: Keep Providence Beautiful).

Halper, Emanuel B.: *Shopping Center and Store Leases* (New York: Law Journal Seminars-Press, Inc., 1984).

Kately, Richard, and Lachman, M. Leanne: Asset Management: The Key to Profitable Real Estate Investment, *Commercial Investment Real Estate Journal* 5(4):46–53, Fall 1986.

Leasing Retail Space (Chicago: Institute of Real Estate Management, 1990).

Levin, Michael S.: *Measuring the Fiscal Impact of a Shopping Center on Its Community* (New York: International Coucil of Shopping Centers, 1975).

Maccardini, Rebecca L.: *Merchants' Association or Marketing Fund: How to Make the Choice* (New York: International Council of Shopping Centers).

Managing the Shopping Center (Chicago: Institute of Real Estate Management, 1983).

1991 National Benchmarks of Shopping Patterns (Indianapolis: Stillerman Jones & Company, Inc., 1991).

Parking Requirements for Shopping Centers: Summary Recommendations and Research Study Report (Washington, D.C.: ULI—The Urban Land Institute, 1982).

Principles of Real Estate Management, Thirteenth Edition (Chicago: Institute of Real Estate Management, 1991).

Rategan, Cathie: Coping with Catastrophe—What to Do When Hell Freezes Over, *Journal of Property Management* 54:19–22, May–June 1989.

Roca, Rubin A.: *Market Research for Shopping Centers* (New York: International Council of Shopping Centers, 1980).

Roof Maintenance (Englewood, Colo.: The Roofing Industry Educational Institute, 1988).

Schwanke, Dean: *Mixed-Use Development Handbook* (Washington, D.C.: ULI—The Urban Land Institute, 1987).

Senn, Mark A.: *Commercial Real Estate Leases: Forms, Second Edition* (New York: John Wiley & Sons, Inc., 1990).

Senn, Mark A.: *Commercial Real Estate Leases: Preparation and Negotiation, Second Edition* (New York: John Wiley & Sons, Inc., 1990).

Shopping Center Study Lease: 1987 Edition (New York: International Council of Shopping Centers, 1987).

Special Report: Mixed-Use Projects, Moving to the Suburbs, *Shopping Centers Today* May 1990, p. 162.

Thomas, Laura: Thermal Storage Systems, *Journal of Property Management* 54:43–44, July–Aug 1989.

20 Ways to Conserve Energy in Office Buildings, Shopping Centers, and Other Commercial Properties (Chicago: Institute of Real Estate Management).

Wachsberger, Barry: Roof Maintenance and Inspection, *Journal of Property Management* 56:35–37, Mar–Apr 1991.

Watson, John A.: *Commercial Roofing Systems* (Reston, Va.: Reston Publishing Company, Inc., 1984).

Witherspoon, Robert E., et al.: *Mixed-Use Development: New Ways of Land Use* (Washington, D.C.: ULI—The Urban Land Institute, 1976).

Magazines and Newsletters

AndrewsReport (Indianapolis: Report Communications, monthly).

Building Operating Management (Milwaukee, Wis.: Trade Press Publishing Company, monthly).

CarlsonReport (Indianapolis: Report Communications, monthly).

Chain Store Age Executive (with *Shopping Center Age*) (New York: Lebhar-Friedman, Inc., monthly).

JonesReport (Indianapolis: Report Communications, monthly).

Journal of Property Management (Chicago: Institute of Real Estate Management, bimonthly).

Management Insights (San Francisco: American Building Maintenance Industries, quarterly).

Monitor, formerly *National Mall Monitor* (Clearwater, Fla.: National Mall Monitor, bimonthly).

Shopping Centers Today (New York: International Council of Shopping Centers, monthly).

Shopping Center World (Atlanta, Ga.: Communication Channels, Inc., monthly).

Urban Land (Washington, D.C.: ULI—The Urban Land Institute, monthly).

Market Research

The U.S. Department of Commerce, Bureau of the Census, compiles demographic data on an ongoing basis. *The Census Catalog and Guide* is published every decade. The *Census of Retail Trade* is published every five years in years ending in two and seven. *Current Business Reports* compiles data on monthly retail trade sales and inventories. *American Housing Survey* compiles data on housing quality and costs, neighborhood quality, personal income, and other statistics of interest to retailers. The *CPI Detailed Report* is a monthly report of changes in the Consumer Price Index. The Bureau of Labor Statistics conducts and publishes a *Survey of Consumer Expenditures* that describes American spending patterns by merchandise categories. Updated census data are published each year in *Statistical Abstract of the United States* available from the Government Printing Office in Washington, D.C.

In addition, there are numerous nongovernmental sources for demographic data. *American Demographics* and *The Numbers News* are published monthly by American Demographics Press in Ithaca, New York. *Metro Insights* is published annually by DRI/McGraw-Hill in Lexington, Massachusetts. *Rand McNally Commercial Atlas & Marketing Guide* is published annually by Rand McNally & Company in Skokie, Illinois. The *REIS Reports* covering retail market analyses for major metropolitan areas are issued from New York City. *Survey of Buying Power,* published annually as a supplement to *Sales and Marketing Management* (New York: Bill Communications Inc.), provides information related to sales performance, market potential, marketing strategies, and selection of advertising media and markets.

Targeted data compilations that focus census statistics are available from several private companies, including the following:

CACI in Fairfax, Virginia
CDP Marketing Information Corporation in Hauppauge, New York
Claritas in Alexandria, Virginia
Donnelley Marketing Information Services in Stamford, Connecticut
Intelligent Charting, Inc., in Perth Amboy, New Jersey
National Decision Systems in Encinitas, California
Survey Sampling, Inc., in Fairfield, Connecticut
Urban Decision Systems, Inc., in Los Angeles, California

Directories and other listings of retailers and leasing information are published periodically. Most are issued annually; a few are published twice a year or on another schedule. Many are special issues of trade magazines.

The Book on Value Retailing (St. Petersburg, Fla.: *Value Retail News*).

Lists off-price and outlet discount tenants, with their existing locations and people to contact.

Centermation Systems Food Court Special Report.

An annual survey published in *CarlsonReport* (Indianapolis: Report Communications).

Chain Store Guide—Directory of Leading Chain Stores in the United States (New York: Business Guides, Inc., annual).

A listing of chain stores with five or more locations—by category and by state—showing company name, address and telephone number, number of stores, area of activity, and people to contact.

Dealmakers Weekly.

A newsletter published 48 times a year and affiliated with TKC Consulting, Center Leasing & Development Corp.

Directory of Major Malls (Spring Valley, New York: JOMURPA Publishing Inc., annual).

A listing of shopping centers (existing and planned), developers, retailers, and markets in the United States and Canada.

Directory of Shopping Centers in the United States (Chicago: National Research Bureau, division of Automated Marketing Systems, Inc., annual).

A three-volume compilation of information on shopping centers (size, tenants, age, ownership, etc.), leasing agents, and other center personnel.

Factory Outlet World: Third Edition (Suffern, New York: DPN Enterprises, Inc., 1985).

A listing of retailers, developers, centers, and services to the off-price/outlet industry.

The Franchise Annual Directory (Lewiston, N.Y.: Info Franchise News).

A listing of hundreds of franchise opportunities.

Leasing Opportunities (New York: International Council of Shopping Centers).

Published annually, this book lists retailers with expansion plans for the coming year, giving space and location requirements and type of center desired.

Retail Tenant Directory.

An annual listing of tenants in large and small shopping centers in the United States published by *Monitor* magazine.

Also available are reports of surveys of operating income and expenses for shopping centers and for various retailers. Such information is useful for comparison purposes; however, the reader should bear in mind that the passage of time renders such data less reliable for current planning.

Buildings: The Facilities Construction & Management Magazine (Cedar Rapids, Iowa: Stamats Communications, Inc., monthly).

January issue includes a nationwide survey of percentage rental rates paid by various categories of retailers.

Dollars & Cents of Shopping Centers: 1990—A Study of Receipts and Expenses in Shopping Center Operations (Washington, D.C.: ULI—The Urban Land Institute, 1990).

Published every three years, this comprehensive report analyzes super regional, regional, community, and neighborhood shopping centers in the United States with comparisons of income and expenses by geographic area and age, including sales and rent data for various types of merchandise categories commonly found in each type of center (department stores, other anchors, and shops). Information on Canadian centers is also included. Supplementary data cover tenant classifications, new leases, parking, food courts, promotional entities (merchants' associations and marketing funds), and mall expenses for HVAC, security, and snow removal.

The Urban Land Institute also periodically issues various special reports of comparison data on other types of shopping centers. The following are currently available: *Dollars & Cents of Convenience Centers: 1990; Dollars & Cents of Fashion Malls: 1990; Dollars & Cents of Off-Price Shopping Centers* (1986); *Dollars & Cents of Super Community Centers: 1990; Dollars & Cents of Superstore Centers: 1990.*

Fairchild's Financial Manual of Retail Stores (New York: Fairchild Publications, Book Division, annual).

A survey of the operating income and expenses of retail stores.

Income/Expense Analysis: Shopping Centers—Open and Enclosed (Chicago: Institute of Real Estate Management, annual).

A new resource on shopping center financial data, this publication provides timely information focused on income and expenses.

Shopping Center Operating Cost Report (New York: International Council of Shopping Centers, periodic).

Professional Organizations

The Institute of Real Estate Management (IREM) is an association of property management professionals, including shopping center managers. Headquartered in Chicago, Illinois, IREM offers courses and seminars on property management topics and publishes numerous books and periodicals, including the annual *Income/Expense Analysis: Shopping Centers—Open and Enclosed* and the bimonthly *Journal of Property Management (JPM)*. "Leasing and Management of Shopping Centers and Retail Space" is one of a series of courses that lead toward the CERTIFIED PROPERTY MANAGER® (CPM®) designation. In addition, monthly meetings of local chapters provide opportunities to hear timely speakers and network with other shopping center management professionals.

The International Council of Shopping Centers (ICSC) holds national and regional meetings and offers courses on shopping center marketing, leasing, management, and development. Headquartered in New York City, ICSC publishes *Leasing Opportunities*, an annual directory of shopping centers and retailers, and *Research Quarterly*, a report of shopping center statistics (size, sales, vacancies, etc.) as they are changing. They offer two designations: Certified Shopping Center Manager (CSM) and Certified Marketing Director (CMD).

The Urban Land Institute (ULI), an association of developers, architects, and others interested in land use, is headquartered in Washington, D.C. They publish *Dollars & Cents of Shopping Centers* and a series of *Dollars & Cents* special reports on fashion malls and other specialty retail centers comparing income and expenses with particular focus on individual merchandise categories.

ULI and ICSC have done considerable research on shopping center parking requirements. Information on other aspects of parking design, including parking for handicapped people, may be sought from the Institute of Transportation Engineers in Washington, D.C., publishers of *ITE Journal.*

Glossary

ACCREDITED MANAGEMENT ORGANIZATION® (AMO®) A designation conferred by the Institute of Real Estate Management on real estate management firms that are under the direction of a CERTIFIED PROPERTY MANAGER® and comply with stipulated requirements as to accounting procedures, performance, and protection of funds entrusted to them.

Adaptive use Conversion of an existing structure for a new use, e.g., a former post office converted to a shopping center.

Asset management A specialized field of property management that involves the supervision of an owner's real estate assets at the investment level. An *asset manager* typically has a more active role in the acquisition, disposition, and divestiture of the real estate investment than a property manager normally does and may have only a superficial involvement with day-to-day operations. (See also *property management*.)

Base rent Minimum monthly rent payments as set forth in a retail lease, exclusive of pass-through expenses, percentage rents, and other additional charges. (See also *minimum rent*.)

Breakpoint In retail leases, the point at which the tenant's percentage rent (percentage rate times sales) is equal to the base rent and beyond which the tenant will begin to pay overages; also called *natural breakpoint* and calculated by dividing the percentage rate into the base rent amount. Sometimes tenant and landlord negotiate an *artificial breakpoint* that allows the tenant to begin paying percentage rent either before or after the natural breakpoint is reached.

Build-to-suit   An arrangement between a shopping center developer and a large space user (supermarket, department store, fast food franchise, bank, etc.) whereby the developer agrees to construct the tenant's building according to the tenant's detailed specifications. The tenant then leases the building and the site from the developer.

Capitalization rate   A percentage rate of return used to determine the value of a property based on its income stream; also called *cap rate*.

Cash flow   The amount of cash available after all payments have been made for operating expenses and debt service (mortgage payment of principal and interest).

Center court   In an enclosed mall, a location midway between two department store anchors.

CERTIFIED PROPERTY MANAGER® (CPM®)   The professional designation conferred by the Institute of Real Estate Management on those individuals who distinguish themselves in the areas of education, experience, and ethics in property management.

Common area agreement   A separate agreement, usually between an anchor tenant and a shopping center owner, that sets standards for maintenance of the common area and states how the related expenses will be distributed between the parties. It may also prohibit the shopping center owner from making changes to the common areas (e.g., relocating entrances or adding a pad or outlot building) without the written approval of each signatory to the agreement. Such an agreement may also be established among multiple owners of a mixed-use development (MXD) or other similar property, in which case it may also address removal of the common area manager for nonperformance.

Community shopping center   A shopping center commonly anchored by a junior department store, discount store, or variety store and having 150,000–400,000 square feet of GLA, often configured as a large open-air strip with three or more anchors.

Construction loan   A short-term loan covering the cost to develop a project, usually funded by one or more commercial banks.

Consumer Price Index (CPI)   A measure of consumer purchasing power by comparing the current costs of goods and services to those of a selected base year. The CPI is published monthly by the U.S. Department of Labor, Bureau of Labor Statistics, and often used as the basis for rental rate increases.

Convenience center   A small shopping center (5,000–50,000 square feet of GLA), sometimes anchored by a quick-stop food store and usually occupied by service-oriented businesses; often designed in a strip.

Cost-benefit analysis   A projection of the impact of a particular change on operating income (NOI) and cash flow, comparing that impact to the cost of making the change.

Demographic profile   The social and economic statistics of a specific population, including population size and density and characteristics of individuals such as age, education, occupation, and income.

Depreciation   In real estate, the loss of value due to all causes, including physical deterioration (ordinary wear and tear), structural defects, and changing economic and market conditions (see also *obsolescence*). The tax deduction that allows for exhaustion of property by allocation of its cost over its estimated useful life.

Effective gross income   The estimated gross income less allowances for vacancies and rent losses; the total amount of income actually collected during a reporting period.

Enclosure   The conversion of part of the common area of an open shopping center to a fully enclosed mall by addition of a roof and walls.

Equity   The interest or value that an owner has in real estate over and above the mortgage and other financial liens against it; outright ownership.

Estoppel certificate   A document by which the tenant states the terms of the lease, including the amount of rent to be paid over the entire term of the lease; commonly requested by the landlord in conjunction with a transfer of ownership or in relation to financing.

Exclusive   A right granted to the tenant that restricts the owner from leasing space in the same shopping center to other retailers that sell similar merchandise, usually defined in an *exclusive use* clause. Care must be taken in granting exclusives because such limitation of competition may violate antitrust regulations. When granted, exclusives must be taken into account when prospecting for and leasing to additional retail tenants.

Food court   An area in a shopping center, usually in an enclosed mall, where different kinds of foods are available from individual vendors selling from separate stalls; typically there is a shared (common) seating area for customers.

Franchise   An exclusive right to sell a product or perform a service; in retailing, an individual purchases this right from a chain store or other type of parent corporation and operates the store according to the rules and regulations of the franchisor.

Frontage   The section of a store that faces the street or the pedestrian walkway in a mall; also refers to window display area and entrance.

Gross leasable area (GLA)   The size of an individual tenant's space, usually measured in square feet. The total square footage of floor space in all store areas of a shopping center (excluding common area space); also called floor area.

Gross lease   A lease whereby the landlord (lessor) is responsible for paying all property expenses (e.g., taxes, insurance, utilities, repairs, etc.), and these costs are factored into the rent paid by the tenant (lessee). (Compare *net lease*.)

Ground lease   A lease for land only.

Institute of Real Estate Management (IREM)   A professional association of men and women who meet established standards of experience, education, and ethics with the objective of continually improving their respective managerial skills by mutual education and exchange of ideas and experience. The Institute is an affiliate of the NATIONAL ASSOCIATION OF REALTORS®. (See also *CERTIFIED PROPERTY MANAGER®*.)

Insurance   A means of reducing economic risk in which funds are accumulated from a group of insured parties and used to pay the losses of an individual member of the group. As a form of risk management, insurance substitutes regular payment of insurance premiums for the unpredictable cost of an economic loss, based on the probability of a particular type of loss occurring.

Investment value   The price that an investor bound by special circumstances and restraints will agree to pay. (Compare *market value*.)

Lease   A contract between the property owner or landlord (lessor) and a tenant (lessee) that transfers to the tenant the right to use a piece of property for a specified period of time under certain conditions.

Leasing agent   The individual directly responsible for renting space in a shopping center. Leasing agents may be employed by brokerage firms, management organizations, or development companies; in some states, they are required to be licensed as real estate brokers.

Management agreement   A legal contract between the owner of a property and a person who agrees to manage it. This agreement establishes the manager's duties, authority, and compensation and states the owner's obligations to insure the property, provide sufficient funds for its operation, and assure its compliance with building and construction codes and environmental regulations.

Management fee   The monetary consideration paid monthly or otherwise for the performance of management duties, usually defined in the management agreement as a percentage of the gross rental income of the property and/or as a minimum monthly amount.

Marketing   Promotion of a store or retail center through advertising and public relations programs.

Marketing fund   An account controlled by the landlord that is specifically for funding shopping center promotions and advertising and to which all merchants in the center must contribute a predetermined amount as stated in their leases. (Compare *merchants' association*.)

Market rent   The rent a retail site could command under prevailing market conditions.

Market research   The gathering of information about a trade area and a particular retail site—usually pertaining to population, economy, local industries, per capita expenditures, competing retail sites, and sales potential.

Market share   The portion of consumer dollars spent on a particular merchandise category that a given retailer can capture.

Market value   The price at which a seller would willingly sell an item (e.g., a property) and a buyer would willingly buy it in an open market.

Merchandising   The buying, promoting, and selling of goods.

Merchants' association   An organization formed in shopping centers and controlled by the tenants to plan promotions and advertisements for the good of the center as a whole and usually established as a not-for-profit corporation. All tenants are required to participate, and both tenants and landlord pay dues. (Compare *marketing fund*.)

Minimum rent   The rent which will always be due each month in a tenant's lease term, regardless of sales volume and exclusive of any additional charges; often used in conjunction with a percentage rent arrangement; sometimes called fixed minimum rent. (See also *base rent*.)

Mixed-use development (MXD)   A large-scale real estate project having three or more significant revenue-producing uses (e.g., retail, office, residential, hotel, recreation), incorporating significant physical and functional integration of project components (thus an intensive use of land), and conforming to a coherent plan.

Modernization   The removal or upgrading of original or existing features of a property, primarily to reflect technological improvements such as energy-saving equipment.

Mortgage   A written instrument that creates a lien upon real estate as security for the payment of a specified debt. See also *permanent loan*.

Multi-use development   A term applied to multiple uses of a single site and encompassing densely configured developments that achieve physical and functional integration but include only two uses, mixed-use developments as such, and developments with two or more uses but lacking physical and functional integration (usually because of large scale, low density, or lack of a coherent plan). (Compare *mixed-use development*.)

Negotiation   The process of bargaining between landlord and tenant to reach a mutually profitable agreement on rental rates, term of the lease, and other points.

Neighborhood center   A shopping center typically anchored by a supermarket or drugstore and having 50,000–150,000 square feet of GLA.

Net lease   A lease under which the tenant pays a prorated share of some or all operating expenses. In retail leasing, the tenant pays a prorated share of property taxes under a net lease, prorated shares of both property taxes and insurance under a net-net lease, and prorated shares of all operating expenses (including common area maintenance) under a triple-net lease. (Compare *gross lease*.)

Net operating income (NOI)   The money available to an owner or developer after deducting a property's operating expenses from its effective gross income. (Debt service is deducted from NOI to determine cash flow.)

Obsolescence Lessening of value due to being out-of-date (obsolete) as a result of changes in design and use; an element of depreciation. *Physical obsolescence* (deterioration) results from deferred maintenance; *functional obsolescence* is an internal condition of a property related to its design or use; and *economic obsolescence* is an inability to generate enough income to offset operating expenses, usually due to conditions external to the property (changes in populations and/or land uses, legislation, etc.).

Occupancy cost The retail tenant's cost for the leased space, including base and percentage rent plus pass-through prorations (operating expenses, taxes, insurance, CAM costs).

Off-price center A type of specialized shopping center whose tenants offer brand-name merchandise at large discounts (20%–60%) off normal retail prices because special bulk purchases allow cost savings to be passed on to the customer. (Compare *outlet center.*)

Operating expenses All expenditures made in connection with operating a property with the exceptions of debt service and income taxes.

Option In a retail lease, a statement of the tenant's right to obtain a specific condition within a specified time (typically covering renewal, extension of the term, expansion of the space, or cancellation of the lease); often incorporated into the lease as an addendum.

Outlet center A type of specialized shopping center dominated by factory outlet stores that sell manufacturers' surplus merchandise (factory seconds, irregulars, or overruns); usually the manufacturer operates the store, eliminating the retail markup. (Compare *off-price center.*)

Outlot In a shopping center, a site that is not attached to the main center; also called out parcel or *pad* space. The term is often applied to freestanding space in the parking lot.

Overage See *percentage rent.*

Parking area ratio The relationship between the square footage of the parking area and the square footage of the building.

Parking index The number of parking spaces per 1,000 square feet of GLA in a shopping center.

Pass-through charges The portion of operating expenses of the property that is prorated among the tenants, usually including real estate taxes, insurance on the property, and common area maintenance (CAM) costs; also sometimes called tenant charges and billback items. (See also *net lease.*)

Percentage rent Rent paid by a tenant based on a percentage of gross sales or net income; often set against a guaranteed minimum or base rent and therefore considered *overage.*

Permanent loan   A long-term loan used to finance the purchase of an existing project or to replace the construction loan for a new development; a mortgage.

Points   An upfront percentage fee paid for a loan—one point equals one percent of the face value of the loan—that increases the yield to the lender.

Power center   A large strip shopping center anchored by several large promotional, warehouse, or specialty stores that dominate their merchandising categories and having very few small shops; originally called *promotional centers.*

Preleasing   The leasing of a large retail project before and during construction to assure a high occupancy level when completed; often required to obtain financing.

Pro forma   According to form; in development, a statement of estimated costs and projected income (a budget).

Property management   The operation of income-producing real estate as a business, including leasing, rent collection, maintenance of the property, and general administration. Usually, this is performed by a person other than the owner, someone who acts as the owner's agent—a professional property manager.

Property manager   The person who supervises the day-to-day operations of a property (e.g., a shopping center) according to the owner's objectives.

Pro rata share   The tenant's share of operating expenses, HVAC charges, common area maintenance (CAM) costs, taxes, insurance, etc., computed as a percentage by dividing the gross leasable area (GLA) of the tenant's space by the GLA of the shopping center.

Prospecting   The search for potential tenants by advertising, referrals, canvassing, and cooperation with other brokers.

Psychographic profile   An analysis of the trade area that goes beyond numbers and dollars to examine values, attitudes, and similar phenomena. (See also *demographic profile.*)

Qualification   The process of evaluating a prospective tenant to determine its ability to fulfill the terms of the lease, especially the payment of rent and other charges. Retail tenants are also evaluated on their ability as merchants and their compatibility with the array of tenants in the shopping center.

Reciprocal easement agreement (REA)   In shopping centers, an agreement between anchor tenant(s) and landlord regarding rights of use of each other's property, specifically the use of each other's parking area for customer parking.

Recycling   The reprocessing of various materials (e.g., paper, glass, aluminum, and various types of plastic) into usable products.

Regional center   A large shopping center anchored by two or three major retailers, at least one of which is a full-line department store, and usually developed as enclosed malls having 400,000–1,000,000 square feet of GLA.

Rehabilitation   The restoration of a property to its original condition, without changing its basic use.

Retailing   The selling of goods and services to the ultimate consumer. (See also specialized terminology in appendix A.)

Sales analysis   A comparative evaluation of tenants' sales for specified periods (e.g., one-month or one-year intervals) to measure growth and change, commonly on a per-square-foot basis. In shopping centers, sales analysis is used to evaluate prospective tenants, compare retailers within merchandise categories, and measure the success of the center as a whole.

Sales potential   The total number of consumer dollars available to retailers for the entire trade area.

Sales tax   A tax on the transfer of personal property (as distinguished from a tax on the property itself), usually measured as a percentage of the purchase price. It is added to the selling price and collected by the seller for the governmental agency (state, local) imposing it.

Sales volume   The total dollar sales for a specified period, usually a year; also stated in dollars per square foot and often used as a measure of a retailer's success and for comparison of retailers to each other and within their merchandise categories.

Shell space   The condition of a tenant's space before occupancy and before any tenant improvements to it. For retail space, definition may vary with regional location and type of shopping center.

Shopping center   A group of commercial establishments planned, developed, owned, and managed as a unit related in location, size, and type of shops to the trade area the unit serves and providing on-site parking in definite relationship to the types and sizes of stores.

Specialty center   A type of shopping center often dominated by food and gift tenants and having 50,000–300,000 square feet of GLA. Many such centers have been created by conversion of an existing old building (adaptive use) in a tourist-oriented area, usually perpetuating an architectural theme suggested by the site; also known as theme or festival shopping centers.

Strip center   A shopping area consisting of a group of stores in a row.

Super regional center   A shopping center anchored by at least four full-line department stores and having more than 1,000,000 square feet of GLA.

Temporary tenant   A tenant that rents for a short period of time, often on a seasonal or month-to-month basis, usually occupying a kiosk or cart in the common area. A temporary tenant program may also be called a specialty leasing program.

Tenant improvement allowance   Funds allowed by the landlord for the tenant's use in improving the shell space prior to move in, the amount being negotiable.

Tenant mix   The combination of retailers and service vendors leasing space in a shopping center.

Trade area   The geographic area from which a shopping center will obtain most of its customers, usually subdivided into primary, secondary, and tertiary trade area zones. The size of the trade area depends on the type of center, location of competition, and other factors.

Traffic count   The number of automobiles passing an intersection or point along a street within a given period of time; in a mall, the number of pedestrians entering the shopping center. In shopping center development, these counts are used by market researchers to determine whether a site will support a proposed center.

Use clause   A lease provision that restricts a retail tenant's use of the rented space by indicating what can and cannot be sold.

Vacancy rate   The ratio of vacant space to total rentable space (GLA), expressed as a percentage.

Valuation   The determination of value or worth. Valuation of real estate is done by a professional appraiser. There are three approaches to determining property value. In the *cost approach*, the value of real property is based on the cost to replace the improvements on it—either to reproduce the improvements using the same materials or to replace them using modern materials and techniques. In the *market approach*, value is determined by comparing the property to similar properties that have been sold recently. In the *income approach*, value is based on the property's ability to generate income. All three approaches should be used to determine value most accurately.

Workletter   An addendum to the tenant improvement clause of a retail lease that lists in detail all the work to be done for the tenant by the landlord.

Zoning   A legal mechanism whereby local governments regulate the use of privately owned real property to prevent conflicting land uses and promote orderly development.

Index